AMERICA FIRSTHAND

READINGS
IN
AMERICAN
HISTORY

A MERICA FIRSTHAND

Volume II *FROM RECONSTRUCTION*
TO THE PRESENT

ROBERT D. MARCUS

State University of New York College at Brockport

and

DAVID BURNER

State University of New York at Stony Brook

ST. MARTIN'S PRESS
New York

Editor: Don Reisman
Project Management: Susan Hunsberger/Editing, Design & Production, Inc.
Cover Design: Darby Downey
Cover Art: *Brooklyn Bridge* by Milton Bond. Reverse glass, 16 × 20. © 1882 Jay America's
Folk Heritage Gallery.

Library of Congress Catalog Card Number: 87-60518

For information, write:
St. Martin's Press, Inc.
175 Fifth Avenue
New York, NY 10010

ISBN: 0-312-00432-X

Preface

America Firsthand is a response to the growing difficulty of teaching and learning American history. While virtually no one uses the term "relevant" anymore, the old issue of the usability of the past continues to torment teachers and writers of history. Historians wonder who is listening to them besides other historians; students question why they must study what is passed and gone. In recent years, this problem has increased. With the vast expansion of subject matter, historians have less and less of either a shared language or an implied synthesis or consensus around which to argue. Not long ago, any American historian could expect to be able to read and understand the writing of almost any other American historian. Today many of the languages are technical, employing terms either created to express new sensibilities, or borrowed from the language of statistics or other social sciences.

And learning, of course, is always harder than teaching. Students understandably object to synthesizing a field in fragments (less understandable are objections to reading and to writing). However, like their professors, students must draw *their own* threads through the past, whatever color these threads may be. Otherwise, it is all gray on gray.

Students need to find exemplars of themselves in the past, and *America Firsthand* is an effort to help them discover how the diversities of recent scholarship can respond to that need. The focus is on people, mostly real people, but occasionally fictional characters whose depiction influenced the imagination of real people. Included are memoirs, letters, diaries, oral histories, speeches, testimonies, and pieces of fiction, the rich store that historians of the last quarter of a century have learned to find, read, and interpret. Individuals are presented insofar as possible in their own words and in selections long enough to be memorable, personal, and immediate. The accounts of indentured servants, runaway slaves, cowboys, factory workers, civil rights activists, business people, and many others offer students possible identifications while providing teachers with entries for the diverse kinds of analyses that have flourished in recent decades in American historical writing. They can also serve as occasions for student essays and research projects.

We have included enough political documents to maintain the traditional markers of United States history, which continue to provide a useful political and narrative spine. While the readings convey the experiences and forces of specific personalities, they include observations on the debates in the first meetings of the United States Senate, on the war of 1812, and on the style and policy of President John F. Kennedy. All teachers and students must struggle with the problem of connecting traditional chronology with the new materials of social history, and no formula for doing that is without its problems. We have, however, offered a set of connections that will be workable for many courses. Careful headnotes and questions at the end of each section help make the essential links.

This book explores the many ways of being an American, the many minds and personalities that make up a diverse history and nation. We see the American experience through the eyes of varied people who have in common the fact that, in some form, they have left behind vivid records of the times in which they lived. These personal, eyewitness recollections serve as fertile ground in which students can begin to root their interest in history.

Acknowledgments

The authors wish to thank the following individuals who reviewed *America Firsthand* for St. Martin's Press: John Barnard, Oakland University; Virginia Bernhard, University of St. Thomas; Mario S. De Pillis, University of Massachusetts, Amherst; Leornard Dinnerstein, University of Arizona; Hency C. Ferrell, Jr., East Carolina University; Patrick J. Furlong, Indiana University at South Bend; Barbara L. Green, Texas Tech University; Maurine Greenwald, University of Pittsburgh; Patrick F. Palermo, University of Dayton; Nancy Rachels, Hillsborough Community College; James E. Sefton, California State University, Northridge; G. L. Seligmann, Jr., University of North Texas; Curtis Solberg, Santa Barbara City College.

Contents

AMERICA FIRSTHAND

PART I | RECONSTRUCTION AND THE WESTERN FRONTIER

The crisis provoked by slavery and sectionalism was resolved only by war. The impact of war we see both in Small's memoirs of a prisoner of war and in the account of the devastation wrought by William T. Sherman's march through Georgia. This was the first modern war and it speeded the transformation of American life into something that we can recognize as modern.

Victory for the Union did not resolve questions about the role of black men and women in American life. Three new amendments to the constitution initiated a revolution which, more than a century later, is far from over. In the selections that follow, we see the first painful and difficult reactions to these changes as black and white Southerners react to Reconstruction. We also witness how the revolution in race relations carried with it striking changes in the most important forms of property and economic relations: ownership of the land and the crops planted on it. By the 1880's, sharecropping, governed by instruments like the Grimes Sharecrop contract, had emerged as the principal replacement for slavery.

The completion of the first transcontinental railroad link in 1869, and the renewed movement westward that it generated, fundamentally altered the western United States. The destruction of western buffalo herds, as shown in the writings of W.S. Glenn, E.N. Andrews, and John Cook, meant the collapse of the Indian culture based on hunting the buffalo. The increase of white settlers delivered the final blow.

Industries such as buffalo hunting, the large-scale commercial raising of cattle, and mining—combined with the warfare between whites and Indians—made the late nineteenth century a legendary era of western violence. Nat Love's attitudes and adventures are representative of the more romantic views of the

1

western cowboy. Famous as "Deadeye Dick," Love was one of the about 25 percent of cowboys who were black.

The main motive of cowboys, however, was less romantic violence than the pursuit of economic fortune, the search for new means of livelihood, or, simply, a stable income. The workaday existence of Andy Adams provides one example of the existence of routine in what was ordinarily thought of as an extraordinary, adventuresome life.

Presaged by the attitudes of buffalo hunter John Cook was the tragedy of the Wounded Knee massacre. The late nineteenth century marked the final shunting of Indians to reservations often far distant from their ancestral homes. A selection containing Indian testimony and the ballad of a cavalry soldier shows contrasting views of what stands as one of the most dismal events in Indian-white relations.

1 | In the Track of Sherman's Army

Sidney Andrews, a Northern journalist, visited the Carolinas and Georgia shortly after the end of the Civil War. His dispatches were published as The South Since the War. *His description of Columbia, South Carolina, provides a dramatic picture of defeat. Ironically, accounts like this succeeded to some extent in arousing sympathy for the suffering South, and made many Northerners hesitate over the vigorous Reconstruction that, however necessary to help the freed blacks seemed hard to impose on the white South.*

Columbia, September 12, 1865.
The war was a long time in reaching South Carolina, but there was vengeance in its very breath when it did come,—wrath that blasted everything it touched, and set Desolation on high as the genius of the State. "A brave people never before made such a mistake as we did," said a little woman who sat near me in the cars while coming up from Charleston; "it mortifies me now, every day I live, to think how well the Yankees fought. We had no idea they could fight half so well." In such humiliation as hers is half the lesson of the war for South Carolina.

Columbia is in the heart of Destruction. Being outside of it, you can only get in through one of the roads built by Ruin. Being in it, you can only get out over one of the roads walled by Desolation. You go north thirty-two miles, and find the end of one railroad; southeast thirty miles, and find the end of another; south forty-five miles, and find the end of a third; southwest fifty miles, and meet a fourth; and northwest twenty-nine miles, and find the end of still another. Sherman came in here, the papers used to say, to break up the railroad system of the seaboard States of the Confederacy. He did his work so thoroughly that half a dozen years will nothing more than begin to repair the damage, even in this regard.

The railway section of the route from Charleston lies mostly either in a pine barren or a pine swamp, though after passing Branchville we came into a more open and rolling country, with occasional signs of life.

Sidney Andrews. The South Since the War: As Shown by Fourteen Weeks of Travel and Observation in Georgia and the Carolinas. *(Boston, Ticknor and Fields, 1866), pp. 28–37.*

Yet we could not anywhere, after we left the immediate vicinity of the city, see much indication of either work or existence. The trim and handsome railway stations of the North, the little towns strung like beads on an iron string, are things unknown here. In the whole seventy-seven miles there are but two towns that make any impression on the mind of a stranger,—Summerville and George's,—and even these are small and unimportant places. Elsewhere we stopped, as it appeared, whenever the train-men pleased,—the "station" sometimes existing only in the consciousness of the engineer and conductor.

Branchville was, however, noticeable because of the place it once occupied in Northern anxiety. There is where Sherman was to meet his fate. Have we forgotten how the Richmond papers of early February spoke? They were not at liberty to mention the preparations, etc., but they might say, etc., and the Yankee nation would have sore cause to remember Branchville, etc. Unfortunately, however, Sherman flanked Branchville, just as he had other places of thrice its importance, and it missed the coveted renown. It is nothing but a railroad junction in a pine barren, with a long, low station-house and cotton warehouse, and three or four miserable dwellings.

I found the railroad in better condition than I supposed that I should. The rails are very much worn, but the roadbed is in fair order for nearly the entire distance. The freight-cars seemed in passably good repair; but the passenger-coaches were the most wretched I ever saw,— old, filthy, and rickety. On our train was one new feature,—a colored man and his wife, whose duty it was to wait on the passengers.

I came up from Orangeburg, forty-five miles, by "stage," to wit, an old spring-covered market-wagon, drawn by three jaded horses and driven by Sam, freedman, late slave,—of the race not able to take care of themselves, yet caring, week in and week out, for the horses and interests of his employer as faithfully and intelligently as any white man could. There were six of us passengers, and we paid ten dollars each passage-money. We left Orangeburg at four, P.M.; drove eight miles; supped by the roadside; drove all night; lunched at sunrise by a muddy brook; and reached Columbia and breakfast at eleven, A.M., thankful that we had not broken down at midnight, and had met only two or three minor accidents. I am quite sure there are more pleasant ways of travelling than by "stage" in South Carolina at the present time. Thirty-two miles of the forty-five lie in such heavy and deep sand that no team can travel faster than at a moderate walk. For the other thirteen miles the road is something better, though even there it is the exception and not the rule to trot your mules. The river here was formerly spanned by an elegant and expensive bridge, but the foolish Rebels burned it; and the crossing of the Congaree is now effected in a ferry, the style and management of which would disgrace any backwoods settlement of the West.

The "Shermanizing process," as an ex-Rebel colonel jocosely called it, has been complete everywhere. To simply say that the people hate that officer is to put a fact in very mild terms. Butler is, in their estimation, an angel when compared to Sherman. They charge the latter with the entire work and waste of the war so far as their State is concerned,— even claim that Columbia was burned by his express orders. They pronounce his spirit "infernal," "atrocious," "cowardly," "devilish," and would unquestionably use stronger terms if they were to be had. I have been told by dozens of men that he couldn't walk up the main street of Columbia in the daytime without being shot; and three different gentlemen, residing in different parts of the State, declare that Wade Hampton expresses a purpose to shoot him at sight whenever and wherever he meets him. Whatever else the South Carolina mothers forget, they do not seem likely in this generation to forget to teach their children to hate Sherman.

Certain bent rails are the first thing one sees to indicate the advent of his army. They are at Branchville. I looked at them with curious interest. "It passes my comprehension to tell what became of our railroads," said a travelling acquaintance; "one week we had passably good roads, on which we could reach almost any part of the State, and the next week they were all gone,—not simply broken up, but gone; some of the material was burned, I know, but miles and miles of iron have actually disappeared, gone out of existence." Branchville, as I have already said, was flanked, and the army did not take it in the line of march, but some of the boys paid it a visit.

At Orangeburg there is ample proof that the army passed that way. About one third of the town was burned. I found much dispute as to the origin of the fire, and while certain fellows of the baser sort loudly assert that it was the work of the Yankee, others of the better class express the belief that it originated with a resident who was angry at the Confederate officers. Thereabouts one finds plenty of railroad iron so bent and twisted that it can never again be used. The genius which our soldiers displayed in destroying railroads seems remarkable. How effectually they did it, when they undertook the work in earnest, no pen can make plain. "We could do something in that line, we thought," said an ex-Confederate captain, "but we were ashamed of ourselves when we saw how your men could do it."

We rode over the road where the army marched. Now and then we found solitary chimneys, but, on the whole, comparatively few houses were burned, and some of those were fired, it is believed, by persons from the Rebel army or from the neighboring locality. The fences did not escape so well, and most of the planters have had these to build during the summer. This was particularly the case near Columbia. Scarcely a tenth of that destroyed appears to have been rebuilt, and thousands of acres of land of much richness lie open as a common.

There is great scarcity of stock of all kinds. What was left by the Rebel conscription officers was freely appropriated by Sherman's army, and the people really find considerable difficulty not less in living than in travelling. Milk, formerly an article much in use, can only be had now in limited quantities: even at the hotels we have more meals without than with it. There are more mules than horses, apparently; and the animals, whether mules or horses, are all in ill condition and give evidence of severe overwork.

Columbia was doubtless once the gem of the State. It is as regularly laid out as a checker-board,—the squares being of uniform length and breadth and the streets of uniform width. What with its broad streets, beautiful shade-trees, handsome lawns, extensive gardens, luxuriant shrubbery, and wealth of flowers, I can easily see that it must have been a delightful place of residence. No South-Carolinian with whom I have spoken hesitates an instant in declaring that it was the most beautiful city on the continent; and, as already mentioned, they charge its destruction directly to General Sherman.

It is now a wilderness of ruins. Its heart is but a mass of blackened chimneys and crumbling walls. Two thirds of the buildings in the place were burned, including, without exception, everything in the business portion. Not a store, office, or shop escaped; and for a distance of three fourths of a mile on each of twelve streets there was not a building left. "They destroyed everything which the most infernal Yankee ingenuity could devise means to destroy," said one gentleman to me; "hands, hearts, fire, gunpowder, and behind everything the spirit of hell, were the agencies which they used." I asked him if he wasn't stating the case rather strongly; and he replied that he would make it stronger if he could. The residence portion generally escaped conflagration, though houses were burned in all sections except the extreme northeastern.

Every public building was destroyed, except the new and unfinished state-house. This is situated on the summit of tableland whereon the city is built, and commands an extensive view of the surrounding country, and must have been the first building seen by the victorious and on-marching Union army. From the summit of the ridge, on the opposite side of the river, a mile and a half away, a few shells were thrown at it, apparently by way of reminder, three or four of which struck it, without doing any particular damage. With this exception, it was unharmed, though the workshops, in which were stored many of the architraves, caps, sills, &c., were burned,—the fire, of course, destroying or seriously damaging their contents. The poverty of this people is so deep that there is no probability that it can be finished, according to the original design, during this generation at least.

The ruin here is neither half so eloquent nor touching as that at Charleston. This is but the work of flame, and might have mostly been brought about in time of peace. Those ghostly and crumbling walls and those long-deserted and grass-grown streets show the prostration of a community,—such prostration as only war could bring.

I find a commendable spirit of enterprise, though, of course, it is enterprise on a small scale, and the enterprise of stern necessity. The work of clearing away the ruins is going on, not rapidly or extensively, to be sure, but something is doing, and many small houses of the cheaper sort are going up. Yet, at the best, this generation will not ever again see the beautiful city of a year ago. Old men and despondent men say it can never be rebuilt. "We shall have to give it up to the Yankees, I reckon," said one of two gentlemen conversing near me this morning. "Give it up!" said the other; "they've already moved in and taken possession without asking our leave." I guess the remark is true. I find some Northern men already here, and I hear of more who are coming.

Of course there is very little business doing yet. The city is, as before said, in the heart of the devastated land. I judge that twenty thousand dollars would buy the whole stock of dry goods, groceries, clothing, &c. in store. The small change of the place is made in shinplasters, printed on most miserable paper, and issued by the various business men, "redeemable in United States currency when presented in sums of two dollars and upwards." "Greenbacks" and national currency notes pass without question in the city, but are looked upon with suspicion by the country people. "Having lost a great deal by one sort of paper, we propose to be careful now," they say. Occasionally one sees a State banknote, but they pass for only from twenty-five to sixty or sixty-five cents on the dollar. There is none of the Confederate money in circulation; though I judge, from what I hear, that considerable quantities of it are hoarded up in the belief that things will somehow take such a turn as to one day give it value.

There is a certain air of easy dignity observable among the people that I have not found elsewhere in the State,—not even in Charleston itself. Something of this is probably due to the fact that the capital is located here; but more of it, probably, to the existence of Columbia College. It was before the war a very flourishing institution, but has been closed during the last three years. The old but roomy buildings are in part occupied by the military authorities, partly by the professors and officers of the college, and are partly closed. No indication is given as to the time of reopening the school. It is said by residents that the city contained some of the finest private libraries in the South; but these, with one or two exceptions, were burned.

The women who consider it essential to salvation to snub or insult Union officers and soldiers at every possible opportunity do not seem as numerous as they appeared to be in Charleston; and indeed marriages between soldiers and women of the middle class are not by any means the most uncommon things in the world; while I notice, in a quiet, unobservant manner, as even the dullest traveller may, that at least several very elegant ladies do not seem at all averse to the attentions of the gentlemen of shoulderstraps. Can these things be, and not overcome the latent fire of Rebellion?

In coming up from Charleston I learned a great many things by conversation with persons, and by listening to conversation between people; and these are some of the more important facts thus learned.

Thus, one man insisted with much vehemence that cotton is king, and that a resolution on the part of the South not to sell any for a year would bring the North upon its knees.

Another man was very confident that the North depends entirely upon the cotton trade for a living, and that a failure to get at least one million bales before spring will bring a tremendous financial crash.

Another gravely asserted that a state of anarchy prevails in the entire North; that the returned soldiers are plundering and butchering indiscriminately; and that there has recently been a most bloody riot in Boston.

Another, and a man of much apparent intelligence, informed me that the negroes have an organized military force in all sections of the State, and are almost certain to rise and massacre the whites about Christmas time.

Another had heard, and sincerely believed, that General Grant's brother-in-law is an Indian, and is on his staff, and that the President had issued an order permitting the General's son to marry a mulatto girl whom he found in Virginia.

A woman, evidently from the country districts, stated that there had been a rising of the negroes in Maryland; that a great many whites had been killed; and that some considerable portion of Baltimore and many of the plantations had been seized by the negroes.

And, finally, an elderly gentleman who represented himself as a cotton factor, declared that there would be a terrible civil war in the North within two years; that England would compel the repudiation of our National debt and the assumption of the Confederate debt for her guaranty of protection.

The people of the central part of the State are poor, wretchedly poor; for the war not only swept away their stock and the material resources of their plantations, but also all values,—all money, stocks, and bonds,—and generally left nothing that can be sold for money but cotton, and only a small proportion of the landholders have any of that. Therefore there is for most of them nothing but the beginning anew of life, on the strictest personal economy and a small amount of money borrowed in the city. It would be a benefit of hundred of millions of dollars if the North could be made to practise half the economy which poverty forces upon this people.

They are full of ignorance and prejudices, but they want peace and quiet, and seem not badly disposed toward the general government. Individuals there are who rant and rave and feed on fire as in the old days, but another war is a thing beyond the possibilities of time. So far as any fear of that is concerned we may treat this State as we please,— hold it as a conquered province or restore it at once to full communion in the sisterhood of States. The war spirit is gone, and no fury can re-enliven it.

The spirit of oppression still exists, however, and military authority cannot be withdrawn till the relation between employer and employed is put upon a better basis. On the one hand, the negro in the country districts must be made to understand, what he has already been taught in the city, that freedom does not mean idleness. On the other hand, the late master should specially be made to understand that the spirit of slavery must go to the grave with the thing itself. It will not be an easy work to teach either class its chief lesson. We must have patience,— patience, and faith that neither faints nor falters.

2 | Blacks' Reactions to Reconstruction

The Reconstruction period remains a subject of intense historical debate. The Thirteenth, Fourteenth, and Fifteenth Amendments to the U.S. Constitution asserted an equality between the races that was not realized in fact. At first the federal government vigorously supported the Freedman's Bureau and the efforts of Reconstruction governments in southern states to help the freed slaves, but within about a decade those efforts were abandoned as the northern public lost interest.

The social revolution brought about by emancipation caused severe problems for both blacks and whites. Just as the slaves' experiences had varied widely, so the newly freed blacks responded to their new situation in many different ways. Their needs were rarely understood by a public ill-prepared to accept blacks as equals or to support the long-term federal intervention that was required to make freedom an economic and social reality.

FELIX HAYWOOD From San Antonio, Texas. Born in Raleigh, North Carolina. Age at Interview: 88

The end of the war, it come just like that—like you snap your fingers. . . . How did we know it! Hallelujah broke out—

> Abe Lincoln freed the nigger
>   With the gun and the trigger;
> And I ain't going to get whipped any more.
>   I got my ticket,
>   Leaving the thicket,
>   And I'm a-heading for the Golden Shore!

Soldiers, all of a sudden, was everywhere—coming in bunches, crossing and walking and riding. Everyone was a-singing. We was all walking on golden clouds. Hallelujah!

Botkin, B.A. (editor), Lay My Burden Down: A Folk History of Slavery. (Chicago, University of Chicago Press, 1945), pp. 65–70, 223–224, 241–242, 246–247. Copyright © 1989 by Curtis Brown, Ltd.

> Union forever,
>   Hurrah, boys, hurrah!
> Although I may be poor,
>   I'll never be a slave—
> Shouting the battle cry of freedom.

Everybody went wild. We felt like heroes, and nobody had made us that way but ourselves. We was free. Just like that, we was free. It didn't seem to make the whites mad, either. They went right on giving us food just the same. Nobody took our homes away, but right off colored folks started on the move. They seemed to want to get closer to freedom, so they'd know what it was—like it was a place or a city. Me and my father stuck, stuck close as a lean tick to a sick kitten. The Gudlows started us out on a ranch. My father, he'd round up cattle—unbranded cattle—for the whites. They was cattle that they belonged to, all right; they had gone to find water 'long the San Antonio River and the Guadalupe. Then the whites gave me and my father some cattle for our own. My father had his own brand—7 B)—and we had a herd to start out with of seventy.

We knowed freedom was on us, but we didn't know what was to come with it. We thought we was going to get rich like the white folks. We thought we was going to be richer than the white folks, 'cause we was stronger and knowed how to work, and the whites didn't, and they didn't have us to work for them any more. But it didn't turn out that way. We soon found out that freedom could make folks proud, but it didn't make 'em rich.

Did you ever stop to think that thinking don't do any good when you do it too late? Well, that's how it was with us. If every mother's son of a black had thrown 'way his hoe and took up a gun to fight for his own freedom along with the Yankees, the war'd been over before it began. But we didn't do it. We couldn't help stick to our masters. We couldn't no more shoot 'em than we could fly. My father and me used to talk 'bout it. We decided we was too soft and freedom wasn't going to be much to our good even if we had a education.

/   /   /

WARREN MCKINNEY, *From Hazen, Arkansas. Born in South Carolina. Age at Interview: 85.*

I was born in Edgefield County, South Carolina. I am eighty-five years old. I was born a slave of George Strauter. I remembers hearing them say, "Thank God, I's free as a jay bird." My ma was a slave in the field. I was eleven years old when freedom was declared. When I was little, Mr. Strauter whipped my ma. It hurt me bad as it did her. I hated him. She was crying. I chunked him with rocks. He run after me, but he didn't catch me. There was twenty-five or thirty hands that worked in the field. They raised wheat, corn, oats, barley, and cotton. All the children that couldn't work stayed at one house. Aunt Mat kept the babies and small children that couldn't go to the field. He had a gin and a shop. The shop was at the fork of the roads. When the war come on, my papa went to build forts. He quit Ma and took another woman. When the war close, Ma took her four children, bundled 'em up and went to Augusta. The government give out rations there. My ma washed and ironed. People died in piles. I don't know till yet what was the matter. They said it was the change of living. I seen five or six wooden, painted coffins piled up on wagons pass by our house. Loads passed every day like you see cotton pass here. Some said it was cholera and some took consumption. Lots of the colored people nearly starved. Not much to get to do and not much houseroom. Several families had to live in one house. Lots of the colored folks went up North and froze to death. They couldn't stand the cold. They wrote back about them dying. No, they never sent them back. I heard some sent for money to come back. I heard plenty 'bout the Ku Klux. They scared the folks to death. People left Augusta in droves. About a thousand would all meet and walk going to hunt work and new homes. Some of them died. I had a sister and brother lost that way. I had another sister come to Louisiana that way. She wrote back.

I don't think the colored folks looked for a share of land. They never got nothing 'cause the white folks didn't have nothing but barren hills left. About all the mules was wore out hauling provisions in the army. Some folks say they ought to done more for the colored folks when they left, but they say they was broke. Freeing all the slaves left 'em broke.

That reconstruction was a mighty hard pull. Me and Ma couldn't live. A man paid our ways to Carlisle, Arkansas, and we come. We started working for Mr. Emenson. He had a big store, teams, and land. We liked it fine, and I been here fifty-six years now. There was so much wild game, living was not so hard. If a fellow could get a little bread and a place to stay, he was all right. After I come to this state, I voted some. I have farmed and worked at odd jobs. I farmed mostly. Ma went back to her old master. He persuaded her to come back home. Me and her went back and run a farm four or five years before she died. Then I come back here.

/   /   /

LEE GUIDON, From South Carolina. Born in South Carolina. Age at Interview: 89.

Yes, ma'am, I sure was in the Civil War. I plowed all day, and me and my sister helped take care of the baby at night. It would cry, and me bumping it [in a straight chair, rocking]. Time I git it to the bed where its mama was, it wake up and start crying all over again. I be so sleepy. It was a puny sort of baby. Its papa was off at war. His name was Jim

Cowan, and his wife Miss Margaret Brown 'fore she married him. Miss Lucy Smith give me and my sister to them. Then she married Mr. Abe Moore. Jim Smith was Miss Lucy's boy. He lay out in the woods all time. He say no need in him gitting shot up and killed. He say let the slaves be free. We lived, seemed like, on 'bout the line of York and Union counties. He lay out in the woods over in York County. Mr. Jim say all they fighting 'bout was jealousy. They caught him several times, but every time he got away from 'em. After they come home Mr. Jim say they never win no war. They stole and starved out the South. . . .

After freedom a heap of people say they was going to name their-selves over. They named theirselves big names, then went roaming round like wild, hunting cities. They changed up so it was hard to tell who or where anybody was. Heap of 'em died, and you didn't know when you hear about it if he was your folks hardly. Some of the names was Abraham, and some called theirselves Lincum. Any big name 'cept-ing their master's name. It was the fashion. I heard 'em talking 'bout it one evening, and my pa say, "Fine folks raise us and we gonna hold to our own names." That settled it with all of us. . . .

I reckon I do know 'bout the Ku Kluck. I knowed a man named Alfred Owens. He seemed all right, but he was a Republican. He said he was not afraid. He run a tanyard and kept a heap of guns in a big room. They all loaded. He married a Southern woman. Her husband either died or was killed. She had a son living with them. The Ku Kluck was called Upper League. They get this boy to unload all the guns. Then the white men went there. The white man give up and said, "I ain't got no gun to defend myself with. The guns all unloaded, and I ain't got no powder and shot." But the Ku Kluck shot in the houses and shot him up like lacework. He sold fine harness, saddles, bridles—all sorts of leather things. The Ku Kluck sure run them outen their country. They say they not going to have them round, and they sure run them out, back where they came from. . . .

For them what stayed on like they were, Reconstruction times 'bout like times before that 'cepting the Yankee stole out and tore up a scandalous heap. They tell the black folks to do something, and then come white folks you live with and say Ku Kluck whup you. They say leave, and white folks say better not listen to them old Yankees. They'll git you too far off to come back, and you freeze. They done give you all the use they got for you. How they do? All sorts of ways. Some stayed at their cabins glad to have one to live in and farmed on. Some running round begging, some hunting work for money, and nobody had no money 'cepting the Yankees, and they had no homes or land and mighty little work for you to do. No work to live on. Some going every day to the city. That winter I heard 'bout them starving and freezing by the wagon loads.

I never heard nothing 'bout voting till freedom. I don't think I ever voted till I come to Mississippi. I votes Republican. That's the party of my color, and I stick to them as long as they do right. I don't dabble in white folks' business, and that white folks' voting is their business. If I vote, I go do it and go on home.

I been plowing all my life, and in the hot days I cuts and saws wood. Then when I gets outa cotton-picking, I put each boy on a load of wood and we sell wood. The last years we got $3 a cord. Then we clear land till next spring. I don't find no time to be loafing. I never missed a year farming till I got the Bright's disease [one of several kinds of kidney ailments] and it hurt me to do hard work. Farming is the best life there is when you are able. . . .

When I owned most, I had six head mules and five head horses. I rented 140 acres of land. I bought this house and some other land about. The anthrax killed nearly all my horses and mules. I got one big fine mule yet. Its mate died. I lost my house. My son give me one room, and he paying the debt off now. It's hard for colored folks to keep anything. Somebody gets it from 'em if they don't mind.

The present times is hard. Timber is scarce. Game is about all gone. Prices higher. Old folks cannot work. Times is hard for younger folks too. They go to town too much and go to shows. They going to a tent show now. Circus coming, they say. They spending too much money for foolishness. It's a fast time. Folks too restless. Some of the colored folks work hard as folks ever did. They spends too much. Some folks is lazy. Always been that way.

I signed up to the government, but they ain't give me nothing 'cepting powdered milk and rice what wasn't fit to eat. It cracked up and had black something in it. A lady said she would give me some shirts that was her husband's. I went to get them, but she wasn't home. These heavy shirts give me heat. They won't give me the pension, and I don't know why. It would help me buy my salts and pills and the other medicines like Swamp Root. They won't give it to me.

TOBY JONES, From Madisonville, Texas. Born in
South Carolina. Age at Interview: 87.

I worked for Massa 'bout four years after freedom, 'cause he forced me to, said he couldn't 'ford to let me go. His place was near ruint, the fences burnt, and the house would have been, but it was rock. There was a battle fought near his place, and I taken Missy to a hideout in the mountains to where her father was, 'cause there was bullets flying everywhere. When the war was over, Massa come home and says, ''You son of a gun, you's supposed to be free, but you ain't, 'cause I ain't gwine give you freedom.'' So I goes on working for him till I gits the chance to steal a hoss from him. The woman I wanted to marry, Govie, she 'cides to come to Texas with me. Me and Govie, we rides that hoss 'most a hundred miles, then we turned him a-loose and give him a scare back to his house, and come on foot the rest the way to Texas.

All we had to eat was what we could beg, and sometimes we went three days without a bite to eat. Sometimes we'd pick a few berries. When we got cold we'd crawl in a brushpile and hug up close together to keep warm. Once in awhile we'd come to a farmhouse, and the man let us sleep on cottonseed in his barn, but they was far and few between, 'cause they wasn't many houses in the country them days like now.

When we gits to Texas, we gits married, but all they was to our wedding am we just 'grees to live together as man and wife. I settled on some land, and we cut some trees and split them open and stood them on end with the tops together for our house. Then we deadened some trees, and the land was ready to farm. There was some wild cattle and hogs, and that's the way we got our start, caught some of them and tamed them.

I don't know as I'spected nothing from freedom, but they turned us out like a bunch of stray dogs, no homes, no clothing, no nothing, not 'nough food to last us one meal. After we settles on that place, I never seed man or woman, 'cept Govie, for six years, 'cause it was a long ways to anywhere. All we had to farm with was sharp sticks. We'd stick holes and plant corn, and when it come up we'd punch up the dirt round it. We didn't plant cotton, 'cause we couldn't eat that. I made bows and arrows to kill wild game with, and we never went to a store for nothing. We made our clothes out of animal skins.

WHY ADAM KIRK WAS A DEMOCRAT

(House Report no. 262, 43 Cong., 2 Sess., p. 106. Statement of an Alabama Negro. [1874])

A white man raised me. I was raised in the house of old man Billy Kirk. He raised me as a body servant. The class that he belongs to seems nearer to me than the northern white man, and actually, since the war, everything I have got is by their aid and their assistance. They have helped me raise up my family and have stood by me, and whenever I want a doctor, no matter what hour of the day or night, he is called in whether I have got a cent or not. And when I want any assistance I can get it from them. I think they have got better principles and better character than the republicans.

Walter L. Fleming (editor), Documentary History of Reconstruction, Volume Two. *(Gloucester, Massachusetts, Peter Smith, 1960), p. 87.*

3 | White Southerners' Reaction to Reconstruction

The Congressional Joint Committee of Fifteen, assembled to examine Southern representation in Congress, was named in December 1865 and served as the Republican response to President Andrew Johnson's lenient plan of Reconstruction. In 1866, the committee held hearings as part of its effort to develop the Fourteenth Amendment. Congress had already, despite the President's veto, enlarged the scope of the Freedmen's Bureau to care for displaced ex-slaves and to try by military commission those accused of depriving freedmen of civil rights.

The testimony of white Southerners, three samples of which are presented below, indicate how difficult it was for the white South to accept the idea of black equality. Congress's reconstruction policy, more stringent than Johnson's but still cautious, appeared radical, even unthinkable, to most white Southerners and probably to many Northerners. Reading such testimony, one begins to understand why the nation has found it so difficult to carry out the mandate of the Fourteenth and Fifteenth Amendments.

B. R. GRATTAN

Washington, D.C., February 10, 1866

Question: Where do you reside?
Answer: Richmond, Virginia.
Question: Are you a native of Virginia?
Answer: Yes, sir: I was raised in the valley of Virginia.
Question: Do you hold any public position?
Answer: I am a member of the present house of delegates of Virginia.
Question: Is that the only public position you have held?
Answer: I held the office of reporter to the court of appeals since January, 1844.

The Report of the Committees of the House of Representatives Made During the First Session, Thirty-Ninth Congress, 1865–'66. Volume II. (Washington, D.C., Government Printing Office, 1866), Grattan: pp. 161–164; Forshey: pp. 129–132; Sinclair: 168–171.

Question: I speak of two classes of people in Virginia for the sake of convenience, not with a view of offending anybody. I speak of secessionists and Union men. By secessionists I mean those who have directly or indirectly favored the rebellion; and by Union men I mean those who opposed the rebellion; and by the rebellion I mean the war which has taken place between the two sections of the country. What is the general feeling among the secessionists of Virginia towards the government of the United States, so far as your observation extends?

Answer: So far as I know, the sentiment is universal that the war has decided the question of secession entirely, that it is no longer an open question, and that we are all prepared to abide by the Union and live under it.

Question: You mean to be understood as saying that they suppose that the sword has settled the abstract right of secession?

Answer: Yes; we consider that we put it to the arbitrament of the sword, and have lost.

Question: What proportion of the legislature of Virginia are original secessionists, have in view the definitions I gave?

Answer: I would suppose that there are few members of the legislature who are less able to judge of that matter than myself, for my acquaintance as a member is very limited; but I should suppose, from the general sentiments of the people of Virginia, that while probably a very large proportion of those who are now members of the legislature were not in favor of secession or a dissolution of the Union originally, yet nearly all of them went with their State when it went out. They went heartily with it.

Question: How have the results of the war affected the feelings of Virginians generally? What is the sentiment left in their hearts in regard to satisfaction or dissatisfaction with the government of the United States—love or hatred, respect or contempt?

Answer: I cannot undertake to say generally; my intercourse is very limited. I would rather suppose, however, that while the feeling against the government was originally very strong, that feeling has been very much modified; it is nothing like as strong as it was, and is gradually declining.

Question: You think that the feeling is gradually changing from dislike to respect?

Answer: Yes, I think so.

Question: Have you any reason to suppose that there are persons in Virginia who still entertain projects of a dissolution of the Union?

Answer: None whatever. I do not believe that there is an intelligent man in the State who does.

/   /   /

Question: What has been, in your judgment, the effect, in the main, of President Johnson's liberality in bestowing pardons and amnesties on rebels?

Answer: I think it has been very favorable; I think President Johnson has commended himself very heartily. There is a very strong feeling of gratitude towards President Johnson.

/   /   /

Question: What, in your judgment, would be the consequences of such an infranchisement: would it produce scenes of violence between the two races?

Answer: I believe it would. I have very great apprehension that an attempt of that sort would lead to their extermination, not immediately, but to their gradual extinction. It would set up really an antagonistic interest, which would probably be used as a power, because I have no doubt that the negro vote would be under the influence of white people. You are to recollect that this is not simply a prejudice between the white and black races. It has grown to be a part of our nature to look upon them as an inferior; just as much a part of our nature as it is a part of the nature of other races to have enmity to each other; for instance, between the Saxon Irish and the Celtic Irish, or between the English and the French. You must change that nature, and it takes a long time to do it. I believe that if you place the negro on a footing of perfect equality with the white, it would actually increase the power of the white race, which would control the negro vote; yet it seems to me that nothing can reconcile the white people to that short of equal political power, and I fear, therefore, very much the consequences of any attempt of that sort upon the black race in Virginia.

Question: Would not that prejudice become modified a great deal in case the blacks should be educated and rendered more intelligent than they are now?

Answer: You would have to change their skin before you can do it. I beg leave to say this, so far from there being any unkind feeling to the negro, I believe that there is, on the part of the white race, towards the negro, no feeling but that of kindness, sympathy, and pity, and that there is every disposition to ameliorate their condition and improve it as much as possible; but it is that difference which has existed so long in their obvious distinction of color and condition—

Question: But suppose the condition of the negro should change?

Answer: The condition is annexed to the color. We are accustomed to see the color in the condition.

/   /   /

Question: Is there a general repugnance on the part of whites to the acquisition and enjoyment of property by the blacks?

Answer: I do not know. I do not think there is. Far from it. We would be very glad to see them all doing well and improving their condition.

Question: Do you find a similar repugnance to the acquisition of knowledge by blacks?

Answer: No, sir; far from it; on the contrary, we are trying, so far as we can, to educate them; but we are too poor ourselves to do much in educating other people, and they are certainly too poor to educate themselves.

Question: You would, then, anticipate a struggle of races in case the right of suffrage was given to the blacks?

Answer: Yes, sir; I think so.

Question: You would not anticipate it in case the blacks should vote in the interests of the white race?

Answer: As I said before, I believe that if the blacks are left to themselves, if all foreign influence were taken away, the whites would control their vote. It is not in that the difficulty lies, but it is in the repugnance which the white race would feel to that sort of political equality. It is the same sort of repugnance which a man feels to a snake. He does not feel any animosity to the snake, but there is a natural shrinking from it; that is my feeling. While I think I have as much sympathy for the black race, and feel as much interest in them as anybody else, while I can treat them kindly and familiarly, still the idea of equality is one which has the same sort of shrinking for me, and is as much a part of my nature, as was the antagonism between Saxon and Celt in Ireland.

Question: You are aware that that state of feeling does not exist in Ireland, England, or Scotland towards the blacks?

Answer: No; because they never had them; because they never saw them in their constant condition. So that difference of alienation between Saxon and Celt does not exist here, but it exists in Ireland. It is where that has been the feeling operating for so long that it has become a part of our nature. It is not a simple prejudice, but it becomes part of the nature of the man. . . .

Question: You have not much reason to expect that the legislature of Virginia will adopt this constitutional amendment in case it shall pass both houses of Congress?

Answer: I cannot speak for others, but for myself I say certainly not. No political power would ever induce me to vote for it. That form is much more objectionable than even a proposition to make them voters. It is giving you all the advantages of numbers, while you are taking that from us which, according to the original constitution, we had—three-fifths of the slave population—and no political power will force me to consent to that.

CALEB G. FORSHEY

Washington, D.C., March 28, 1966

Question: Where do you reside?
Answer: I reside in the State of Texas.
Question: How long have you been a resident of Texas?
Answer: I have resided in Texas and been a citizen of that State for nearly thirteen years.
Question: What opportunities have you had for ascertaining the temper and disposition of the people of Texas towards the government and authority of the United States?
Answer: For ten years I have been superintendent of the Texas Military Institute, as its founder and conductor. I have been in the confederate service in various parts of the confederacy; but chiefly in the trans-Mississippi department, in Louisiana and Texas, as an officer of engineers. I have had occasion to see and know very extensively the condition of affairs in Texas, and also to a considerable extent in Louisiana. I think I am pretty well-informed, as well as anybody, perhaps, of the present state of affairs in Texas.
Question: What are the feelings and views of the people of Texas as to the late rebellion, and the future condition and circumstances of the State, and its relations to the federal government?
Answer: After our army had given up its arms and gone home, the surrender of all matters in controversy was complete, and as nearly universal, perhaps, as anything could be. Assuming the matters in controversy to have been the right to secede, and the right to hold slaves, I think they were given up teetotally, to use a strong Americanism. When you speak of feeling, I should discriminate a little. The feeling was that of any party who had been cast in a suit he had staked all upon. They did not return from feeling, but from a sense of necessity, and from a judgment that it was the only and necessary thing to be done, to give up the contest. But when they gave it up, it was without reservation; with a view to look forward, and not back. That is my impression of the manner in which the thing was done. There was a public expectation that in some very limited time there would be a restoration to former relations; and in such restoration they felt great interest, after the contest was given up. The expectation was, and has been up to the present time, that there would be a speedy and immediate restoration. It was the expectation of the people that, as soon as the State was organized as proposed by the President, they would be restored to their former relations, and things would go on as before.

/   /   /

Question: What is your opinion of a military force under the authority of the federal government to preserve order in Texas and to protect those who have been loyal, both white and black, from the aggressions of those who have been in the rebellion?

Answer: My judgment is well founded on that subject: that wherever such military force is and has been, it has excited the very feeling it was intended to prevent; that so far from being necessary it is very pernicious everywhere, and without exception. The local authorities and public sentiment are ample for protection. I think no occasion would occur, unless some individual case that our laws would not reach. We had an opportunity to test this after the surrender and before any authority was there. The military authorities, or the military officers, declared that we were without laws, and it was a long time before the governor appointed arrived there, and then it was some time before we could effect anything in the way of organization. We were a people without law, order, or anything; and it was a time for violence if it would occur. I think it is a great credit to our civilization that, in that state of affairs, there was nowhere any instance of violence. I am proud of it, for I expected the countrary; I expected that our soldiers on coming home, many of them, would be dissolute, and that many of them would oppress the class of men you speak of; but it did not occur. But afterwards, wherever soldiers have been sent, there have been little troubles, none of them large; but personal collisions between soldiers and citizens.

Question: What is your opinion as to the necessity and advantages of the Freedmen's Bureau, or an agency of that kind, in Texas?

Answer: My opinion is that it is not needed; my opinion is stronger than that—that the effect of it is to irritate, if nothing else. While in New York city recently I had a conversation with some friends from Texas, from five distant points in the State. We met together and compared opinions; and the opinion of each was the same, that the negroes had generally gone to work since January; that except where the Freedmen's Bureau had interfered, or rather encouraged troubles, such as little complaints, especially between negro and negro, the negro's disposition was very good, and they had generally gone to work, a vast majority of them with their former masters. I was very gratified to learn that from districts where I feared the contrary. Still this difference was made, particularly by Mr. Carpenter, from Jefferson, the editor of the Jefferson Herald. He said that in two or three counties where they had not been able to organize the Freedmen's Bureau, there had been no trouble at all; nearly all the negroes had gone to work. The impression in Texas at present is that the negroes under the influence of the Freedmen's Bureau do worse than without it.

I want to state that I believe all our former owners of negroes are the friends of the negroes; and that the antagonism paraded in the papers of the north does not exist at all. I know the fact is the very converse of that; and good feeling always prevails between the masters and the slaves. But the negroes went off and left them in the lurch; my own family was an instance of it. But they came back after a time, saying they had been free enough and wanted a home.

Question: Do you think those who employ the negroes there are willing to make contracts with them, so that they shall have fair wages for their labor?

Answer: I think so; I think they are paid liberally, more than the white men in this country get; the average compensation to negroes there is greater than the average compensation of free laboring white men in this country. It seems to have regulated itself in a great measure by what each neighborhood was doing; the negroes saying, "I can get thus and so at such a place." Men have hired from eight to fifteen dollars per month during the year, and women at about two dollars less a month; house-servants at a great deal more.

Question: Do the men who employ the negroes claim to exercise the right to enforce their contract by physical force?

Answer: Not at all; that is totally abandoned; not a single instance of it has occurred. I think they still chastise children, though. The negro parents often neglect that, and the children are still switched as we switch our own children. I know it is done in my own house; we have little house-servants that we switch just as I do our own little fellows.

Question: What is your opinion as to the respective advantages to the white and black races, of the present free system of labor and the institution of slavery?

Answer: I think freedom is very unfortunate for the negro; I think it is sad; his present helpless condition touches my heart more than anything else I ever contemplated, and I think that is the common sentiment of our slaveholders. I have seen it on the largest plantations, where the negro men had all left, and where only women and children remained, and the owners had to keep them and feed them. The beginning certainly presents a touching and sad spectacle. The poor negro is dying at a rate fearful to relate.

I have some ethnological theories that may perhaps warp my judgment; but my judgment is that the highest condition the black race has ever reached or can reach, is one where he is provided for by a master race. That is the result of a great deal of scientific investigation and observation of the negro character by me ever since I was a man. The labor question had become a most momentous one, and I was studying it. I undertook to investigate the condition of the negro from statistics under various circumstances, to treat it purely as a matter of statistics from the census tables of this country of ours. I found that the free blacks of the north decreased 8 per cent.; the free blacks of the south increased 7 or 8 per cent., while the slaves by their sides increased 34 per cent. I inferred from the doctrines of political economy that the race is in the best condition when it procreates the fastest; that, other things being equal, slavery is of vast advantage to the negro. I will mention one or two things in connexion with this as explanatory of that result. The negro will not take care of his offspring unless required to do it, as compared with the whites. The little children will die; they do die, and hence the necessity of very rigorous regulations on our plantations which we have adopted in our nursery system.

Another cause is that there is no continence among the negroes. All the continence I have ever seen among the negroes has been enforced upon plantations, where it is generally assumed there is none. For the sake of procreation, if nothing else, we compel men to live with their wives. The discipline of the plantation was more rigorous, perhaps, in regard to men staying with their wives, than in regard to anything else; and I think the procreative results, as shown by the census tables, is due in a great measure to that discipline.

I think they are very much better off in having homes than the free blacks are. The free blacks in Louisiana, where we had 34,000, with a great deal of blood of the whites in them, and therefore a great deal of white sense, were nothing like so happy and so well off as our slaves are. My observation for many years leads me to this conclusion.

Question: What is the prevailing inclination among the people of Texas in regard to giving the negroes civil or political rights and privileges?

Answer: I think they are all opposed to it. There are some men—I am not among them—who think that the basis of intelligence might be a good basis for the elective franchise. But a much larger class, perhaps nine-tenths of our people, believe that the distinctions between the races should not be broken down by any such community of interests in the management of the affairs of the State. I think there is a very common sentiment that the negro, even with education, has not a mind capable of appreciating the political institutions of the country to such an extent as would make him a good associate for the white man in the administration of the government. I think if the vote was taken on the question of admitting him to the right of suffrage there would be a very small vote in favor of it—scarcely respectable: that is my judgment.

/   /   /

REVEREND JAMES SINCLAIR

Washington, D.C., January 29, 1866

[James Sinclair, a Scottish born minister who served on the Freedmen's Bureau in 1865, had been living in North Carolina for nine years. Though a slaveholder himself, Sinclair opposed succession. This led to the loss of his church and his eventual arrest during the war. In contrast to the testimony of Caleb Forshey, Sinclair's description of relations between whites and blacks suggests that, in some cases, paternalism has been replaced by outright enmity. An outsider in the South both during and after the conflict, Sinclair offers a point of view that seems the most pessimistic in its assessment of whether the wounds of the war would heal in the near future.]

Question: What is generally the state of feeling among the white people of North Carolina towards the government of the United States?

Answer: That is a difficult question to answer, but I will answer it as far as my own knowledge goes. In my opinion, there is generally among the white people not much love for the government. Though they are willing, and I believe determined, to acquiesce in what is inevitable, yet so far as love and affection for the government is concerned, I do not believe that they have any of it at all, outside of their personal respect and regard for President Johnson.

Question: How do they feel towards the mass of the northern people—that is, the people of what were known formerly as the free States?

Answer: They feel in this way: that they have been ruined by them. You can imagine the feelings of a person towards one whom he regards as having ruined him. They regard the northern people as having destroyed their property or taken it from them, and brought all the calamaties of this war upon them.

Question: How do they feel in regard to what is called the right of secession?

Answer: They think that it was right . . . that there was no wrong in it. They are willing now to accept the decision of the question that has been made by the sword, but they are not by any means converted from their old opinion that they had a right to secede. It is true that there have always been Union men in our State, but not Union men without slavery, except perhaps among Quakers. Slavery was the central idea even of the Unionist. The only difference between them and the others upon that question was, that they desired to have that institution under the aegis of the Constitution, and protected by it. The secessionists wanted to get away from the north altogether. When the secessionists precipitated our State into rebellion, the Unionists and secessionists went together, because the great object with both was the preservation of slavery by the preservation of State sovereignty. There was another class of Unionists who did not care anything at all about slavery, but they were driven by the other whites into the rebellion for the purpose of preserving slavery. The poor whites are to-day very much opposed to conferring upon the negro the right of suffrage; as much so as the other classes of the whites. They believe it is the intention of government to give the negro rights at their expense. They cannot see it in any other light than that as the negro is elevated they must proportionately go down. While they are glad that slavery is done away with, they are as bitterly opposed to conferring the right of suffrage on the negro as the most prominent secessionists; but it is for the reason I have stated, that they think rights conferred on the negro must necessarily be taken from them, particularly the ballot, which was the only bulwark guarding their superiority to the negro race.

Question: In your judgment, what proportion of the white people of North Carolina are really, and truly, and cordially attached to the government of the United States?

Answer: Very few, sir; very few.

Question: Judging from what you have observed of the feelings of the people of that State, what would be their course in case of a war between the United States and a foreign government?

Answer: I can only tell you what I have heard young men say there; perhaps it was mere bravado. I have heard them say that they wished to the Lord the United States would get into a war with France or England; they would know where they would be. I asked this question of some of them: If Robert E. Lee was restored to his old position in the army of the United States, and he should call on you to join him to fight for the United Sates and against a foreign enemy, what would you do? They replied, "Wherever old Bob would go we would go with him."

Question: Have you heard such remarks since the war is over, as that they wished the United States would get into a war with England and France?

Answer: Oh, yes, sir; such remarks are very common. I have heard men say, "May my right hand wither and my tongue cleave to the roof of my mouth if I ever lift my arm in favor of the United States."

Question: Did you ever hear such sentiments rebuked by by-standers?

Answer: No, sir; it would be very dangerous to do so.

Question: Is the Freedmen's Bureau acceptable to the great mass of the white people in North Carolina?

Answer: No, sir; I do not think it is; I think the most of the whites wish the bureau to be taken away.

Question: Why do they wish that?

Answer: They think that they can manage the negro for themselves: that they understand him better than northern men do. They say, "Let us understand what you want us to do with the negro—what you desire of us; lay down your conditions for our re-admission into the Union, and then we will know what we have to do, and if you will do that we will enact laws for the government of these negroes. They have lived among us, and they are all with us, and we can manage them better than you can." They think it is intefering with the rights of the State for a bureau, the agent and representative of the federal government, to overslaugh the State entirely, and interfere with the regulations and administration of justice before their courts.

Question: Is there generally a willingness on the part of the whites to allow the freedmen to enjoy the right of acquiring land and personal property?

Answer: I think they are very willing to let them do that, for this reason; to get rid of some portion of the taxes imposed upon their property by the government. For instance, a white man will agree to sell a negro some of his land on condition of his paying so much a year on it, promising to give him a deed of it when the whole payment is made, taking his note in the mean time. This relieves that much of the land from taxes to be paid by the white man. All I am afraid of is, that the negro is too eager to go into this thing; that he will ruin himself, get himself into debt to the white man, and be forever bound to him for the debt and never get the land. I have often warned them to be careful what they did about these things.

Question: There is no repugnance on the part of the whites to the negro owning land and personal property?

Answer: I think not.

Question: Have they any objection to the legal establishment of the domestic relations among the blacks, such as the relation of husband and wife, of parent and child, and the securing by law to the negro the rights of those relations?

Answer: That is a matter of ridicule with the whites. They do not believe the negroes will ever respect those relations more than the brutes. I suppose I have married more than two hundred couples of negroes since the war, but the whites laugh at the very idea of the thing. Under the old laws a slave could not marry a free woman of color; it was made a penal offence in North Carolina for any one to perform such a marriage. But there was in my own family a slave who desired to marry a free woman of color, and I did what I conceived to be my duty, and married them, and I was presented to the grand jury for doing so, but the prosecuting attorney threw out the case and would not try it. In former times the officiating clergyman marrying slaves, could not use the usual formula: "Whom God has joined together let no man put asunder;" you could not say, "According to the ordinance of God I pronounce you man and wife; you are no longer two but one." It was not legal for you to do so.

Question: What, in general, has been the treatment of the blacks by the whites since the close of hostilities?

Answer: It has not generally been of the kindest character, I must say that; I am compelled to say that.

Question: Are you aware of any instance of personal ill treatment towards the blacks by the whites?

Answer: Yes, sir.

Question: Give some instances that have occurred since the war.

Answer: [Sinclair describes the beating of a young woman across her buttocks in graphic detail.]

Question: What was the provocation, if any?

Answer: Something in regard to some work, which is generally the provocation.

Question: Was there no law in North Carolina at that time to punish such an outrage?

Answer: No, sir; only the regulations of the Freedmen's Bureau; we took cognizance of the case. In old times that was quite allowable; it is what was called "paddling."

Question: Did you deal with the master?

Answer: I immediately sent a letter to him to come to my office, but he did not come, and I have never seen him in regard to the matter since. I had no soldiers to enforce compliance, and I was obliged to let the matter drop.

Question: Have you any reason to suppose that such instances of cruelty are frequent in North Carolina at this time—instances of whipping and striking?

Answer: I think they are; it was only a few days before I left that a woman came there with her head all bandaged up, having been cut and bruised by her employer. They think nothing of striking them.

Question: And the negro has practically no redress?

Answer: Only what he an get from the Freedmen's Bureau.

Question: Can you say anything further in regard to the political condition of North Carolina—the feeling of the people towards the government of the United States?

Answer: I for one would not wish to be left there in the hands of those men; I could not live there just now. But perhaps my case is an isolated one from the position I was compelled to take in that State. I was persecuted, arrested, and they tried to get me into their service; they tried everything to accomplish their purpose, and of course I have rendered myself still more obnoxious by accepting an appointment under the Freedmen's Bureau. As for myself I would not be allowed to remain there. I do not want to be handed over to these people. I know it is utterly impossible for any man who was not true to the Confederate States up to the last moment of the existence of the confederacy, to expect any favor of these people as the State is constituted at present.

Question: Suppose the military pressure of the government of the United States should be withdrawn from North Carolina, would northern men and true Unionists be safe in that State?

Answer: A northern man going there would perhaps present nothing obnoxious to the people of the State. But men who were born there, who have been true to the Union, and who have fought against the rebellion, are worse off than northern men. And Governor Holden will never get any place from the people of North Carolina, not even a constable's place.

Question: Why not?

Answer: Because he identified himself with the Union movement all along after the first year of the rebellion. He has been a marked man; his printing office has been gutted, and his life has been threatened by the soldiers of the rebellion. He is killed there politically, and never will get anything from the people of North Carolina, as the right of suffrage exists there at present. I am afraid he would not get even the support of the negro, if they should be allowed to vote, because he did not stand right up for them as he should have done. In my opinion, he would have been a stronger man than ever if he had.

Question: Is it your opinion that the feelings of the great mass of the white people of North Carolina are unfriendly to the government of the United States?

Answer: Yes, sir, it is; they have no love for it. If you mean by loyalty, acquiescence in what has been accomplished, then they are all loyal; if you mean, on the other hand, that love and affection which a child has for its parent even after he brings the rod of correction upon him, then they have not that feeling. It may come in the course of time.

/   /   /

Question: In your judgment, what effect has been produced by the liberality of the President in granting pardons and amnesties to rebels in that State—what effect upon the public mind?

Answer: On my oath I am bound to reply exactly as I believe; that is, that if President Johnson is ever a candidate for re-election he will be supported by the southern States, particularly by North Carolina; but that his liberality to them has drawn them one whit closer to the government than before, I do not believe. It has drawn them to President Johnson personally, and to the democratic party, I suppose.

Question: Has that clemency had any appreciable effect in recovering the real love and affection of that people for the government?

Answer: No, sir; not for the government, considered apart from the person of the Executive.

Question: Has it had the contrary effect?

Answer: I am not prepared to answer that question, from the fact that they regard President Johnson as having done all this because he was a southern man, and not because he was an officer of the government.

/   /   /

4 | A Sharecrop Contract

The ending of slavery and the impoverishment of the South in the aftermath of the Civil War seriously disrupted Southern agriculture. Five years after the war's end, Southern cotton production was still only about half of what it had been in the 1850s. The large plantations, no longer tended by gangs of slaves or hired freedmen, were broken up into smaller holdings, but the capital required for profitable agriculture meant that control of farming remained centralized in a limited elite of merchants and larger landholders.

Various mechanisms arose to finance Southern agriculture. Tenants worked on leased land. Small landowners gave liens on their crops to get financing. But the most common method of financing agriculture was sharecropping. Agreements like the Grimes family's sharecrop contract determined the economic life of thousands of poor rural families in the southern United States after the Civil War. Families, black and white, lacking capital for agriculture, were furnished the seed, implements, and a line of credit for food and other necessities to keep them through the growing season. Accounts were settled in the winter after crops were in. Under these conditions a small number of farmers managed to make money and eventually become landowners, and the larger part found themselves in ever deeper debt at the end of the year with no choice but to contract again for the next year.

To every one applying to rent land upon shares, the following conditions must be read, and *agreed to.*

To every 30 or 35 acres, I agree to furnish the team, plow, and farming implements, except cotton planters, and I *do not* agree to furnish a cart to every cropper. The croppers are to have half of the cotton, corn and fodder (and peas and pumpkins and potatoes if any are planted) if the following conditions are complied with, but—if not—they are to have only two fifths ($\frac{2}{5}$). Croppers are to have no part or interest in the cotton seed raised from the crop planted and worked by them. No vine crops of any description, that is, no watermelons, muskmelons, . . . squashes or anything of that kind, except peas and pumpkins, and po-

From the Grimes Family Papers (#3357), 1882. Held in the Southern Historical Collection, University of North Carolina, Chapel Hill.

tatoes, are to be planted in the cotton or corn. All must work under my direction. All plantation work to be done by the croppers. My part of the crop to be *housed* by them, and the fodder and oats to be hauled and put in the house. All the cotton must be topped about 1st August. If any cropper fails from any cause to save all the fodder from his crop, I am to have enough fodder to make it equal to one half of the whole if the whole amount of fodder had been saved.

For every mule or horse furnished by me there must be 1000 good sized rails . . . hauled, and the fence repaired as far as they will go, the fence to be torn down and put up from the bottom if I so direct. All croppers to haul rails and work on fence wherever I may order. Rails to be split when I may say. Each cropper to clean out every ditch in his crop, and where a ditch runs between two croppers, the cleaning out of that ditch is to be divided equally between them. Every ditch bank in the crop must be shrubbed down and cleaned off before the crop is planted and must be cut down every time the land is worked with his hoe and when the crop is "laid by," the ditch banks must be left clean of bushes, weeds, and seeds. The cleaning out of all ditches must be done by the first of October. The rails must be split and the fence repaired before corn is planted.

Each cropper must keep in good repair all bridges in his crop or over ditches that he has to clean out and when a bridge needs repairing that is outside of all their crops, then any one that I call on must repair it.

Fence jams to be done as ditch banks. If any cotton is planted on the land outside of the plantation fence, I am to have *three fourths* of all the cotton made in those patches, that is to say, no cotton must be planted by croppers in their home patches.

All croppers must clean out stables and fill them with straw, and haul straw in front of stables whenever I direct. All the cotton must be manured, and enough fertilizer must be brought to manure each crop highly, the croppers to pay for one half of all manure bought, the quantity to be purchased for each crop must be left to me.

No cropper to work off the plantation when there is any work to be done on the land he has rented, or when his work is needed by me or other croppers. Trees to be cut down on Orchard, House field & Evanson fences, leaving such as I may designate.

Road field to be planted from the *very edge of the ditch to the fence,* and all the land to be planted close up to the ditches and fences. *No stock of any kind* belonging to croppers to run in the plantation after crops are gathered.

If the fence should be blown down, or if trees should fall on the fence outside of the land planted by any of the croppers, any one or all that I may call upon must put it up and repair it. Every cropper must feed, or have fed, the team he works, Saturday nights, Sundays, and every morning before going to work, beginning to feed his team (morning, noon, and night *every day* in the week) on the day he rents and feeding it to and including the 31st day of December. If any cropper shall from any cause fail to repair his fence as far as 1000 rails will go, or shall fail to clean out any part of his ditches, or shall fail to leave his ditch banks, any part of them, well shrubbed and clean when his crop is laid by, or shall fail to clean out stables, fill them up and haul straw in front of them whenever he is told, he shall have only two-fifths ($\frac{2}{5}$) of the cotton, corn, fodder, peas and pumpkins made on the land he cultivates.

If any cropper shall fail to feed his team Saturday nights, all day Sunday and all the rest of the week, morning/noon, and night, for every time he so fails he must pay me five cents.

No corn nor cotton stalks must be burned, but must be cut down, cut up and plowed in. Nothing must be burned off the land except when it is *impossible* to plow it in.

Every cropper must be responsible for all gear and farming implements placed in his hands, and if not returned must be paid for unless it is worn out by use.

Croppers must sow & plow in oats and haul them to the crib, but *must have no part of them.* Nothing to be sold from their crops, nor fodder nor corn to be carried out of the fields until my rent is all paid, and all amounts they owe me and for which I am responsible are paid in full.

I am to gin & pack all the cotton and charge every cropper an eighteenth of his part, the cropper to furnish his part of the bagging, ties, & twine.

The sale of every cropper's part of the cotton to be made by me when and where I choose to sell, and after deducting all they may owe me and all sums that I may be responsible for on their accounts, to pay them their half of the net proceeds. Work of every description, particularly the work on fences and ditches, to be done to my satisfaction, and must be done over until I am satisfied that it is done as it should be.

No wood to burn, nor light wood, nor poles, nor timber for boards, nor wood for any purpose whatever must be gotten above the house occupied by Henry Beasley—nor must any trees be cut down nor any wood used for any purpose, except for firewood, without my permission.

5 | On Buffaloes and Indians

The great herds of buffalo on the western plains were essential to the Plains Indians, providing them with food, shelter, and fuel. In the twenty years after the Civil War, though, with buffalo hides in fashion in white society, professional hunters and so-called sportsmen nearly extinguished the species in one of the great ecological disasters in history. It has been estimated that thirteen-million animals were exterminated by 1883, when extinction threatened and buffalo became too scarce to be hunted profitably. Ironically, it was principally the herds of buffalo saved for "wild west" shows, such as that of Wild Bill Cody, that allowed the limited survival of the species.

In the first reading, W. Skelton Glenn describes commercial buffalo hunting. His 1910 memoirs, which most likely describe a hunt taking place in Texas sometime in 1876 or 1877, provide an account of the use of new, technologically superior rifles that greatly facilitated the buffalo's rapid decline. The second selection, by E. N. Andrews, documents the hunt of buffalo for sport. As Andrews documents the brutality of the kill, he is wistful and somewhat regretful about the encroachment of white civilization onto Indian lands. However, John Cook expresses little sentimental concern about the Indians. The fact that the decline of the Indians was linked to the destruction of their food resources provided an incentive against the conservation of the buffalo herds. Influenced by the conservative social Darwinism of the late nineteenth century, Cook saw the decline of the buffalo and the Indians as an event that not only was inevitable, but it would lead to the establishment of a more advanced civilization on the North American continent.

W. SKELTON GLENN*

There was several methods to kill [buffalos] and each [hunter] adopted his own course and plan. They would get together and while one gained a point from another, he, in turn, would gain a point from him. One method was to run beside them, shooting them as they ran. Another was to shoot from the rear, what was termed tail shooting: [always

*From Strickland, Rex W., editor, "The Recollections of W. S. Glenn, Buffalo Hunter," Panhandle-Plains Historical Review 22 (1949), pp. 20–26. Courtesy of Panhandle-Plains Historical Society.

shooting] the hindmost buffalo and when a day's hunt was done, they would be strung on the ground for a mile or more, from ten to fifteen yards apart.

We first noticed that the buffaloes always went around a ravine or gulch, unless going for water straight down a bluff; and as the buffalo always followed these trails a man on foot by a mere cut-off of a hundred yards could cut him off. That is why they was so far apart in tail-hunting, as it was called.

/   /   /

Another method of hunting was to leave your horse out of sight after you had determined the direction and course of the wind, and then get as near as possible. If the herd was lying at rest, he would pick out some buffalo that was standing up on watch and shoot his ball in the side of him so that it would not go through, but would lodge in the flesh; as on many times it had been proven by men [who were] well hid and the wind taking the sound of the gun and the whizz of the bullet off, [that] if a ball passed through a buffalo the herd would stampede and run for miles. A buffalo shot in this manner would merely hump up his back as if he had the colic and commence to mill round and round in a slow walk. The other buffalo sniffing the blood and following would not be watching the hunter, and he would continue to shoot the outside cow buffalo; if there were old cows they would take them as there would be some two or three offsprings following her. If she would hump up, he would know that he had the range, and in this way hold the herd as long as they acted in this way as well as the well trained cowpuncher would hold his herd, only the hunter would use his gun. This was termed mesmerising the buffalo so that we could hold them on what we termed a stand, which afterwards proved to be the most successful way of killing the buffalo.

It was not always the best shot but the best hunter that succeeded, that is, the man who piled his buffalo in a pile so as to be more convenient for the skinner to get at and not have to run all over the country.

/   /   /

The hunter was hired by the piece: if robe hides were worth $3.00, [he was] given twenty-five cents for every one that he killed and was brought in by the skinners—was tallied up at camp. It was the camp rustler's business to keep tally of the number of hides killed each day. If the hides were worth $2.50, he [the hunter] got 20 cents; $2.00, he got 15 cents; $1.50, he got 10 cents; and $1.00, he got 5 cents.

/   /   /

. . . . At the Doby Walls fight [i.e., the Adobe Walls, June 27, 1874], the hunters [used] all classes of guns, such as the Spencer, Springfield, Winchester and six-shooters, also all classes of buffalo guns, including a new sample 45, which Sharp had just sent out, . . . [Billy Dixon's famous long shot, so Glenn says, was made with the new 45-caliber Sharp.] Still some were not satisfied, so went outside and stepped off a 150 yards and commenced to pile dry bull hides ten in a bunch, and began to shoot with all four guns—as they went through so easily, they added more and continued to add until they had shot through 32 [hides] and one bullet stook in the thirty-third one and it proved to be the new gun. All had to have a shot with the new gun and as it gave entire satisfaction, they sent word back that this was the gun for the buffalo, and all of them ordered a gun. Sharp began to manufacture these rifles as fast as he could in various lengths and this gun, as it afterwards proved, was the cause of the extermination of the buffalo, as before this they had increased faster than killed out as it took too many shots to get a buffalo.

/   /   /

I have seen their bodies so thick after being skinned, that they would look like logs where a hurricane had passed through a forrest [sic]. If they were lying on a hillside, the rays of the sun would make it look like a hundred glass windows. These buffalo would lie in this way until warm weather, drying up, and I have seen them piled fifty or sixty in a pile where the hunter had made a stand. As the skinner commenced on the edge, he would have to roll it out of the way to have room to skin the next, and when finished they would be rolled up as thick as saw logs around a mill. In this way a man could ride over a field and pick out the camps that were making the most money out of the hunt.

These hides, like all other commodities would rise and fall in price and we had to be governed by the prices [in the] East. This man, J. R. Loganstein, that run the hunt, has known them to be shipped to New York, then to Liverpool and back again in order to raise the price or corner the market. . . .

We will now describe a camp outfit. They would range from six to a dozen men, there being one hunter who killed the buffalo and took out the tongues, also the tallow. As the tallow was of an oily nature, it was equal to butter; [it was used] for lubricating our guns and we loaded our own shells, each shell had to be lubricated and [it] was used also for greasing wagons and also for lights in camp. Often chunks as large as an ear of corn were thrown on the fire to make heat. This [i.e., the removal of the tallow] had to be done while the meat was fresh, the hunter throwing it into a tree to wind dry; if the skinner forgot it, it would often stay there all winter and still be good to eat in the spring and better to eat after hanging there in the wind a few days.

We will return to the wagon man. [There were] generally two men to the wagon and their business was to follow up the hunter, if they were not in sight after the hunter had made a killing, he would proceed in their direction until he had met them, and when they would see him, he would signal with his hat where the killing was. If they got to the buffalo when they were fresh, their duty was to take out all the humps, tongues and tallow from the best buffalo. The hunter would then hunt more if they did not have hides enough to make a load or finish their day's work.

A remarkable good hunter would kill seventy-five to a hundred in a day, an average hunter about fifty, and a common one twenty-five, some hardly enough to run a camp. It was just like in any other business. A good skinner would skin from sixty to seventy-five, an average man from thirty to forty, and a common one from fifteen to twenty-five. These skinners were also paid by the hide[,] about five cents less than the hunter was getting for killing, being furnished with a grind stone, knives and steel and a team and wagon. The men were furnished with some kind of a gun, not as valuable as Sharp's rifle, to kill cripples with, also kips and calves that were standing around. In several incidents [instances?] it has been known to happen while the skinner was busy, they would slip up and knock him over. Toward the latter part of the hunt, when all the big ones were killed, I have seen as many as five hundred up to a thousand in a bunch, nothing but calves and have ridden right up to them, if the wind was right.

/   /   /

E. N. ANDREWS*

Excursions over the "Plains" are becoming so common as to excite little or no attention. One can now ride over that broad expanse extending beyond the borders of civilization on the east, to and beyond the Rocky Mountains, in the most elegant coaches drawn by the untiring horse of iron.

In boyhood, when on some gunning excursion for game so infinitesimal as to be unworthy of mention, it was considered unwise to reveal a favorable resort, lest other Nimrods [hunters] should go and steal our honors. But on the occasion referred to in this sketch, having had our views philanthropic enlarged a little, we shall not hesitate to tell, from actual observations, something of the Indian hunting-grounds of the Plains, which form the open porch to the mountains. It will, however, be as impossible to describe the scenes we saw, or the impressions produced, as it is for the poet fully to paint with words all the finer emotions of his soul.

*From E. N. Andrews, "A Buffalo Hunt by Rail," Kansas Magazine 3 (May 1873), pp. 450–455.

Although these excursions are of common occurrence since the laying of the rails, and will ever continue so, yet to the writer the trip revealed scenes and events altogether new and striking, and such as can never be forgotten. We played a little on the border-lands; while the limitless area, where roam the Indian and his counterpart the buffalo, together with the wolf, the prairie-dog and the antelope, swift of foot, extends hundreds of miles farther westward, and thousands northward and southward.

Our excursion party, organized for the benefit of a church in that place, and numbering about three hundred, left Lawrence, Kansas, Tuesday, A.M., at 10 o'clock, October 6, 1868, by the Kansas Pacific Railway. Our train consisted of five passenger coaches, one smoking car, one baggage and one freight car. The two latter were used for the commissary, although on our way back the freight car was devoted to another purpose.

The Lawrence Cornet Band, which went along, entertained us upon the platform while our large company were undergoing the slow process of shipment. Our engine (all honor to her for having "done what she could") being of rather a consumptive tendency, drew us not very rapidly toward the Occident, especially along the inevitably upward acclivities which lay in her track toward the Rocky Mountains. . . .

There were seventy-five or eighty guns on board, and the writer bagged the first game, namely, one quail, while the train stopped near a plowed field. He does not boast of this, however, as most of the guns were rifles, while he had a shot-and-rifle combined—the right kind for a variety of game. . . .

It was now tea time; the day had been comfortable and pleasant. One of those rare sunset scenes which are not uncommon to the people of Kansas, greeted our sight, to describe which were impossible. Suffice it to say, that the golden flood which extended eastward along the northern horizon, gradually ended in a distinctly violet hue, while the dark clouds above seemed to compress this evening glory, as they shut down from above, within the compass of a narrow space, making the scene more intense. But as joy and beauty are often accompanied by tears, so did not this day close without a change. We went on to Ellsworth, where we spent the night, arranging our seats, (for there were no sleeping-cars,) as best we could for a night's rest. At nine o'clock the wind had changed from south to north, and howled frightfully, as if to blow the cars from the track. The rain came, beating through every crevice; the lightning flashed, the temperature became quite cold, and there was a prospect of an uncomfortable night. But fires were kindled, and we rested as well as we could, with feet as high as our heads, while we wished for day.

At 5 o'clock A.M., on Wednesday, we left Ellsworth, near which is Fort Harker, and proceeded. The all-important question, revealing very plainly the thought and desire of all, was: "Where shall we see the buffalo?'' ''Are there any buffalo about here?'' These and similar interrogatories were put to everybody we could find, especially to the colored soldiers or guards at the various water-tanks. When told that we should soon see the ''animals,'' all were on the *qui vive*; the rifles were made ready; all eyes were strained lest some object should escape our notice. And it is no wonder that there was this hopeful expectancy, for most of us had probably never seen the bison, the mythic autocrat of the Plains! Nor did we anticipate a very near proximity to any large number of those animals. For one, however, I ardently desired to see a buffalo, a single one, at least, before the close of my mortal existence, especially since this is so peculiarly an American animal. . . .

We now arrived at Fort Hays and Hays City, the latter a poor gambling-place. Indeed, these frontier towns seem mostly to have been inhabited for the purpose of gambling with and thus robbing men coming in from the mines, or with cattle from over the Plains.

Here we were informed that there were plenty of buffalo twenty-five miles ahead! Could we believe it? We rolled onward on the iron [railroad] track, but looked in vain on either side for the chief object of attraction. A few were seen in the dim distance; but this was an aggravation. We continued to shoot at prairie-dogs, and gathered, when the train stopped at the water-tanks, the cactus,—the kind called prickly-pear. There is also another kind, the sword-cactus, growing in this region. We met another train which had on board several quarters of buffalo-meat, also General Sheridan. But the latter seemed of little account to us buffalo-hunters, just then, since we had seen the tracks or evidences of the ''animals.'' We were now told that ten miles farther on we should find them.

With minds still dubious on the subject, when near the 325th milestone, (counting from State Line on the Missouri River, where the road begins,) we began to see buffalo near at hand, or within a quarter of a mile of the track. But what a sight was gradually unfolded to our vision! In the distance, as if upon a gentle slope, we beheld at least a thousand buffalo feeding, though this was not a circumstance to that which followed. For ten miles vast numbers continued in sight; and not only for this short (?) distance, but for forty miles, buffalo were scattered along the horizon, some nearer and others more remote. In estimating the number, the only fitting word was ''innumerable;'' one hundred thousand was too small a number, a million would be more correct. Besides, who could tell how many miles those herds, or *the* herd, extended beyond the visible horizon? It were vain to imagine! Antelope and wolves continued to be seen here and there, the latter skulking near the carcasses of buffalo scattered all along the Plains near the track. . . .

Another thing noticeable: what gives to the telegraph-poles in this region that smooth, greasy appearance a few feet from the base? That is where the animals have rubbed themselves when passing. Thanks to you, O Telegraph Company, in behalf of the bison. This is a rare luxury for our shaggy-coated herds which inhabit where no trees are. But while noticing this appearance of the poles, a suggestive thought came into my mind. Is not this pushing and rubbing of the buffalo against the telegraph poles, in his onward march northward or southward over his own long-inhabited feeding-grounds, an effort of his nature to repel the encroachments of civilization, as fitly embodied in this pioneer agency of electricity? So it seemed. And is it strange that the herdsmen of these animals, the red men, should also refuse to stand and look with complacency upon the on-reaching iron trail of the white man, bearing the shrieking locomotive far out into the depths of his hunting-ground, and disturbing the quiet and sanctity of that boundless realm? Without apologizing for the cowardly depredations and hostile demonstrations of the Indian, who was then on the "war-path," we can yet see something that may, from his stand-point, look like a provocation sufficient to warrant all this hostility.

But to return to the actual sights and the sports of our party. At about 6:30 o'clock on Wednesday evening, October 7th, though not anticipating any sport at close quarters, (since we were told that on the morrow the train would return to the hunting-ground, so that we could have all day with the buffalo and hunt to our satisfaction,) when at the 365th mile-post we saw buffalo near at hand. Three bulls were on the left of the track, though nearly all that we had seen were on the right, or north of that barrier, while now on their southward course, feeding in their slow advance toward winter-quarters in Texas or New Mexico. Of those three noble wanderers, one was doomed to fall before the bullets of the excursionists. They all kept pace with the train for at least a quarter of a mile, while the boys blazed away at them without effect. It was their design to get ahead of the train and cross over to the main body of their fellows; and they finally accomplished their object. The cow-catcher, however, became almost a bull-catcher, for it seemed to graze one as he passed on the jump. As soon as the three were well over upon the right, they turned backward, at a small angle away from the train, and then it was that powder and ball were brought into requisition! Shots enough were fired to rout a regiment of men. Ah! see that bull in advance there; he has stopped a second; he turns a kind of reproachful look toward the train; he starts again on the lope a step or two; he hesitates; poises on the right legs; a pail-full of blood gushes warm from his nostrils; he falls flat upon the right side, dead. One of the remaining companions turns a farewell look upon the vanquished one, and then starts off over the prairie toward the herd. We had expected no such coup d'essai on that day, expecially so late in the evening, and the pleasure and excitement were all the greater because so unexpected. The engineer was kind enough to shut off the steam; the train stopped, and such a scrambling and screeching was never before heard on the Plains, except among the red men, as we rushed forth to see our first game lying in his gore. The writer had the pleasure of first putting hands on the dark locks of the noble monster who had fallen so bravely. Another distinguished himself by mounting the fallen brave. Then came the ladies; a ring was formed; the cornet band gathered around, and, as if to tantalize the spirits of all departed buffalo, as well as Indians, played Yankee Doodle. I thought that "Hail to the Chief," would have done more honor to the departed.

And now butcher-knives and butchers were in requisition. "Let us eviscerate and carry home this our first captive without further mutilation, that we may give our friends the pleasure of seeing the dimensions of the animal." This seemed a good plan, and we proceeded to carry it out. After the butchers had done their work, a rope was attached to the horns, and the animal, weighing about fifteen hundred pounds, was dragged to the cars and thence lifted on board the freight-car, a few of our party climbing upon the top of the car, the better to pull on the rope. It was now getting dark, and as the head of that huge horned creature was being drawn up to the car-door, I thought I had never before seen any object that came so near my idea of the Prince of Darkness, as it seemed to look out over the crowd who were uplifting him.

"Monstrum horrendum, ingens!"

Our game being thus, after much effort, well bagged, we moved on again with a general feeling of immense satisfaction. "Glory enough for one day," thought we; "now what shall the morrow reveal?" . . .

JOHN R. COOK*

That evening there was a general discussion in regard to the main subject in hunters' minds. Colorado had passed stringent laws that were practically prohibitory against buffalo-killing; the Legislature of Kansas did the same; the Indian Territory was patrolled by United States marshals. And all the venturesome hunters from eastern Colorado, western Kansas, the Platte, Solomon and Republican rivers country came to Texas to follow the chase for buffalo-hides.

The Texas Legislature, while we were here among the herds, to destroy them, was in session at Austin, with a bill drawn up for their protection. General Phil. Sheridan was then in command of the military department of the Southwest, with headquarters at San Antonio. When he heard of the nature of the Texas bill for the protection of the buffaloes, he went to Austin, and, appearing before the joint assembly of the House and Senate, so the story goes, told them that they were making a sentimental mistake by legislating in the interest of the buffalo. He told them that instead of stopping the hunters they ought to give them

*John R. Cook, The Border and the Buffalo: An Untold Story of the Southwest Plains. (Topeka, Kansas, Crane and Company, 1907), pp. 112–115, 290–291.

a hearty, unanimous vote of thanks, and appropriate a sufficient sum of money to strike and present to each one a medal of bronze, with a dead buffalo on one side and a discouraged Indian on the other.

He said: "These men have done in the last two years and will do more in the next year, to settle the vexed Indian question, than the entire regular army has done in the last thirty years. They are destroying the Indians' commissary; and it is a well-known fact that an army losing its base of supplies is placed at a great disadvantage. Send them powder and lead, if you will; but, for the sake of a lasting peace, let them kill, skin, and sell until the buffaloes are exterminated. Then your prairies can be covered with speckled cattle, and the festive cowboy, who follows the hunter as a second forerunner of an advanced civilization."

His words had the desired effect, and for the next three years the American bison traveled through a hail of lead.

The next morning our outfit pulled out south, and that day we caught up with and passed through many straggling bands of these solemn-looking but doomed animals. And thus we traveled by easy stages four days more.

Arriving on the breaks of the Salt fork of the Brazos river, we realized that we were in the midst of that vast sea of animals that caused us gladness and sorrow, joy, trouble and anxiety, but independence, for the succeeding three years. We drove down from the divide, and, finding a fresh spring of water, went into camp at this place. We decided to scout the country around for a suitable place for a permanent camp.

/   /   /

I had killed wild turkeys in southwest Missouri, also in southeastern Kansas, and had always looked upon them as a wary game bird. But here, turkey, turkey! Manifesting at all times and places a total indifference to our presence. At first we killed some of them, but after cooking and attempting to eat them we gave it up. Their meat was bitter and sickening, from eating china-berries (the fruit of *Sapindus marginatus*, or soapberry trees).

So we passed and repassed them; and they did the same, and paid no attention whatever to us.

/   /   /

Deer were simply too easy to find; for they were ever present. The same with antelope, bear, panther, mountain lion or cougar, raccoon, polecat, swift coyotes and wolves—they were all here.

And at times I asked myself: "What would you do, John R. Cook, if you had been a child of this wonderfully prolific game region, your ancestors, back through countless ages, according to traditional history, having roamed these vast solitudes as free as the air they breathed?

What would you do if some outside interloper should come in and start a ruthless slaughter upon the very soil you had grown from childhood upon, and that you believed you alone had all the rights by occupancy that could possibly be given one? Yes, what would you do?''

But there are two sides to the question. It is simply a case of the survival of the fittest. Too late to stop and moralize now. And sentiment must have no part in our thoughts from this time on. We must have these 3361 hides that this region is to and did furnish us inside of three months, within a radius of eight miles from this main camp. So at it we went. And Hart, whom we will hereafter call Charlie, started out, and in two hours had killed sixty-three bison.

/   /   /

The summer of 1877 is on record as being the last of the Comanches in the rôle of raiders and scalpers; and we hunters were justly entitled to credit in winding up the Indian trouble in the great State of Texas, so far as the Kiowas and Comanches were concerned. Those Indians had been a standing menace to the settlement of 90,000 square miles of territory in Texas and New Mexico.

And to-day, 1907, it is a pleasing thought to the few surviving hunters of the old Southwest to know that the entire country of the then vast unsettled region is now dotted over with thousands of peaceful, prosperous homes.

/   /   /

The last great slaughter of the buffaloes was during the months of December, 1877, and January, 1878, more than one hundred thousand buffalo-hides being taken by the army of hunters during that fall and winter. That winter and spring many families came onto the range and selected their future homes, and killed buffaloes for hides and meat. More meat was cured that winter than the three previous years all put together.

In the spring of 1877 but few buffalo went north of Red river. The last big band of these fast-diminishing animals that I ever saw was ten miles south of the Mustang Spring, going southwest. They never came north again. And I afterward learned that the remnant of the main herd that were not killed crossed the Rio Grande and took to the hills of Chihuahua in old Mexico. This last view was in February, 1878. During the rest of the time that I was on the range, the hunters could only see a few isolated bands of buffaloes. And if one heard of a herd which contained fifty head he would not only look, but be surprised.

/   /   /

ANDY ADAMS

6 | The Life of a Cowboy

Born in Indiana just before the Civil War, Andy Adams went west in 1882. For the next eight years, he took part in some of the last drives that moved cattle over the trails from Texas to the railheads in Kansas for shipment to Chicago slaughterhouses. Although The Log of a Cowboy *(1903) is a historical novel, it has a firm base in facts about the West. Adams' version of the cowboy life is the realistic workaday one—a tough, lonely, grubby job that few men took by choice. The American public has generally preferred the more dashing, violent, and romantic depiction of cowboys that stems from Owen Wister's bestselling novel* The Virginian, *which appeared the year before* The Log of a Cowboy *and spawned an unending legacy of novels, cowboy movies, television shows, and cigarette commercials.*

In spite of any effort on our part, the length of the days made long drives the rule. The cattle could be depended on to leave the bed ground at dawn, and before the outfit could breakfast, secure mounts, and overtake the herd, they would often have grazed forward two or three miles. Often we never threw them on the trail at all, yet when it came time to bed them at night, we had covered twenty miles. They were long, monotonous days; for we were always sixteen to eighteen hours in the saddle, while in emergencies we got the benefit of the limit. We frequently saw mirages, though we were never led astray by shady groves of timber or tempting lakes of water, but always kept within a mile or two of the trail. The evening of the third day after Forrest left us, he returned as we were bedding down the cattle at dusk [and] resumed his place with the herd. He had not even reached the Solomon River, but had stopped with a herd of Millet's on Big Boggy. This creek he reported as bottomless, and the Millet herd as having lost between forty and fifty head of cattle in attempting to force it at the regular crossing the day before his arrival. They had scouted the creek both up and down since without finding a safe crossing. It seemed that there had been unusually heavy June rains through that section, which accounted for Boggy being

Andy Adams, The Log of a Cowboy: A Narrative of the Old Trail Days *(Boston, Houghton Mifflin Company, 1903) pp. 210–223, 230–231.*

in its dangerous condition. Millet's foreman had not considered it necessary to test such an insignificant stream until he got a couple of hundred head of cattle floundering in the mire. They had saved the greater portion of the mired cattle, but quite a number were trampled to death by the others, and now the regular crossing was not approachable for the stench of dead cattle. Flood knew the stream, and so did a number of our outfit, but none of them had any idea that it could get into such an impassable condition as Forrest reported.

The next morning Flood started to the east and Priest to the west to look out a crossing, for we were then within half a day's drive of the creek. Big Boggy paralleled the Solomon River in our front, the two not being more than five miles apart. The confluence was far below in some settlements, and we must keep to the westward of all immigration, on account of the growing crops in the fertile valley of the Solomon. On the westward, had a favorable crossing been found, we would almost have had to turn our herd backward, for we were already within the half circle which this creek described in our front. So after the two men left us, we allowed the herd to graze forward, keeping several miles to the westward of the trail in order to get the benefit of the best grazing. Our herd, when left to itself, would graze from a mile to a mile and a half an hour, and by the middle of the forenoon the timber on Big Boggy and the Solomon beyond was sighted. On reaching this last divide, some one sighted a herd about five or six miles to the eastward and nearly parallel with us. As they were three or four miles beyond the trail, we could easily see that they were grazing along like ourselves, and Forrest was appealed to to know if it was the Millet herd. He said not, and pointed out to the northeast about the location of the Millet cattle, probably five miles in advance of the stranger on our right. When we overtook our wagon at noon, McCann, who had never left the trail, reported having seen the herd. They looked to him like heavy beef cattle, and had two yoke of oxen to their chuck wagon, which served further to proclaim them as strangers.

Neither Priest nor Flood returned during the noon hour, and when the herd refused to lie down and rest longer, we grazed them forward till the fringe of timber which grew along the stream loomed up not a mile distant in our front. From the course we were traveling, we would strike the creek several miles above the regular crossing, and as Forrest reported that Millet was holding below the old crossing on a small rivulet, all we could do was to hold our wagon in the rear, and await the return of our men out on scout for a ford. Priest was the first to return, with word that he had ridden the creek out for twenty-five miles and had found no crossing that would be safe for a mud turtle. On hearing this, we left two men with the herd, and the rest of the outfit took the wagon, went on to Boggy, and made camp. It was a deceptive-looking stream, not over fifty or sixty feet wide. In places the current barely moved, shallowing and deepening, from a few inches in places to several feet in others, with an occasional pool that would swim a horse. We probed it with poles until we were satisfied that we were up against a proposition different from anything we had yet encountered. While we were discussing the situation, a stranger rode up on a fine roan horse, and inquired for our foreman. Forrest informed him that our boss was away looking for a crossing, but we were expecting his return at any time; and invited the stranger to dismount. He did so, and threw himself down in the shade of our wagon. He was a small, boyish-looking fellow, of sandy complexion, not much, if any, over twenty years old, and smiled continuously.

"My name is Pete Slaughter," said he, by way of introduction, "and I've got a herd of twenty-eight hundred beef steers, beyond the trail and a few miles back. I've been riding since daybreak down the creek, and I'm prepared to state that the chance of crossing is as good right here as anywhere. I wanted to see your foreman, and if he'll help, we'll bridge her. I've been down to see this other outfit, but they ridicule the idea, though I think they'll come around all right. I borrowed their axe, and to-morrow morning you'll see me with my outfit cutting timber to bridge Big Boggy. That's right, boys; it's the only thing to do. The trouble is I've only got eight men all told. I don't aim to travel over eight or ten miles a day, so I don't need a big outfit. You say your foreman's name is Flood? Well, if he don't return before I go, some of you tell him that he's wasting good time looking for a ford, for there ain't none."

In the conversation which followed, we learned that Slaughter was driving for his brother Lum, a widely known cowman and drover, whom we had seen in Dodge. He had started with the grass from north Texas, and by the time he reached the Platte, many of his herd would be fit to ship to market, and what were not would be in good demand as feeders in the corn belt of eastern Nebraska. He asked if we had seen his herd during the morning, and on hearing we had, got up and asked McCann to let him see our axe. This he gave a critical examination, before he mounted his horse to go, and on leaving said,—

"If your foreman don't want to help build a bridge, I want to borrow that axe of yours. But you fellows talk to him. If any of you boys has ever been over on the Chisholm trail, you will remember the bridge on Rush Creek, south of the Washita River. I built that bridge in a day with an outfit of ten men. Why, shucks! if these outfits would pull together, we could cross to-morrow evening. Lots of these old foremen don't like to listen to a cub like me, but, holy snakes! I've been over the trail oftener than any of them. Why, when I wasn't big enough to make a hand with the herd,—only ten years old,—in the days when we drove to Abilene, they used to send me in the lead with an old cylinder gun to shoot at the buffalo and scare them off the trail. And I've made the trip every year since. So you tell Flood when he comes in, that Pete Slaughter was here, and that he's going to build a bridge, and would like to have him and his outfit help."

Had it not been for his youth and perpetual smile, we might have taken young Slaughter more seriously, for both Quince Forrest and The Rebel remembered the bridge on Rush Creek over on the Chisholm. Still there was an air of confident assurance in the young fellow; and the fact that he was the trusted foreman of Lum Slaughter, in charge of a valuable herd of cattle, carried weight with those who knew that drover. The most unwelcome thought in the project was that it required the swinging of an axe to fell trees and to cut them into the necessary lengths, and, as I have said before, the Texan never took kindly to manual labor. But Priest looked favorably on the suggestion, and so enlisted my support, and even pointed out a spot where timber was most abundant as a suitable place to build the bridge.

/ / /

The next morning young Slaughter was at our camp before sunrise, and never once mentioning his business or waiting for the formality of an invitation, proceeded to pour out a tin cup of coffee and otherwise provide himself with a substantial breakfast. There was something amusing in the audacity of the fellow which all of us liked, though he was fifteen years the junior of our foreman. McCann pointed out Flood to him, and taking his well-loaded plate, he went over and sat down by our foreman, and while he ate talked rapidly, to enlist our outfit in the building of the bridge. During breakfast, the outfit listened to the two bosses as they discussed the feasibility of the project,—Slaughter enthusiastic, Flood reserved, and asking all sorts of questions as to the mode of procedure. Young Pete met every question with promptness, and assured our foreman that the building of bridges was his long suit. After breakfast, the two foremen rode off down the creek together, and within half an hour Slaughter's wagon and *remuda* pulled up within sight of the regular crossing, and shortly afterwards our foreman returned, and ordered our wagon to pull down to a clump of cottonwoods which grew about half a mile below our camp. Two men were detailed to look after our herd during the day, and the remainder of us returned with our foreman to the site selected for the bridge. On our arrival three axes were swinging against as many cottonwoods, and there was no doubt in any one's mind that we were going to be under a new foreman for that day at least. Slaughter had a big negro cook who swung an axe in a manner which bespoke him a job for the day, and McCann was instructed to provide dinner for the extra outfit.

The side chosen for the bridge was a miry bottom over which oozed three or four inches of water, where the width of the stream was about sixty feet, with solid banks on either side. To get a good foundation was the most important matter, but the brush from the trees would supply the material for that; and within an hour, brush began to arrive, dragged from the pommels of saddles, and was piled into the stream. About this time a call went out for a volunteer who could drive oxen, for the darky was too good an axeman to be recalled. As I had driven oxen as a boy, I was going to offer my services, when Joe Stallings eagerly volunteered in order to avoid using an axe. Slaughter had some extra chain, and our four mules were pressed into service as an extra team in snaking logs. As McCann was to provide for the inner man, the mule team fell to me; and putting my saddle on the nigh wheeler, I rode jauntily past Mr. Stallings as he trudged alongside his two yoke of oxen.

/   /   /

Pete Slaugher was a harsh master, considering he was working volunteer labor; but then we all felt a common interest in the bridge, for if Slaughter's beeves could cross, ours could, and so could Millet's. All the men dragging brush changed horses during dinner, for there was to be no pause in piling in a good foundation as long as the material was at hand. Jacklin and his outfit returned, ten strong, and with thirty men at work, the bridge grew. They began laying the logs on the brush after dinner, and the work of sodding the bridge went forward at the same time. The bridge stood about two feet above the water in the creek, but when near the middle of the stream was reached, the foundation gave way, and for an hour ten horses were kept busy dragging brush to fill that sink hole until it would bear the weight of the logs. We had used all the acceptable timber on our side of the stream for half a mile either way, and yet there were not enough logs to complete the bridge. When we lacked only some ten or twelve logs, Slaughter had the boys sod a narrow strip across the remainng brush, and the horsemen led their mounts across to the farther side. Then the axe-men crossed, felled the nearest trees, and the last logs were dragged up from the pommels of our saddles.

It now only remained to sod over and dirt the bridge thoroughly. With only three spades the work was slow, but we cut sod with axes, and after several hours' work had it finished. The two yoke of oxen were driven across and back for a test, and the bridge stood it nobly. Slaughter then brought up his *remuda*, and while the work of dirting the bridge was still going on, crossed and recrossed his band of saddle horses twenty times. When the bridge looked completed to every one else, young Pete advised laying stringers across on either side; so a number of small trees were felled and guard rails strung across the ends of the logs and staked. Then more dirt was carried in on tarpaulins and in gunny sacks, and every chink and crevice filled with sod and dirt. It was now getting rather late in the afternoon, but during the finishing touches, young Slaughter had dispatched his outfit to bring up his herd; and at the same time Flood had sent a number of our outfit to bring up our cattle. Now Slaughter and the rest of us took the oxen, which we had unyoked, and went out about a quarter of a mile to meet his herd coming up. Turning the oxen in the lead, young Pete took one point and Flood the other, and pointed in the lead cattle for the bridge. On reaching it the cattle hesitated for a moment, and it looked as though they were going to balk, but finally one of the oxen took the lead, and they began to cross in almost Indian file. They were big four and five year old beeves, and too many of them on the bridge at one time might have sunk it, but Slaughter rode back down the line of cattle and called to the men to hold them back.

"Don't crowd the cattle," he shouted. "Give them all the time they want. We're in no hurry now; there's lots of time."

They were a full half hour in crossing, the chain of cattle taking the bridge never for a moment being broken. Once all were over, his men rode to the lead and turned the herd up Boggy, in order to have it well out of the way of ours, which were then looming up in sight. Slaughter asked Flood if he wanted the oxen; and as our cattle had never seen a bridge in their lives, the foreman decided to use them; so we brought them back and met the herd, now strung out nearly a mile. Our cattle were naturally wild, but we turned the oxen in the lead, and the two bosses again taking the points, moved the herd up to the bridge. The oxen were again slow to lead out in crossing, and several hundred head of cattle had congested in front of the new bridge, making us all rather nervous, when a big white ox led off, his mate following, and the herd began timidly to follow. Our cattle required careful handling, and not a word was spoken as we nursed them forward, or rode through them to scatter large bunches. A number of times we cut the train of cattle off entirely, as they were congesting at the bridge entrance, and, in crossing, shied and crowded so that several were forced off the bridge into the mire. Our herd crossed in considerably less time than did Slaughter's beeves, but we had five head to pull out; this, however, was considered nothing, as they were light, and the mire was as thin as soup. Our wagon and saddle horses crossed while we were pulling out the bogged cattle, and about half the outfit, taking the herd, drifted them forward towards the Solomon.

/   /   /

It was now late in the evening, and as we had to wait some little time to get our own horses, we stayed for supper. It was dark before we set out to overtake the herd, but the trail was plain, and letting our horses take their own time, we jollied along until after midnight. We might have missed the camp, but, by the merest chance, Priest sighted our camp-fire a mile off the trail, though it had burned to embers. On reaching camp, we changed saddles to our night horses, and, calling Officer, were ready for our watch. We were expecting the men on guard to call us any minute, and while Priest was explaining to Officer the trouble we had had in crossing the Millet herd, I dozed off to sleep there as I sat by the rekindled embers. In that minute's sleep my mind wandered in a dream to my home on the San Antonio River, but the next moment I was aroused to the demands of the hour by The Rebel shaking me and saying,—

"Wake up, Tom, and take a new hold. They're calling us on guard. If you expect to follow the trail, son, you must learn to do your sleeping in the winter."

7 | Deadwood Dick

While black Americans rarely appear in "Westerns" as anything but cooks and clowns, about twenty to twenty-five percent of the cowboys who drove cattle on the long trails were black, as were a similar proportion of western cavalry men in the United States Army during the taming of the last Indian frontier.

The most famous of the black cowboys—famous in part because he wrote a vivid autobiography—was Nat Love, who became known as Deadwood Dick. Born a slave in 1854, he "struck out of Kansas" in 1869 to escape discrimination and the lack of schools for black children. On the cow trails, though, Nat found race to be no barrier. He shot and boasted with the best and became an expert Indian fighter.

The era of the cattle trails was short. By the late 1880s, railroads had replaced cowpunchers in moving western beef to Eastern consumers. Nat Love quit the trails in 1890 and found that the best opportunity for a black man— even in the West—was as a Pullman car porter.

We arrived in Deadwood in good condition without having had any trouble with the Indians on the way up. We turned our cattle over to their new owners at once, then proceeded to take in the town. The next morning, July 4th, the gamblers and mining men made up a purse of $200 for a roping contest between the cow boys that were then in town, and as it was a holiday nearly all the cow boys for miles around were assembled there that day. It did not take long to arrange the details for the contest and contestants, six of them being colored cow boys, including myself. Our trail boss was chosen to pick out the mustangs from a herd of wild horses just off the range, and he picked out twelve of the most wild and vicious horses that he could find.

The conditions of the contest were that each of us who were mounted was to rope, throw, tie, bridle and saddle and mount the particular horse picked for us in the shortest time possible. The man accomplishing the feat in the quickest time to be declared the winner.

It seems to me that the horse chosen for me was the most vicious of

Nat Love, The Life and Adventures of Nat Love Better Known in the Cattle Country as "Deadwood Dick" by Himself *(Los Angeles, 1907), pp. 91, 93, 95, 97, 98–99, 101, 103–105.*

49

the lot. Everything being in readiness, the "45" cracked and we all sprang forward together, each of us making for our particular mustang.

I roped, threw, tied, bridled, saddled and mounted my mustang in exactly nine minutes from the crack of the gun. The time of the next nearest competitor was twelve minutes and thirty seconds. This gave me the record and championship of the West, which I held up to the time I quit the business in 1890, and my record has never been beaten. It is worthy of passing remark that I never had a horse pitch with me so much as that mustang, but I never stopped sticking my spurs in him and using my quirt on his flanks until I proved his master. Right there the assembled crowd named me Deadwood Dick and proclaimed me champion roper of the western cattle country.

The roping contest over, a dispute arose over the shooting question with the result that a contest was arranged for the afternoon, as there happened to be some of the best shots with rifle and revolver in the West present that day. Among them were Stormy Jim, who claimed the championship; Powder Horn Bill, who had the reputation of never missing what he shot at; also White Head, a half breed, who generally hit what he shot at, and many other men who knew how to handle a rifle or 45-colt.

The range was measured off 100 and 250 yards for the rifle and 150 for the Colt 45. At this distance a bulls eye about the size of an apple was put up. Each man was to have 14 shots at each range with the rifle and 12 shots with the Colts 45. I placed every one of my 14 shots with the rifle in the bulls eye with ease, all shots being made from the hip; but with the 45 Colts I missed it twice, only placing 10 shots in the small circle, Stormy Jim being my nearest competitor, only placing 8 bullets in the bulls eye clear, the rest being quite close, while with the 45 he placed 5 bullets in the charmed circle. This gave me the championship of rifle and revolver shooting as well as the roping contest, and for that day I was the hero of Deadwood, and the purse of $200 which I had won on the roping contest went toward keeping things moving, and they did move as only a large crowd of cattle men can move things. This lasted for several days when most of the cattle men had to return to their respective ranches, as it was the busy season, accordingly our out- fit began to make preparations to return to Arizona.

In the meantime news had reached us of the Custer massacre, and the indignation and sorrow was universal, as General Custer was per- sonally known to a large number of the cattle men of the West. But we could do nothing now, as the Indians were out in such strong force. There was nothing to do but let Uncle Sam revenge the loss of the Gen- eral and his brave command, but it is safe to say not one of us would have hesitated a moment in taking the trail in pursuit of the blood thirsty red skins had the opportunity offered.

Everything now being in readiness with us we took the trail home-

ward bound, and left Deadwood in a blaze of glory. On our way home
we visited the Custer battle field in the Little Big Horn Basin.

There was ample evidence of the desperate and bloody fight that
had taken place a few days before. We arrived home in Arizona in a
short time without further incident, except that on the way back we met
and talked with many of the famous Government scouts of that region,
among them Buffalo Bill (William F. Cody), Yellow Stone Kelley, and
many others of that day, some of whom are now living, while others
lost their lives in the line of duty, and a finer or braver body of men
never lived than these scouts of the West. It was my pleasure to meet
Buffalo Bill often in the early 70s, and he was as fine a man as one could
wish to meet, kind, generous, true and brave.

Buffalo Bill got his name from the fact that in the early days he was
engaged in hunting buffalo for their hides and furnishing U. P. Railroad
graders with meat, hence the name Buffalo Bill. Buffalo Bill, Yellowstone
Kelley, with many others were at this time serving under Gen. C. C.
Miles.

The name of Deadwood Dick was given to me by the people of
Deadwood, South Dakota, July 4, 1876, after I had proven myself worthy to carry it, and after I had defeated all comers in riding, roping,
and shooting, and I have always carried the name with honor since that
time.

We arrived at the home ranch again on our return from the trip to
Deadwood about the middle of September, it taking us a little over two
months to make the return journey, as we stopped in Cheyenne for
several days and at other places, where we always found a hearty welcome, especially so on this trip, as the news had preceded us, and I
received enough attention to have given me the big head, but my head
had constantly refused to get enlarged again ever since the time I sam-
pled the demijohn in the sweet corn patch at home.

Arriving at home, we received a send off from our boss and our
comrades of the home ranch, every man of whom on hearing the news
turned loose his voice and his artillery in a grand demonstration in my
honor.

But they said it was no surprise to them, as they had long known
of my ability with the rope, rifle and 45 Colt, but just the same it was
gratifying to know I had defeated the best men of the West, and brought
the record home to the home ranch in Arizona. After a good rest we
proceeded to ride the range again, getting our herds in good condition
for the winter now at hand.

/   /   /

It was a bright clear fall day, October 4, 1876, that quite a large number of us boys started out over the range hunting strays which had been

lost for some time. We had scattered over the range and I was riding along alone when all at once I heard the well known Indian war whoop and noticed not far away a large party of Indians making straight for me. They were all well mounted and they were in full war paint, which showed me that they were on the war path, and as I was alone and had no wish to be scalped by them I decided to run for it. So I headed for Yellow Horse Canyon and gave my horse the rein, but as I had considerable objection to being chased by a lot of painted savages without some remonstrance, I turned in my saddle every once in a while and gave them a shot by way of greeting, and I had the satisfaction of seeing a painted brave tumble from his horse and go rolling in the dust every time my rifle spoke, and the Indians were by no means idle all this time, as their bullets were singing around me rather lively, one of them passing through my thigh, but it did not amount to much. Reaching Yellow Horse Canyon, I had about decided to stop and make a stand when one of their bullets caught me in the leg, passing clear through it and then through my horse, killing him. Quickly falling behind him I used his dead body for a breast work and stood the Indians off for a long time, as my aim was so deadly and they had lost so many that they were careful to keep out of range.

But finally my ammunition gave out, and the Indians were quick to find this out, and they at once closed in on me, but I was by no means subdued, wounded as I was and almost out of my head, and I fought with my empty gun until finally overpowered. When I came to my senses I was in the Indians' camp.

My wounds had been dressed with some kind of herbs, the wound in my breast just over the heart was covered thickly with herbs and bound up. My nose had been nearly cut off, also one of my fingers had been nearly cut off. These wounds I received when I was fighting my captors with my empty gun. What caused them to spare my life I cannot tell, but it was I think partly because I had proved myself a brave man, and all savages admire a brave man and when they captured a man whose fighting powers were out of the ordinary they generally kept him if possible as he was needed in the tribe.

Then again Yellow Dog's tribe was composed largely of half breeds, and there was a large percentage of colored blood in the tribe, and as I was a colored man they wanted to keep me, as they thought I was too good a man to die. Be that as it may, they dressed my wounds and gave me plenty to eat, but the only grub they had was buffalo meat which they cooked over a fire of buffalo chips,* but of this I had all I wanted to eat. For the first two days after my capture they kept me tied hand and foot. At the end of that time they untied my feet, but kept my hands tied for a couple of days longer, when I was given my freedom, but was

---

*Dried buffalo manure, commonly used as fuel

always closely watched by members of the tribe. Three days after my capture my ears were pierced and I was adopted into the tribe. The operation of piercing my ears was quite painful, in the method used, as they had a small bone secured from a deer's leg, a small thin bone, rounded at the end and as sharp as a needle. This they used to make the holes, then strings made from the tendons of a deer were inserted in place of thread, of which the Indians had none. Then horn ear rings were placed in my ears and the same kind of salve made from herbs which they placed on my wounds was placed on my ears and they soon healed.

The bullet holes in my leg and breast also healed in a surprisingly short time. That was good salve all right. As soon as I was well enough I took part in the Indian dances. One kind or another was in progress all the time. The war dance and the medicine dance seemed the most popular. When in the war dance the savages danced around me in a circle, making gestures, chanting, with every now and then a blood curdling yell, always keeping time to a sort of music provided by stretching buffalo skins tightly over a hoop.

When I was well enough I joined the dances, and I think I soon made a good dancer. The medicine dance varies from the war dance only that in the medicine dance the Indians danced around a boiling pot, the pot being filled with roots and water and they dance around it while it boils. The medicine dance occurs about daylight.

I very soon learned their ways and to understand them, though our conversation was mostly carried on by means of signs. They soon gave me to understand that I was to marry the chief's daughter, promising me 100 ponies to do so, and she was literally thrown in my arms; as for the lady she seemed perfectly willing if not anxious to become my bride. She was a beautiful woman, or rather girl; in fact all the squaws of this tribe were good looking, out of the ordinary, but I had other notions just then and did not want to get married under such circumstances, but for prudence sake I seemed to enter into their plans, but at the same time keeping a sharp lookout for a chance to escape. I noted where the Indians kept their horses at night, even picking out the handsome and fleet Indian pony which I meant to use should opportunity occur, and I seemed to fall in with the Indians' plans and seemed to them so contented that they gave me more and more freedom and relaxed the strict watch they had kept on me, and finally in about thirty days from the time of my capture my opportunity arrived.

My wounds were now nearly well, and gave me no trouble. It was a dark, cloudy night, and the Indians, grown careless in their fancied security, had relaxed their watchfulness. After they had all thrown themselves on the ground and the quiet of the camp proclaimed them all asleep I got up and crawling on my hands and knees, using the greatest caution for fear of making a noise, I crawled about 250 yards to where the horses were picketed, and going to the Indian pony I had already picked out I slipped the skin thong in his mouth which the Indians use for a bridle, one which I had secured and carried in my shirt for some time for this particular purpose, then springing to his back I made for the open prairie in the direction of the home ranch in Texas, one hundred miles away. All that night I rode as fast as my horse could carry me and the next morning, twelve hours after I left the Indians camp I was safe on the home ranch again. And my joy was without bounds, and such a reception as I received from the boys. They said they were just one day late, and if it hadn't been for a fight they had with some of the same tribe, they would have been to my relief. As it was they did not expect to ever see me again alive. But that they know that if the Indians did not kill me, and gave me only half a chance I would get away from them, but now that I was safe home again, nothing mattered much and nothing was too good for me.

It was a mystery to them how I managed to escape death with such wounds as I had received, the marks of which I will carry to my grave and it is as much a mystery to me as the bullet that struck me in the breast just over the heart passed clear through, coming out my back just below the shoulder. Likewise the bullet in my leg passed clear through, then through my horse, killing him.

Those Indians are certainly wonderful doctors, and then I am naturally tough as I carry the marks of fourteen bullet wounds on different part of my body, most any one of which would be sufficient to kill an ordinary man, but I am not even crippled. It seems to me that if ever a man bore a charm I am the man, as I have had five horses shot from under me and killed, have fought Indians and Mexicans in all sorts of situations, and have been in more tight places than I can number. Yet I have always managed to escape with only the mark of a bullet or knife as a reminder. The fight with the Yellow Dog's tribe is probably the closest call I ever had, and as close a call as I ever want.

The fleet Indian pony which carried me to safety on that memorable hundred mile ride, I kept for about five years. I named him "The Yellow Dog Chief." And he lived on the best the ranch afforded, until his death which occurred in 1881, never having anything to do except an occasional race, as he could run like a deer. I thought too much of him to use him on the trail and he was the especial pet of every one on the home ranch, and for miles around.

I heard afterwards that the Indians persued me that night for quite a distance, but I had too much the start and besides I had the fastest horse the Indians owned. I have never since met any of my captors of that time. As they knew better than to venture in our neighborhood again. My wound healed nicely, thanks to the good attention the Indians gave me. My captors took everything of value I had on me when captured. My rifle which I especially prized for old associations sake; also my forty fives, saddle and bridle, in fact my whole outfit leaving me only the few clothes I had on at the time.

My comrades did not propose to let this bother me long, however, because they all chipped in and bought me a new outfit, including the best rifle and revolvers that could be secured, and I had my pick of the ranch horses for another mount. During my short stay with the Indians I learned a great deal about them, their ways of living, sports, dances, and mode of warfare which proved of great benefit to me in after years. The oblong shields they carried were made from tanned buffalo skins and so tough were they made that an arrow would not pierce them although I have seen them shoot an arrow clean through a buffalo. Neither will a bullet pierce them unless the ball hits the shield square on, otherwise it glances off.

All of them were exceedingly expert with the bow and arrow, and they are proud of their skill and are always practicing in an effort to excel each other. This rivalry extends even to the children who are seldom without their bows and arrows.

They named me Buffalo Papoose, and we managed to make our wants known by means of signs. As I was not with them a sufficient length of time to learn their langauge, I learned from them that I had killed five of their number and wounded three while they were chasing me and in the subsequent fight with my empty gun. The wounded men were hit in many places, but they were brought around all right, the same as I was. After my escape and after I arrived home it was some time before I was again called to active duty, as the boys would not hear of me doing anything resembling work, until I was thoroughly well and rested up. But I soon began to long for my saddle and the range.

And when orders were received at the ranch for 2000 head of cattle, to be delivered at Dodge City, Kansas, I insisted on taking the trail again. It was not with any sense of pride or in bravado that I recount here the fate of the men who have fallen at my hand.

It is a terrible thing to kill a man no matter what the cause. But as I am writing a true history of my life, I cannot leave these facts out. But every man who died at my hands was either seeking my life or died in open warfare, when it was a case of killing or being killed.

8 | The Wounded Knee Massacre

By the mid-1880s, the Plains Indians were a defeated people largely confined to reservations. Then, in 1888, a new religion arose, the so-called Ghost Dance, which promised a return to the order existing before the coming of the white man. Warriors on the Sioux reservation in Dakota, encouraged by the still defiant, if defeated, Sitting Bull, began to believe that wearing garments painted with sacred symbols would render the white man's bullets harmless.

Skirmishes between young braves and the army led to several deaths, including that of Sitting Bull. Then troops of the Seventh Cavalry—Custer's old regiment—began searching for arms in an Indian village at Wounded Knee Creek. A shot rang out and the troops began indiscriminately killing the largely disarmed and already surrendered braves, while cannon raked the teepees occupied by women and children. On December 29, 1890, the army slaughtered every Indian in sight. Women and children were hunted down as far as three miles away from the village. Yet throughout the Ghost Dance excitement, not a single Indian raid had occurred on a white settlement.

The ballad, "The Indian Ghost Dance and War," written by W. H. Prather, a black private in the Ninth Cavalry, long remained popular in army barracks. The Indian accounts were recorded stenographically at a council held by delegations of Sioux Indians with the Commissioner of Indian Affairs in Washington in 1891.

W. H. PRATHER*

The Red Skins left their Agency, the Soldiers left their Post,
   All on the strength of an Indian tale about Messiah's ghost
Got up by savage chieftains to lead their tribes astray;
   But Uncle Sam wouldn't have it so, for he ain't built that way.
They swore that this Messiah came to them in visions sleep,
   And promised to restore their game and Buffalos a heap,
So they must start a big ghost dance, then all would join their band,
   And may be so we lead the way into the great Bad Land.

---

*James Mooney, The Ghost-Dance Religion and Wounded Knee. (New York, Dover Publications, 1973) pp. 883–886. Reprinted from The Ghost-Dance Religion and the Sioux Outbreak of 1890 (Washington, D.C., Government Printing Office, 1896).

Chorus:
They claimed the shirt Messiah gave, no bullet could go through,
    But when the Soldiers fired at them they saw this was not true.
The Medicine man supplied them with their great Messiah's grace,
    And he, too, pulled his freight and swore the 7th hard to face.

About their tents the Soldiers stood, awaiting one and all,
    That they might hear the trumpet clear when sounding General call
Or Boots and Saddles in a rush, that each and every man
    Might mount in haste, ride soon and fast to stop this devilish band
But Generals great like Miles and Brooke don't do things up that way,
    For they know an Indian like a book, and let him have his sway
Until they think him far enough and then to John they'll say,
    "You had better stop your fooling or we'll bring our guns to play."
Chorus.—They claimed the shirt, etc.

The 9th marched out with splendid cheer the Bad Lands to explo'e—
    With Col. Henry at their head they never fear the foe;
So on they rode from Xmas eve 'till dawn of Xmas day;
    The Red Skins heard the 9th was near and fled in great dismay;
The 7th is of courage bold both officers and men,
    But bad luck seems to follow them and twice has took them in;
They came in contact with Big Foot's warriors in their fierce might
    This chief made sure he had a chance of vantage in the fight.
Chorus.—They claimed the shirt, etc.

A fight took place, 'twas hand to hand, unwarned by trumpet call,
    While the Sioux were dropping man by man—the 7th killed them all,
And to that regiment be said "Ye noble braves, well done,
    Although you lost some gallant men a glorious fight you've won."
The 8th was there, the sixth rode miles to swell that great command
    And waited orders night and day to round up Short Bull's band.
The Infantry marched up in mass the Cavalry's support,
    And while the latter rounded up, the former held the fort.
Chorus.—They claimed the shirt, etc.

E battery of the 1st stood by and did their duty well,
    For every time the Hotchkiss barked they say a hostile fell.
Some Indian soldiers chipped in too and helped to quell the fray,
    And now the campaign's ended and the soldiers marched away.
So all have done their share, you see, whether it was thick or thin,
    And all helped break the ghost dance up and drive the hostiles in.
The settlers in that region now can breathe with better grace;
    They only ask and pray to God to make John hold his base.
Chorus.—They claimed the shirt, etc.
                                    (W. H. Prather, I, 9th Cavalry).

THE INDIAN STORY OF WOUNDED KNEE*

TURNING HAWK, Pine Ridge (Mr Cook, interpreter): Mr Commissioner, my purpose to-day is to tell you what I know of the condition of affairs at the agency where I live. A certain falsehood came to our agency from the west which had the effect of a fire upon the Indians, and when this certain fire came upon our people those who had farsightedness and could see into the matter made up their minds to stand up against it and fight it. The reason we took this hostile attitude to this fire was because we believed that you yourself would not be in favor of this particular michief-making thing; but just as we expected, the people in authority did not like this thing and we were quietly told that we must give up or have nothing to do with this certain movement. Though this is the advice from our good friends in the east, there were, of course, many silly young men who were longing to become identified with the movement, although they knew that there was nothing absolutely bad, nor did they know there was anything absolutely good, in connection with the movement.

In the course of time we heard that the soldiers were moving toward the scene of trouble. After awhile some of the soldiers finally reached our place and we heard that a number of them also reached our friends at Rosebud. Of course, when a large body of soldiers is moving toward a certain direction they inspire a more or less amount of awe, and it is natural that the women and children who see this large moving mass are made afraid of it and be put in a condition to make them run away. At first we thought that Pine Ridge and Rosebud were the only two agencies where soldiers were sent, but finally we heard that the other agencies fared likewise. We heard and saw that about half our friends at Rosebud agency, from fear at seeing the soldiers, began the move of running away from their agency toward ours (Pine Ridge), and when they had gotten inside of our reservation they there learned that right ahead of them at our agency was another large crowd of soldiers, and while the soldiers were there, there was constantly a great deal of false rumor flying back and forth. The special rumor I have in mind is the threat that the soldiers had come there to disarm the Indians entirely and to take away all their horses from them. That was the oft-repeated story.

So constantly repeated was this story that our friends from Rosebud, instead of going to Pine Ridge, the place of their desti-

*[From the Report of the Commissioner of Indian Affairs for 1891, volume 1, pages 179–181. Extracts from verbatim stenographic report of council held by delegations of Sioux with Commissioner of Indian Affairs, at Washington, February 11, 1891.]

nation, veered off and went to some other direction toward the "Bad Lands." We did not know definitely how many, but understood there were 300 lodges of them, about 1,700 people. Eagle Pipe, Turning Bear, High Hawk, Short Bull, Lance, No Flesh, Pine Bird, Crow Dog, Two Strike, and White Horse were the leaders.

Well, the people after veering off in this way, many of them who believe in peace and order at our agency, were very anxious that some influence should be brought upon these people. In addition to our love of peace we remembered that many of these people were related to us by blood. So we sent out peace commissioners to the people who were thus running away from their agency.

I understood at the time that they were simply going away from fear because of so many soldiers. So constant was the word of these good men from Pine Ridge agency that finally they succeeded in getting away half of the party from Rosebud, from the place where they took refuge, and finally were brought to the agency at Pine Ridge. Young-Man-Afraid-of-his-Horses, Little Wound, Fast Thunder, Louis Shangreau, John Grass, Jack Red Cloud, and myself were some of these peace-makers.

The remnant of the party from Rosebud not taken to the agency finally reached the wilds of the Bad Lands. Seeing that we had succeeded so well, once more we sent to the same party in the Bad Lands and succeeded in bringing these very Indians out of the depths of the Bad Lands and were being brought toward the agency. When we were about a day's journey from our agency we heard that a certain party of Indians (Big Foot's band) from the Cheyenne River agency was coming toward Pine Ridge in flight.

CAPTAIN SWORD: Those who actually went off of the Cheyenne River agency probably number 303, and there were a few from the Standing Rock reserve with them, but as to their number I do not know. There were a number of Ogalallas, old men and several school boys, coming back with that very same party, and one of the very seriously wounded boys was a member of the Ogalalla boarding school at Pine Ridge agency. He was not on the warpath, but was simply returning home to his agency and to his school after a summer visit to relatives on the Cheyenne river.

TURNING HAWK: When we heard that these people were coming toward our agency we also heard this. These people were coming toward Pine Ridge agency, and when they were almost on the agency they were met by the soldiers and surrounded and finally taken to the Wounded Knee creek, and there at a given time their guns were demanded. When they had delivered them up, the men were separated from their families, from their tipis, and taken to a certain spot. When the guns were thus taken and the men thus separated, there was a crazy man, a young man of very bad influence and in fact a nobody, among that bunch of Indians fired his gun, and of course the firing of a gun must have been the breaking of a military rule of some sort, because immediately the soldiers returned fire and indiscriminate killing followed.

SPOTTED HORSE: This man shot an officer in the army; the first shot killed this officer. I was a voluntary scout at that encounter and I saw exactly what was done, and that was what I noticed; that the first shot killed an officer. As soon as this shot was fired the Indians immediately began drawing their knives, and they were exhorted from all sides to desist, but this was not obeyed. Consequently the firing began immediately on the part of the soldiers.

TURNING HAWK: All the men who were in a bunch were killed right there, and those who escaped that first fire got into the ravine, and as they went along up the ravine for a long distance they were pursued on both sides by the soldiers and shot down, as the dead bodies showed afterwards. The women were standing off at a different place from where the men were stationed, and when the firing began, those of the men who escaped the first onslaught went in one direction up the ravine, and then the women, who were bunched together at another place, went entirely in a different direction through an open field, and the women fared the same fate as the men who went up the deep ravine.

AMERICAN HORSE: The men were separated, as has already been said, from the women, and they were surrounded by the soldiers. Then came next the village of the Indians and that was entirely surrounded by the soldiers also. When the firing began, of course the people who were standing immediately around the young man who fired the first shot were killed right together, and then they turned their guns, Hotchkiss guns, etc., upon the women who were in the lodges standing there under a flag of truce, and of course as soon as they were fired upon they fled, the men fleeing in one direction and the women running in two different directions. So that there were three general directions in which they took flight.

There was a woman with an infant in her arms who was killed as she almost touched the flag of truce, and the women and children of course were strewn all along the circular village until they were dispatched. Right near the flag of truce a mother was shot down with her infant; the child not knowing that its mother was dead was still nursing, and that especially was a very sad sight. The women as they were fleeing with their babies were killed together, shot right through, and the women who were very heavy with child were also killed. All the Indians fled in these three directions, and after most all of them had been killed a cry was made that all those who were not killed or wounded should come forth and they would be safe. Little boys who were not wounded came out of their places of refuge, and as soon as they came in sight a number of soldiers surrounded them and butchered them there.

Of course we all feel very sad about this affair. I stood very loyal to the government all through those troublesome days, and believing so much in the government and being so loyal to it, my disappointment was very strong, and I have come to Washington with a very great blame on my heart. Of course it would have been all right if only the men were killed; we would feel almost grateful for it. But the fact of the killing of the women, and more especially the killing of the young boys and girls who are to go to make up the future strength of the Indian people, is the saddest part of the whole affair and we feel it very sorely.

I was not there at the time before the burial of the bodies, but I did go there with some of the police and the Indian doctor and a great many of the people, men from the agency, and we went through the battlefield and saw where the bodies were from the track of the blood.

TURNING HAWK: I had just reached the point where I said that the women were killed. We heard, besides the killing of the men, of the onslaught also made upon the women and children, and they were treated as roughly and indiscriminately as the men and boys were.

Of course this affair brought a great deal of distress upon all the people, but especially upon the minds of those who stood loyal to the government and who did all that they were able to do in the matter of bringing about peace. They especially have suffered much distress and are very much hurt at heart. These peace-makers continued on in their good work, but there were a great many fickle young men who were ready to be moved by the change in the events there, and consequently, in spite of the great fire that was brought upon all, they were ready to assume any hostile attitude. These young men got themselves in readiness and went in the direction of the scene of battle so they might be of service there. They got there and finally exchanged shots with the soldiers. This party of young men was made up from Rosebud, Ogalalla (Pine Ridge), and members of any other agencies that happened to be there at the time. While this was going on in the neighborhood of Wounded Knee—the Indians and soldiers exchanging shots—the agency, our home, was also fired into by the Indians. Matters went on in this strain until the evening came on, and then the Indians went off down by White Clay creek. When the agency was fired upon by the Indians from the hillside, of course the shots were returned by the Indian police who were guarding the agency buildings.

Although fighting seemed to have been in the air, yet those who believed in peace were still constant at their work. Young-Man-Afraid-of-his-Horses, who had been on a visit to some other agency in the north or northwest, returned, and immediately went out to the people living about White Clay creek, on the border of the Bad Lands, and brought his people out. He succeeded in obtaining the consent of the people to come out of their place of refuge and return to the agency. Thus the remaining portion of the Indians who started from Rosebud were brought back into the agency. Mr Commissioner, during the days of the great whirlwind out there, those good men tried to hold up a counteracting power, and that was "Peace." We have now come to realize that peace has prevailed and won the day. While we were engaged in bringing about peace our property was left behind, of course, and most of us have lost everything, even down to the matter of guns with which to kill ducks, rabbits, etc, shotguns, and guns of that order. When Young-Man-Afraid brought the people in and their guns were asked for, both men who were called hostile and men who stood loyal to the government delivered up their guns.

Questions for Part I

1 What was the "Shermanizing process" as Southerners saw it? Does Andrews's account make you feel sympathetic toward the defeated South? Why or why not?

2 Based on the evidence you have read, what were some of the attitudes and expectations among the freedmen after the Civil War?

3 Did Southern whites accept the consequences of the Civil War? Explain.

4 What kind of life would a sharecropping family lead? Give details.

5 What, if anything, does the whites' hunting of buffalo say about the character of white civilization as it moved westward across America? Compare it with the Indians' way of life.

6 Describe the life of a cowboy as it is depicted by Andy Adams and Nat Love. Which account seems more realistic? How do you account for the differences?

7 Why do you think the Wounded Knee Massacre occurred? Why do you think Indians have in recent years made Wounded Knee an important symbol of their history?

PART II | AN AGE OF ECONOMIC EXPANSION

In pre-Civil War America an ideology of "producerism" sought to define a common element in the economic contribution of workers, farmers, and entrepreneurs. This producerism held true even though, among these groups, roles underwent so much shifting that men—and sometimes women—had multiple functions in the economy. Workers dreamed of operating small businesses. Farmers, as one commentator ironically noted, cultivated the soil and, increasingly, (thinking of themselves as entrepreneurs going beyond self-sufficiency and selling their goods on the open market) "the main chance."

In the post-Civil War era, the harsher outlines of modern industrial society emerged. Different interests led to different ideologies. The Labor Movement grew on the recognition that "once a worker" most likely meant "always a worker," particularly when this was applied to women, children, immigrants, and members of other groups for whom opportunities for a different life would not often materialize. And farmers began to see themselves as distinct from an urbanizing and industrializing America.

In the readings that follow, Andrew Carnegie articulates the emerging ideology of business—an ideology that stresses individual integrity and vision. However, while the owner or entrepreneur of a business might have faced liberation from conventions of the past, large-scale, "rationally operated" business, such as the John Wanamaker department store, placed limits on worker initiative. This is also seen in the strictures contained in the manual for the employees (most of whom were women) of the Siegel and Cooper department store. And, of course, as the readings on child labor testify, millions of children worked as well—sacrificing both the pleasures of childhood and the opportunity to be educated for a different way of life as adults. Some common folk found opportunities to sell, to save, to advance, or to organize themselves and their brethren. Examples of this can be seen in the autobiography of Mother Jones and in the various

65

reminiscences of working Americans. Finally, even as immigrants such as the ones described by O. E. Rölvaag tried to make their farms succeed against the backdrop of harsh climates and lonely surroundings, the family farm as a representative American institution had already begun its decline. The sentiments of struggling farmers are expressed in the letters of Halvor Harris and other supporters of late nineteenth-century populism.

Sharpening the tension of American society were the massive surges of immigration in the 1880s and in the early years of the twentieth century. In contrast to earlier immigrants (from Northern and Western Europe), the new immigrants were, more frequently, from Southern and Eastern Europe. These people looked different, they sounded different, and their culture seemed very different.

The first victims of nativist resentment were the Chinese, whose economic role on the West coast (they supposedly took railroad and other jobs away from white Americans) led to a ten-year prohibition, through Federal legislation enacted in 1882, of new immigrants from China to the United States. The new European immigrants of the late nineteenth century raised further anti-nativist sentiment that was to continue well into the 1920s and 1930s. The children of these later immigrants doubted they could meld into American society as easily as did children in earlier generations. The painful manifestations of these fears are revealed in the series of letters to the Jewish Daily Forward.

ANDREW CARNEGIE

9 | Climbing the Ladder

Andrew Carnegie (1835-1919), the great industrialist and philanthropist, delivered the following address in 1885 to students at a business school in Pittsburgh. Its optimism and explanation of success in terms of character rather than circumstance or inherited advantages makes it typical of American success literature. As advice, it differs little from what one might have heard in a school commencement speech at any time in the past hundred years. Carnegie, though, gave the message authenticity, because he was that rare case: the very rich man who actually did begin poor and without connections.

Movie buffs have applied Carnegie's advice to another class on the make, the gangsters of the depression era. Edward G. Robinson's "Little Rico," for instance, followed Carnegie to the line: In the opening of the movie Little Caesar Rico robs a filling station, following Carnegie's advice to "begin at the beginning and occupy the most subordinate positions." After the gas station robbery, Rico goes to a diner with his pal and complains, "We nobodies." "Be Somebody," he says to his pal, and he dreams of being a big Chicago mobster. "Aim high," advises Carnegie. Rico becomes a professional of sorts, a professional killer. Rico never drank; Carnegie said, "The destroyer of young men is the drinking of alcohol." Rico avoids women, another Carnegie precept. Rico, too, was singleminded; Carnegie wrote, "And here is the great secret: concentrate your energy, thought and capital exclusively on the business in which you are engaged."

THE ROAD TO BUSINESS SUCCESS: A TALK TO YOUNG MEN

It is well that young men should begin at the beginning and occupy the most subordinate positions. Many of the leading business men of Pittsburgh had a serious responsibility thrust upon them at the very threshold of their career. They were introduced to the broom, and spent the first hours of their business lives sweeping out the office. I notice we have janitors and janitresses now in offices, and our young men unfortunately miss that salutary branch of a business education. But if

From an address to Curry Commercial College, Pittsburgh, June 23, 1885. Published in Andrew Carnegie, The Empire of Business. (New York, Doubleday, Page, and Co., 1902) pp. 3-18.

by chance the professional sweeper is absent any morning the boy who has the genius of the future partner in him will not hesitate to try his hand at the broom. The other day a fond fashionable mother in Michigan asked a young man whether he had ever seen a young lady sweep in a room so grandly as her Priscilla. He said no, he never had, and the mother was gratified beyond measure, but then said he, after a pause, "What I should like to see her do is sweep out a room." It does not hurt the newest comer to sweep out the office if necessary. I was one of those sweepers myself, and who do you suppose were my fellow sweepers? David McCargo, now superintendent of the Alleghany Valley Railroad; Robert Pitcairn, Superintendent of the Pennsylvania Railroad, and Mr. Moreland, City Attorney. We all took turns, two each morning did the sweeping; and now I remember Davie was so proud of his clean white shirt bosom that he used to spread over it an old silk bandana handkerchief which he kept for the purpose, and we other boys thought he was putting on airs. So he was. None of us had a silk handkerchief.

Assuming that you have all obtained employment and are fairly started, my advice to you is "aim high." I would not give a fig for the young man who does not already see himself the partner or the head of an important firm. Do not rest content for a moment in your thoughts as head clerk, or foreman, or general manager in any concern, no matter how extensive. Say each to yourself. "My place is at the top." *Be king in your dreams.* Make your vow that you will reach that position, with untarnished reputation, and make no other vow to distract your attention, except the very commendable one that when you are a member of the firm or before that, if you have been promoted two or three times, you will form another partnership with the loveliest of her sex—a partnership to which our new partnership act has no application. The liability there is never limited.

Let me indicate two or three conditions essential to success. Do not be afraid that I am going to moralize, or inflict a homily upon you. I speak upon the subject only from the view of a man of the world, desirous of aiding you to become successful business men. You all know that there is no genuine, praiseworthy success in life if you are not honest, truthful, fair-dealing. I assume you are and will remain all these, and also that you are determined to live pure, respectable lives, free from pernicious or equivocal associations with one sex or the other. There is no creditable future for you else. Otherwise your learning and your advantages not only go for naught, but serve to accentuate your failure and your disgrace. I hope you will not take it amiss if I warn you against three of the gravest dangers which will beset you in your upward path.

The first and most seductive, and the destroyer of most young men, is the drinking of liquor. I am no temperance lecturer in disguise, but a man who knows and tells you what observation has proved to him; and I say to you that you are more likely to fail in your career from acquiring the habit of drinking liquor than from any, or all, the other temptations likely to assail you. You may yield to almost any other temptation and reform—may brace up, and if not recover lost ground, at least remain in the race and secure and maintain a respectable position. But from the insane thirst for liquor escape is almost impossible. I have known but few exceptions to this rule. First, then, you must not drink liquor to excess. Better if you do not touch it at all—much better; but if this be too hard a rule for you then take your stand firmly here:—Resolve never to touch it except at meals. A glass at dinner will not hinder your advance in life or lower your tone; but I implore you hold it inconsistent with the dignity and self-respect of gentlemen, with what is due from yourselves to yourselves, being the men you are, and especially the men you are determined to become, to drink a glass of liquor at a bar. Be far too much of the gentleman ever to enter a bar-room. You do not pursue your careers in safety unless you stand firmly upon this ground. Adhere to it and you have escaped danger from the deadliest of your foes.

The next greatest danger to a young business man in this community I believe to be that of speculation. When I was a telegraph operator here we had no Exchanges in the City, but the men or firms who speculated upon the Eastern Exchanges were necessarily known to the operators. They could be counted on the fingers of one hand. These men were not our citizens of first repute: they were regarded with suspicion. I have lived to see all of these speculators irreparably ruined men, bankrupt in money and bankrupt in character. There is scarcely an instance of a man who has made a fortune by speculation and kept it. Gamesters die poor, and there is certainly not an instance of a speculator who has lived a life creditable to himself, or advantageous to the community. The man who grasps the morning paper to see first how his speculative ventures upon the Exchanges are likely to result, unfits himself for the calm consideration and proper solution of business problems, with which he has to deal later in the day, and saps the sources of that persistent and concentrated energy upon which depend the permanent success, and often the very safety, of his main business.

The speculator and the business man tread diverging lines. The former depends upon the sudden turn of fortune's wheel; he is a millionaire to-day, a bankrupt to-morrow. But the man of business knows that only by years of patient, unremitting attention to affairs can he earn his reward, which is the result, not of chance, but of well-devised means for the attainment of ends. During all these years his is the cheering thought that by no possibility can he benefit himself without carrying prosperity to others. The speculator on the other hand had better never have lived so far as the good of others or the good of the community is concerned. Hundreds of young men were tempted in this city not long since to gamble in oil, and many were ruined; all were injured whether they lost or won.

/   /   /

The third and last danger against which I shall warn you is one which has wrecked many a fair craft which started well and gave promise of a prosperous voyage. It is the perilous habit of indorsing—all the more dangerous, inasmuch as it assails one generally in the garb of friendship. It appeals to your generous instincts, and you say, "How can I refuse to lend my name only, to assist a friend?" It is because there is so much that is true and commendable in that view that the practice is so dangerous. Let me endeavor to put you upon safe honourable grounds in regard to it. I would say to you to make it a rule now, *never indorse:* but this is too much like never taste wine, or never smoke, or any other of the "nevers." They generally result in exceptions. You will as business men now and then probably become security for friends. Now, here is the line at which regard for the success of friends should cease and regard for your own honour begins.

If you owe anything, all your capital and all your effects are a solemn trust in your hands to be held inviolate for the security of those who have trusted you. Nothing can be done by you with honour which jeopardizes these first claims upon you. When a man in debt indorses for another, it is not his own credit or his own capital he risks, it is that of his own creditors. He violates a trust. Mark you then, never indorse until you have cash means not required for your own debts, and never indorse beyond those means.

/   /   /

I beseech you avoid liquor, speculation and indorsement. Do not fail in either, for liquor and speculation are the Scylla and Charybdis of the young man's business sea, and indorsement his rock ahead.

Assuming you are safe in regard to these your gravest dangers, the question now is how to rise from the subordinate position we have imagined you in, through the successive grades to the position for which you are, in my opinion, and, I trust, in your own, evidently intended. I can give you the secret. It lies mainly in this. Instead of the question, "What must I do for my employer?" substitute "What can I do?" Faithful and conscientious discharge of the duties assigned you is all very well, but the verdict in such cases generally is that you perform your present duties so well that you had better continue performing them. Now, young gentlemen, this will not do. It will not do for the coming partners. There must be something beyond this. We make Clerks, Bookkeepers, Treasurers, Bank Tellers of this class, and there they remain to the end of the chapter. The rising man must do something exceptional, and beyond the range of his special department. *He must attract attention.* A shipping clerk, he may do so by discovering in an invoice an error with which he has nothing to do, and which has escaped the attention of the proper party. If a weighing clerk, he may save for the firm by doubting the adjustment of the scales and having them corrected, even if this be the province of the master mechanic. If a messenger boy, even he can lay the seed of promotion by going beyond the letter of his intructions in order to secure the desired reply. There is no service so low and simple, neither any so high, in which the young man of ability and willing disposition cannot readily and almost daily prove himself capable of greater trust and usefulness, and, what is equally important, show his invincible determination to rise. Some day, in your own department, you will be directed to do or say something which you know will prove disadvantageous to the interest of the firm. Here is your chance. Stand up like a man and say so. Say it boldly, and give your reasons, and thus prove to your employer that, while his thoughts have been engaged upon other matters, you have been studying during hours when perhaps he thought you asleep, how to advance his interests. You may be right or you may be wrong, but in either case you have gained the first condition of success. You have attracted attention. Your employer has found that he has not a mere hireling in his service, but a man; not one who is content to give so many hours of work for so many dollars in return, but one who devotes his spare hours and constant thought to the business. Such an employee must perforce be thought of, and thought of kindly and well. It will not be long before his advice is asked in his special branch, and if the advice given be sound, it will soon be asked and taken upon questions of broader bearing. This means partnership; if not with present employers then with others. Your foot, in such a case, is upon the ladder; the amount of climbing done depends entirely upon yourself.

One false axiom you will often hear, which I wish to guard you against: "Obey orders if you break owners." Don't you do it. This is no rule for you to follow. Always break orders to save owners. There never was a great character who did not sometimes smash the routine regulations and make new ones for himself. The rule is only suitable for such as have no aspirations, and you have not forgotten that you are destined to be owners and to make orders and break orders. Do not hesitate to do it whenever you are sure the interests of your employer will be thereby promoted and when you are so sure of the result that you are willing to take the responsibility. You will never be a partner unless you know the business of your department far better than the owners possibly can. When called to account for your independent action, show him the result of your genius, and tell him that you knew that it would be so; show him how mistaken the orders were. Boss your boss just as soon as you can; try it on early. There is nothing he will like so well if he is the right kind of boss; if he is not, he is not the man for you to remain with—leave him whenever you can, even at a present sacrifice, and find one capable of discerning genius. Our young partners in the Carnegie firm have won their spurs by showing that we did not know half as well what was wanted as they did. Some of them have acted upon occasion with me as if they owned the firm and I was but some airy New Yorker presuming to advise upon what I knew very little about. Well, they are not interfered with much now. They were the true bosses—the very men we were looking for.

There is one sure mark of the coming partner, the future million-naire; his revenues always exceed his expenditures. He begins to save early, almost as soon as he begins to earn. No matter how little it may be possible to save, save that little. Invest it securely, not necessarily in bonds, but in anything which you have good reason to believe will be profitable, but no gambling with it, remember. A rare chance will soon present itself for investment. The little you have saved will prove the basis for an amount of credit utterly surprising to you. Capitalists trust the saving young man. For every hundred dollars you can produce as the result of hard-won savings, Midas, in search of a partner, will lend or credit a thousand; for every thousand, fifty thousand. It is not capital that your seniors require, it is the man who has proved that he has the business habits which create capital, and to create it in the best of all possible ways, as far as self-discipline is concerned, is, by adjusting his habits to his means. Gentlemen, it is the first hundred dollars saved which tells. Begin at once to lay up something. The bee predominates in the future millionnaire.

Of course there are better, higher aims than saving. As an end, the acquisition of wealth is ignoble in the extreme; I assume that you save and long for wealth only as a means of enabling you the better to do some good in your day and generation. Make a note of this essential rule: Expenditure always within income.

You may grow impatient, or become discouraged when year by year you float on in subordinate positions. There is no doubt that it is becom-ing harder and harder as business gravitates more and more to immense concerns, for a young man without capital to get a start for himself, and in this city especially where large capital is essential, it is unusually difficult. Still, let me tell you for your encouragement, that there is no country in the world, where able and energetic young men can so read-ily rise as this, nor any city where there is more room at the top. Young men give all kinds of reasons why in their cases failure was clearly attrib-utable to exceptional circumstances which render success impossible. Some never had a chance, according to their own story. This is simply nonsense. No young man ever lived who had not a chance, and a splen-did chance, too, if he ever was employed at all.

/ / /

The young man who never had a chance is the same young man who has been canvassed over and over again by his superiors, and found desti-tute of necessary qualifications, or is deemed unworthy of closer rela-

tions with the firm, owing to some objectionable act, habit, or association, of which he thought his employers ignorant.

/   /   /

And here is the prime condition of success, the great secret: concentrate your energy, thought, and capital exclusively upon the business in
which you are engaged. Having begun in one line, resolve to fight it
out on that line, to lead in it; adopt every improvement, have the best
machinery, and know the most about it.

The concerns which fail are those which have scattered their capital,
which means that they have scattered their brains also. They have investments in this, or that, or the other, here, there and everywhere.
"Don't put all your eggs in one basket" is all wrong. I tell you "put all
your eggs in one basket, and then watch that basket." Look round you
and take notice; men who do that do not often fail. It is easy to watch
and carry the one basket. It is trying to carry too many baskets that
breaks most eggs in this country. He who carries three baskets must put
one on his head, which is apt to tumble and trip him up. One fault of
the American business man is lack of concentration.

To summarize what I have said: Aim for the highest; never enter a
bar-room; do not touch liquor, or if at all only at meals; never speculate;
never indorse beyond your surplus cash fund; make the firm's interest
yours; break orders always to save owners; concentrate; put all your
eggs in one basket, and watch that basket; expenditure always within
revenue; lastly, be not impatient, for, as Emerson says, "no one can
cheat you out of ultimate success but yourselves."

/   /   /

JOHN WANAMAKER AND THE
SIEGEL AND COOPER
DEPARTMENT STORE

10 | The Business of Selling

Buying and selling in America was once an informal affair. In small stores, the owners family were in constant attendance to run the business. Merchants and customers chatted and haggled—as they still do in much of the world. The development of the department store was a giant step toward making selling impersonal and predictable, accomplished through intermediaries who were simply employees. The next step was advertising, establishing brand standards and prices before the customer even entered the shop. We are so used to the modern world of sales and advertising that it is hard to imagine how new it once was.

John Wanamaker (1838–1922) pioneered the "new kind of store" (as he advertised it in 1877), which quickly became known as the "department store": a collection of specialty shops under one roof and one management. Relying heavily on newspaper advertising and training programs for his employees, Wanamaker set many of the directions that large-scale retailing followed in the twentieth century. In the next selection, Wanamaker discusses this new kind of store. The second reading features a manual for the employees of the Siegel and Cooper department store.

THE EVOLUTION OF MERCANTILE BUSINESS*

Address of Hon. John Wanamaker, Philadelphia

As late as forty years ago, or before the war, the transaction of business in producing and distributing merchandise required many agencies: the manufacturer, importer, commission men, bankers, jobbers, commercial travelers, and retailers.

Until twenty years ago trade rules limited the sales of manufacturers to commission men, and those of commission houses to jobbers, so that the only market door open to retailers was the jobbers, whose goods were loaded, when they reached the retailer, with three or four unavoid-

*John Wanamaker, "The Evolution of Mercantile Business," In Corporations and Public Welfare Addresses at the Annual Meeting of the American Academy of Political and Social Science, Philadelphia, 1900. (New York, McClure, Philips and Company, 1900) pp. 124–128, 130–133.

able profits incident to passing the various fixed stages toward the consumer.

The conditions governing the placing of goods in the retailer's hands were not only heavily weighted with expense, but, in the main, the retail merchant was badly handicapped as a rule by

(a) Small capital, commonly borrowed by long credit for merchandise.

(b) Necessity of selling upon credit.

(c) Necessity for larger percentage of profit.

(d) Impossibility of utilizing to advantage store and people all seasons of the year.

(e) Non-accumulation of capital.

The consequence was, according to accepted statistics, that but four out of every hundred merchants succeeded in business. Getting a mere living forty years ago was generally secured in part by the occupancy of a part of the store premises as a residence. Naturally, an undercurrent of discontent with these conditions manifested itself, protesting against two or more prices for the same article, meagre assortments of goods, high prices and the custom that probably grew out of one rate to cash buyers and a different rate to buyers upon credit.

The Centennial Exposition of 1876 was, in my judgment, the moving cause of a departure toward general business by single ownership. The rising tide of popular desire to assemble under one roof articles used in every home and with freedom to purchase was a constant suggestion in 1876, not alone because of its convenience, but because to some degree it would form a permanent and useful exibition. This idea culminated in the formation of a Permanent Exhibition Company, which succeeded the Centennial. Being located in Fairmount Park and not in a business centre, and without skilled management, the scheme was abandoned in a short time.

Up to 1877, so far as now known, no extensive, well-systemized mercantile retail establishment upon a large scale existed in the United States. The nearest approach was the A. T. Stewart store in New York, which limited itself to dry goods of the higher class.

/   /   /

The tendency of the age toward simplification of business systems and to remove unnecessary duplication of expenses, awakened throughout the United States a keen study of means to bring about a closer alliance with the producer and consumer. Almost simultaneously in a number of cities, long-established stores gradually enlarged and new stores sprang up to group at one point masses of merchandise in more or less variety. The movement everywhere arrested attention and provoked discussion because of the approval and practical support of the people at large.

Though there probably was never a time in any city that there were not bankruptcies of merchants and vacant stores, yet after the opening of the large stores, it everywhere became common with storekeepers and renters to charge all the causes of disaster to the large stores, then and now commonly called departent stores, and an unsuccessful effort was made to decry them as monopolies.

For the time being, and even now, to some extent, prejudice and perhaps unconscious selfishness blinds a part of every community upon public questions. The inequality of talents and the unequal application of individuals must always carry some to the top and others to the lower places in all pursuits of life. The highest statesmanship thus far known has not been able anywhere in the world to maintain a permanent equilibrium for the slow, slovenly and misplaced workers with the thrifty, well-trained and properly fitted toilers, and criticism begins whenever and wherever one man and his family gathers a business that outgrows their own hands.

Whoever conquers a higher place than his neighbor is supposed to face a commanding position, that at least makes his business way more difficult with his fellow tradesmen. Doubtless there must be some disadvantages arising from large single businesses of every kind. The growth of our splendid free libraries will to a certain extent curtail the sale of books and affect other established libraries; the ever enlarging and wonderful facilities and inexpensiveness of the universities and colleges of learning will interfere to some degree with many private academies and schools. . . . The trolley affected the business of the horse dealer. The large stores certainly affect a certain part of the small stores. Neither well-dressed ignorance nor well-satisfied storekeeping ownership can argue down that fact.

In the olden times when any city was smaller the advent of even one more small store affected every other store in the block in which it located, mayhap in the entire city. The thing to be considered, and considered fairly from every point of view, is what the large single ownership businesses contribute to the well-being of the public to counterbalance any disadvantages arising from them.

First of all it must be remembered that society is not constituted for the benefit of any one particular class of the population. Economic questions cannot be voted on by any 10 per cent of the people; the other 90 per cent must have their say. Without sentiment or prejudice, the interests of all must be justly weighed and the greatest good of the greatest number must be gained.

I respectfully submit that the evolution in mercantile business during the last quarter of a century has been wrought not by combinations of capital, corporations or trusts, but by the natural growth of individual mercantile enterprises born of new conditions out of the experience, mistakes and losses of old-time trading . . . ; that thus far the enlarged retailing has practically superseded agents, commission houses, importers and large and small jobbers, thereby saving rentals, salaries and various expenses of handling.

/ / /

I contend that the department store development would not be here but for its service to society; that it has done a public service in retiring middlemen; that its organization neither denies rights to others nor claims privileges of state franchises, or favoritism of national tariff laws; that if there is any suffering from it it is by the pressure of competition, and not from the pressure of monopoly; that so long as competition is not suppressed by law, monopolies cannot exist in storekeeping. . . .

I hold that the evolution in trade was inevitable, because it was water-logged by old customs that overtaxed purchasers; that there was at work for a long time a resistless force moving towards the highest good of humanity; that the profit therefrom to individuals who have risked their own capital, as any man may still do if he chooses, has been insignificant, compared to the people benefited both by the cheapening of the comforts of life and by the improved condition of persons employed.

/ / /

I believe the new American system of storekeeping is the most powerful factor yet discovered to compel minimum prices. . . . It is a noticeable fact that lowered prices stimulate consumption and require additional labor in producing, transporting and distributing. The care of such large stocks, amounting in one single store upon an average at all times to between four and five millions of dollars, and the preparation of and handling from reserves to forward stocks, require large corps of men. Under old conditions of storekeeping a man and his wife or daughter did all the work between daylight and midnight. The new systems make shorter hours of duty and thus the number of employes is increased, while many entirely new avenues of employment for women are opened, as typewriters, stenographers, cashiers, check-clerks, inspectors, wrappers, mailing clerks and the like. The division of labor creates many places for talented and high-priced men, whose salaries range alongside of presidents of banks and trust companies and similar important positions. It is universally admitted that the sanitary conditions that surround the employes of the large stores are better than in the old-time smaller stores and that employes are considerably better paid.

/ / /

What is the effect of the modern retail store upon competition? Are its tendencies monopolistic in the control of merchandise or of trade? I counted yesterday the number of mercantile licenses of dealers, places and stores in Philadelphia in the year 1870. There were 16,560. To-day I obtained the number of notices of mercantile licenses thus far sent out in Philadelphia representing the stores and places of business, and the figures given me are a minimum of 34,000, with an additional number yet to be issued.

The population in 1870 was 674,022, twenty years later it was 1,046,964, and is now variously estimated at from 1,250,000 to 1,300,000. The number of stores in 1870 (16,560) to the population of that date was 245 for every 10,000, while at the maximum estimate for 1900 the number of stores is 267 for every 10,000 persons. The increase in the number of business dealers has more than kept pace with the growth of the population.

/   /   /

If all the storekeepers of any one city were to combine, such a combination would not stand twelve months because of the power of manufacturers to become retailers, and further, such a city of combinations would be overwhelmed with independent storekeepers from every other city, who would very properly expect and command the support of the people.

RULES AND REGULATIONS FOR THE SIEGEL AND COOPER EMPLOYEES

GENERAL INSTRUCTIONS

Deportment

We want it said of our employees, that they are a credit to the house. Be civil and polite to your superiors. Should those in authority not be civil to you, "Obey," and if grievance warrants, see Superintendent. Under no circumstances are you to refuse to do what you are told to do by one superior in authority. Should you be reported for not obeying, you will lose your position, even if circumstances warranted your actions. After doing as told, then if order was unjust, or uncalled for, see Superintendent, who will always uphold you if in the right.

Rules and Regulations for the Government of the Employees of The Siegel and Cooper Company of New York. (New York, Siegel and Cooper Company, 1900), passim.

Buyers, assistant buyers and floor managers being in sectional command, their orders must be obeyed. Appeal can be made in writing if possible, to Superintendent.

Not Permitted

Buyers and floor managers will be held accountable and blamed if anyone under their control is found chewing gum, tobacco, or eating while back of counters. Anyone acting thus will be discharged.

Things Not To Do

Do not stand in groups.
Do not chew gum, read books or sew.
Do not giggle, flirt or idle away your time.
Do not walk together through the store.
Do not be out of your place.
Do not be late at any time.
Do not take over fifteen minutes on a pass.
Do not make a noise when going up in elevators.
Do not push when going into elevators, but always stand in line.
Do not talk across aisle, or in a loud voice.
Do not gossip; mind your own affairs, and you will have enough to do.
Do not sit in front of counter.
Do not tell customer the article asked for is "Out of date." In other words, that they don't know what they want.

Try To Be

Polite, neat; dress in black.
Serious in your work.
Punctual, obliging, painstaking.
Keep your stock in good order, and follow the rules of the house, which, if obeyed, simply means that you are doing right, and if you do what you feel *is right* you will find that you are obeying the rules.

System Of The House

Learn all the details.
Know how to make out all checks.
If you don't know, ask.
Ask reasons, so you not only know how, but why you must comply exactly and not omit some little thing, which to us may be important.
Always write legibly. Auditing girls are instructed to send all illegi-

ble checks to Superintendent. Superintendent, on noting your day's sales filled with illegible figures and addresses, is apt to ask Auditing room for sales of a week back. If the week's sales show carelessness or incompetence, clerk will be dismissed, as we cannot permit illegible records.

/   /   /

Wrong

It is wrong to *destroy the property of others.*

Any destructiveness or vandalism on the part of employees should be reported, which report will be received in confidence by the Superintendent.

/   /   /

Clever People Are Appreciated

Anyone employed by our firm, who has an idea that would improve existing conditions in any department, will be received in confidence by the Superintendent, who will value such information.

/   /   /

Elevator Attendants

We have one man in full charge, whose orders must be obeyed. Your duty as an elevator man calls for more than the ordinary amount of intelligence. Your pace is to run your car properly, call off the floors, and be polite. You are not to talk back to customers, or slam the door in their faces. *Be polite;* but of course you cannot wait for people all day.

Don't make customers angry by brusk talk. If they are slow getting in or out, say, "Step lively, please." Always say "Please."

/   /   /

Late

If we opened at 10 A.M. some people would come late. We are rigid in our rule that you be on time. You should be here by 8 A.M.; after 8:05 you will be "late." Doors will be closed at 8:10, and employees coming after 8:10 will be told to come at noon, and therefore lose half a day's pay.

Rules Regarding Time Card

Name, number, date, and lunch hour, must be written in ink on time card before noon on each Monday. Cards must be carried on person.

When coming late, cards must be surrendered to time keeper at once.

To Our Employees in General: A Few Words of Advice

Character and Habits

You may be bright, energetic and a valuable employee, yet your services may be undesirable if you haven't a good character, or if your habits are questionable. We may suffer temporarily, but we soon find out, and the main and real sufferer is the person involved. You stand or fall by your own actions. Remember that judgment is passed on truth, and right will always triumph.

As you rise step by step, it is because of ability and character, but no matter how high you do get, laxity in either may be your downfall and ruination for life.

You would be very much surprised if you knew the trouble and expense we go to, to find out "character and habits." Detectives you don't know, often are detailed to report all of your doings for a week.

Don't flirt. Remember the esteem which is due to all self-respecting persons, and ever remember the ill comments which follow idle gossip.

Don't lie. It takes more lies to back it up, which finally brings the house down on your head.

Don't live beyond your income, or go into debt. Cultivate saving. No matter what your wages are, you should save a part for a rainy day. It is not only the amount, but the habit formed, which will prove valuable to you.

/   /   /

Don't Borrow Or Lend

Don't loan money even to your best friend. You are apt to lose both your money and your friend if you do.

/   /   /

Never Call Anyone

By his or her first name; that is childish and unbusinesslike.
Be dignified; it shows respect and adds to your good sense.
Be precise in these little courtesies.

/   /   /

Merit Wins

We want you to have in mind that those in authority are always on the
alert to gauge the merits of employees and to advance them, as vacan-
cies occur, so that conscientious work and proper efforts in the interest
of the firm may not be lost, and good seed sown will in time reap ample
harvest.

Thus, work here is not like the drudgery in a small store—where
one has little hope of advancement, where the hours are from 6 A.M. to
9 P.M., where possibilities are limited and much menial work is expected. Here you receive a liberal business training, and surroundings
that should ever arouse hope and ambition; for on all sides you can see
people in positions of trust and holding the confidence of the firm, who,
only a few years ago were in the ranks, just as you are now. But these
were men and women of purpose and faith in their work, and ever at
work, their merit won out.

/   /   /

11 | Testimony on Child Labor

Children have been working in factories since the advent of the Industrial Revolution. The opportunity to provide work for women and children was one of the arguments made in favor of "manufacturing establishments" by Alexander Hamilton in his Report on Manufacturing *in 1791. Organized efforts to regulate and restrict child labor finally began in the 1880s but had limited success and that only in the North. The Progressive movement worked to outlaw child labor, but the 1916 federal law to that effect was declared unconstitutional by the Supreme Court in* Hammer v. Dagenhart *in 1918. Federal efforts to outlaw child labor succeeded only in 1938.*

The three documents that follow illustrate the phenomenon of child labor. The first is from the important Report of the Committee of the U.S. Senate Upon the Relations Between Labor and Capital, Hearings Held in 1883; *the latter two are from a New York State Legislative Committee Hearing in 1896.*

Augusta, Ga., *November* 23, 1883.*

Otis G. Lynch sworn and examined.

By the Chairman:

Q: What is your occupation?

A: I am superintendent of the Enterprise Manufacturing Company.

Q: How long have you been superintendent of that company?

A: I have been superintendent of the Enterprise Company for something over two and one-half years.

Q: Please state where you were born and what has been your experience in manufacturing?

A: I was born in Otsego County, New York, I came to Augusta twenty-eight years ago.

Q: Had you any knowledge of manufacturing when you came here?

A: Yes; I had worked some in the mills in Oneida County, New

From Report of the Committee of the Senate Upon the Relations Between Labor and Capital and Testimony Taken by the Committee. Volume IV, (Washington, D.C., Government Printing Office, 1885), pp. 748–749, 752–753.

York. I commenced the business in the county in which I was born, at the age of about ten, and I have been in the same business ever since, except during short periods when I went to school about six months at a time when I was a boy. For a good many years I was employed in a subordinate position in the Augusta factory and afterwards I got to be the overseer.

Q: You have worked your way up, as Mr. Hickman says a man will?

A: Yes, sir; as some men will.

Q: What is the capital stock of the Enterprise Company?

A: Five hundred thousand dollars.

Q: What is the annual product?

A: We run 602 looms at the present time.

Q: How many bales of lint cotton do you work up?

A: About 6,200 a year.

Q: How much help do you employ?

A: We have, I think, 485 on our pay-roll.

Q: How many of those are men?

A: I cannot answer that exactly; about one-seventh.

Q: The rest are women and children, I suppose?

A: Yes, sir.

Q: How many of them would you class as women and how many as children?

A: I think about one-third of the remainder would be children and two-thirds women. That is about the proportion.

Q: What is the average wages that you pay?

A: Eighty-two cents a day for the last six months, or in that neighborhood.

Q: What do the women make a day?

A: About $1.

Q: And the men?

A: Do you mean common laborers?

Q: Yes; the average wages of your laborers.

A: About $1 a day.

Q: What do the children make on an average?

A: About from 35 to 75 cents a day.

Q: You employ children of ten years and upward?

A: Yes, sir.

Q: Do you employ any below the age of ten?

A: No.

Q: About what proportion of the men in your employ can read and write; I mean who can read well enough to read the Constitution of the United States, or the New Testament, or a newspaper and understand what they are about?

A: I think about two-thirds of them can do it.

Q: What proportion of the women?

A: Not so large a proportion; I should think, probably, one-half of them.

Q: You think that one-half of the female operatives in your employ can read a common book, one of the novels of the day, or a history of the United States, and understand it?

A: I think that one-half of them may be said to know how to read, but that is a rough guess on my part.

Q: What proportion of the children can read or write?

A: Most of them can read. They nearly all go to Sunday school.

Q: Do they learn to read in the Sunday schools?

A: Yes, sir; if they have not learned elsewhere before they come to the mill.

Q: Then, reading and writing are taught in the Sunday schools?

A: Yes; reading is. I think a larger porportion of the children than of the grown people can read intelligently.

/   /   /

Q: What is your experience as to the employment of child labor?

A: What do you mean?

Q: I mean is it a good thing according to your experience that children of from ten to fifteen years of age should work in the factories?

A: Yes, sir; I think it is.

Q: Do you think it is a good thing that they should work eleven hours a day all the year around?

A: I think it would be better for them if they were not compelled to work at all, but—

Q: (Interposing.) You would want them to work a part of the time in order to learn a business for life, would you not?

A: Yes, sir. Circumstances now force them into the mills. They come in with their mothers.

Q: I understand that as a matter of fact, in the present condition of these people it is a necessity that they shall have employment, and that the employment of the children of a family oftentimes prevents the whole family from becoming paupers; but setting aside this temporary necessity, do you think it well that children between the ages of say ten and fourteen years should be required to work more than about half the time in a factory?

A: Well, I don't know that I can answer that question satisfactorily. I don't know whether they should be compelled to work at all in the factory unless circumstances made it necessary.

Q: You think, I suppose, that it would be better for the children to have a chance to be outdoors?

A: Yes, sir.

Q: But the testimony is that many of those children seem to enjoy their work in the factory.

A: Oh, yes. It is not laborious work, and it is not continuous; there is more or less rest as they go along.

Q: Not much play, I suppose?

A: Some little; not much. Of course, we have discipline in the mill, but the labor is not continuous or excessive.

Q: Do the children remain in the mill during the whole eleven hours as the older operatives do?

A: Yes.

Q: How as to their chance of getting some education in your free schools?

A: Well, in individual cases they sometimes quit the mill and go to school—some of them do.

Q: For how long periods?

A: Indefinite periods. Some of the parents take their children out when they feel that they can do without them for a while and send them to school, and afterwards when it becomes necessary they send them back to the mill again. There is no rule about it.

Q: But most of them remain in the mill one year after another, I suppose.

A: Oh, yes; but they change a good deal out and in.

*The following reading is part of a report of a committee of the Assembly of the State of New York. **

The inquiry into the condition of manufacturing places in the city of New York, and the condition and circumstances of the persons who worked therein, has involved the inquiry into branches of State and city government which are naturally and indissolubly connected therewith. The education and health of the persons who work in manufacturing establishments, as well as the sanitary arrangements and conditions existing therein, have necessarily become a part of the committee's inquiry, and the committee has found that the welfare of the working people depends not upon the wisdom, adequacy and enforcement of the Factory Law alone, but in addition upon proper and adequate education and health laws.

The opinion of the committee presented in its preliminary report, that large numbers of children were employed in manufacturing places contrary to law, has been amply confirmed by its further and fuller investigations. The committee stamps the employment of child labor un-

*From Documents of the Assembly of the State of New York, *119th Session, 1896, Volume 23, No. 97, Part I (Albany, Wynkoop Hallenback Crawford Company, 1896), pp. 5–7, 460–465.*

der the statutory age as one of the most extensive evils now existing in the city of New York, and an evil which is a constant and grave menace to the welfare of its people. Many children were found by the diligent efforts of the committee's subpoena servers and brought before the committee, who were under the requisite age, and many others were seen by members of the committee upon their investigation tours. These children were undersized, poorly clad and dolefully ignorant, unacquainted with the simplest rudiments of a common school education, having no knowledge of the simplest figures and unable in many cases to write their own names in the native or any other language.

The following illustrations, of the many which could be cited, will suffice to corroborate the broad statement contained in the previous sentence:

Eva Lunsky testified as follows:

Q: When were you born?
A: I don't know.
Q: Nobody has ever told you?
A: No, sir.
Q: Did your mamma ever tell you when you were born?
A: She told me, but I have forgotten.
Q: You don't know whether you ever had a birthday party or not?
A: Yes, sir; I have had a birthday party.
Q: When?
A: Last year.
Q: How old were you last year?
A: I was 15.
Q: Was it in the winter time?
A: It was in the summer time.
Q: And you don't know the month?
A: No, sir.
Q: Do you know when the Fourth of July is?
A: No, sir.
Q: Do you know when the summer time is when they fire off fire crackers; don't they have any down your way? (The witness gave no answer.)
Q: Did you ever go to school in this country?
A: I went only three months.
Q: When was that, Eva?
A: That was last summer.
Q: What time in the summer was it that you went there; what months, do you know?
A: No.
Q: Do you know the names of the summer months?
A: No, sir.
Q: What month is this; do you know what month this is?
A: No.

Again, Fannie Harris, who earned two dollars per week, of which her mother allowed her two cents a week for spending money, testified:

Q: Now, have you been to school in this country?
A: No.
Q: Can you read?
A: I can read a little, not much.
Q: What can you read—can you read "dog?"
A: No, sir.
Q: Do you know how to spell dog?
A: I went to night school.
Q: Do you know how to spell dog?
A: I have forgotten it since night school stopped.
Q: Can you spell "cat?"
A: Yes, sir.
Q: How do you spell it?
A: I have forgot.
Q: When did you have a birthday; did you have a birthday lately?
A: No, sir.
Q: Did you ever have a birthday?
A: No, sir.
Q: You know what a birthday is, don't you, Fannie?
A: Yes, sir.
Q: What is that?
A: The day that you were born.
Q: Now, didn't you have a birthday?
A: I never had a birthday because we have not any money to make a birthday.
Q: That is, you never had a little party?
A: No, sir.
Q: A birthday is a day when you have a little party, is it not?
A: Yes, sir.
Q: Does your mamma work?
A: Now she ain't working, because I am working, but before, when I didn't work, she worked.
Q: Your mamma is not sick, is she?
A: No, sir.
Q: And your mamma wants you to go to work?
A: Yes, sir; sure she does; and I want to go to work myself.
Q: And if you don't go to work then your mamma will have to go to work?
A: Sure.
Q: Now, Fannie, when will you be 15 years of age?
A: I don't know.
Q: Are you 15 now?
A: No, sir.

Q: And this paper (showing age certificate) your mamma gave you, did she?

A: I went to a lawyer and paid twenty-five cents and he gave me it.

/   /   /

Abraham Rose, having been called as a witness (not sworn) testified as follows:

Examination by Mr. Mayer:

Q: You are not afraid of me, are you?

A: I can't understand English.

Q: You are not afraid of me, are you?

A: No.

Q: Will you tell me the truth in everything I ask you?

A: I will.

Q: What is going to happen to you if you do not tell the truth? (The examination of this witness was conducted with the aid of an interpreter.)

A: He knows that; he knows he will be punished if he don't tell the truth.

Q: Where do you live?

A: Five Norfolk street.

Q: Where do you work?

A: By Mr. Levi.

Q: Where is his place of business?

A: Thirty-one Hester street.

Q: Where were you born?

A: I don't know.

Q: Where were you born?

A: I was born in Gallacia.

Q: Is your papa alive?

A: Yes, sir.

Q: What does he do?

A: My father is living and working; he is a peddler.

Q: How much does Levi pay you every week?

A: He pays me two dollars a week.

Q: When do you go to work in the morning?

A: At seven o'clock.

Q: When do you go home?

A: At six o'clock.

Q: Do you get any time for dinner in the middle of the day?

A: Yes, sir.

Q: Do you go home for dinner?

A: I go home to dinner.

Q: Do you take dinner with your mother?

A: I live with my mother, and my mother gives me to eat.
Q: What do you do with the two dollars you get every week?
A: I give it to my mother.
Q: Does your mother give you any money to spend?
A: She don't give me nothing but one penny.
Q: One penny every week?
A: Every week one penny.
Q: When were you confirmed?
A: One year.
Q: Now, who told you to tell us that?
A: Nobody told me.
Q: What synagogue were you confirmed in?
A: I was confirmed in Europe—not here.
Q: When did you come from Europe?
A: About six months I am here.
Q: And is your father here only the same time?
A: My father and mother came here with me.
Q: What time of the year was it that you were confirmed?
A: He was confirmed about the fall or winter; he was confirmed about December.
Q: Last December?
A: Before that—about a couple of weeks before that; I was confirmed a year previous to last December.
Q: Now, you must be 13 years old to be confirmed, must you not?
A: I was 13 years old when I was confirmed.
Q: How old must a boy be when he is confirmed?
A: Thirteen years old.
Q: How long have you been working for Levi?
A: Two months and a half I am working for Mr. Levi.
Q: Did you work for anybody else in this country?
A: Yes, sir; someone else.
Q: Who else—where does he live?
A: His name was Levi too.
Q: Where does he live?
A: In Montgomery street, but I don't remember the number.
Q: How much did this man pay you—the first Levi?
A: One dollar and a half a week.
Q: And did you work just as long as you are working now?
A: Yes, sir; I did.
Q: What do you do now—what is the kind of work you do?
A: I am pulling bastings.
Q: And you do that all day long?
A: Sometimes if there is nothing why I do nothing, but all the time there is nothing but bastings pulling.
Q: He keeps you busy all day long?

A: There is only one finisher present and she can't give me work enough to pull bastings out.

Q: Can you write your name in English?

A: I can read it in Polish.

Q: Can you write your name in English?

A: I don't know whether I could or not.

Q: You can not, can you?

A: No.

Q: Now, do you know what day to-day is?

A: Yes, sir.

Q: What day is today?

A: Monday.

Q: What month is this month?

A: I don't know what month it is.

Q: Can you write anything in Polish?

A: Yes, sir; I can write in Polish my name, my address, etc.

Q: Anything else?

A: I can write a little, but not very good.

Q: Can you add up?

A: I could, but I have forgotten.

Q: Do you know how much two and three make?

A: Yes, sir.

Q: How much?

A: Five.

Q: How much does five and seven make?

A: Five and seven makes twelve.

Q: Were you ever in school in this country?

A: No, sir; I was not.

Q: Who told you that you were 14 years old?

A: I know that by when I was confirmed; I am 13 years old, and I am confirmed one year, and therefore I know I am 14 years old; that is the only reason I know I am 14 years old.

Q: Did you and Levi have a talk before you came down here to-day?

A: No, sir; I have not spoken to Mr. Levi before I came here.

Q: Who told you how to get here?

A: My boss brought me here.

Q: What did he say to you on the way down from the shop?

A: A man brought me here to-day that came for me—a man that brought me here.

Q: You were down in the other building last Saturday, were you not?

A: I was last Saturday with my boss in the other building.

Q: Did he say anything to you last Saturday?

A: No; he said nothing to me last Saturday.

Nathan Levi, having been called as a witness and duly sworn by the chairman, testified as follows:

Examination by Mr. Mayer:

Q: What is your full name?
A: Nathan Levi.
Q: Where do you live?
A: Thirty-one Hester street.
Q: Now, Levi, this little boy Abraham Rose who was on the stand is employed by you, is he not?
A: Yes, sir.
Q: How old is he?
A: His father told me—
Q: How old is he?
A: I don't know.
Q: When did the father tell you that?
A: He told me that.
Q: Talk so we can understand you.
A: Yes, sir; when he came to me to work I asked him how old he was and he told me he was 14 years old, and I take him to work.
Q: He told you he was 14 years old; when was he 14?
A: About ten weeks ago.
Q: Was he 14 years old just before the Jewish holiday?
A: Yes, sir.
Q: Before what holiday?
A: Ten weeks before; he came up to me to work and I asked him how old he was and he told me 14 years.
Q: Now, when was he 14 years old; did the father tell you that?
A: No, sir; I don't ask him for that.
Q: Did you not ask the father to go before a notary public; you didn't ask him to swear to the boy's age?
A: No, sir.
Q: Have you done anything else except ask the father how old he was?
A: I told him to bring me a ticket.
Q: Has he brought you any ticket?
A: No, sir.
Q: Have you done anything else to find out how old he is?
A: No, sir.
Q: How long has he been with you?
A: Ten weeks.
Q: How much would you have to pay a boy 16 years old to do the same work that this little boy is doing?
A: All the same.
Q: You would pay a boy 16 years old two dollars, would you?
A: For this work I don't pay any more.

By Mr. Wilks:

Q: Can you get a boy 16 years old to work for that?
A: Yes, sir.

By Mr. Mayer:

Q: Did you ever have one?
A: Yes sir; I had a boy 16 years old.
Q: What was his name?
A: I couldn't remember his name.
Q: When did you keep him?
A: When I lived in East New York.
Q: When did you keep the boy that was 16 years old?
A: Before my present boy came to me.
Q: So you had this 16-year-old boy about two months ago, did you?
A: Yes, sir.
Q: What did he leave you for?
A: I don't know why.
Q: What were you paying when he left?
A: Two dollars a week.
Q: How old was he?
A: Sixteen years old.
Q: How do you know he was 16?
A: He brought me a ticket.
Q: He brought you a ticket, did he?
A: Yes, sir.
Q: Why didn't you ask for a ticket from this little boy?
A: I asked him for a ticket.
Q: You never asked for one, did you?
A: I asked the father for a ticket.
Q: He has been with you for ten weeks?
A: Yes, sir.
Q: Was there never a factory inspector in your place?
A: No, sir.
Q: How long have you been doing business where you are now?
A: Five years.
Q: And there never has been a factory inspector there?
A: No, sir.
Q: Do you know what a factory inspector is?
A: Yes, sir.
Q: There never was a factory inspector to see you?
A: No, sir.
Q: Not in five years?
A: I don't live there five years.

Q: How long have you been in this place, No. 11 Norfolk street?
A: Only about four months.
Q: In No. 11 Norfolk street; that is where you have your workshop now?
A: Yes, sir.
Q: Where were you before that?
A: In East New York.
Q: How long were you there?
A: About a year and a half.
Q: What do you mean by telling me nobody has been to see you for five years?
A: There was a lady in East New York.
Q: But there has been nobody here in Norfolk street?
A: No, sir.
Q: Do you know what can be done to you for employing this boy?
A: No, sir; I don't know.
Q: Did you ever try to find out?
A: No, sir.
Q: Do you know whether you have a right to employ that boy?
A: I asked for a ticket.
Q: Do you know whether you have a right to employ that boy?
A: If he is 14 years old then I can take him to work.
Q: Is that all you know; if he is under 16 years of age and can not write a sentence in English can you employ him?
A: I don't know that.
Q: Did the factory inspector tell you that?
A: No, sir.
Q: Has there ever been an inspector from the board of health where you are now?
A: No, sir.

12 | Organizing the Coal Miners

Irish-born Mary Harris Jones is a legendary figure in the history of American labor, particularly of the United Mine Workers. Courageous, a powerful speaker, and possessed of boundless energy, she was universally known as Mother Jones. (Her real motherhood was tragic: Her husband and all four of her children died during the Memphis yellow-fever epidemic of 1864.) In the 1870s, she emerged as an organizer, principally in the mining unions, and she worked, it seemed, everywhere. Her personal odyssey and the history of American labor for half a century merged. This small woman—her handsome face and sparkling gray eyes wreathed in a perennial black bonnet, her speech picturesque, her voice a high falsetto—was present: at the great rail strike in Pittsburgh in 1877, at the Haymarket massacre in Chicago in 1886, at the rail strike in Birmingham in 1894, at the national coal strikes of 1900 and 1902 (where she organized the miners' wives to march with mops and brooms), at the West Virginia coal strike of 1912–1913 (presented in the following reading), at the New York garment workers and street-car strikes of 1915–1916, and at the great steel strike of 1919. Her autobiography is indispensable for capturing the first heroic age of American labor.

Tom Haggerty was in charge of the Fairmont field. One Sunday morning, the striking miners of Clarksburg started on a march of Monongha to get out the miners in the camps along the line. We camped in the open fields and held meetings on the road sides and in barns, preaching the gospel of unionism.

The Consolidated Coal Company that owns the little town of New England forbade the distribution of the notices of our meeting and arrested any one found with a notice. But we got the news around. Several of our men went into the camp. They went in twos. One pretended he was deaf and the other kept hollering in his ear as they walked around, "Mother Jones is going to have a meeting Sunday afternoon outside the town on the sawdust pile." Then the deaf fellow would ask him what he said and he would holler to him again. So the word got around the entire camp and we had a big crowd.

Mary Field Parton, editor, Autobiography of Mother Jones, *Chicago, 1925.*

When the meeting adjourned, three miners and myself set out for Fairmont City. The miners, Jo Battley, Charlie Blakley and Barney Rice walked but they got a little boy with a horse and buggy to drive me over. I was to wait for the boys just outside the town, across the bridge, just where the interurban car comes along.

The little lad and I drove along. It was dark when we came in sight of the bridge which I had to cross. A dark building stood beside the bridge. It was the Coal Company's store. It was guarded by gunmen. There was no light on the bridge and there was none in the store.

A gunman stopped us. I could not see his face.

"Who are you?" said he.

"Mother Jones," said I, "and a miner's lad."

"So that's you, Mother Jones," said he rattling his gun.

"Yes, it's me," I said, "and be sure you take care of the store to-night. Tomorrow I'll have to be hunting a new job for you."

I got out of the buggy where the road joins the Interurban tracks, just across the bridge. I sent the lad home.

"When you pass my boys on the road tell them to hurry up. Tell them I'm waiting just across the bridge."

There wasn't a house in sight. The only people near were the gunmen whose dark figures I could now and then see moving on the bridge. It grew very dark. I sat on the ground, waiting. I took out my watch, lighted a match and saw that it was about time for the interurban.

Suddenly the sound of "Murder! Murder! Police! Help!" rang out through the darkness. Then the sound of running and Barney Rice came screaming across the bridge toward me. Blakley followed, running so fast his heels hit the back of his head. "Murder! Murder!" he was yelling.

I rushed toward them. "Where's Jo?" I asked.

"They're killing Jo—on the bridge—the gunmen."

At that moment the Interurban car came in sight. It would stop at the bridge. I thought of a scheme.

I ran onto the bridge, shouting, "Jo! Jo! The boys are coming. They're coming! The whole bunch's coming. The car's most here!"

Those bloodhounds for the coal company thought an army of miners was in the Interurban car. They ran for cover, barricading themselves in the company's store. They left Jo on the bridge, his head broken and the blood pouring from him. I tore my petticoat into strips, bandaged his head, helped the boys to get him on to the Interurban car, and hurried the car into Fairmont City.

We took him to the hotel and sent for a doctor who sewed up the great, open cuts in his head. I sat up all night and nursed the poor fellow. He was out of his head and thought I was his mother.

The next night Tom Haggerty and I addressed the union meeting, telling them just what had happened. The men wanted to go clean up the gunmen but I told them that would only make more trouble. The meeting adjourned in a body to go see Jo. They went up to his room, six or eight of them at a time, until they had all seen him.

We tried to get a warrant out for the arrest of the gunmen but we couldn't because the coal company controlled the judges and the courts.

Jo was not the only man who was beaten up by the gunmen. There were many and the brutalities of these bloodhounds would fill volumes.

In Clarksburg, men were threatened with death if they even billed meetings for me. But the railway men billed a meeting in the dead of night and I went in there alone. The meeting was in the court house. The place was packed. The mayor and all the city officials were there.

"Mr. Mayor," I said, "will you kindly be chairman for a fellow American citizen?"

He shook his head. No one would accept my offer.

"Then," said I, "as chairman of the evening, I introduce myself, the speaker of the evening, Mother Jones."

13 | Letters from Six Farm Men and Women

Hard times on the farm fueled the Populist movement of the late nineteenth century. One sees the reality behind the political slogans of the era in letters written by farm men and women to Populist newspapers or Populist politicians. The first letter is from Minnesota; the second from Nebraska; the third from North Dakota; the fourth from a Nebraskan preparing to move to the Oklahoma Territory; and the fifth and sixth are from Kansas. Although the spelling and grammar in the letters are far from exemplary, the farmers concerns—the cost of land, railroad rates, credit rates, drought—are real and compelling. The farmers found expression not only in the Populist or People's party, but in the 1896 capture of the Democratic party by the followers of William Jennings Bryan.

HALVOR HARRIS*

In the minds of the forlorne and the unprotected Poor People of this and other states I might say I am one of those Poor and unprotected. One of those which have settled upon the socalled Indemnity Land of the Minn St Paul and Manitoba now the great Northern [Railroad]. I settled on this Land in good Faith Built House and Barn Broken up Part of the Land. Spent years of hard Labor in grubing fencing and Improving are they going to drive us out like tresspassers wife and children a sickly wife with Poor Health enough Before and give us away to the Corporations how can we support them. When we are robed of our means. they will shurely not stand this we must Decay and Die from Woe and Sorrow We are Loyal Citicens and do Not Intend to Intrude on any R.R. Corporation we Believed and still do Believe that the RR Co has got No Legal title to this Land in question We Love our wife and children just as Dearly as any of you But how can we protect them give them education as they should wen we are driven from sea to sea. . . .

*Halvor Harris to Ignatius Donnelly, January 29, 1891, Donnelly Papers, Minnesota Historical Society.

W. M. TAYLOR*

This season is without a parallel in this part of the country. The hot winds burned up the entire crop, leaving thousands of families wholly destitute, many of whom might have been able to run through this crisis had it not been for the galling yoke put on them by the money loaners and sharks—not by charging 7 per cent. per annum, which is the lawful rate of interest, or even 10 per cent., but the unlawful and inhuman country destroying rate of 3 per cent. a month, some going still farther and charging 50 per cent per annum. We are cursed, many of us financially, beyond redemption, not by the hot winds so much as by the swindling games of the bankers and money loaners, who have taken the money and now are after the property, leaving the farmer moneyless and homeless. . . . I have borrowed for example $1,000. I pay $25 besides to the commission man. I give my note and second mortgage of 3 per cent of the $1,000, which is $30 more. Then I pay 7 per cent. on the $1,000 to the actual loaner. Then besides all this I pay for appraising the land, abstract, recording, etc., so when I have secured my loan I am out the first year $150. Yet I am told by the agent who loans me the money, he can't stand to loan at such low rates. This is on the farm, but now comes the chattel loan. I must have $50 to save myself. I get the money; my note is made payable in thirty or sixty days for $35, secured by chattel of two horses, harness and wagon, about five times the value of the note. The time comes to pay, I ask for a few days. No I can't wait; must have the money. If I can't get the money, I have the extreme pleasure of seeing my property taken and sold by this iron handed money loaner while my family and I suffer.

W. T. McCULLOCH**

As We are about to have our first great Battle in this State between Corporate Greed, and the great Plain People, the Strugle will be a Desperate one, and must be fought to a finish. Determining, whether it shall be Masters, and Slaves, or a free People. in fact as well as in Name. And few, Reading thinking Men in America, Deny the Slavery of the Masses. to the Money Power of our Country, and a large Portion of our People, having lost all faith in our present Political Parties. for any Reforms. that would wrest the Masses of our People from Corporate Greed. Or give them any Rights, that Corporate Greed would have to respect   It does not appear, that we are Destined to Slavery of one Kind or another, For

*W. M. Taylor to editor, Farmer's Alliance (Lincoln), January 10, 1891, Nebraska Historical Society.
**W. T. McCulloch to Ignatius Donnelly, April, 1892, Donnelly Papers, Minnesota Historical Society.

the Slavery of to Day. Is but of a little different Kind from that of old. While in former Days it was necessary, that the Masters Keep within reach of their Slaves. in order to reap the Profits of their Toil. . . . And there is no Denying. that the Masses have literally slept, the Sleep that brings on Tenantry and Serfdom. and the Partizan Hireling Press have depended upon our Ignorance, and their Power to fool us, and have taken unto themselves. leases, for Prevarication. Missrepresentation and Slander. which is a Menace. to the Moral. Social and financial welfare of every Honest Citizen, and Bodes the Destruction of this Republic. and our People must be put on their guard. Taught not, only the remedy but how to apply it, in order to rid our Land of this Blighting. Blasting Curse, which is undermining. Honest true Manhood in every Department of Life. where they Will not be made Jumping Jacks, at their Beck or call.

M. F. BLANKENSHIP*

I had a mortgage on my team, like all my brother farmers, of $64.50. I was given to understand that this must be paid. To borrow money was out of the question. Nothing was left for me to do but haul off corn, hogs, etc., and pay it. I went to work, hauled off my corn and hogs and sold my hay and paid it. I had made calculations and found I would have no feed, seed, or even bread and meat. . . . I did not know what to do. I received a letter from my uncle in Oklahoma, stating there was plenty of work here at good wages. There was no work, as you all know, in Custer county. After taking all things in careful consideration I concluded I would come to Oklahoma where I could get work. Before reaching this conclusion it cost me many a bitter tear and sleepless night.

SUSAN ORCUTT**

I take my Pen In hand to let you know that we are Starving to death It is Pretty hard to do without any thing to Eat hear in this God for saken country we would of had Plenty to Eat if the hail hadent cut our rye down and ruined our corn and Potatoes   I had the Prettiest Garden that you Ever seen and the hail ruined It and I have nothing to look at My Husband went a way to find work and came home last night and told me that we would have to Starve   he has bin in ten countys and did not Get no work   It is Pretty hard for a woman to do with out any

*M. F. Blankenship to editor, Custer County Beacon (Broken Bow, Nebraska), March 24, 1892, Nebraska Historical Society.
**Susan Orcutt to Lorenzo D. Lewelling, June 29, 1894, Lewelling Papers, Kansas State Historical Society.

thing to Eat when She dosent no what minute She will be confined to bed If I was In Iowa I would be all right I was born there and raised there I havent had nothing to Eat to day and It is three oclock[.]

W. R. CHRISTY*

We are worried over what our Poor People of our county are to do for fuel to keep them warm this winter. . . . there are at least $\frac{2}{3}$ of the People that have to depend on Cow chips for fuel & as the cattle had to be Sold off verry close that its been difficult to get them. Some have went as far as 13 miles to get them. the thermometer this morning was 16 below zero & .4 or 5 inches of snow on the ground, under those circumstances what are the People to do. at this time our coal dealers have not all told more than 100 bushels of coal on hand & it cant be bought for less than 40¢ per hundred in Less than ton lots.

*W. R. Christy to L. P. Broad, December 28, 1894, Lewelling Papers, Kansas State Historical Society.

O. E. RÖLVAAG

14 | Immigrants on the Prairie

O. E. Rölvaag, born in a small fishing village in the far north of Norway, emigrated to the United States in 1896. His novel, Giants in the Earth, *draws on his first three years in the United States, which he spent on an uncle's farm in South Dakota. Although Rölvaag received most of his education in the United States (and became a professor of Norwegian literature at his alma mater, St. Olaf College), he wrote originally in Norwegian, first for a predominantly Norwegian-American and later a predominantly Norwegian audience.*

Giants in the Earth *is one of the best portraits we have of American pioneer life, and in English translation, done partly by Rölvaag himself, the novel is a classic of American literature. Its picture of the psychological effect of the treeless prairie on immigrants cut off both from a familiar environment and a familiar culture remains an unforgettable account of the pain that accompanied the accomplishments of pioneering. The selection begins with the thoughts of Beret, the immigrant wife and mother. Other characters in the story are two neighbors, Sörine and Kjersti.*

In a certain sense, she had to admit to herself, it was lovely up here. The broad expanse stretching away endlessly in every direction, seemed almost like the ocean—especially now, when darkness was falling. It reminded her strongly of the sea, and yet it was very different. . . . This formless prairie had no heart that beat, no waves that sang, no soul that could be touched . . . or cared. . . .

The infinitude surrounding her on every hand might not have been so oppressive, might even have brought her a measure of peace, if it had not been for the deep silence, which lay heavier here than in a church. Indeed, what was there to break it? She had passed beyond the outposts of civilization; the nearest dwelling places of men were far away. Here no warbling of birds rose on the air, no buzzing of insects sounded[1]; even the wind had died away; the waving blades of grass that trembled to the faintest breath now stood erect and quiet, as if listening, in the great hush of the evening. . . . All along the way, coming out, she had noticed this strange thing: the stillness had grown deeper, the silence more depressing, the farther west they journeyed; it must have been over two weeks now since she had heard a bird sing! Had they travelled into some nameless, abandoned region? Could no living thing exist out here, in the empty, desolate, endless wastes of green and blue? . . . How *could* existence go on, she thought, desperately? If life is to thrive and endure, it must at least have something to hide behind! . . .

The children were playing boisterously a little way off. What a terrible noise they made! But she had better let them keep on with their play, as long as they were happy. . . . She sat perfectly quiet, thinking of the long, oh, so interminably long march that they would have to make, back to the place where human beings dwelt. It would be small hardship for her, of course, sitting in the wagon; but she pitied Per Hansa and the boys—and then the poor oxen! . . . He certainly would soon find out for himself that a home for men and women and children could never be established in this wilderness. . . . And how could she bring new life into the world out here! . . .

Slowly her throughts began to centre on her husband; they grew warm and tender as they dwelt on him. She trembled as they came. . . .

But only for a brief while. As her eyes darted nervously here and there, flitting from object to object and trying to pierce the purple dimness that was steadily closing in, a sense of desolation so profound settled upon her that she seemed unable to think at all. It would not do to gaze any longer at the terror out there, where everything was turning to grim and awful darkness. . . . She threw herself back in the grass and looked up into the heavens. But darkness and infinitude lay there, also—the sense of utter desolation still remained. . . . Suddenly, for the first time, she realized the full extent of her loneliness, the dreadful nature of the fate that had overtaken her. Lying there on her back, and staring up into the quiet sky across which the shadows of night were imperceptibly creeping, she went over in her mind every step of their wanderings, every mile of the distance they had travelled since they had left home. . . .

/ / /

Now she was lying here on a little green hillock, surrounded by the open, endless prairie, far off in a spot from which no road led back!

---

1. Original settlers are agreed that there was neither bird nor insect life on the prairie, with the exception of mosquitoes, the first year that they came. (Note by Rölvaag.)

. . . It seemed to her that she had lived many lives already, in each one of which she had done nothing but wander and wander, always straying farther away from the home that was dear to her.

She sat up at last, heaved a deep sigh, and glanced around as if waking from a dream. . . . The unusual blending of the gentle and forceful in her features seemed to be thrown into relief by the scene in which she sat and the twilight hovering about her, as a beautiful picture is enhanced by a well-chosen frame.

The two boys and their little sister were having great fun up here. So many queer things were concealed under the tufts of grass. Store-Hans came running, and brought a handful of little flat, reddish chips of stone that looked as though they had been carved out of the solid rock; they were pointed at one end and broadened out evenly on both sides, like the head of a spear. The edges were quite sharp; in the broad end a deep groove had been filed. Ole brought more of them, and gave a couple to his little sister to play with. . . . The mother sat for a while with the stones in her lap, where the children had placed them; at last she took them up, one by one, and examined them closely. . . . These must have been formed by human hands, she thought.

Suddenly Ole made another rare discovery. He brought her a larger stone, that looked like a sledge hammer; in this the groove was deep and broad.

The mother got up hastily.

"Where are you finding these things?"

The boys at once took her to the place; in a moment she, too, was standing beside the little hollow at the brow of the hill, which the men had discovered the night before; the queer stones that the children had been bringing her lay scattered all around.

"Ole says that the Indians made them!" cried Store-Hans, excitedly. "Is it true, mother? . . . Do you suppose they'll ever come back?"

"Yes, maybe—if we stay here long enough. . . . " She remained standing awhile beside the hollow; the same thought possessed her that had seized hold of her husband when he had first found the spot—here a human being lay buried. Strangely enough, it did not frighten her; it only showed her more plainly, in a stronger, harsher light, how unspeakably lonesome this place was.

/   /   /

Per Hansa [Beret's husband] came home late the following afternoon; he had so many words of praise for what she and the boys had accomplished while he had been gone, that he fairly bewildered her. Now it had taken possession of him again—that indomitable, conquering mood which seemed to give him the right of way wherever he went, whatever he did. Outwardly, at such times, he showed only a buoyant recklessness, as if wrapped in a cloak of gay, wanton levity; but down beneath all this lay a stern determination of purpose, a driving force, so strong that she shrank back from the least contact with it.

To-day he was talking in a steady stream.

"Here is the deed to our kingdom, Beret-girl! See to it that you take good care of the papers. . . . Isn't it stranger than a fairy tale, that a man can have such things here, just for the taking? . . . Yes—and years after he won the princess, too!" He cocked his head on one side. "I'll tell you what, it seems so impossible and unheard of, that I can't quite swallow it all yet. . . . What do you say, my Beret-girl?"

Beret stood smiling at him, with tears in her eyes, beside the improvised house that she had made; there was little for her to say. And what would be the use of speaking now? He was so completely wrapped up in his own plans that he would not listen nor understand. It would be wrong, too, to trouble him with her fears and misgivings. . . . When he felt like this he was so tender to her, so cheerful, so loving and kind. . . . How well she knew Per Hansa! . . .

"What are you thinking about it all, my Beret-girl?" He flung his arm around her, whirled her off her feet, and drew her toward him.

"Oh, Per, it's only this—I'm so afraid out here!" She snuggled up against him, as if trying to hide herself. "It's all so big and open . . . so empty. . . . Oh, Per! Not another human being from here to the end of the world!"

/   /   /

. . . No, the days would not pass! . . . Why, here it was, only the middle of November! It seemed to Per Hansa, as he sat by the table puffing his pipe and following Beret around with his eyes, that many winters must have gone by already.

/   /   /

But . . . other days followed. Per Hansa remained idle and had nothing to do but look at his wife. He looked and looked, until he had to face the hard fact that something was wrong.

. . . Had she ever been so brooding and taciturn when she was with child before? He could talk to the boys about the future until they would be completely carried away by his visions; but whenever he tried to draw her into the conversation he failed completely—failed, no matter which tack he took nor how hard he tried. He understood it clearly: it wasn't because she did not want to respond—she *couldn't*! . . . The pain of it surged through him like a wave. God in Heaven, had she grown so weak and helpless! . . . She wasn't even able to take nourishment. . . . There Beret sat in the room with them, within four paces—yet she was far, far away. He spoke to her now, to her alone, but could not

make her come out of the enchanted ring that lay about her. . . . When
he discovered this, it hurt him so that he could have shrieked. . . .

. . . Another queer thing, she was always losing the commonest
objects—completely losing them, though they were right at hand. He
had seen it happen several times without taking much notice; but by
and by it began to occur so frequently that he was forced to pay attention. She would put a thing down, merely turn around, and then go
about searching for it in vain; and the thing would lie exactly where she
had placed it, all the time. . . . This happened again and again; sometimes it struck them all as very funny. . . . "It looks as if your eyes were
in your way, Mother!" Store-Hans once exclaimed, laughing so heartily
that the others had to join in; but Per Hansa soon noticed that she was
hurt when they made fun of her.

One day she was looking for the scissors. She had been sitting by
the stove, mending a garment; had risen to put on more fuel; and when
she sat down again had been unable to find her scissors, which she held
all the while in her hand. She searched diligently, and asked the others
to help her. Suddenly Ole discovered the scissors in his mother's hand;
he ran up to her and jerked them away; the boy was roaring with
laughter. . . . Then she burst into violent tears, laid her work aside,
threw herself down on the bed, and buried her face in the pillow. All
three menfolk felt painfully embarrassed.

/   /   /

Winter was ever tightening its grip. The drifting snow flew wildly
under a low sky, and stirred up the whole universe into a whirling mass;
it swept the plain like the giant broom of a witch, churning up a flurry
so thick that people could scarcely open their eyes.

As soon as the weather cleared icy gusts drove through every chink
and cranny, leaving white frost behind; people's breaths hung frozen
in the air the moment it was out of the mouth; if one touched iron, a
piece of skin would be torn away.

At intervals a day of bright sunshine came. Then the whole vast
plain flittered with the flashing brilliance of diamonds; the glare was so
strong that it burnt the sight; the eyes saw blackness where there was
nothing but shining white.

/   /   /

Now she found plenty of time to remember how her parents had
begged and threatened her to break with him; she recalled all that they
had said, turning it over in her mind and examining it minutely. . . .
Per Hansa was a shiftless fellow, they had told her; he drank; he fought;
he was wild and reckless; he got himself tangled up in all sorts of
brawls; no honourable woman could be happy with such a man. He
probably had affairs with other women, too, whenever he had a

chance. . . . All the other accusations she knew to be true; but not the last—no, not the last! She alone among women held his heart. The certainty of this fact had been the very sweetness of life to her. . . . What did she care for the rest of it! All was as nothing compared with this great certainty. . . . Ah, no—she knew it well enough: for him she was the only princess!

But now she understood clearly all that her parents had done to end it between them, and all the sacrifices they had been willing to make; she had not realized it at the time. . . . Oh, those kind-hearted parents on whom she had turned her back in order that she might cleave to him: how they must have suffered! The life which she and he had begotten in common guilt they had offered to take as their own, give it their name and their inheritance, and bring it up as their very child. They had freely offered to use their hard-earned savings to send her away from the scene of her shame. . . *so* precious had she been to them! But she had only said no, and no, and *no*, to all their offers of sacrifice and love! . . . Had there ever been a transgression so grievous as hers!

/   /   /

. . . When Per Hansa had come home from Lofoten that spring and announced in his reckless, masterful way, that he was off for America: would Beret come now, or wait until later? . . . Well, there hadn't been a "no" in her mouth then! There she had sat, with three children in a nice little home which, after the manner of simple folk, they had managed to build. . . . But she had risen up, taken the children with her, and left it all as if nothing mattered but him!

. . . How her mother had wept at that time! . . . How her father had grieved when they had left! Time after time he had come begging to Per Hansa, offering him all that he had—boat and fishing outfit, house and farm—if only he would settle down in Norway and not take their daughter from them forever. . . . But Per Hansa had laughed it all aside! There had been a power in his unflinching determination which had sent hot waves through her. She must have led a double life at that time; she had been sad with her parents but had rejoiced with Per Hansa. He had raged like a storm through those days, wild and reckless—and sometimes ruthless, too. . . . No!—he had cried—they would just make that little trip across the ocean! America—that's the country where a poor devil can get ahead! Besides, it was only a little way; if they didn't like it, they could drift back on the first fair western breeze! . . . So they had sold off everything that they had won with so much toil, had left it all like a pair of worn-out shoes—parents, home, fatherland, and people. . . . And she had done it gladly, even rejoicingly! . . . Was there ever a sin like hers?

/   /   /

. . . Then she had arrived in America. The country did not at all come up to her expectations; here, too, she saw enough of poverty and grinding toil. What did it avail, that the rich soil lay in endless stretches? More than ever did she realize that "man liveth not by bread alone!" . . . Even the bread was none too plentiful at times. . . .

Beyond a doubt, it was Destiny that had brought her thither. . . . Destiny, the inexorable law of life, which the Lord God from eternity had laid down for every human being, according to the path He knew would be taken. . . . Now punishment stood here awaiting her—the punishment for having broken God's commandment of filial obedience. . . . Throughout the fall she had been reckoning up her score, and it came out exactly thus: Destiny had so arranged everything that the punishment should strike her all the more inevitably. Destiny had cast her into the arms of Per Hansa—and she did not regret it! Destiny had held up America as an enticing will-o'-the-wisp—and they had followed! . . .

But no sooner had they reached America than the west-fever had smitten the old settlements like a plague. Such a thing had never happened before in the history of mankind; people were intoxicated by bewildering visions; they spoke dazedly, as though under the force of a spell. . . . "Go west! . . . Go west, folks! . . . The farther west, the better the land!" . . . Men beheld in feverish dreams the endless plains, teeming with fruitfulness, glowing, out there where day sank into night—a Beulah Land of corn and wine! . . . She had never dreamed that the good Lord would let such folly loose among men. Were it only the young people who had been caught by the plague, she would not have wondered; but the old had been taken even worse. . . . "Now we're bound west?" said the young. . . . "Wait a minute—we're going along with you!" cried the old, and followed after. . . . Human beings gathered together, in small companies and large—took whatever was movable along, and left the old homestead without as much as a sigh! Ever westward led the course, to where the sun glowed in matchless glory as it sank at night; people drifted about in a sort of delirium, like sea birds in mating time; then they flew toward the sunset, in small flocks and large—always toward Sunset Land. . . . Now she saw it clearly: here on the trackless plains, the thousand-year-old hunger of the poor after human happiness had been unloosed!

Into this feverish atmosphere they had come. Could Destiny have spun his web more cunningly? She remembered well how the eyes of Per Hansa had immediately begun to gleam and glow! . . . And the strange thing about this spell had been that he had become so very kind under it. How playfully affectionate he had grown toward her during the last winter and spring! It had been even more deliciously sweet to give herself to him then, than back in those days when she had first won him. Was it not worth all the care and sorrow in the world to taste such bliss, she had often asked herself—but had been unable to answer.

But—then it had happened: this spring she had been gotten with child again. . . . Let no one tell her that this was not Destiny!

She had urged against this last journey; she had argued that they must tarry where they were until she had borne the child. One year more or less would make no difference, considering all the land there was in the west. . . . Hans Olsa, however, had been ready to start; and so there had been no use in trying to hold back Per Hansa. All her misgiving he had turned to sport and laughter, or playful love; he had embraced her, danced around with her, and become so roguish that she had been forced to laugh with him. . . . "Come here, *Litagod*—now we're gone!" . . . She well recalled how lovely this endearing term had sounded in her ears, the first night he had used it. . . .

/ / /

About noon of Christmas Eve the air suddenly cleared. An invisible fan was pushed in under the thick, heavy curtain that hung trembling between earth and heaven—made a giant sweep, and revealed the open, blue sky overhead. The sun shone down with powerful beams, and started a slight trickling from the eaves. Toward evening, it built a golden fairy castle for itself out yonder, just beyond Indian Hill.

/ / /

She was fully rational, and asked the neighbour women to leave the room for a moment, as she had something to say to her husband. She spoke with great composure; they obeyed immediately. When the door closed behind them Beret rose and came over to him, her face distorted. She laid a hand on each of his shoulders, and looked deep into his eyes, then clasped her hands behind his neck and pulled him violently toward her. Putting his arms firmly around her, he lifted her up gently and carried her to the bed; there he laid her down. He started to pull the covers over her. . . . But she held on to him; his solicitous care she heeded not at all.

When he had freed himself, she spoke brokenly, between gasps:
. . . "To-night I am leaving you. . . . Yes, I must leave you. . . . I know this is the end! The Lord has found me out because of my sins. . . . It is written, 'To fall into the hands of the living God!' . . . Oh!—it is terrible! . . . I can't see how you will get along when you are left alone . . . though I have only been a burden to you lately. . . . You had better give And-Ongen to Kjersti . . . she wants a child so badly—she is a kind woman. . . . You must take the boys with you—and *go away from here!* . . . How lonesome it will be for me . . . to lie here all alone!"

Tears came to her eyes, but she did not weep; between moans she went on strongly and collectedly:
"But promise me one thing: put me away in the big chest! . . . I

have emptied it and made it ready. . . . Promise to lay me away in the big chest, Per Hansa! . . . And you must be sure to dig the grave deep! . . . You haven't heard how terribly the wolves howl at night! . . . Promise to take plenty of time and dig deep down—do you hear!"

His wife's request cut Per Hansa's heart like sharp ice; he threw himself on his knees beside the bed and wiped the cold perspiration from her face with a shaking hand.

. . ."There now, blessed Beret-girl of mine!". . . . His words sounded far off—a note of frenzy in them. . . . "Can't you understand that this will soon be over? . . . To-morrow you'll be as chipper as a lark again!"

Her terror tore her only the worse. Without heeding his words, she spoke with great force out of the clearness of her vision:

"I shall die to-night. . . . Take the big chest! . . . At first I thought of asking you not to go away when spring came . . . and leave me here alone. . . . But that would be a sin! . . . I tell you, you *must go!* . . . Leave as soon as spring comes! Human beings cannot exist here! . . . They grow into beasts. . . . "

The throes were tearing her so violently now that she could say no more. But when she saw him rise she made a great effort and sat up in bed.

. . . "Oh!—don't leave me!—don't go away! . . . Can't you see how sorely I need you? . . . And now I shall die! . . . Love me—oh, do love me once more, Per Hansa!" . . . She leaned her body toward him. . . . "You must go back to Norway. . . . Take the children with you . . . let them grow up there. Ask father and mother to forgive me! . . . Tell father that I am lying in the big chest! . . . Can't you stay with me to-night . . . stay with me and love me? . . . Oh!—*there they come for me!*"

Beret gave a long shriek that rent the night. Then she sobbed violently, praying that they should not take her away from Per Hansa. . . .

Per Hansa leaped to his feet, and found his voice.

"Satan—now you shall leave her alone!" he shouted, flinging the door open and calling loudly to the women outside. Then he vanished into the darkness.

/   /   /

Per Hansa walked to and fro outside the hut all night long; when he heard some one coming he would run away into the darkness. He could not speak to a living soul to-night. As soon as the visitor had gone he would approach the hut again, circle around it, stop, and listen. Tears were streaming down his face, though he was not aware of it. . . . Every shriek that pierced the walls of the hut drove him off as if a whip had struck him; but as soon as it had died out, something would draw him back again. At intervals he went to the door and held it ajar. . . . What did Per Hansa care for custom and decency, now that his Beret lay struggling with death! . . . Each time Sörine came to the door; each time she shook her head sadly, and told him there was no change yet; it was doubtful if Beret would be able to pull through; no person could endure this much longer; God have mercy on all of them!

That was all the comfort Sörine could give him. . . . Then he would rush off into the darkness again, to continue his endless pacing; when daylight came they found a hard path tramped into the snow around the hut.

The night was well-nigh spent when the wails in there began to weaken—then died out completely, and did not come again. Per Hansa crept up to the door, laid his ear close to it, and listened. . . . So now the end had come! His breath seemed to leave him in a great sob. The whole prairie began to whirl around with him; he staggered forward a few steps and threw himself face downward on the snow.

. . . But then suddenly things didn't seem so bad to him . . . really not so bad. . . . He saw a rope . . . a rope. . . . It was a good, strong rope that would hold anything. . . . It hung just inside the barn door— and the crossbeam ran just *there!* . . . No trick at all to find these things. Per Hansa felt almost happy at the thought; that piece of rope was good and strong—and the crossbeam ran just *there!*

. . . A door opened somewhere; a gleam of light flashed across the snow, and vanished. Some one came out of the hut quietly—then stopped, as if searching.

"Per Hansa!" a low voice called. . . . "Per Hansa, where are you?" . . . He rose and staggered toward Kjersti like a drunken man.

"You must come in at once!" she whispered, and hurried in before him.

The light was dim in there; nevertheless it blinded him so strongly that he could not see a thing. He stood a moment leaning against the door until his eyes had grown accustomed to it. . . . A snug, cosy warmth enveloped him; it carried with it an odd, pleasant odour. The light, the warmth, and the pleasant smell overcame him like sweet sleep that holds a person who has been roused, but who does not care to awaken just yet.

"How is it?" he heard a man's voice ask. Then he came back to his senses. . . . Was that he himself speaking? . . .

"You'll have to ask Sörrina," Kjersti answered.

Sörine was tending something on the bed; not until now did he discover her—and wake up completely. . . . What was this? . . . the expression on her face? Wasn't it beaming with motherly goodness and kindliness?

"Yes, here's your little fellow! I have done all I know how. Come and look at him. . . . It's the greatest miracle I ever saw, Per Hansa, that you didn't lose your wife to-night, and the child too! . . . I pray the Lord I never have to suffer so!"

"Is there any hope?" was all Per Hansa could gasp—and then he clenched his teeth.

"It looks so, now—but you had better christen him at once. . . . We had to handle him roughly, let me tell you."

"*Christen him?*" Per Hansa repeated, unable to comprehend the words.

"Why, yes, of course. I wouldn't wait, if he were mine."

Per Hansa heard no more—for now Beret turned her head and a wave of such warm joy welled up in him that all the ice melted. He found himself crying softly, sobbing like a child. . . . He approached the bed on tiptoe, bent over it, and gazed down into the weary, pale face. It lay there so white and still; her hair, braided in two thick plaits, flowed over the pillow. All the dread, all the tormenting fear that had so long disfigured her features, had vanished completely. . . . She turned her head a little, barely opened her eyes and said, wearily:

"Oh, leave me in peace, Per Hansa. . . . Now I was sleeping so well."

. . . The eyelids immediately closed.

/   /   /

Per Hansa stood for a long time looking at his wife, hardly daring to believe what he saw. She slept peacefully; a small bundle lay beside her, from which peeped out a tiny, red, wrinkled face. . . .

15 | The Threat to the "White Goddess"

"Unguarded Gates," written in 1885, is a poetic expression of opposition to unrestricted immigration. Its author, Thomas Bailey Aldrich, was a member of the social elite of New York and Boston who, although he lived near the immigrants' ghettos, never sought to understand their culture, ignored their economic contributions, and saw them only as a social problem. Aldrich reflected the concerns felt by many Americans over the so-called new immigration from southern and eastern Europe. Beginning in the 1880s, this human tide exceeded immigration from northern and western Europe. As this influx reached its peak in the period from 1905 to 1914, sentiments like Aldrich's became more prominent and led ultimately to the immigration restriction "quota" laws of 1921 and 1924.

Unguarded Gates

Wide open and unguarded stand our gates,
  Named of the four winds, North, South, East, and
  West;
Portals that lead to an enchanted land
  Of cities, forests, fields of living gold,
Vast prairies, lordly summits touched with snow,
  Majestic rivers sweeping proudly past
The Arab's date-palm and the Norseman's pine—
  A realm wherein are fruits of every zone,
Airs of all climes, for lo! throughout the year
  The red rose blossoms somewhere—a rich land,
A later Eden planted in the wilds,
  With not an inch of earth within its bound
But if a slave's foot press it sets him free.
  Here, it is written, Toil shall have its wage,
And Honor honor, and the humblest man
  Stand level with the highest in the law.
Of such a land have men in dungeons dreamed,
  And with the vision brightening in their eyes
Gone smiling to the fagot and the sword.

Thomas Bailey Aldrich, Unguarded Gates and Other Poems. (Boston, Houghton, Mifflin and Company, 1895), pp. 15-17.

Wide open and unguarded stand our gates,
    And through them presses a wild motley throng—
Men from the Volga and the Tartar steppes,
    Featureless figures of the Hoang-Ho,
Malayan, Scythian, Teuton, Kelt, and Slav,
    Flying the Old World's povery and scorn;
These bringing with them unknown gods and rites,
    Those, tiger passions, here to stretch their claws.
In street and alley what strange tongues are loud,
    Accents of menace alien to our air,
Voices that once the Tower of Babel knew!
    O Liberty, white Goddess! is it well
To leave the gates unguarded? On thy breast
    Fold Sorrow's children, soothe the hurts of fate,
Lift the down-trodden, but with hand of steel
    Stay those who to thy sacred portals come
To waste the gifts of freedom. Have a care
    Lest from thy brow the clustered stars be torn
And trampled in the dust. For so of old
    The thronging Goth and Vandal trampled Rome,
And where the temples of the Cæsars stood
    The lean wolf unmolested made her lair.

HENRY PRATT FAIRCHILD

16 | An Argument against the Melting Pot

Henry Pratt Fairchild was a widely published New York University sociologist and an authority on immigration and demography during a career spanning most of the first half of the twentieth century. He presented careful, scholarly arguments against unlimited immigration and the melting pot ideology that supported it. (Fairchild explains the "melting pot" image at the beginning of the reading.) Like Aldrich, Fairchild feared the radical changes in American character, culture, and ideas that he thought would result from the large number of what he termed "unassimilable" immigrants arriving from Southern and Eastern Europe as well as from Asia. Although this article was published in 1926, the ideas Fairchild expressed had by then been aired for many years and were embodied in the Immigration Restriction Act of 1924. That law attempted to fix the ethnic mix of the American population at what its proportions were in 1890—before the bulk of the "new immigration" had arrived.

These were the facts which gave to Israel Zangwill's little drama, "The Melting-Pot", when it appeared in 1909, a significance quite disproportionate to its literary importance. For one hundred years and more a stream of immigration had been pouring into the United States in constantly increasing volume. At first this movement had attracted little attention, and such feelings as it aroused were mainly those of complacency and satisfaction. As the decades rolled by certain features of the movement created considerable consternation and a demand sprang up for some form of governmental relief. In time this relief was granted, and the popular concern died down. In general, however, during practically the whole of the nineteenth century the attitude of the American people toward immigration was one of easy-going, tolerant indifference when it was not actually welcome. But as the century drew to a close evidences of popular uneasiness and misgiving began to display themselves. These were due in part to changes in the social and economic situation in the United States, in part to changes in the personal and social characteristics of the immigrants, and in part to repeated warnings

From The Melting Pot Mistake *by Henry Pratt Fairchild, pp. 9–12, 245–246, 253–255, 257–261. Copyright 1926 by Walter Lippmann. By permission of Little, Brown and Company.*

issued by those whose professional activities and opportunities gave them a wider access to the facts of immigration than was possible to the average citizen. In particular the American people began to ponder about the ultimate effect upon its own vitality and solidarity of this stupendous injection of foreign elements. Could we stand it, and if so, how long? Were not the foundations of our cherished institutions already partially undermined by all these alien ideas, habits, and customs? What kind of a people were we destined to become physically? Was the American nation itself in danger? Immigration became a great public problem, calling for judgment.

Then came the symbol, like a portent in the heavens. America is a Melting-Pot. Into it are being poured representatives of all the world's peoples. Within its magic confines there is being formed something that is not only uniform and homogeneous but also finer than any of the separate ingredients. The nations of the world are being fused into a new and, choicer nation, the United States.

The figure was a clever one—picturesque, expressive, familiar, just the sort of thing to catch the popular fancy and lend itself to a thousand uses. It swept over this country and other countries like wild fire. As always, it was welcomed as a substitute for both investigation and thought. It calmed the rising wave of misgiving. Few stopped to ask whether it fitted the phenomena of assimilation. Few inquired whether Mr. Zangwill's familiarity with the intricate facts of immigration were such as to justify him in assuming the heavy responsibility of interpreter. America was a Melting-Pot, the apparent evidences of national disintegration were illusions, and that settled it.

It would be hard to estimate the influence of the symbol of the melting pot in staving off the restriction of immigration. It is certain that in the popular mind it offsets volumes of laboriously compiled statistics and carefully reasoned analyses. It is virtually beyond question that restriction would have come in time in any case. How soon it would have come without the Great War [World War I] must remain a matter of conjecture. Be that as it may, when the concussions of that conflict had begun to die down the melting pot was discovered to be so badly cracked that it is not likely ever to be dragged into service again. Its day was over. But this did not mean that the real facts of immigration had suddenly become public property. Our symbol had been shattered, but we had not yet, as a people, been able to undertake the extensive investigation necessary to reveal the true nature of the case. The history of post-war movements is replete with evidences of the gross misconceptions of the meaning and processes of assimilation which characterized many even of those who devoted themselves directly to the problem. Even to-day, in spite of the fact that there is perhaps no other great public problem on which the American people is so well educated as on immigration, there is yet great need of a clearer understanding of the tremendous task that still confronts us. We know now that the Melting-Pot did not melt, but we are not entirely sure why.

/   /   /

The central idea of the melting-pot symbol is clearly the idea of unification. That is an idea which needs no logical demonstration to command general acceptance. Every one realizes, almost intuitively, that in any community, particularly a democratic one, unity is one of the essentials of stability, order, and progress. Every American citizen will admit without argument that if immigration threatens the national unity of the United States it is a matter of grave concern. The purpose of the melting-pot figure was to convince the American people that immigration did not threaten its unity, but tended to produce an even finer type of unity. It failed because it did not take account of the true nature of group unity, of the conditions of its preservation, or of the actual consequences of such inroads upon unity as are involved in an immigration movement.

As we survey the world of to-day we are impressed with the fact that group unity is one of the most important factors with which mankind has to reckon. We see the human species divided up into numerous well-defined units,

/   /   /

Why should we take the pains deliberately to reach out after the friendship of those to whom we are not attracted? This natural process operates at both ends of the assimilation nexus. The foreigner no less than the native limits his close associations to those with whom he feels at home.

The plain truth, which needs to be engraved deeply on the consciousness of every one interested in Americanization, is that assimilation takes place only under certain conditions, that these conditions do not exist in the United States at the present time, and that they can not be created by any deliberate programs devised for the purpose. The barriers to assimilation are found in certain inherent characteristics of human nature, particularly those concerned with group organization. We may, or may not, admire these characteristics. This is of no practical importance as long as they exist. Abraham Lincoln once said, "A universal feeling, whether well or ill-founded, can not be safely disregarded." We can not frame immigration policies on the basis of an imaginary human nature which we might regard as more admirable than that which exists.

/   /   /

It has been repeatedly stated that the consequence of nonassimilation is the destruction of nationality. This is the central truth of the whole problem of immigration and it cannot be overemphasized. An immigration movement that did not involve nonassimilation might be tolerated, though it might have other evil consequences which would condemn it. But an immigration movement that does involve nonassimilation—like the movement to the United States during the last fifty years at least—is a blow at the very heart of nationality and can not be endured if nationality is conceived to have any value whatsoever. The American nationality has already been compared to a plant. There is, indeed, a striking parallelism between a nation and a noble tree—for instance, one of our own incomparable redwoods—which may be followed a little further, not with any expectation or desire of popularizing a new symbol, but merely for the clarification that it affords.

A nation, like a tree, is a living vital thing. Growth is one of its conditions of life, and when it ceases to grow there is good reason to fear that it is about to decay and die. Every nation, like every tree, belongs to a certain general type, but it is also uniquely individual within that type. Its peculiar form is determined by various forces, some of which are internal and some external. No nation need fear the changes which come as the result of the operation of natural, wholesome internal forces, that is to say, the ideas and activities of its own true members. These forces may, in the course of time, produce a form and character wholly different from the original, just as the mature plant may have an entirely different aspect from the seedling. This is nothing to be dreaded or opposed. No change that represents the natural evolution of internal forces need be dreaded. But there are other forces which originate without which threaten not only the form and character but also the vigor and perhaps the very life of the nation. Some of these are the forcible attacks of other nations, like the crowding of trees upon each other, or the unwholesome influence of alien ideas which may be compared with harsh and uncongenial winds which blow upon trees, dwarfing and distorting them.

Most dangerous of all however, are those foreign forces which, among trees, are represented by minute hostile organisms that make their way into the very tissue of the tree itself and feed upon its life substances, and among nations to alien individuals who are accepted as immigrants and by a process of "boring from within" (in something much more than a mere trade-union sense) sap the very vitality of their host. In so doing the immigrants may be merely following out their natural and defensible impulses without any hostility toward the receiving nation, any more than the parasites upon a tree may be considered to have any hostility to the tree. Nor can the immigrants, any more than the parasites, be expected to foresee that their activities will eventually destroy the very organism upon which they depend for their existence. The simple fact is that they are alien particles, not assimilated, and therefore wholly different from the foreign particles which the tree takes in the form of food, and transforms into cells of its own body.

/   /   /

These considerations do not in any measure justify treating the alien as if he had no rights and were not entitled to express himself on any subject, as has sometimes been done by overzealous partriots under the stress of acute national hysteria. But they do justify the exercise of a wholly different type of control over the public utterances of aliens from that imposed upon citizens, and even more the exclusion of those who in the nature of the case are likely to indulge in un-American utterances because they are imbued with un-American ideas.

There are, it should be noted, a few foreigners whose attitude toward the United States is more positively destructive than that of those who simply can not understand America because they are not Americans. Among this number are those, very few altogether, who make it their business to launch direct attacks upon the fundamental form and institutions of the American government. To them the deportation acts may most appropriately be applied. But much more dangerous are those who insolently regard the United States as a mere economic catch basin, to which they have come to get out of it what they can, confessing no obligation to it, recognizing no claim on its part to the preservation of its own identity, displaying no intention to contribute to its development or to remain permanently as a part of it. One type of this group looks forward to a return to the native land as soon as America has been bled of all it has to offer. Another type looks upon America as a sort of no man's land, or every man's land, upon which they can develop a separate group existence along any lines that they see fit. For instance, we are told upon the best of authority that there has already developed in the United States a distinct Polish-American society, which is neither truly Polish nor truly American, but which has a vigorous and distinct character and existence of its own.

More dangerous, however, than any foreign elements, are certain individuals of native birth who in an excess of zeal for the foreigner, emanating, it may be presumed, from a misguided and sentimental though well-meaning reaction from the attitude of ethno-centric superiority so characteristic of many Americans, go to the extreme of denying any merit in American institutions, and ignoring any claim on the part of America to the perpetuation of its peculiar existence. They are ready to throw any and all distinctly American characteristics into the discard if only we can absorb the "dear foreigners" into our midst. They applaud any expression of national pride on the part of a foreigner as an evidence of sturdy and commendable patriotism, but condemn a similar expression on the part of an American as narrow bigotry.

/   /   /

The central factor in the world organization of the present is nationalism. Strong, self-conscious nationalities are indispensable to the efficient ordering and peaceful promotion of international relations. Every well-developed nationality is a priceless product of social evolution. Each has its peculiar contribution to make to future progress. The destruction of any one would be an irreparable loss to mankind.

Among the nations of the world America stands out unique, and in many ways preëminent. Favored by Nature above all other nations in her physical endowment, favored by history in the character of her people and the type of her institutions, she has a rôle to play in the development of human affairs which no other nation can play. Foremost in this rôle is the development of true democracy. In America the stage is set more favorably than anywhere else for the great drama of the common man. Here if anywhere the conditions are auspicious for the upward movement of the masses. If democracy fails in America, where shall we look for it to succeed? Any program or policy which interferes in the slightest degree with the prosecution of this great enterprise must be condemned as treason to our high destiny. Any yielding to a specious and superficial humanitarianism which threatens the material, political, and social standards of the average American must be branded as a violation of our trust. The highest service of America to mankind is to point the way, to demonstrate the possibilities, to lead onward to the goal of human happiness. Any force that tends to impair our capacity for leadership is a menace to mankind and a flagrant violation of the spirit of liberalism.

Unrestricted immigration was such a force. It was slowly, insidiously, irresistibly eating away the very heart of the United States. What was being melted in the great Melting Pot, losing all form and symmetry, all beauty and character, all nobility and usefulness, was the American nationality itself.

ABRAHAM CAHAN

17 | A Bintel Brief

Years before "Ann Landers" and "Dear Abby," there was "A Bintel Brief."
In 1906 the Jewish Daily Forward, a Yiddish-language newspaper addressing
the large community of Jewish immigrants in New York City, began running an
advice column, "A Bintel Brief" [bundle of letters]. The paper's editor was
Abraham Cahan, who also wrote several novels about immigrant life. Cahan
contributed some of the letters as well as the responses. "A Bintel Brief" gave
advice on all kinds of personal problems. The following excerpts from the early
years of the column offer fascinating glimpses into Jewish immigrant life at the
turn of the century, particularly the tensions resulting from the desire to enjoy
full equality and opportunity in a new land, and the need—for at least of some
immigrants—to maintain continuity with native traditions and beliefs.

Worthy Editor,
   We are a small family who recently came to the "Golden Land."
My husband, my boy and I are together, and our daughter lives in
another city.
   I had opened a grocery store here, but soon lost all my money. In
Europe we were in business; we had people working for us and paid
them well. In short, there we made a good living but here we are badly
off.
   My husband became a peddler. The "pleasure" of knocking on
doors and ringing bells cannot be known by anyone but a peddler. If
anybody does buy anything "on time," a lot of the money is lost, because there are some people who never intend to pay. In addition, my
husband has trouble because he has a beard, and because of the beard
he gets beaten up by the hoodlums.
   Also we have problems with our boy, who throws money around.
He works every day till late at night in a grocery for three dollars a week.
I watch over him and give him the best because I'm sorry that he has

Isaac Metzker, A Bintel Brief: Sixty Years of Letters from the Lower East Side to the Jewish
Daily Forward. (New York, Doubleday and Company, 1971), pp. 42–44, 49–51, 54–55, 58–59,
63–64, 68–70, 109–110, 117–118. Copyright by the Jewish Daily Forward. Used by permission.

to work so hard. But he costs me plenty and he borrows money from everybody. He has many friends and owes them all money. I get more and more worried as he takes here and borrows there. All my talking doesn't help. I am afraid to chase him away from home because he might get worse among strangers. I want to point out that he is well versed in Russian and Hebrew and he is not a child any more, but his behavior is not that of an intelligent adult.

I don't know what to do. My husband argues that he doesn't want to continue peddling. He doesn't want to shave off his beard, and it's not fitting for such a man to do so. The boy wants to go to his sister, but that's a twenty-five-dollar fare. What can I do? I beg you for a suggestion.

Your Constant reader,
F.L.

ANSWER:
Since her husband doesn't earn a living anyway, it would be advisable for all three of them to move to the city where the daughter is living. As for the beard, we feel that if the man is religious and the beard is dear to him because the Jewish law does not allow him to shave it off, it's up to him to decide. But if he is not religious, and the beard interferes with his earnings, it should be sacrificed.

Dear Editor,

For a long time I worked in a shop with a Gentile girl, and we began to go out together and fell in love. We agreed that I would remain a Jew and she a Christian. But after we had been married for a year, I realized that it would not work.

I began to notice that whenever one of my Jewish friends comes to the house, she is displeased. Worse yet, when she sees me reading a Jewish newspaper her face changes color. She says nothing, but I can see that she has changed. I feel that she is very unhappy with me, though I know she loves me. She will soon become a mother, and she is more dependent on me than ever.

She used to be quite liberal, but lately she is being drawn back to the Christian religion. She gets up early Sunday mornings, runs to church and comes home with eyes swollen from crying. When we pass a church now and then, she trembles.

Dear Editor, advise me what to do now. I could never convert, and there's no hope for me to keep her from going to church. What can we do now?

Thankfully,
A Reader

ANSWER:
Unfortunately, we often hear of such tragedies, which stem from marriages between people of different worlds. It's possible that if this couple were to move to a Jewish neighborhood, the young man might have more influence on his wife.

Dear Friend Editor,
Since your worthy newspaper has made it a policy in the "Bintel Brief" to allow everyone to state his opinions, ask questions and request advice, I hope you will allow me, too, to convey some part of my tragic life.

Thirteen years ago I loved and married a quiet young girl, and even in bad times we lived in peace and serenity. I worked hard. My wife devoted herself to our three children and the housekeeping.

A few years ago a brother of mine came to America too, with a friend of his. I worked in a shop, and as I was no millionaire, my brother and his friend became our boarders. Then my trouble began. The friend began earning good money. He began to mix in the household affairs and to buy things for my wife.

Neighbors began to whisper that my wife was carrying on an affair with this boarder, but I had no suspicions of my wife, whom I loved as life itself. I didn't believe them. Nevertheless I told her that people were talking. She swore to me that it was a lie, and evil people were trying to make bad blood between us. She cried as she spoke to me, and I believed her.

But people did not stop talking, and as time went on I saw that my wife was a common liar and that it was all true. My brother took it badly, because he had brought trouble into my home, and in remorse and shame, shot himself. He wounded himself and is left paralyzed on one side of his body. It was a terrible scandal. Good friends mixed in, made peace between us, and for the children's sake we remained together. I promised never to mention the tragic story and she promised to be a loyal wife to me and a good mother to the children she still loves deeply.

Again I worked long and hard, and with the aid of money I borrowed from friends I opened a stationery store. But my wife couldn't restrain herself and betrayed me again. She didn't give up her lover, but ran around with him day and night. I was helpless, because I had to be in the store at all times so she did as she pleased.

Again there was a scandal and her lover fled to Chicago. This was of little avail, because when my wife went to the country for the summer she left the children with the woman who rented her the rooms, and went to him for two weeks.

In short, I sold the store and everything is ruined. I gave her a thousand dollars and all her household effects. She and the children are now with him.

I know, dear Editor, that you cannot advise me now, but for me it's enough that I can pour out my suffering on paper. I can't find a place for myself. I miss the children. Life is dark and bitter without them. I hope that my wife will read my letter in the *Forward* and that she will blush with shame.

With respect, your reader who longs
for his wife and dear children,
B.R.

Dear Editor,

I, too, want to take advantage of this opportunity to tell about my troubles, and I ask you to answer me.

Eight months ago I brought my girlfriend from Russia to the States. We had been in love for seven years and were married shortly after her arrival. We were very happy together until my wife became ill. She was pregnant and the doctors said her condition was poor. She was taken to the hospital, but after a few days was sent home. At home, she became worse, and there was no one to tend her.

You can hardly imagine our bitter lot. I had to work all day in the shop and my sick wife lay alone at home. Once as I opened the door when I came home at dinnertime, I heard my wife singing with a changed, hoarse voice. I was terror-stricken, and when I ran to her I saw she was out of her head with fever.

Imagine how I felt. My wife was so ill and I was supposed to run back to the shop because the last whistle was about to blow. Everybody was rushing back to work, but I couldn't leave. I knew that my boss would fire me. He had warned me the day before that if I came late again he would't let me in. But how could I think of work now, when my wife was so ill? Yet without the job what would happen? There would not be a penny coming into the house. I stayed at my wife's bedside and didn't move till four o'clock.

Suddenly I jumped up and began to run around the room, in despair. My wife's singing and talking drove me insane. Like a madman I ran to the door and locked it. I leaped to the gas jet, opened the valve, then lay down in the bed near my wife and embraced her. In a few minutes I was nearer death than she.

Suddenly my wife cried out, "Water! water!" I dragged myself from the bed. With my last ounce of strength I crept to the door and opened it, closed the gas valve, and when I came to, gave her milk instead of water. She finished a glassful and wanted more, but there wasn't any more so I brought her some seltzer. I revived myself with water, and both of us slowly recovered.

The next morning they took my wife to the hospital, and after a stay of fourteen days she got well. Now I am happy that we are alive, but I keep thinking of what almost happened to us. Until now I never told anyone about it, but it bothers me. I have no secrets from my wife, and I want to know whether I should now tell her all, or not mention it. I beg you to answer me.

                                                          The Newborn

ANSWER:
This letter depicting the sad life of the worker is more powerful than any protest against the inequality between rich and poor. The advice to the writer is that he should not tell his wife that he almost ended both their lives. This secret may be withheld from his beloved wife, since it is clear he keeps it from her out of love.

                    /   /   /

Dear Editor,
    I am a girl from Galicia and in the shop where I work I sit near a Russian Jew with whom I was always on good terms. Why should one worker resent another?
    But once, in a short debate, he stated that all Galicians were no good. When I asked him to repeat it, he answered that he wouldn't retract a word, and that he wished all Galician Jews dead.
    I was naturally not silent in the face of such a nasty expression. He maintained that only Russian Jews are fine and intelligent. According to him, the *Galitzianer* are inhuman savages, and he had the right to speak of them so badly.
    Dear Editor, does he really have a right to say this? Have the Galician Jews not sent enough money for the unfortunate sufferers of the pogroms in Russia? When a Gentile speaks badly of Jews, it's immediately printed in the newspapers and discussed hotly everywhere. But that a Jew should express himself so about his own brothers is nothing? Does he have a right? Are Galicians really so bad? And does he, the Russian, remain fine and intelligent in spite of such expressions?
    As a reader of your worthy newspaper, I hope you will print my letter and give your opinion.

                                            With thanks in advance,
                                                          B.M.

ANSWER:
    The Galician Jews are just as good and bad as people from other lands. If the Galicians must be ashamed of the foolish and evil ones among them, then the Russians, too, must hide their heads in shame

because among them there is such an idiot as the acquaintance of our letter writer.

Worthy Editor,

I am eighteen years old and a machinist by trade. During the past year I suffered a great deal, just because I am a Jew.

It is common knowledge that my trade is run mainly by the Gentiles and, working among the Gentiles, I have seen things that cast a dark shadow on the American labor scene. Just listen:

I worked in a shop in a small town in New Jersey, with twenty Gentiles. There was one other Jew besides me, and both of us endured the greatest hardships. That we were insulted goes without saying. At times we were even beaten up. We work in an area where there are many factories, and once, when we were leaving the shop, a group of workers fell on us like hoodlums and beat us. To top it off, we and one of our attackers were arrested. The hoodlum was let out on bail, but we, beaten and bleeding, had to stay in jail. At the trial, they fined the hoodlum eight dollars and let him go free.

After that I went to work on a job in Brooklyn. As soon as they found out that I was a Jew they began to torment me so that I had to leave the place. I have already worked at many places, and I either have to leave, voluntarily, or they fire me because I am a Jew.

Till now, I was alone and didn't care. At this trade you can make good wages, and I had enough. But now I've brought my parents over, and of course I have to support them.

Lately I've been working on one job for three months and I would be satisfied, but the worm of anti-Semitism is beginning to eat at my bones again. I go to work in the morning as to Gehenna, and I run away at night as from a fire. It's impossible to talk to them because they are common boors, so-called "American sports." I have already tried in various ways, but the only way to deal with them is with a strong fist. But I am too weak and there are too many.

Perhaps you can help me in this matter. I know it is not an easy problem.

Your reader,
E.H.

ANSWER:
In the answer, the Jewish machinist is advised to appeal to the United Hebrew Trades and ask them to intercede for him and bring up charges before the Machinists Union about this persecution. His attention is also drawn to the fact that there are Gentile factories where Jews and Gentiles work together and get along well with each other.

Finally it is noted that people will have to work long and hard before this senseless racial hatred can be completely uprooted.

Worthy Editor,

I was born in America and my parents gave me a good education. I studied Yiddish and Hebrew, finished high school, completed a course in bookkeeping and got a good job. I have many friends, and several boys have already proposed to me.

Recently I went to visit my parents' home town in Russian Poland. My mother's family in Europe had invited my parents to a wedding, but instead of going themselves, they sent me. I stayed at my grandmother's with an aunt and uncle and had a good time. Our European family, like my parents, are quite well off and they treated me well. They indulged me in everything and I stayed with them six months.

It was lively in the town. There were many organizations and clubs and they all accepted me warmly, looked up to me—after all, I was a citizen of the free land, America. Among the social leaders of the community was an intelligent young man, a friend of my uncle's, who took me to various gatherings and affairs.

He was very attentive, and after a short while he declared his love for me in a long letter. I had noticed that he was not indifferent to me, and I liked him as well. I looked up to him and respected him, as did all the townsfolk. My family became aware of it, and when they spoke to me about him, I could see they thought it was a good match.

He was handsome, clever, educated, a good talker and charmed me, but I didn't give him a definite answer. As my love for him grew, however, I wrote to my parents about him, and then we became officially engaged.

A few months later we both went to my parents in the States and they received him like their own son. My bridegroom immediately began to learn English and tried to adjust to the new life. Yet when I introduced him to my friends they looked at him with disappointment. "This 'greenhorn' is your fiancé?'' they asked. I told them what a big role he played in his town, how everyone respected him, but they looked at me as if I were crazy and scoffed at my words.

At first I thought, Let them laugh, when they get better acquainted with him they'll talk differently. In time, though, I was affected by their talk and began to think, like them, that he really was a "greenhorn" and acted like one.

In short, my love for him is cooling off gradually. I'm suffering terribly because my feelings for him are changing. In Europe, where everyone admired him and all the girls envied me, he looked different. But, here, I see before me another person.

I haven't the courage to tell him, and I can't even talk about it to my parents. He still loves me with all his heart, and I don't know what to do. I choke it all up inside myself, and I beg you to help me with advice in my desperate situation.

Respectfully,
A Worried Reader

ANSWER:
The writer would make a grave mistake if she were to separate from her bridegroom now. She must not lose her common sense and be influenced by the foolish opinions of her friends who divided the world into "greenhorns" and real Americans.

We can assure the writer that her bridegroom will learn English quickly. He will know American history and literature as well as her friends do, and be a better American than they. She should be proud of his love and laugh at those who call him "greenhorn."

/   /   /

Dear Editor,
We, the unfortunates who are imprisoned on Ellis Island, beg you to have pity on us and print our letter in your worthy newspaper, so that our brothers in America may know how we suffer here.

The people here are from various countries, most of them are Russian Jews, many of whom can never return to Russia. These Jews are deserters from the Russian army and political escapees, whom the Czar would like to have returned to Russia. Many of the families sold everything they owned to scrape together enough for passage to America. They haven't a cent but they figured that, with the help of their children, sisters, brothers and friends, they could find means of livelihood in America.

You know full well how much the Jewish immigrant suffers till he gets to America. First he has a hard enough time at the borders, then with the agents. After this he goes through a lot till they send him, like baggage, on the train to a port. There he lies around in the immigrant sheds till the ship finally leaves. Then follows the torment on the ship, where every sailor considers a steerage passenger a dog. And when, with God's help, he has endured all this, and he is at last in America, he is given for "dessert" an order that he must show that he possesses twenty-five dollars.

But where can we get it? Who ever heard of such an outrage, treating people so? If we had known before, we would have provided for it somehow back at home. What nonsense this is! We must have the money on arrival, yet a few hours later (when relatives come) it's too late. For this kind of nonsense they ruin so many people and send them back to the place they escaped from.

It is impossible to describe all that is taking place here, but we want to convey at least a little of it. We are packed into a room where there is space for two hundred people, but they have crammed in about a thousand. They don't let us out into the yard for a little fresh air. We lie about on the floor in the spittle and filth. We're wearing the same shirts for three or four weeks, because we don't have our baggage with us.

Everyone goes around dejected and cries and wails. Women with little babies, who have come to their husbands, are being detained. Who can stand this suffering? Men are separated from their wives and children and only when they take us out to eat can they see them. When a man wants to ask his wife something, or when a father wants to see his child, they don't let him. Children get sick, they are taken to a hospital, and it often happens that they never come back.

Because today is a holiday, the Fourth of July, they didn't send anyone back. But Tuesday, the fifth, they begin again to lead us to the "slaughter," that is, to the boat. And God knows how many Jewish lives this will cost, because more than one mind dwells on the thought of jumping into the water when they take him to the boat.

All our hope is that you, Mr. Editor, will not refuse us, and print our letter which is signed by many immigrants. The women have not signed, because they don't let us get to them.

This letter is written by one of the immigrants, a student from Petersburg University, at Castle Garden, July 4, 1909, on the eve of the fast day of *Shivah Asar B'Tamuz* [the seventeenth day of the month of *Tamuz*, when Jews fast in memory of Nebuchadnezzar's siege and destruction of Jerusalem].

Alexander Rudnev

One hundred immigrants, aged from eight to fifty-eight, had signed this letter (each one had included his age). To stir up public opinion and the Jewish organizations, the letter was printed on page 1 with an appeal for action to help the unfortunates. To affirm the authenticity of the facts in the letter, the *Forward* stated that in the English press it had been announced that during the previous week six hundred detained immigrants had been sent back. And on the day the letter from the one hundred was printed, they were sending back two hundred and seventy people.

The *Forward* had previously printed many protests against the unjust treatment of the immigrants confined on Ellis Island, also against the fact that masses were being sent back, and the *Forward* was not silent on this letter.

Dear Editor,

Since I do not want my conscience to bother me, I ask you to decide whether a married woman has the right to go to school two evenings a week. My husband thinks I have no right to do this.

I admit that I cannot be satisfied to be just a wife and mother. I am still young and I want to learn and enjoy life. My children and my house are not neglected, but I go to evening high school twice a week. My husband is not pleased and when I come home at night and ring the bell, he lets me stand outside a long time intentionally, and doesn't hurry to open the door.

Now he has announced a new decision. Because I send out the laundry to be done, it seems to him that I have too much time for myself, even enough to go to school. So from now on he will count out every penny for anything I have to buy for the house, so I will not be able to send out the laundry any more. And when I have to do the work myself there won't be any time left for such "foolishness" as going to school. I told him that I'm willing to do my own washing but that I would still be able to find time for study.

When I am alone with my thoughts, I feel I may not be right. Perhaps I should not go to school. I want to say that my husband is an intelligent man and he wanted to marry a woman who was educated. The fact that he is intelligent makes me more annoyed with him. He is in favor of the emancipation of women, yet in real life he acts contrary to his beliefs.

Awaiting your opinion on this, I remain,

Your reader,
The Discontented Wife

ANSWER:
Since this man is intelligent and an adherent of the women's emancipation movement, he is scolded severely in the answer for wanting to keep his wife so enslaved. Also the opinion is expressed that the wife absolutely has the right to go to school two evenings a week.

Dear Editor,

I plead with you to open your illustrious newspaper and take in my "Bintel Brief" in which I write about my great suffering.

A long gloomy year, three hundred and sixty-five days, have gone by since I left my home and am alone on the lonely road of life. Oh, my poor dear parents, how saddened they were at my leaving. The leave-taking, their seeing me on my way, was like a silent funeral.

There was no shaking of the alms box, there was no grave digging and no sawing of boards, but I, myself, put on the white shirt that was wet with my mother's tears, took my pillow, and climbed into the wagon. Accompanying me was a quiet choked wail from my parents and friends.

The wheels of the wagon rolled farther and farther away. My mother and father wept for their son, then turned with heavy hearts to the empty house. They did not sit *shive* even though they had lost a child.

I came to America and became a painter. My great love for Hebrew, for Russian, all of my other knowledge was smeared with paint. During the year that I have been here I have had some good periods, but I am not happy, because I have no interest in anything. My homesickness and loneliness darken my life.

Ah, home, my beloved home. My heart is heavy for my parents whom I left behind. I want to run back, but I am powerless. I am a coward, because I know that I have to serve under *"Fonie"* [the Czar] for three years. I am lonely in my homesickness and I beg you to be my counsel as to how to act.

Respectfully,
V.A.

ANSWER:
The answer states that almost all immigrants yearn deeply for dear ones and home at first. They are compared with plants that are transplanted to new ground. At first it seems that they are withering, but in time most of them revive and take root in the new earth.

The advice to this young man is that he must not consider going home, but try to take root here. He should try to overcome all these emotions and strive to make something of himself so that in time he will be able to bring his parents here.

18 | WPA Interviews

In the 1930s, the federal Works Progress Administration (WPA) was responsible for thousands of public projects designed to improve American life and give the unemployed jobs. The WPA did lasting work in the construction of buildings, roads, and other public works, but it also hired artists, writers, scholars, and journalists to produce plays, paint murals on public buildings, write guides to the states, organize local history archives, and conduct oral history interviews. The WPA cultural programs produced a renewed interest in American social history and popular culture and promoted respect for the lives of poor working people.

The interviews conducted by the WPA were to be an invaluable collection of impressions by average Americans. Some, like the following, go as far back in time as the late nineteenth and early twentieth centuries. Caution is in order in considering the material presented by these interviews. People often were talking about events from ten, twenty, or even fifty years earlier in their lives; their memories may have been faulty or colored by the passage of time. Also, the interviewers had the prejudices and the particular political ideologies—generally some distance to the left of center—of their era. Nonetheless, the voices heard in the interviews are well worth listening to.

MORRIS HOROWITZ: A PEDDLER

How did I happen to become a peddler? When I came to Chicago in 1870, there was nothing else to do. I was eighteen years old. I had learned no trade in Russia. The easiest thing to do was to peddle. People coming to America today have a much harder time. There are better houses to live in and nearly everybody has a bathtub, but there are no jobs. In the old days, if you had a few dollars, you could buy some dry goods and peddle. But today you must know a trade or have a profession; otherwise you have no chance.

I went to live with an aunt and uncle when I first came to Chicago.

Ann Banks, First-Person America (New York, Alfred A. Knopf, 1980) pp. 31–35, 39–43, 184–187, 201–205, 245–247, 250–252. Copyright © 1980 by Ann Banks. Reprinted by permission of Alfred A. Knopf, Inc.

They lived in a small four-room house on Fourth Avenue. They had four children but they managed to rent one room to two roomers. I shared the bed with these two men. The day after I got to Chicago my uncle asked me if I had any money. I told him I had ten dollars. He told me to invest it in dry goods and start peddling. I peddled in Chicago till after the fire of 1871. There were not many stores, so I had no trouble selling my goods. I used to make from six to ten dollars a week. I paid my aunt three dollars a week for food and lodging and I saved the rest. I had the responsibility of bringing my father, two sisters, and two brothers to America.

It was the great fire of 1871 that made me a country peddler. I remember the fire very well. It was in October. We used to go to bed early, because the two roomers had to go to work very early. We were getting ready to go to bed, when we heard the fire bells ringing. I asked the two men if they wanted to see where the fire was.

"Why should I care as long as our house is not on fire," one of the men said. "There is a fire every Monday and Thursday in Chicago." But I wanted to see the fire, so I went out into the street. I saw the flames across the river, but I thought that since the river was between the fire and our house, there was nothing to worry about. I went back to bed. The next thing I knew my two bedfellows were shaking me. "Get up," they cried. "The whole city is on fire! Save your things! We are going to Lincoln Park."

I jumped out of bed and pulled on my pants. Everybody in the house was trying to save as much as possible. I tied my clothes in a sheet. With my clothes under my arm and my pack on my back, I left the house with the rest of the family. Everybody was running north. People were carrying all kinds of crazy things. A woman was carrying a pot of soup, which was spilling all over her dress. People were carrying cats, dogs, and goats. In the great excitement people saved worthless things and left behind good things. I saw a woman carrying a big frame in which was framed her wedding veil and wreath. She said it would have been bad luck to leave it behind.

When we came to Lake Street I saw all the wagons of Marshall Field and Company [the firm was then called Field, Leiter and Company] lined up in front. Men were carrying the goods out of the building and loading everything into the wagons. The merchandise was taken to the streetcar barns on State near Twentieth Street; a couple of weeks later, Marshall Field started doing business there.

No one slept that night. People gathered on the streets and all kinds of reasons were given for the fire. I stood near a minister talking to a group of men. He said the fire was sent by God as a warning that the people were wicked. He said there were too many saloons in Chicago, too many houses of prostitution. A woman who heard this said that a fire started in a barn was a direct warning from God since Jesus was also born in a barn. I talked to a man who lived next door to Mrs.

O'Leary, and he told me that the fire started in Mrs. O'Leary's barn. She went out to milk the cow when it was beginning to get dark. The cow kicked the lamp over and that's how the fire started. There were all kinds of songs made up about the fire. Years after, people were still singing songs about it. You remember the song "Hot Time in the Old Town?" Well there was a song made up to that tune. These are the words:

> One moonlit night while the families were in bed,
>   Mrs. O'Leary took a lantern to the shed,
> The cow kicked it over, winked her eye and said:
> There'll be a hot time in the old town tonight,
>   my baby.

Since many homes were burned, many people left the city. Some went to live with relatives in other cities. A great many men became country peddlers. There were thousands of men walking from farm to farm with heavy packs on their backs. These peddlers carried all kinds of merchandise, things they thought farmers and their families could use.

There was no rural mail delivery in those days. The farmers very seldom saw a newspaper and were hungry for news. They were very glad to see a peddler from any large city. They wanted to hear all about the great fire. When I told a farmer that I was from Chicago, he was very glad to see me. You see, I was a newspaper and a department store.

The farms were ten, fifteen, twenty, and even thirty miles apart. It would take a day sometimes to walk from one farm to the next. I used to meet peddlers from all over. It was not an easy life, but we made pretty good money. Most of the men had come from Europe and had left their families behind. We were all trying to save enough money to bring relatives to America.

The living expenses of the peddlers were very little. The farmers' wives always gave us plenty of food. I did not eat anything that was not kosher, but I could eat eggs and there were plenty of them. There was fresh milk and bread and butter. The farmers always gave us a place to sleep. In the summer we slept in the hayloft. In the winter, if there was no spare bed, we would sleep on the floor. When the farmer had no extra blankets, we slept with our clothes on to keep warm.

I had a customer in Iowa and I used to get to his farm once a year. He had a nice six-room house, and it was one of the few places where I could have a bed to sleep in. When I got to the place after a year's absence, there was no house. The ground was covered with snow. . . . My friend the farmer came out of a dugout. I asked him what had happened to his house.

"Oh, we had a terrible storm about four months ago, and the house blew away," said the farmer. "We are living in this dugout; it isn't as nice as the house was, but it's safe and warm. Come on in."

I had never been in a dugout and I was surprised to see how nice the farmer and his wife had fixed up this hole in the ground. Seven people were living in this dugout, but they made room for me. The farmers were very lonely during the long winters, and they were glad to have anybody come to their homes.

After carrying the pack on my back for two years, I decided to buy a horse and wagon. Many other peddlers got the same idea. I used to meet the small covered wagons as they drove about the country. I had now been peddling for five years and had saved enough money to bring my father, brothers, and sisters to Chicago. By that time a great many new houses had been built and we rented a four-room house on Maxwell Street. My oldest brother started peddling. One of my sisters started working in a clothing factory, while the other one kept house.

After my father had been in Chicago a few months, he wanted to go to Burlington, Iowa, to see a friend who had been his neighbor in Russia. When he got there, he met this friend's daughter and decided that I ought to marry her. So I went to Burlington, met the girl, and I agreed with my father. The young lady and I were married in 1875. I rented a small house near my father's home and we furnished it. I believe we had the first rug in the neighborhood. We were very proud of our first American home. It was the beginning of a good life. I stayed home for a week with my young wife. It was my first vacation since I had come to America. Then I started off again in my wagon. During the fifty years that I peddled, I always went home for all the Jewish holidays and when a baby was born. I would stay home a week and then was off again.

Many of the men who carried packs on their backs and in covered wagons became very rich. They learned American business ways. Some of them opened small stores which their wives looked after while the men were on the road. When the stores showed a good profit, they would quit peddling. Some of the largest departments stores in the country were started by men who peddled with packs on their backs.

I never got rich. My wife and I raised six children. When my sisters and brothers got married, my father came to live with us. Then one of my sisters died and her children came to live with us. Then my wife brought her parents to America and they lived with us. Then we wanted our children to have an education, so we sent them to college. There never was enough money left to start any kind of business. But I feel that we made a good investment.

PHILIPPE LEMAY: A FRENCH-CANADIAN TEXTILE WORKER

When we landed at Lowell in 1864, there were very few French Canadians. Many more came after the Civil War was over. I was only eight years old, but that didn't stop me from going to work. My first job as a textile worker was in the Lawrence mill, Number Five, where I worked as a doffer [a worker who removes filled bobbins from spindles] for about three years. In 1872, when I was sixteen, our family moved to Manchester.

Here I started in a card room as roping and bobbin boy, but I wanted to be a fly-spinner, making cotton into thread, ready for the weave room. It wasn't until 1875 that I got my chance. How I landed in Number One spinning mill of the Amoskeag, where no French Canadian could be hired before, is a story in itself.

Each spring and fall, it seems, the older immigrants had a touch of homesickness. Most of them still had farms in old Quebec, so they went back to Canada twice a year. They had to make many sacrifices to save up enough money to pay railroad fares and other necessary expenses. While there, they visited friends and relatives, but their principal reason was a serious one. At heart, they were still farmers like their ancestors, and they wanted to get something out of those farms, some of which had been in the family for many generations. In the spring, they attended to the ploughing, harrowing, and sowing; in the fall, to the harvesting of the crops.

While they were absent from the mills, other hands had their chance to work. That's how I got into spinning. The overseer was out sick and the second hand hired me. When the boss came back, I was giving all my attention to my work and not losing a minute. But the overseer didn't look pleased when his assistant told him my name. He wanted to know why I had been hired when he didn't want any Frenchman working in his mill. The second hand said he'd discharge me right away and I felt that my dream of becoming a fly-spinner was coming to an end quickly. I kept on working. The boss looked at me, seemed to think twice before he spoke, and then said: "Don't do it now; wait until Smith comes back to work."

Smith did come back and I was out of a job, but not for long. The boss was sorry to let me go, that was plain. He took my address and said he'd let me know as soon as he needed me. He had changed his mind about hiring French Canadians after he had seen one of them work. The very next day he sent for me and after that I had a regular job in the Amoskeag. That same boss hired many of my people, and that is the point I want to bring out in my story.

Later, I was transferred to Number Four mill. One day, another overseer tried to get me, and when I spoke of leaving, the boss of Number Four wouldn't hear of it. To keep me, he offered me extra pay if I would do the work of a sickly operative who had to loaf at times, and more extra pay if I wanted to take the place of a third hand once in a while. I accepted, and as long as the arrangement lasted I got two dollars a day and a little more. I was finally given a regular job as third hand, quite a promotion for a French Canadian at the time. In 1881 I was made second hand, and in 1901, overseer in Number One spinning mill.

It was a big event when I was appointed overseer of the One and Eight spinning mills. There was to be a vacancy very shortly. I knew about it and, convinced that no one would say a good word for me, I decided to speak for myself. I asked the super if he wouldn't give me the chance. He was so surprised that he couldn't speak for a long time, or so it seemed to me. He was looking at me as if he had been struck by thunder and lightning. What! A Frenchman had the crust to think he could be an overseer! That was something unheard of, absolutely shocking. When he recovered enough to speak, he told me he'd think it over, turned his back on me, and walked off. He was certainly upset.

The next day, he came to me and, with a doubting expression still spread all over his face, said he'd try me for six months. But I didn't want six months, I answered back. I wasn't going to clog up that spinning department. Either I was the man for the job, I said, or I wasn't. One month: that's all I wanted to show what I could do. The super seemed to be wondering again but answered it was all right with him. So I became the overseer of Number One spinning, where I had made my shaky debut in 1875.

That was another step ahead for the French Canadians, but this time it was an awful scandal. The sad news didn't take long to spread. Americans and Irish were mad clean through. The Irish, it seemed, were afraid that we had come to take their jobs away from them in the mills and tried hard to send us back to Canada by making life impossible for us in America. They looked at me and spoke to me only when they were strictly obliged to, but there was no more friendship. I, a Frenchman, had jumped over the heads of others who thought themselves the only ones entitled to the job of overseer. Here was a sin that could not be forgiven, and what was the world coming to, anyway?

Later, several other French-Canadian textile workers got well-deserved promotions. One of my own second hands was a boss just three days. Then he came back to his old job with me after telling the superintendent that he'd be happier and healthier that way. "An overseer has too many worries," he said. So my friend had the distinction of being the first French Canadian to refuse an overseer's job.

I liked the people who were with me in the mills and I sympathized with them. I helped them as anybody else would have done in my place. Didn't I, when I was a boss, hide some who weren't quite sixteen, when inspectors visited the mills? If boys and girls were big and strong enough to work, even if they were a little under the legal age, I gave them a chance to keep their jobs. I started working in the Lowell mills when I was only eight years old, and I could understand. Their parents were poor and needed every cent they could get. So I'd tell these younger workers to keep out of sight until the inspector had gone away. There was no harm to anybody in that, and it did a lot of good. Besides, the law wasn't so strict in those days.

That strike of 1922 was really a terrible thing. It lasted nearly ten months and was the worst thing that ever happened. It was bad for the city, its merchants, tenement owners, business in general. It destroyed Amoskeag's trade. The company never recovered from the blow and kept going down until it had to close its doors [in 1936]. But my sympathy goes first to all the workers, for they suffered the most. They lost all their savings, went deep in debt, and lived on canned beans while the hope of winning the fight was kept dangling before their eyes. They were told almost every day by the strike leaders to be patient and tighten their belts because victory was in sight. But there was no victory, only defeat for all concerned.

As an overseer, I couldn't join their ranks in the union nor help them in any way, but neither could I be against them. As a boy, a young man, and a middle-aged man with a family, I had worked long hours for anything but high wages. I knew what it meant to be poor, what sacrifices must be made if you want to lay something aside for a rainy day. The workers wanted more pay; I would have given them a living wage if it had been in my power to do so, every worker having a right to that. They wanted shorter hours; I would have given them a reasonable work week if I had anything to say about it. Even as a second hand and an overseer, I never forgot my humble beginning and always considered myself a textile worker. Those strikers were textile workers too, and I was sorry for them.

J. C. JULIAN: TOBIES

If I tell you about tobies, I don't want you to be talking about them to nobody else. If you do, don't tell nobody I was the one who told you. It's against the laws of the state of Oklahoma, and lots of other states, to sell tobies. They claim us toby-sellers are running a racket, deceiving the people, that there ain't nothing to tobies. But I know better, and you ought to know better.

You believe in luck, don't you? Sure you do! Everybody believes there's such a thing as luck. You know yourself, things don't just happen. Some people are lucky and some people ain't so lucky, and all people sometime or other have luck. A toby helps people to be lucky. If you want something real bad, you don't get what you want without some help. That's where my tobies come in. I sell them for just one dollar, but they're worth fifty times that amount. And I guarantee my tobies. But don't never let nobody else touch your toby. If you do, the toby will lose its charm.

A toby is a lucky charm. It's what you put in them that does the trick. It ain't just everybody that knows how to make them. It took me a long time to learn. I put eight things in my tobies. The most important thing is high-john-the-conqueror. It's a kind of lucky root. Then I put in a four-leaf clover, five-finger grass, a white powder, a black powder, and a pink powder. That white powder costs plenty, over twenty dollars an ounce. I don't put in much, just a smidgen. I don't recollect the name of them powders, but you can get them at any lucky shop. I put two more things in my tobies; they've slipped my mind for the present.

You put all these things in a little fancy colored bag, known as a lucky bag. Then I usually wrap the lucky bag in cellophane, and tie it up with pretty ribbon. The cellophane keeps the lucky bag clean, and helps to keep it from wearing out. I'd show you my toby, but it would take all the luck out of it, showing it to someone else. One quick peek wouldn't hurt very much, but like a fool when I changed my pants this morning, I forgot and left my toby in the right-hand pocket. It's a wonder I ain't been run down by a car.

The last time I got careless and left my toby home, I damn near got myself killed. I ought to of had better sense than to go to a dance sober and without my toby. I knew I didn't have it with me when I reached for my change to get into the dance. If I hadn't of been sober, I couldn't of got drunk. And if I had had my toby with me, I wouldn't of got in that fight. And even if I couldn't of kept out of the fight, I wouldn't of been the one to get all cut up.

I sold a toby to a woman in Walters, down in Cotten County. She had been full of religion when she was a young gal, but when she married, God left her. Her husband was a poor cotton farmer and had to make whiskey on the side to make a living. This old gal got a liking for whiskey and she could drink ten men under the table. All this drinking led to looseness, and she started trifling on her old man. Then she did get herself in a fix. One day it come to her that she was going to have a baby. She knew her old man was suspicious of her conduct, and if the kid didn't look something like him, he'd break her neck, or run her off. It scared her so bad that she gave up drinking and trifling and started going to church, but it didn't do no good. She couldn't get salvation. It just wouldn't come to her.

The woman was just about dead with worry when I hit town. She heard through one of my customers that I sold tobies that never failed, and she looked me up. I sold her one for five dollars, but it was worth five hundred to her. When her baby was born, it looked like her. That toby sure enough saved that woman from shame and a good beating, maybe death itself. But my tobies never fail—never fail! Of course, if you don't put no faith in a toby, a toby won't help you none. It's like everything else: you've got to put faith in it or you won't get no results.

Here's my sales talk:

"Put up and built by the Seven Sisters at the Crackerjack Drug Store at New Orleans, Louisiana. My toby will bring you Honor, Riches, and Happiness. It will help you Win in all Games. It will bring you Health and Wealth. It will Protect you against Evil Spirits and Witchcraft. Thieves nor Enemies cannot bother you. Now listen, everything you turn your hand to Prospers you and makes you Money. You succeed in

your Trade, Job, or Business. You got Seven Wishes to make with each
Lucky Bag. Hold the Bag in your Left hand, blow your hot breath on it
Three times, and Make your Wish, and see if it don't come to Pass be-
fore the Seventh day is gone.

"To hold your True Loved one. To get anyone you love. To Protect
yourself against all Law. To Kill all Voodoo and Witchcraft. Buy a toby.
Just One Dollar. And if you ain't satisfied with my Toby, I give you your
Money back. Don't be Foolhardy. Don't run no Risk. Keep a Toby on
your person all the Time. Just One Dollar. But it's worth Fifty."

I've sold tobies to all kinds of folks. I've sold them to politicians and
big businessmen, to gamblers, and to thieves. I've sold lot of them to
folks wanting to get married, and to folks who don't want to get married
but want to live like married folks. But the poor whites and the poor
Negroes are my best customers. It ain't because they're dumber than
rich folks. Some of them ain't as dumb. And young man, let me tell
you right now, it's the dumb folks that don't buy tobies to help them.
Understand that right off! Poor folks need more luck than rich folks.
That's the reason they buy more tobies.

"DOC" VAN ASTINE: A CIRCUS TROUPER

At an early age I had a yearning for the show business. School didn't
interest me a bit. I hated books. I wasn't a danged bit interested in reading about what somebody else did, or where they went, or what they
saw. I wanted to go, do, and see things for myself, and I couldn't think
of any better way to satisfy my ambition than to join up with a circus.

Come a day, once, when I was a young gaffer in my early teens, I
had a chance to run away with the Mighty Yankee Robinson Circus. The
lure of sawdust and spangles was much stronger than family ties or the
red schoolhouse, so off I went.

I was hired as a block boy to help set up and tear down the blues
[seats]. There wasn't no commoner job, but I remember how proud and
thrilled I was merely to touch anything that was a part of the circus.

I was only there four days when I was dragged home to the family
fireside and my place at the table, but not without a trip to the barn first,
where my father strapped me around the legs and across the back with
a tie-strap until I weren't hardly able to navigate. As tough a lickin as
the old man gave me, I soon forgot it—but I didn't forget my first four
days with the circus.

I remember how I gazed in awe at the performers, and to think I
was so close to them. I seen a lot of beautiful women in my day, but I
don't believe I ever seen a woman in my later life that looked so beautiful to me as them circus women did. I had the feeling that they was
queens, or goddesses, or something too beautiful to belong to the world.

And I recall the thrill of thrills when a clown—circus folks call the funny men Joeys—said, "Hey, lad, run out to a butcher shop and get me a pound of lard." The Joeys used lard for taking off their makeup. I was so excited at having a performer actually speak to me that I couldn't say yes or no. But with the ten-cent piece he give me clutched in my fist, I run like lightning to the nearest butcher shop. Boy, oh boy, was I happy.

When I went back to school after my four days with the circus, I cut quite a figure among my schoolmates. Being with a circus made me a hero, and did I glory in it. I knew that when I got a little bit older I was going to join up with a circus and be showman for always and always.

There just ain't no comparison between the circus of today and the circus of the past. The circus in this day and age seems really to be the stupendous, gigantic, colossal exhibition the advance billing and the "barkers," "spielers," and "grinders" claim for it. The circus your grandfather went to see as a boy was nothing more than a variety, or vaudeville, show under canvas. Pretty near all the acts they done in the circus could have been put on in even the ordinary theaters of that time, but the kids of today ain't so wide-eyed and amazed at what they see at a circus as they was a quarter of a century ago. So many marvelous things goes on all the time in this day and age that kids probably expect more from a circus now than it's humanly possible to give.

The people who works for the circuses today is all trained specialists. Everybody has only one job, and he's supposed to do that one thing well. The old-time trouper was a Jack-of-all-trades. He could shoe a horse, if he had to, he could clown, drive a ten-horse team, lay out canvas, and fill in at anything around the lot except perhaps aerial acrobatics, and believe it or not, many of the old-timers could even double in acrobatics.

Circus people in the old days was considered social outcasts. "Decent" people wouldn't have nothing to do with troupers. This brought the show folks closer together; made em clannish. Circus people was just like one big family, and was always a good lot, always willing to help each other over the bumps. People don't look at it the way they used to, anymore, but circus people is still clannish just the same.

My family was determined that I was going to be a doctor, like my old man. In them days, anybody that thought they was cut out for it could be a doctor if they wanted to. All you needed was a little schooling and be handy around sick folks and not be afraid of the sight of blood. All medicine was bitter if it was any good, and if they didn't know what ailed a person they drew some blood. Then he either got better or worse, as God willed. I might have made a good doctor at that, if I only could have got show business off my mind.

When I got a few years older, I was able to out-talk the old folks and get my own way. I give up all thought of pill-rolling and left home to join a circus. I stuck with circuses for nearly sixty years of my life and I worked on all the big shows one time or another. Studying for a doctor, though, give me the nickname, "Doc," and that's the name I'm knowed by wherever on this globe a "big top" is being raised.

A "Hey Rube" is practically unknown today. A Hey Rube was a fight between the circus folks and the town yokels. Those ruckuses used to come regularly every so often in the old days. Many of the Hey Rubes was started by folks figgering they wasn't getting all the circus advertised; if the stupendous wasn't stupendous enough, the gigantic wasn't gigantic enough, the colossal wasn't colossal enough, or the "largest in captivity" wasn't large enough, the town folks felt like they had grounds for a fight. Another common cause of a Hey Rube was because petty thieves, purse-snatchers, and pickpockets followed circuses from town to town. The circus got blamed for what them slickers did, but there was nothing they could do about it. When the crooks hit a crowd too hard, and too many people got plucked, the town folk got together and tried to take it out on the circus people. Pretty near every Hey Rube I ever seen ended with the town folks coming out second best physically, although the circus usually lost out financially. Lawsuits always followed a Hey Rube, usually by some innocent bystanders who got hurt in the scramble, and circus people had no chance for a square deal in a prejudiced small-town court.

The circus had always been one of the world's most progressive enterprises. New inventions, if they was something the circus could use, was grabbed up by the circus as soon as they come out. The circus was always away ahead of anybody else in lighting equipment. Modern methods and high specialization has made it a lot easier for the circus man. Transportation is improved, and accommodations is a lot better than they was. You don't have to be tough inside and out to troupe with a circus nowadays. In the old days any handler of circus stock knowed how to mix up a batch of kerosene or paregoric liniment to dope an ailing animal. Nowadays the big show troupes a staff of veterinarians, and each valuable animal is watched as close and its diet figured out as carefully as for the Dionne quints.

I got a lot of respect for Clyde Beattie and other of today's animal trainers, but I don't think there is any comparison between the temper and ferocity of jungle-born cats that the old-time trainer faced twice a day, and the animals born in captivity that the present-day trainers work with. You don't hardly ever hear of a trainer getting killed in an exhibition cage today; but in the old days I have seen trainers torn to ribbons in the twinkling of an eye.

The circus reached its greatest size in 1908 when Ringling Brothers introduced the first "spec," or spectacle. Since that year the spec was a feature with all circuses. The first spec was called "King Solomon" and later "Arabian Nights," and others. I was boss canvasman for many years with a number of different circuses. Boss canvasman is a good job on a big show and pays from seventy-five to a hundred dollars a week.

I made quite a lot of money in my day, but I haven't got anything to show for it now.

The show business may be a hard life, but if I had it all to do over again I would still want you to give me the same route.

NORBERTO DIAZ: EYEWITNESS TO A MURDER*

Every time I pass in front of the Cuban Club I think of Isleno. The other day I was down to the beach and seen the palm tree where he was hung. It's funny, but that was the first coconut palm to die from the disease that's killing most all the palm trees on the island. I believe Isleno's *brujo* [ghost] is killing the palm trees, too. People say the whole island's cursed and that's why there is so much bad luck and people do not have enough to eat.

Isleno's curse has already killed five of the Ku Klux Klan who beat and hung him. He knew who they were and called their names and cursed them for horrible deaths in revenge. He shot the Klan leader himself, one man was blowed up by dynamite when he was working on the bridges, another got caught in the Mattecumbe hurricane, one was ground to pieces under his boat when it went on a reef, and another went fishing and never came back. Isleno's curse killed them all. It's killing another with tuberculosis right now.

I guess I can tell the story as good as anybody. Isleno was a good friend to me; he was a good friend to everybody. He was a Spaniard from the Canary Islands: that's why we called him Isleno. He owned a little coffee shop and had a good business, but he was one of those men what likes to spend their money for a good time, drinking and all that. But he never caused nobody no trouble; all he did was to be happy and enjoy life. Isleno began living with a brown—a mulatto girl. We called her Rosita Negra. They lived in a room right in back of the coffee shop. People talked about his living with a brown, but nobody didn't really think much about it. I think a man's got a right to live with any kind of woman he wants to. If he wants to live with a brown, that ain't nobody's business but his own.

Almost anybody in town can tell you who the Klan members are. I know all them fellows. I think if a man has anything against another man he ought to go up to his face and tell him about it, and not get a whole crowd of men together and hide their faces in pillowcases. Some of the very ones that hung Isleno; I've seem em in Negro jungle houses myself. They try to hide their faces when they see me but I go right up to em and say, "Whacha say, old boy? What're you doing here?" They all jump the fence and put horns on their wives every chance they get.

*The events Diaz described happened on Christmas Eve, 1921. No one was ever arrested for the murder, according to an account in the *Key West Citizen*, 23 December 1977.

That's what makes me so mad, them men killed Isleno for doing the same thing they do. Only difference was Isleno didn't try to hide it. The Klan sent Isleno a warning to get Rosita out of the house. But Isleno. wasn't afraid of nobody. He was a big man, strong as an ox. When he got that warning he just started keeping his gun under the counter of his shop.

Then one night—it was Christmas Eve—about twenty of the Ku Klux Klan came marching down from Duval Street, all dressed in white robes with hoods over their faces and carrying guns and torches. They marched straight for Isleno's shop. He was in bed with Rosita when somebody came to warn him. He ran for his gun, but somebody had already stolen it.

By that time the Klansmen were grabbing him. He put up an awful fight, but they tied him and dragged him to the beach, stripped him, and beat him till his kidneys burst. Isleno fought so hard he got free of the ropes and tore the masks off half a dozen of the men. He cursed them all, swore he'd be revenged and that they'd all die horrible deaths. They beat him some more until he was unconscious, and then hung him up in a tree. He was left for dead but he came to his senses and got loose from the rope somehow, and walked all the way back to his coffee shop. The next morning when I heard Isleno was at his shop I went to see him. His back was a pitiful sight! It looked just like one of those red cube steaks that has been all diced up to make it tender. It was a shame the way they had beat that man! He was in bed and suffering something terrible from the pain of his busted kidney. There was a lot of his friends there to see him, but I couldn't stand it and left.

About twelve o'clock Mr. Ostrom, a leader of the Klan and a very prominent man—was walking past the Cuban Club with his arms full of groceries he was taking home for Christmas dinner. When he stopped across the alley Isleno came out, his pants all bloody in front, and with a revolver in his hand. He shot Mr. Ostrom in the belly five times, and he fell on the sidewalk, begging Isleno not to shoot again.

But Isleno stood there and put five more bullets in the gun and shot Mr. Ostrom five more times. Then he climbed up in the attic of a vacant house and barricaded himself in. The police and the sheriff and the deputies and the National Guards surrounded the place, but Isleno kept them back with his shooting. The sheriff asked him to surrender, but Isleno said he would surrender only to the military commander who was stationed here.

The military man came and promised Isleno protection. When Isleno surrendered, the sheriff promised the military man to protect Isleno if he would turn him over to his custody. So the sheriff took Isleno upstairs in the jail where they beat him some more. After he was unconscious they grabbed him by the heels and dragged him down those iron steps, his head cracking like an egg on every step.

They tied a rope around his neck and pulled his body through the streets behind an automobile and down to the beach. Isleno was already plenty dead, but they hung his body up in a palm tree where it stayed. I don't know how long till the buzzards and smell got so bad they had to cut it down.

LLOYD GREEN: PULLMAN PORTER

"New York"

I'm in New York, but New York ain't in me. You understand? I'm in New York, but New York ain't in me. What do I mean? Listen. I'm from Jacksonville, Florida. Been in New York twenty-five years. I'm a New Yorker! But I'm in New York and New York ain't in me. Yuh understand? Naw, naw, you don't get me. What do they do? Take Lenox Avenue. Take Seventh Avenue. Take Sugar Hill! Pimps. Numbers. Cheating these poor people outa what they got. Shooting, cutting, backbiting, all them things. Yuh see? Yuh see what I mean? *I'm* in New York, but *New York ain't in me*! Don't laugh, don't laugh. I'm laughing but I don't mean it; it ain't funny. Yuh see. I'm on Sugar Hill, but Sugar Hill ain't on me.

I come here twenty-five years ago. Bright lights, pretty women. More space to move around. Son, if I had-a got New York in me I'd a-been dead a long time ago. What happened the other night? Yuh heard about the shooting up here in the Hill. Take that boy. I knowed him! Anybody been around this Hill knows him, n they know he went to a bad man. What'd he do? Now mind yuh now, his brother's a big shot. Makes plenty money. Got a big car an a fine office. But *he* comes up on this Hill tearin up people's property if they don't pay him protection. Last night he walks into this wop's place up the street n tries to tear it up. Now yuh know that's a bad man, gonna tear up the wop's place. Well, he stepped out the door n a bunch of them wops showed up in a car n tried to blow him away. *He* had too much New York. I'm in New York, yuh see? But New York ain't in me! Hell yes, he went and got too much New York, yuh understand what I tryin to tell yuh?

I been in New York twenty-five years! But I ain't never bothered nobody. Ain't never done nothin to nobody. I ain't no bad fellow. Shore I drink. I like good whiskey. I drinks but I ain't drunk. Yuh think I'm drunk? I don't *talk* drunk do I? I drinking n I got money in mah pockets. But I ain't throwing ma money away. Hell, I talking sense, ain't I? Yuh heard me way in yonder didn't yuh? Yuh came to me, heard me. I didn't have to come after yuh, did I? If I hada been talking foolishness yuh wouldn't a paid me no mind. Hell, I know I'm right. I got something to say. I got something to say n I ain't no preacher neither. I'm drinking. I likes to drink. It's good for mah stomach. Good whiskey's good for anybody's stomach. Look at the bottle. Mount Vernon! Good whiskey. What did the saint say? He said a little spirits is good for the stomach, good to warm the spirit. Now where did that come from? Yuh don't know, yuh too young. Yuh young Negroes don't know the Bible. Don't laugh, don't laugh. Look here, I'll tell you somethin:

> Some folks drinks to cut the fool,
> But some folks drinks to think.

> I drinks to think.

Questions for Part II

1 What advice does Carnegie give? What aim does he consider to be higher than accumulating money?

2 What does Wanamaker say are the advantages of the "new store"? Judging from the employee instructions you have read, would you have enjoyed working in the new department stores? Why or why not?

3 Why would the use of child labor have appealed to employers? What are some negative consequences of child labor?

4 The introduction to the Mother Jones reading mentions several labor disputes in which she was involved. What were the issues? Who were the participants? What were the outcomes?

5 Discuss the problems the farm men and women cite in their letters. Compare them with what Bryan said in his Cross of Gold speech in 1896. (Your textbook covers that speech.) What solutions to these problems did the Populists and their supporters propose?

6 What does the selection from *Giants in the Earth* add to your understanding of the difficulties of farm life on the Great Plains in the late nineteenth century?

7 What does the "melting pot" image mean? What reasons do Aldrich and Fairchild give for opposing the "new immigration"? What do you think of these reasons?

8 What kinds of problems are discussed in the "Bintel Brief" reading? How different are they from the problems in the personal advice column in the newspaper you read?

9 From the WPA interviews and other information you may have read, try to form some tentative ideas about what life was like for ordinary Americans seventy-five or one-hundred years ago. Have things changed much since then? One factor you might want to consider is the role of government in everyday life.

PART III | ROOTS OF THE MODERN ERA

Historians have understood the first decades of the twentieth century as an era in which Americans struggled to organize a society that was rapidly changing. While the United States was becoming a major political and military influence in the world at large, its leaders and citizens tried to understand a country that was becoming increasingly diverse in population and increasingly bureaucratic and urban.

In the readings on the Progressive Era (1901–1917) that follow, an American of the late twentieth century will find many descriptions of social ills and problems that have been of recurrent concern in recent American history. Jacob Riis, for example, describes the exploitation of women in the workplace. George Washington Plunkitt, an urban political-machine "boss," offers a view of the political process as a matter of who gets what, but Lincoln Steffens, like many reformers today, labels the Plunkitt perception as corrupt and wonders why the public tolerates it. Upton Sinclair pits workers against new technologies and consumers against products whose dangers they do not necessarily understand. Finally, even though it may seem that descriptions of the Triangle Shirtwaist Factory Fire of 1911 depict workplace hazards of a dramatic and immediate sort that largely have been eliminated by elementary safety inspection laws, problems of workplace safety remain. Modern problems with asbestos and other carcinogens are more subtle, long-term, and difficult to remedy. (And, lest we be too confident about the efficacy of our laws in an era of sporadic enforcement, new workshops employing undocumented immigrants increasingly flaunt even the most elementary safety rules.)

Although all wars generate uncertainty and turmoil, some in American history have ended in great clarity about national mission and purpose. World War I, however, like the later Korean and Vietnamese Wars, encouraged social discontent. The war had to be sold to the American people; it raised the questions of who was an American and who was a hyphenated American (Irish-American, German-American, and so on), and who was loyal and who was not. While

149

some soldiers such as Dick O'Neill went to war rather innocently, they came back far less innocent. At home, the battle over the meaning of the war and the meaning of American loyalty engaged much of American society. Boy Scouts, as will be seen in one reading, were taught to sniff out disloyalty; dissenters were silenced; and some, like Emma Goldman, were deported.

The First World War brought other major domestic changes. Fresh opportunities in war industries and the depredations of the boll weevil on farm crops combined to bring on the great migration of blacks into the northern cities, a migration that would be further fueled by the next great war and the era of cold war prosperity that followed it. The war was one of many forces inducing a higher degree of economic organization in American society as it moved into the age of the "expert." People no longer produced goods for an apparently limitless market; they turned to advertising experts to define both the goods and the market. The role of advertising in American life, defended in the Calkins reading, became an issue of debate in the 1920s, and the argument is not over now. More tentatively, experts, such as those from the Children's Bureau, began to tell women how to be expert homemakers and even how to be good mothers. Americans were developing doubts about whether what had worked for a previous generation would work for them. These doubts fueled the satiric modernism of Sinclair Lewis's Babbitt, *as well as the more sinister reactions of the Ku Klux Klan.*

The assumption that American life meant unending growth, expansion, and prosperity came into question during the Great Depression of the 1930s. As can be seen in Studs Terkel's interviews, everyone was reacting to the same overwhelming set of events, yet the range of experience of the depression was broad. Some people ruminated over lost fortunes on the stock markets; others organized workers; still others drifted from place to place.

World War II helped pull the economy out of the depression. This war focused the American sense of mission rather than eroding it. Yet here, too, civil liberties were violated on a massive scale for Japanese-Americans, and racial prejudice remained a painful issue, sometimes confronted, more often avoided or ignored as the reading on the black baseball leagues suggests. Americans followed the course of the war not only with concern for "the boys" overseas but also with pride in the nation's role in the world. Ernie Pyle's widely read accounts never suggested that these men had died in vain.

19 | *Working Women in New York*

Jacob Riis (1849–1914) emigrated to New York City from Denmark in 1870. As a journalist and reformer, he succeeded in effecting substantial housing reform in the city. His How the Other Half Lives *(1901), from which this reading is taken, is a classic of Progressive era "muckraking," or what would now be called "investigative reporting." In* The Pilgrim's Progress, *the seventeenth-century Puritan parable by John Bunyan, the "Man with the Muck Rake" is so busy looking down that he misses the heaven above him. President Theodore Roosevelt—although a Progressive himself—applied this image to the journalists of his era who specialized in criticizing American institutions. The name, intended to be derisive, not only stuck but became a badge of honor.* How the Other Half Lives, *similar to modern investigative journalism, was accompanied by a set of now-classic photographs that have helped to fix permanently our image of the industrial city of the late nineteenth and early twentieth centuries. In the following selection, Riis discusses the plight of working women.*

Six months have not passed since at a great public meeting in this city, the Working Women's Society reported: "It is a known fact that men's wages cannot fall below a limit upon which they can exist, but woman's wages have no limit, since the paths of shame are always open to her. It is simply impossible for any woman to live without assistance on the low salary a saleswoman earns, without depriving herself of real necessities. . . . It is inevitable that they must in many instances resort to evil." It was only a few brief weeks before that verdict was uttered, that the community was shocked by the story of a gentle and refined woman who, left in direst poverty to earn her own living alone among strangers, threw herself from her attic window, preferring death to dishonor. "I would have done any honest work, even to scrubbing," she wrote, drenched and starving, after a vain search for work in a driving storm. She had tramped the streets for weeks on her weary errand, and the only living wages that were offered her were the wages of sin. The ink was not dry upon her letter before a woman in an East Side tene-

From How the Other Half Lives *(1905) by Jacob A. Riis. Dover Publications, Inc., 180 Varick Street, New York, 10014. Reprinted by permission.*

ment wrote down her reason for self-murder: "Weakness, sleepless-ness, and yet obliged to work. My strength fails me. Sing at my coffin: 'Where does the soul find a home and rest?'" Her story may be found as one of two typical "cases of despair" in one little church community, in the *City Mission Society's Monthly* for last February. It is a story that has many parallels in the experience of every missionary, every police reporter and every family doctor whose practice is among the poor.

It is estimated that at least one hundred and fifty thousand women and girls earn their own living in New York; but there is reason to be-lieve that this estimate falls far short of the truth when sufficient account is taken of the large number who are not wholly dependent upon their own labor, while contributing by it to the family's earnings. These alone constitute a large class of the women wage-earners, and it is characteris-tic of the situation that the very fact that some need not starve on their wages condemns the rest to that fate. The pay they are willing to accept all have to take. What the "everlasting law of supply and demand," that serves as such a convenient gag for public indignation, has to do with it, one learns from observation all along the road of inquiry into these real woman's wrongs. To take the case of the saleswomen for illus-tration: The investigation of the Working Women's Society disclosed the fact that wages averaging from $2 to $4.50 a week were reduced by excessive fines, "the employers placing a value upon time lost that is not given to services rendered." A little girl, who received two dollars a week, made cash-sales amounting to $167 in a single day, while the receipts of a fifteen-dollar male clerk in the same department footed up only $125; yet for some trivial mistake the girl was fined sixty cents out of her two dollars. The practice prevailed in some stores of dividing the fines between the superintendent and the time-keeper at the end of the year. In one instance they amounted to $3,000, and "the superintendent was heard to charge the time-keeper with not being strict enough in his duties." One of the causes for fine in a certain large store was sitting down. The law requiring seats for saleswomen, generally ignored, was obeyed faithfully in this establishment. The seats were there, but the girls were fined when found using them.

Cash-girls receiving $1.75 a week for work that at certain seasons lengthened her day to sixteen hours were sometimes required to pay for their aprons. A common cause for discharge from stores in which, on account of the oppressive heat and lack of ventilation, "girls fainted day after day and came out looking like corpses," was too long service. No other fault was found with the discharged saleswomen than that they had been long enough in the employ of the firm to justly expect an increase of salary. The reason was even given with brutal frankness, in some instances.

These facts give a slight idea of the hardships and the poor pay of a business that notoriously absorbs child-labor. The girls are sent to the store before they have fairly entered their teens, because the money they can earn there is needed for the support of the family. If the boys will not work, if the street tempts them from home, among the girls at least there must be no drones. To keep their places they are told to lie about their age and to say that they are over fourteen. The precaution is usually superfluous. The Women's Investigating Committee found the majority of the children employed in the stores to be under age, but heard only in a single instance of the truant officers calling. In that case they came once a year and sent the youngest children home; but in a month's time they were all back in their places, and were not again disturbed. When it comes to the factories, where hard bodily labor is added to long hours, stifling rooms, and starvation wages, matters are even worse. The Legislature has passed laws to prevent the employment of children, as it has forbidden saloon-keepers to sell them beer, and it has provided means of enforcing its mandate, so efficient, that the very number of factories in New York is *guessed* at as in the neighborhood of twelve thousand. Up till this summer, a single inspector was charged with the duty of keeping the run of them all, and of seeing to it that the law was respected by the owners.

Sixty cents is put as the average day's earnings of the 150,000, but into this computation enters the stylish "cashier's" two dollars a day, as well as the thirty cents of the poor little girl who pulls threads in an East Side factory, and, if anything, the average is probably too high. Such as it is, however, it represents board, rent, clothing, and "pleasure" to this army of workers. Here is the case of a woman employed in the manufacturing department of a Broadway house. It stands for a hundred like her own. She averages three dollars a week. Pays $1.50 for her room; for breakfast she has a cup of coffee; lunch she cannot afford. One meal a day is her allowance. This woman is young, she is pretty. She has "the world before her." Is it anything less than a miracle if she is guilty of nothing worse than the "early and improvident marriage," against which moralists exclaim as one of the prolific causes of the distress of the poor? Almost any door might seem to offer welcome escape from such slavery as this. "I feel so much healthier since I got three square meals a day," said a lodger in one of the Girls' Homes. Two young sewing-girls came in seeking domestic service, so that they might get enough to eat. They had been only half-fed for some time, and starvation had driven them to the one door at which the pride of the American-born girl will not permit her to knock, though poverty be the price of her independence.

The tenement and the competition of public institutions and farmers' wives and daughters, have done the tyrant shirt to death, but they have not bettered the lot of the needle-women. The sweater of the East Side has appropriated the flannel shirt. He turns them out to-day at forty-five cents a dozen, paying his Jewish workers from twety to thirty-five cents. One of these testified before the State Board of Arbitration, during the shirtmakers' strike, that she worked eleven hours in the shop and four at home, and had never in the best of times made over six dollars a week. Another stated that she worked from 4 o'clock in the morning to 11 at night. These girls had to find their own thread and pay for their own machines out of their wages. The white shirt has gone to the public and private institutions that shelter large numbers of young girls, and to the country. There are not half as many shirtmakers in New York to-day as only a few years ago, and some of the largest firms have closed their city shops. The same is true of the manufacturers of underwear. One large Broadway firm has nearly all its work done by farmers' girls in Maine, who think themselves well off if they can earn two or three dollars a week to pay for a Sunday silk, or the wedding outfit, little dreaming of the part they are playing in starving their city sisters. Literally, they sew "with double thread, a shroud as well as a shirt." Their pin-money sets the rate of wages for thousands of poor sewing-girls in New York. The average earnings of the worker on underwear to-day do not exceed the three dollars which her competitor among the Eastern hills is willing to accept as the price of her play. The shirtmaker's pay is better only because the very finest custom work is all there is left for her to do.

Calico wrappers at a dollar and a half a dozen—the very expert sewers able to make from eight to ten, the common run five or six—neckties at from 25 to 75 cents a dozen, with a dozen as a good day's work, are specimens of women's wages. And yet people persist in wondering at the poor quality of work done in the tenements! Italian cheap labor has come of late also to possess this poor field, with the sweater in its train. There is scarce a branch of woman's work outside of the home in which wages, long since at low-water mark, have not fallen to the point of actual starvation. A case was brought to my notice recently by a woman doctor, whose heart as well as her life-work is with the poor, of a widow with two little children she found at work in an East Side attic, making paper-bags. Her father, she told the doctor, had made good wages at it; but she received only five cents for six hundred of the little three-cornered bags, and her fingers had to be very swift and handle the paste-brush very deftly to bring her earnings up to twenty-five and thirty cents a day. She paid four dollars a month for her room. The rest went to buy food for herself and the children. The physician's purse, rather than her skill, had healing for their complaint.

I have aimed to set down a few dry facts merely. They carry their own comment. Back of the shop with its weary, grinding toil—the home in the tenement, of which it was said in a report of the State Labor Bureau: "Decency and womanly reserve cannot be maintained there—what wonder so many fall away from virtue?" Of the outlook, what? Last Christmas Eve my business took me to an obscure street among the West Side tenements. An old woman had just fallen on the door-step, stricken with paralysis. The doctor said she would never again move her right hand or foot. The whole side was dead. By her bedside, in their cheerless room, sat the patient's aged sister, a hopeless cripple, in dumb despair. Forty years ago the sisters had come, five in number then, with their mother, from the North of Ireland to make their home and earn a living among strangers. They were lace embroiderers and found work easily at good wages. All the rest had died as the years went by. The two remained and, firmly resolved to lead an honest life, worked on though wages fell and fell as age and toil stiffened their once nimble fingers and dimmed their sight. Then one of them dropped out, her hands palsied and her courage gone. Still the other toiled on, resting neither by night nor by day, that the sister might not want. Now that she too had been stricken, as she was going to the store for the work that was to keep them through the holidays, the battle was over at last. There was before them starvation, or the poor-house. And the proud spirits of the sisters, helpless now, quailed at the outlook.

These were old, with life behind them. For them nothing was left but to sit in the shadow and wait. But of the thousands, who are travelling the road they trod to the end, with the hot blood of youth in their veins, with the love of life and of the beautiful world to which not even sixty cents a day can shut their eyes—who is to blame if their feet find the paths of shame that are "always open to them?" The very paths that have effaced the saving "limit," and to which it is declared to be "inevitable that they must in many instances resort." Let the moralist answer. Let the wise economist apply his rule of supply and demand, and let the answer be heard in this city of a thousand charities where justice goes begging.

To the everlasting credit of New York's working-girl let it be said that, rough though her road be, all but hopeless her battle with life, only in the rarest instances does she go astray. As a class she is brave, virtuous, and true. New York's army of profligate women is not, as in some foreign cities, recruited from her ranks. She is as plucky as she is proud. That "American girls never whimper" became a proverb long ago, and she accepts her lot uncomplainingly, doing the best she can and holding her cherished independence cheap at the cost of a meal, or of half her daily ration, if need be. The home in the tenement and the traditions of her childhood have neither trained her to luxury nor predisposed her in favor of domestic labor in preference to the shop. So, to the world she presents a cheerful, uncomplaining front that sometimes deceives it. Her courage will not be without its reward. Slowly, as the conviction is thrust upon society that woman's work must enter more and more into its planning, a better day is dawning. The organization of working girls' clubs, unions, and societies with a community of interests, despite the obstacles to such a movement, bears testimony to it, as to the devotion of the unselfish women who have made their poorer sister's cause their own, and will yet wring from an unfair world the justice too long denied her.

20 | The Shame of Philadelphia

The Shame of the Cities (1904) was perhaps the most influential single piece of muckraking. It created reform movements in nearly every city it discussed— even the most shameful of all, Philadelphia. Steffens mixed a realistic description of events with the moral righteousness that the public cherished. Rather than simply blaming corrupt politicians, he stressed the links between supposedly respectable business and political corruption, showing how, in city after city, the "best" elements in society were tied to the "worst." Steffens himself believed that exposure would not force change and that expressions of moral indignation would do little more than ease people's consciences. Despite his doubts, Steffens's writings contributed greatly to the Progressive Movement's partial success in improving municipal government.

PHILADELPHIA: CORRUPT AND CONTENTED
(July, 1903)

Other American cities, no matter how bad their own condition may be, all point with scorn to Philadelphia as worse—"the worst-governed city in the country." St. Louis, Minneapolis, Pittsburg submit with some patience to the jibes of any other community; the most friendly suggestion from Philadelphia is rejected with contempt. The Philadelphians are "supine," "asleep"; hopelessly ring-ruled, they are "complacent." "Politically benighted," Philadelphia is supposed to have no light to throw upon a state of things that is almost universal.

This is not fair. Philadelphia is, indeed, corrupt; but it is not without significance. Every city and town in the country can learn something from the typical political experience of this great representative city. New York is excused for many of its ills because it is the metropolis, Chicago because of its forced development; Philadelphia is our "third largest" city and its growth has been gradual and natural. Immigration has been blamed for our municipal conditions; Philadelphia, with 47 per cent, of its population native-born of native-born parents, is the most

From The Shame of the Cities *(1904) by Lincoln Steffens. Reprinted by Hill and Wang, New York, 1957, pp. 134–141.*

American of our greater cities. It is "good," too, and intelligent. I don't know just how to measure the intelligence of a community, but a Pennsylvania college professor who declared to me his belief in education for the masses as a way out of political corruption, himself justified the "rake-off" of preferred contractors on public works on the ground of a "fair business profit." Another plea we have made is that we are too busy to attend to public business, and we have promised, when we come to wealth and leisure, to do better. Philadelphia has long enjoyed great and widely distributed prosperity; it is the city of homes; there is a dwelling house for every five persons,—men, women, and children,— of the population; and the people give one a sense of more leisure and repose than any community I ever dwelt in. Some Philadelphians account for their political state on the ground of their ease and comfort. There is another class of optimists whose hope is in an "aristocracy" that is to come by and by; Philadelphia is surer that it has a "real aristocracy" than any other place in the world, but its aristocrats, with few exceptions, are in the ring, with it, or of no political use. Then we hear that we are a young people and that when we are older and "have traditions," like some of the old countries, we also will be honest. Philadelphia is one of the oldest of our cities and treasures for us scenes and relics of some of the noblest traditions of "our fair land." Yet I was told how once, "for a joke," a party of boodlers counted out the "divvy" of their graft in unison with the ancient chime of Independence Hall.

Philadelphia is representative. This very "joke," told, as it was, with a laugh, is typical. All our municipal governments are more or less bad, and all our people are optimists. Philadelphia is simply the most corrupt and the most contented. Minneapolis had cleaned up, Pittsburg has tried to, New York fights every other election, Chicago fights all the time. Even St. Louis has begun to stir (since the elections are over), and at the worst was only shameless. Philadelphia is proud; good people there defend corruption and boast of their machine. My college professor, with his philosophic view of "rake-offs," is one Philadelphia type. Another is the man, who, driven to bay with his local pride, says: "At least you must admit that our machine is the best you have ever seen."

Disgraceful? Other cities say so. But I say that if Philadelphia is a disgrace, it is a disgrace not to itself alone, nor to Pennsylvania, but to the United States and to American character. For this great city, so highly representative in other respects, is not behind in political experience, but ahead, with New York. Philadelphia is a city that has had its reforms. Having passed through all the typical stages of corruption, Philadelphia reached the period of miscellaneous loot with a boss for chief thief, under James McManes and the Gas Ring 'way back in the late sixties and seventies. This is the Tweed stage of corruption from which St. Louis, for example, is just emerging. Philadelphia, in two inspiring popular revolts, attacked the Gas Ring, broke it, and in 1885 achieved that dream of American cities—a good charter. The present condition of Philadelphia, therefore, is not that which precedes, but that which follows reform, and in this distinction lies its startling general significance. What has happened since the Bullitt Law or charter went into effect in Philadelphia may happen in any American city "after reform is over."

For reform with us is usually revolt, not government, and is soon over. Our people do not seek, they avoid self-rule, and "reforms" are spasmodic efforts to punish bad rulers and get somebody that will give us good government or something that will make it. A self-acting form of government is an ancient superstition. We are an inventive people, and we all think that we shall devise some day a legal machine that will turn out good government automatically. The Philadelphians have treasured this belief longer than the rest of us and have tried it more often. Throughout their history they have sought this wonderful charter and they thought they had it when they got the Bullitt Law, which concentrates in the mayor ample power, executive and political, and complete responsibility. Moreover, it calls for very little thought and action on the part of the people. All they expected to have to do when the Bullitt Law went into effect was to elect as mayor a good business man, who, with his probity and common sense, would give them that good business administration which is the ideal of many reformers.

The Bullitt Law went into effect in 1887. A committee of twelve—four men from the Union League, four from business organizations, and four from the bosses—picked out the first man to run under it on the Republican ticket, Edwin H. Fitler, an able, upright business man, and he was elected. Strange to say, his administration was satisfactory to the citizens, who speak well of it to this day, and to the politicians also; Boss McManes (the ring was broken, not the boss) took to the next national convention from Philadelphia a delegation solid for Fitler for President of the United States. It was a farce, but it pleased Mr. Fitler, so Matthew S. Quay, the State boss, let him have a complimentary vote on the first ballot. The politicians "fooled" Mr. Fitler, and they "fooled" also the next business mayor, Edwin S. Stuart, likewise a most estimable gentleman. Under these two administrations the foundation was laid for the present government of Philadelphia, the corruption to which Philadelphians seemed so reconciled, and the machine which is "at least the best you have ever seen."

The Philadelphia machine isn't the best. It isn't sound, and I doubt if it would stand in New York or Chicago. The enduring strength of the typical American political machine is that it is a natural growth—a sucker, but deep-rooted in the people. The New Yorkers vote for Tammany Hall. The Philadelphians do not vote; they are disfranchised, and their disfranchisement is one anchor of the foundation of the Philadelphia organization.

This is no figure of speech. The honest citizens of Philadelphia have no more rights at the polls than the negroes down South. Nor do they fight very hard for this basic privilege. You can arouse their Republican ire by talking about the black Republican votes lost in the Southern States by white Democratic intimidation, but if you remind the average Philadelphian that he is in the same position, he will look startled, then say, "That's so, that's literally true, only I never thought of it in just that way." And it is literally true.

The machine controls the whole process of voting, and practices fraud at every stage. The assessor's list is the voting list, and the asessor is the machine's man. "The assessor of a division kept a disorderly house; he padded his lists with fraudulent names registered from his house; two of these names were used by election officers. . . . The constable of the division kept a disreputable house; a policeman was assessed as living there. . . . The election was held in the disorderly house maintained by the assessor. . . . The man named as judge had a criminal charge for a life offense pending against him. . . . Two hundred and fifty-two votes were returned in a division that had less than one hundred legal votes within its boundaries." These extracts from a report of the Municipal League suggest the election methods. The assessor pads the list with the names of dead dogs, children, and non-existent persons. One newspaper printed the picture of a dog, another that of a little four-year-old negro boy, down on such a list. A ring orator in a speech resenting sneers at his ward as "low down" reminded his hearers that that was the ward of Independence Hall, and naming over signers of the Declaration of Independence, he closed his highest flight of eloquence with the statement that "these men, the fathers of American liberty, voted down here once. And," he added, with a catching grin, "they vote here yet." Rudolph Blankenburg, a persistent fighter for the right and the use of the right to vote (and, by the way, an immigrant), sent out just before one election a registered letter to each voter on the rolls of a certain selected division. Sixty-three per cent. were returned marked "not at," "removed," "deceased," etc. From one four-story house where forty-four voters were addressed, eighteen letters came back undelivered; from another of forty-eight voters, came back forty-one letters; from another sixty-one out of sixty-two; from another, forty-four out of forty-seven. Six houses in one division were assessed at one hundred and seventy-two voters, more than the votes cast in the previous election in any one of two hundred entire divisions.

The repeating is done boldly, for the machine controls the election officers, often choosing them from among the fraudulent names; and when no one appears to serve, assigning the heeler ready for the expected vacancy. The police are forbidden by law to stand within thirty feet of the polls, but they are at the box and they are there to see that the machine's orders are obeyed and that repeaters whom they help to furnish are permitted to vote without "intimidation" on the names they, the police, have supplied. The editor of an anti-machine paper who was looking about for himself once told me that a ward leader who knew him well asked him into a polling place. "I'll show you how it's done," he said, and he had the repeaters go round and round voting again and again on the names handed them on slips. "But," as the editor said, "that isn't the way it's done." The repeaters go from one polling place to another, voting on slips, and on their return rounds change coats, hats, etc. The business proceeds with very few hitches; there is more jesting than fighting. Violence in the past has had its effect; and is not often necessary nowadays, but if it is needed the police are there to apply it. Several citizens told me that they had seen the police help to beat citizens or elections officers who were trying to do their duty, then arrest the victim; and Mr. Clinton Rogers Woodruff, the executive counsel of the Municipal League, has published a booklet of such cases. But an official statement of the case is at hand in an announcement by John Weaver, the new machine mayor of Philadelphia, that he is going to keep the police out of politics and away from the polls. "I shall see," he added, "that every voter enjoys the full right of suffrage and that ballots may be placed in the ballot box without fear of intimidation."

But many Philadelphians do not try to vote. They leave everything to the machine, and the machine casts their ballots for them. It is estimated that 150,000 voters did not go to the polls at the last election. Yet the machine rolled up a majority of 130,000 for Weaver, with a fraudulent vote estimated all the way from forty to eighty thousand, and this in a campaign so machine-made that it was called "no contest." Francis Fisher Kane, the Democrat, got 32,000 votes out of some 204,000. "What is the use of voting?" these stay-at-homes ask. A friend of mine told me he was on the lists in the three wards in which he had successively dwelt. He votes personally in none, but the leader of his present ward tells him how he has been voted.

21 | *Honest and Dishonest Graft*

Reformers such as Lincoln Steffens blamed most of the ills of large cities on the political organizations or "machines" that often ran them. In New York City, the most powerful machine was the Democratic Party's "Tammany Hall." The following selection, by Tammany politician George Washington Plunkitt (1843–1924), offers a view of the political machine that differs from that presented by Steffens.

Plunkitt's reflections of his political experience were published, edited, and perhaps embroidered upon by newspaperman William L. Riordon in 1905. Plunkitt's view of American politics directly contravened the opinions typical of the Progressive Era. While the thrust of reformers, through civil service laws and other programs, was to limit the power of political parties and their machines, Plunkitt argued that parties and political machines performed vital functions. "Honest graft" was, he said, the oil that kept the machines, and government, in motion.

HONEST GRAFT AND DISHONEST GRAFT

"Everybody is talkin' these days about Tammany men growin' rich on graft, but nobody thinks of drawin' the distinction between honest graft and dishonest graft. There's all the difference in the world between the two. Yes, many of our men have grown rich in politics. I have myself. I've made a big fortune out of the game, and I'm gettin' richer every day, but I've not gone in for dishonest graft—blackmailin' gamblers, saloon-keepers, disorderly people, etc.—and neither has any of the men who have made big fortunes in politics.

"There's an honest graft, and I'm an example of how it works. I might sum up the whole thing by sayin': 'I seen my opportunities and I took 'em.'

"Just let me explain by examples. My party's in power in the city, and it's goin' to undertake a lot of public improvements. Well, I'm tipped off, say, that they're going to lay out a new park at a certain place.

William L. Riordon, Plunkitt of Tammany Hall. *(New York, McClure, Phillips, and Company, 1905), pp. 3–10, 19–28, 46–55.*

"I see my opportunity and I take it. I go to that place and I buy up all the land I can in the neighborhood. Then the board of this or that makes its plan public, and there is a rush to get my land, which nobody cared particular for before.

"Ain't it perfectly honest to charge a good price and make a profit on my investment and foresight? Of course, it is. Well, that's honest graft.

"Or, supposin' it's a new bridge they're goin' to build. I get tipped off and I buy as much property as I can that has to be taken for approaches. I sell at my own price later on and drop some more money in the bank.

"Wouldn't you? It's just like lookin' ahead in Wall Street or in the coffee or cotton market. It's honest graft, and I'm lookin' for it every day in the year. I will tell you frankly that I've got a good lot of it, too.

"I'll tell you of one case. They were goin' to fix up a big park, no matter where. I got on to it, and went lookin' about for land in that neighborhood.

"I could get nothin' at a bargain but a big piece of swamp, but I took it fast enough and held on to it. What turned out was just what I counted on. They couldn't make the park complete without Plunkitt's swamp, and they had to pay a good price for it. Anything dishonest in that?

"Up in the watershed I made some money, too. I bought up several bits of land there some years ago and made a pretty good guess that they would be bought up for water purposes later by the city.

"Somehow, I always guessed about right, and shouldn't I enjoy the profit of my foresight? It was rather amusin' when the condemnation commissioners came along and found piece after piece of the land in the name of George Plunkitt of the Fifteenth Assembly District, New York City. They wondered how I knew just what to buy. The answer is—I seen my opportunity and I took it. I haven't confined myself to land; anything that pays is in my line.

"For instance, the city is repavin' a street and has several hundred thousand old granite blocks to sell. I am on hand to buy, and I know just what they are worth.

"How? Never mind that. I had a sort of monopoly of this business for a while, but once a newspaper tried to do me. It got some outside men to come over from Brooklyn and New Jersey to bid against me.

"Was I done? Not much. I went to each of the men and said: 'How many of these 250,000 stones do you want?' One said 20,000, and another wanted 15,000, and another wanted 10,000. I said: 'All right, let me bid for the lot, and I'll give each of you all you want for nothin'.

"They agreed, of course. Then the auctioneer yelled: 'How much am I bid for these 250,000 fine pavin' stones?'

" 'Two dollars and fifty cents,' says I.

" 'Two dollars and fifty cents!' screamed the auctioneer. 'Oh, that's a joke! Give me a real bid.'

"He found the bid was real enough. My rivals stood silent. I got the lot for $2.50 and gave them their share. That's how the attempt to do Plunkitt ended, and that's how all such attempts end.

'I've told you how I got rich by honest graft. Now, let me tell you that most politicians who are accused of robbin' the city get rich the same way.

"They didn't steal a dollar from the city treasury. They just seen their opportunities and took them. That is why, when a reform administration comes in and spends a half million dollars in tryin' to find the public robberies they talked about in the campaign, they don't find them.

"The books are always all right. The money in the city treasury is all right. Everything is all right. All they can show is that the Tammany heads of departments looked after their friends, within the law, and gave them what opportunities they could to make honest graft. Now, let me tell you that's never goin' to hurt Tammany with the people. Every good man looks after his friends, and any man who doesn't isn't likely to be popular. If I have a good thing to hand out in private life, I give it to a friend. Why shouldn't I do the same in public life?

"Another kind of honest graft. Tammany has raised a good many salaries. There was an awful howl by the reformers, but don't you know that Tammany gains ten votes for every one it lost by salary raisin'?

"The Wall Street banker thinks it shameful to raise a department clerk's salary from $1500 to $1800 a year, but every man who draws a salary himself says: 'That's all right. I wish it was me.' And he feels very much like votin' the Tammany ticket on election day, just out of sympathy.

"Tammany was beat in 1901 because the people were deceived into believin' that it worked dishonest graft. They didn't draw a distinction between dishonest and honest graft, but they saw that some Tammany men grew rich, and supposed they had been robbin' the city treasury or levyin' blackmail on disorderly houses, or workin' in with the gamblers and lawbreakers.

"As a matter of policy, if nothing else, why should the Tammany leaders go into such dirty business, when there is so much honest graft lyin' around when they are in power? Did you ever consider that?

"Now, in conclusion, I want to say that I don't own a dishonest dollar. If my worst enemy was given the job of writin' my epitaph when I'm gone, he couldn't do more than write:

"'George W. Plunkitt. He Seen His Opportunities, and He Took 'Em.'"

THE CURSE OF CIVIL SERVICE REFORM

"This civil service law is the biggest fraud of the age. It is the curse of the nation. There can't be no real patriotism while is lasts. How are you goin' to interest our young men in their country if you have no offices

to give them when they work for their party? Just look at things in this
city to-day. There are ten thousand good offices, but we can't get at
more than a few hundred of them. How are we goin' to provide for the
thousands of men who worked for the Tammany ticket? It can't be
done. These men were full of patriotism a short time ago. They expected
to be servin' their city, but when we tell them that we can't place them,
do you think their patriotism is goin' to last? Not much. They say:
'What's the use of workin' for your country anyhow? There's nothin'
in the game.' And what can they do? I don't know, but I'll tell you what
I do know. I know more than one young man in past years who worked
for the ticket and was just overflowin' with patriotism, but when he was
knocked out by the civil service humbug he got to hate his country and
became an Anarchist.

"This ain't no exaggeration. I have good reason for sayin' that most
of the Anarchists in this city to-day are men who ran up against civil
service examinations. Isn't it enough to make a man sour on his country
when he wants to serve it and won't be allowed unless he answers a lot
of fool questions about the number of cubic inches of water in the Atlantic and the quality of sand in the Sahara desert? There was once a bright
young man in my district who tackled one of these examinations. The
next I heard of him he had settled down in Herr Most's saloon smokin'
and drinkin' beer and talkin' socialism all day. Before that time he had
never drank anything but whisky. I knew what was comin' when a
young Irishman drops whisky and takes to beer and long pipes in a
German saloon. That young man is to-day one of the wildest Anarchists
in town. And just to think! He might be a patriot but for that cussed
civil service.

Say, did you hear about the Civil Service Reform Association kickin'
because the tax commissioners want to put their fifty-five deputies on
the exempt list, and fire the outfit left to them by Low? That's civil service for you. Just think! Fifty-five Republicans and mugwumps holdin'
$3000 and $4000 and $5000 jobs in the tax department when 1555 good
Tammany men are ready and willin' to take their places! It's an outrage!
What did the people mean when they voted for Tammany? What is representative government, anyhow? Is it all a fake that this is a government of the people, by the people and for the people? If it isn't a fake,
then why isn't the people's voice obeyed and Tammany men put in all
the offices?

"When the people elected Tammany, they knew just what they
were doin'. We didn't put up any false pretences. We didn't go in for
humbug civil service and all that rot. We stood as we have always stood,
for rewardin' the men that won the victory. They call that the spoils
system. All right; Tammany is for the spoils system, and when we go
in we fire every anti-Tammany man from office that can be fired under
the law. It's an elastic sort of law and you can bet it will be stretched to
the limit. Of course the Republican State Civil Service Board will stand

in the way of our local Civil Service Commission all it can; but say!—
suppose we carry the State some time won't we fire the up-State Board
all right? Or we'll make it work in harmony with the local board, and
that means that Tammany will get everything in sight. I know that the
civil service humbug is stuck into the constitution, too, but, as Tim
Campbell said: 'What's the constitution among friends?'

"Say, the people's voice is smothered by the cursed civil service
law; it is the root of all evil in our government. You hear of this thing
or that thing goin' wrong in the nation, the State or the city. Look down
beneath the surface and you can trace everything wrong to civil service.
I have studied the subject and I know. The civil service humbug is un-
derminin' our institutions and if a halt ain't called soon this great republic will tumble down like a Park-avenue house when they were buildin'
the subway, and on its ruins will rise another Russian government.

"This is an awful serious proposition. Free silver and the tariff and
imperialism and the Panama Canal are triflin' issues when compared to
it. We could worry along without any of these things, but civil service
is sappin' the foundation of the whole shootin' match. Let me argue it
out for you. I ain't up on sillygisms, but I can give you some arguments
that nobody can answer.

"First this great and glorious country was built up by political parties; second, parties can't hold together if their workers don't get the
offices when they win; third, if the parties go to pieces, the government
they built up must go to pieces, too; fourth, then there'll be h___ to pay.

"Could anything be clearer than that? Say, honest now; can you
answer that argument? Of course you won't deny that the government
was built up by the great parties. That's history, and you can't go back
of the returns. As to my second proposition, you can't deny that either.
When parties can't get offices, they'll bust. They ain't far from the
bustin' point now, with all this civil service business keepin' most of the
good things from them. How are you goin' to keep up patriotism if this
thing goes on? You can't do it. Let me tell you that patriotism has been
dying out fast for the last twenty years. Before then when a party won,
its workers got everything in sight. That was somethin' to make a man
patriotic. Now, when a party wins and its men come forward and ask
for their reward, the reply is, 'Nothin' doin', unless you can answer a
list of questions about Egyptian mummies and how many years it will
take for a bird to wear out a mass of iron as big as the earth by steppin'
on it once in a century?'

"I have studied politics and men for forty-five years, and I see how
things are driftin'. Sad indeed is the change that has come over the
young men, even in my district, where I try to keep up the fire of patriotism by gettin' a lot of jobs for my constituents, whether Tammany is in
or out. The boys and men don't get excited any more when they see a
United States flag or hear the 'Star Spangled Banner.' They don't care
no more for fire-crackers on the Fourth of July. And why should they?

What is there in it for them? They know that no matter how hard they work for their country in a campaign, the jobs will go to fellows who can tell about the mummies and the bird steppin' on the iron. Are you surprised then that the young men of the country are beginnin' to look coldly on the flag and don't care to put up a nickel for fire-crackers?

"Say, let me tell of one case. After the battle of San Juan Hill, the Americans found a dead man with a light complexion, red hair and blue eyes. They could see he wasn't a Spaniard, although he had on a Spanish uniform. Several officers looked him over, and then a private of the Seventy-first Regiment saw him and yelled, 'Good Lord, that's Flaherty.' That man grew up in my district, and he was once the most patriotic American boy on the West Side. He couldn't see a flag without yellin' himself hoarse.

Now, how did he come to be lying dead with a Spanish uniform on? I found out all about it, and I'll vouch for the story. Well, in the municipal campaign of 1897, that young man, chockful of patriotism, worked day and night for the Tammany ticket. Tammany won, and the young man determined to devote his life to the service of the city. He picked out a place that would suit him, and sent in his application to the head of department. He got a reply that he must take a civil service examination to get the place. He didn't know what these examinations were, so he went, all lighthearted, to the Civil Service Board. He read the questions about the mummies, the bird on the iron, and all the other fool questions—and he left that office an enemy of the country that he had loved so well. The mummies and the bird blasted his patriotism. He went to Cuba, enlisted in the Spanish army at the breakin' out of the war, and died fightin' his country.

That is but one victim of the infamous civil service. If that young man had not run up against the civil examination, but had been allowed to serve his country as he wished, he would be in a good office today, drawin' a good salary. Ah, how many young men have had their patriotism blasted in the same way!

Now, what is goin' to happen when civil service crushes out patriotism? Only one thing can happen: the republic will go to pieces. Then a czar or a sultan will turn up, which brings me to the fourthly of my argument—that is, there will be h___ to pay. And that ain't no lie.

/   /   /

TO HOLD YOUR DISTRICT—STUDY HUMAN NATURE AND ACT ACCORDIN'

"There's only one way to hold a district; you must study human nature and act accordin'. You can't study human nature in books. Books is a hindrance more than anything else. If you have been to college, so much the worse for you. You'll have to unlearn all you learned before you can get right down to human nature, and unlearnin' takes a lot of time. Some men can never forget what they learned at college. Such men may get to be district leaders by a fluke, but they never last.

"To learn real human nature you have to go among the people, see them and be seen. I know every man, woman, and child in the Fifteenth District, except them that's been born this summer—and I know some of them, too. I know what they like and what they don't like, what they are strong at and what they are weak in, and I reach them by approachin' at the right side.

"For instance, here's how I gather in the young men. I hear of a young feller that's proud of his voice, thinks that he can sing fine. I ask him to come around to Washington Hall and join our Glee Club. He comes and sings, and he's a follower of Plunkitt for life. Another young feller gains a reputation as a base-ball player in a vacant lot. I bring him into our base-ball club. That fixes him. You'll find him workin' for my ticket at the polls next election day. Then there's the feller that likes rowin' on the river, the young feller that makes a name as a waltzer on his block, the young feller that's handy with his dukes—I rope them all in by givin' them opportunities to show themselves off. I don't trouble them with political arguments. I just study human nature and act accordin'.

"But you may say this game won't work with the high-toned fellers, the fellers that go through college and then join the Citizens' Union. Of course it wouldn't work. I have a special treatment for them. I ain't like the patent medicine man that gives the same medicine for all diseases. The Citizens' Union kind of a young man! I love him! He's the daintiest morsel of the lot, and he don't often escape me.

"Before telling you how I catch him, let me mention that before the election last year, the Citizens' Union said they had four hundred or five hundred enrolled voters in my district. They had a lovely headquarters, too, beautiful roll-top desks and the cutest rugs in the world. If I was accused of havin' contributed to fix up the nest for them, I wouldn't deny it under oath. What do I mean by that? Never mind. You can guess from the sequel, if you're sharp.

"Well, election day came. The Citizens' Union's candidate for Senator, who ran against me, just polled five votes in the district, while I polled something more than 14,000 votes. What became of the 400 or 500 Citizens' Union enrolled voters in my district? Some people guessed that many of them were good Plunkitt men all along and worked with the Cits just to bring them into the Plunkitt camp by election day. You can guess that way, too, if you want to. I never contradict stories about me, especially in hot weather. I just call your attention to the fact that on last election day 395 Citizens' Union enrolled voters in my district were missin' and unaccounted for.

"I tell you frankly, though, how I have captured some of the Cit-

izens' Union's young men. I have a plan that never fails. I watch the
City Record to see when there's civil service examinations for good
things. Then I take my young Cit in hand, tell him all about the good
thing and get him worked up till he goes and takes an examination. I
don't bother about him any more. It's a cinch that he comes back to me
in a few days and asks to join Tammany Hall. Come over to Washington
Hall some night and I'll show you a list of names on our rolls marked
'C. S.' which means, 'bucked up against civil service.'

"As to the older voters, I reach them, too. No, I don't send them
campaign literature. That's rot. People can get all the political stuff they
want to read—and a good deal more, too—in the papers. Who reads
speeches, nowadays, anyhow? It's bad enough to listen to them. You
ain't goin' to gain any votes by stuffin' the letter boxes with campaign
documents. Like as not you'll lose votes, for there's nothin' a man hates
more than to hear the letter-carrier ring his bell and go to the letter-box
expectin' to find a letter he was lookin' for, and find only a lot of printed
politics. I met a man this very mornin' who told me he voted the Democratic State ticket last year just because the Republicans kept crammin'
his letter-box with campaign documents.

"What tells in holdin' your grip on your district is to go right down
among the poor families and help them in the different ways they need
help. I've got a regular system for this. If there's a fire in Ninth, Tenth,
or Eleventh Avenue, for example, any hour of the day or night, I'm
usually there with some of my election district captains as soon as the
fire-engines. If a family is burned out I don't ask whether they are Republicans or Democrats, and I don't refer them to the Charity Organization Society, which would investigate their case in a month or two and
decide they were worthy of help about the time they are dead from
starvation. I just get quarters for them, buy clothes for them if their
clothes were burned up, and fix them up till they get things runnin'
again. It's philanthropy, but it's politics, too—mighty good politics.
Who can tell how many votes one of the fires bring me? The poor are
the most grateful people in the world, and, let me tell you, they have
more friends in their neighborhoods than the rich have in theirs.

"If there's a family in my district in want I know it before the charitable societies do, and me and my men are first on the ground. I have
a special corps to look up such cases. The consequence is that the poor
look up to George W. Plunkitt as a father, come to him in trouble—and
don't forget him on election day.

"Another thing, I can always get a job for a deservin' man. I make
it a point to keep on the track of jobs, and it seldom happens that I don't
have a few up my sleeve ready for use. I know every big employer in
the district and in the whole city, for that matter, and they ain't in the
habit of sayin' no to me when I ask them for a job.

"And the children—the little roses of the district! Do I forget them?
Oh, no! They know me, every one of them, and they know that a sight

of Uncle George and candy means the same thing. Some of them are the best kind of vote-getters. I'll tell you a case. Last year a little Eleventh Avenue rosebud whose father is a Republican, caught hold of his whiskers on election day and said she wouldn't let go till he'd promise to vote for me. And she didn't.

ON THE SHAME OF THE CITIES

I've been readin' a book by Lincoln Steffens on *The Shame of the Cities.* Steffens means well but, like all reformers, he don't know how to make distinctions. He can't see no difference between honest graft and dishonest graft and, consequent, he gets things all mixed up. There's the biggest kind of a difference between political looters and politicians who make a fortune out of politics by keepin' their eyes wide open. The looter goes in for himself alone without considerin' his organization or his city. The politician looks after his own interests, the organization's interests, and the city's interests all at the same time. See the distinction? For instance, I ain't no looter. The looter hogs it. I never hogged. I made my pile in politics, but, at the same time, I served the organization and got more big improvements for New York City than any other livin' man. And I never monkeyed with the penal code.

22 | Conditions at the Slaughterhouse

The publication of Upton Sinclair's The Jungle *in 1906 was one of the major events of the Progressive Era. Intended as a plea for socialism, the book was read by a shocked public as an expose not of the economic system but of the sanitary conditions in Chicago meatpacking houses. Sinclair himself said that he had taken aim at America's heart and hit instead its stomach. Evidently the empty stomach of the book's immigrant workers Jurgis and Ona mattered less to the public than its own, which it feared might be filled with packinghouse wastes that were mixed with food. Sinclair's book and President Theodore Roosevelt's leadership persuaded Congress to enact the nation's first national pure food and drug and meat inspection laws.*

"They don't waste anything here," said the guide, and then he laughed and added a witticism, which he was pleased that his unsophisticated friends should take to be his own: "They use everything about the hog except the squeal." In front of Brown's General Office building there grows a tiny plot of grass, and this, you may learn, is the only bit of green thing in Packingtown; likewise this jest about the hog and his squeal, the stock in trade of all the guides, is the one gleam of humor that you will find there.

/   /   /

Entering one of the Durham buildings, they found a number of other visitors waiting; and before long there came a guide, to escort them through the place. They make a great feature of showing strangers through the packing plants, for it is a good advertisement. But *ponas* Jokubas whispered maliciously that the visitors did not see any more than the packers wanted them to.

They climbed a long series of stairways outside of the building, to the top of its five or six stories. Here was the chute, with its river of hogs, all patiently toiling upward; there was a place for them to rest to cool off, and then through another passageway they went into a room from which there is no returning for hogs.

It was a long, narrow room, with a gallery along it for visitors. At the head there was a great iron wheel, about twenty feet in circumference, with rings here and there along its edge. Upon both sides of this wheel there was a narrow space, into which came the hogs at the end of their journey; in the midst of them stood a great burly Negro, bare-armed and bare-chested. He was resting for the moment, for the wheel had stopped while men were cleaning up. In a minute or two, however, it began slowly to revolve, and then the men upon each side of it sprang to work. They had chains which they fastened about the leg of the nearest hog, and the other end of the chain they hooked into one of the rings upon the wheel. So, as the wheel turned, a hog was suddenly jerked off his feet and borne aloft.

At the same instant the ear was assailed by a most terrifying shriek; the visitors started in alarm, the women turned pale and shrank back. The shriek was followed by another, louder and yet more agonizing— for once started upon that journey, the hog never came back; at the top of the wheel he was shunted off upon a trolley, and went sailing down the room. And meantime another was swung up, and then another, and another, until there was a double line of them, each dangling by a foot and kicking in frenzy—and squealing. The uproar was appalling, perilous to the eardrums; one feared there was too much sound for the room to hold—that the walls must give way or the ceiling crack. There were high squeals and low squeals, grunts, and wails of agony; there would come a momentary lull, and then a fresh outburst, louder than ever, surging up to a deafening climax. It was too much for some of the visitors—the men would look at each other, laughing nervously, and the women would stand with hands clenched, and the blood rushing to their faces, and the tears starting in their eyes.

Meantime, heedless of all these things, the men upon the floor were going about their work. Neither squeals of hogs nor tears of visitors made any difference to them; one by one they hooked up the hogs, and one by one with a swift stroke they slit their throats. There was a long line of hogs, with squeals and lifeblood ebbing away together; until at last each started again, and vanished with a splash into a huge vat of boiling water.

It was all so very businesslike that one watched it fascinated. It was porkmaking by machinery, porkmaking by applied mathematics. And yet somehow the most matter-of-fact person could not help thinking of the hogs;

/ / /

One could not stand and watch very long without becoming philosophical, without beginning to deal in symbols and similes, and to hear the hog squeal of the universe. Was it permitted to believe that there was nowhere upon the earth, or above the earth, a heaven for hogs, where they were requited for all this suffering? Each one of these hogs was a separate creature. Some were white hogs, some were black; some were brown, some were spotted; some were old, some young; some were long and lean, some were monstrous. And each of them had an individuality of his own, a will of his own, a hope and a heart's desire; each was full of self-confidence, of self-importance, and a sense of dignity. And trusting and strong in faith he had gone about his business, the while a black shadow hung over him and a horrid Fate waited in his pathway. Now suddenly it had swooped upon him, and had seized him by the leg. Relentless, remorseless, it was; all his protests, his screams, were nothing to it—it did its cruel will with him, as if his wishes, his feelings, had simply no existence at all; it cut his throat and watched him gasp out his life. And now was one to believe that there was nowhere a god of hogs, to whom this hog personality was precious, to whom these hog squeals and agonies had a meaning? Who would take this hog into his arms and comfort him, reward him for his work well done, and show him the meaning of his sacrifice? Perhaps some glimpse of all this was in the thoughts of our humble-minded Jurgis, as he turned to go on with the rest of the party, and muttered: "*Dieve*—but I'm glad I'm not a hog!"

The carcass hog was scooped out of the vat by machinery, and then it fell to the second floor, passing on the way through a wonderful machine with numerous scrapers, which adjusted themselves to the size and shape of the animal, and sent it out at the other end with nearly all of its bristles removed. It was then again strung up by machinery, and sent upon another trolley ride; this time passing between two lines of men, who sat upon a raised platform, each doing a certain single thing to the carcass as it came to him. One scraped the outside of a leg; another scraped the inside of the same leg. One with a swift stroke cut the throat; another with two swift strokes severed the head, which fell to the floor and vanished through a hole. Another made a slit down the body; a second opened the body wider; a third with a saw cut the breastbone; a fourth loosened the entrails; a fifth pulled them out—and they also slid through a hole in the floor. There were men to scrape each side and men to scrape the back; there were men to clean the carcass inside, to trim it and wash it. Looking down this room, one saw, creeping slowly, a line of dangling hogs a hundred yards in length; and for every yard there was a man, working as if a demon were after him. At the end of this hog's progress every inch of the carcass had been gone over several times; and then it was rolled into the chilling room, where it stayed for twenty-four hours, and where a stranger might lose himself in a forest of freezing hogs.

Before the carcass was admitted here, however, it had to pass a government inspector, who sat in the doorway and felt of the glands in the neck for tuberculosis. This government inspector did not have the manner of a man who was worked to death; he was apparently not haunted by a fear that the hog might get by him before he had finished his testing. If you were a sociable person, he was quite willing to enter into conversation with you, and to explain to you the deadly nature of the ptomaines which are found in tubercular pork; and while he was talking with you you could hardly be so ungrateful as to notice that a dozen carcasses were passing him untouched. This inspector wore a blue uniform, with brass buttons, and he gave an atmosphere of authority to the scene, and, as it were, put the stamp of official approval upon the things which were done in Durham's.

Jurgis went down the line with the rest of the visitors, staring openmouthed, lost in wonder. He had dressed hogs himself in the forest of Lithuania; but he had never expected to live to see one hog dressed by several hundred men. It was like a wonderful poem to him, and he took it all in guilelessly—even to the conspicuous signs demanding immaculate cleanliness of the employees. Jurgis was vexed when the cynical Jokubas translated these signs with sarcastic comments, offering to take them to the secret rooms where the spoiled meats went to be doctored.

The party descended to the next floor, where the various waste materials were treated. Here came the entrails, to be scraped and washed clean for sausage casings; men and women worked here in the midst of a sickening stench, which caused the visitors to hasten by, gasping. To another room came all the scraps to be "tanked," which meant boiling and pumping off the grease to make soap and lard; below they took out the refuse, and this, too, was a region in which the visitors did not linger. In still other places men were engaged in cutting up the carcasses that had been through the chilling rooms. First there were the "splitters," the most expert workmen in the plant, who earned as high as fifty cents an hour, and did not a thing all day except chop hogs down the middle. Then there were "cleaver men," great giants with muscles of iron; each had two men to attend him—to slide the half carcass in front of him on the table, and hold it while he chopped it, and then turn each piece so that he might chop it once more. His cleaver had a blade about two feet long, and he never made but one cut; he made it so neatly, too, that his implement did not smite through and dull itself— there was just enough force for a perfect cut, and no more. So through various yawning holes there slipped to the floor below—to one room hams, to another forequarters, to another sides of pork. One might go down to this floor and see the pickling rooms, where the hams were put into vats, and the great smoke rooms, with their airtight iron doors. In other rooms they prepared salt pork—there were whole cellars full of it, built up in great towers to the ceiling. In yet other rooms they were putting up meat in boxes and barrels, and wrapping hams and bacon in oiled paper, sealing and labeling and sewing them. From the doors of these rooms went men with loaded trucks, to the platform where freight cars were waiting to be filled; and one went out there and realized with a start that he had come at last to the ground floor of this enormous building.

Then the party went across the street to where they did the killing of beef—where every hour they turned four or five hundred cattle into meat. Unlike the place they had left, all this work was done on one floor; and instead of there being one line of carcasses which moved to the workmen, there were fifteen or twenty lines, and the men moved from one to another of these. This made a scene of intense activity, a picture of human power wonderful to watch. It was all in one great room, like a circus amphitheater, with a gallery for visitors running over the center.

Along one side of the room ran a narrow gallery, a few feet from the floor; into which gallery the cattle were driven by men with goads which gave them electric shocks. Once crowded in here, the creatures were prisoned, each in a separate pen, by gates that shut, leaving them no room to turn around; and while they stood bellowing and plunging, over the top of the pen there leaned one of the "knockers," armed with a sledge hammer, and watching for a chance to deal a blow. The room echoed with the thuds in quick succession, and the stamping and kicking of the steers. The instant the animal had fallen, the "knocker" passed on to another; while a second man raised a lever, and the side of the pen was raised, and the animal, still kicking and struggling, slid out to the "killing bed." Here a man put shackles about one leg, and pressed another lever, and the body was jerked up into the air. There were fifteen or twenty such pens, and it was a matter of only a couple of minutes to knock fifteen or twenty cattle and roll them out. Then once more the gates were opened, and another lot rushed in; and so out of each pen there rolled a steady stream of carcasses, which the men upon the killing beds had to get out of the way.

The manner in which they did this was something to be seen and never forgotten. They worked with furious intensity, literally upon the run—at a pace with which there is nothing to be compared except a football game. It was all highly specialized labor, each man having his task to do; generally this would consist of only two or three specific cuts, and he would pass down the line of fifteen or twenty carcasses, making these cuts upon each. First there came the "butcher," to bleed them; this meant one swift stroke, so swift that you could not see it— only the flash of the knife; and before you could realize it, the man had darted on to the next line, and a stream of bright red was pouring out upon the floor. This floor was half an inch deep with blood, in spite of the best efforts of men who kept shoveling it through holes; it must have made the floor slippery, but no one could have guessed this by watching the men at work.

The carcass hung for a few minutes to bleed; there was no time lost, however, for there were several hanging in each line, and one was always ready. It was let down to the ground, and there came the "heads-man," whose task it was to sever the head, with two or three swift strokes. Then came the "floorsman," to make the first cut in the skin; and then another to finish ripping the skin down the center; and then half a dozen more in swift succession, to finish the skinning. After they were through, the carcass was again swung up; and while a man with a stick examined the skin, to make sure that it had not been cut, and another rolled it up and tumbled it through one of the inevitable holes in the floor, the beef proceeded on its journey. There were men to cut it, and men to split it, and men to gut it and scrape it clean inside. There were some with hose which threw jets of boiling water upon it, and others who removed the feet and added the final touches. In the end, as with the hogs, the finished beef was run into the chilling room, to hang its appointed time.

The visitors were taken there and shown them, all neatly hung in rows, labeled conspicuously with the tags of the government inspec-tors—and some, which had been killed by a special process, marked with the sign of the *kosher* rabbi, certifying that it was fit for sale to the orthodox. And then the visitors were taken to the other parts of the building, to see what became of each particle of the waste material that had vanished through the floor; and to the pickling rooms, and the salt-ing rooms, the canning rooms, and the packing rooms, where choice meat was prepared for shipping in refrigerator cars, destined to be eaten in all the four corners of civilization. Afterward they went outside, wan-dering about among the mazes of buildings in which was done the work auxiliary to this great industry.

/   /   /

The packers had secret mains, through which they stole billions of gallons of the city's water. The newspapers had been full of this scan-dal—once there had even been an investigation, and an actual uncover-ing of the pipes; but nobody had been punished, and the thing went right on. And then there was the condemned meat industry, with its endless horrors. The people of Chicago saw the government inspectors in Packingtown, and they all took that to mean that they were protected from diseased meat; they did not understand that these hundred and sixty-three inspectors had been appointed at the request of the packers, and that they were paid by the United States government to certify that all the diseased meat was kept in the state. They had no authority be-yond that; for the inspection of meat to be sold in the city and state the whole force in Packingtown consisted of three henchmen of the local political machine! And shortly afterward one of these, a physician, made the discovery that the carcasses of steers which had been con-demned as tubercular by the government inspectors, and which there-fore contained ptomaines, which are deadly poisons, were left upon an open platform and carted away to be sold in the city; and so he insisted that these carcasses be treated with an injection of kerosene—and was ordered to resign the same week! So indignant were the packers that they went farther, and compelled the mayor to abolish the whole bureau of inspection; so that since then there has not been even a pretense of any interference with the graft. There was said to be two thousand dollars a week hush money from the tubercular steers alone; and as much again from the hogs which had died of cholera on the trains, and which you might see any day being loaded into boxcars and hauled away to a place called Globe, in Indiana, where they made a fancy grade of lard.

Jurgis heard of these things little by little, in the gossip of those who were obliged to perpetrate them. It seemed as if every time you met a person from a new department, you heard of new swindles and new crimes. There was, for instance, a Lithuanian who was a cattle butcher for the plant where Marija had worked, which killed meat for canning only; and to hear this man describe the animals which came to his place would have been worth while for a Dante or a Zola. It seemed that they must have agencies all over the country, to hunt out old and crippled and diseased cattle to be canned. There were cattle which had been fed on "whisky-malt," the refuse of the breweries, and had become what the men called "steerly"—which means covered with boils. It was a nasty job killing these, for when you plunged your knife into them they would burst and splash foul-smelling stuff into your face; and when a man's sleeves were smeared with blood, and his hands steeped in it, how was he ever to wipe his face, or to clear his eyes so that he could see? It was stuff such as this that made the "embalmed beef" that had killed several times as many United States soldiers as all the bullets of the Spaniards; only the army beef, besides, was not fresh canned, it was old stuff that had been lying for years in the cellars.

/   /   /

There were the men in the pickle rooms, for instance, where old Antanas had gotten his death; scarce a one of these that had not some spot of horror on his person. Let a man so much as scrape his finger pushing a truck in the pickle rooms, and he might have a sore that would put him out of the world; all the joints in his fingers might be eaten by the acid, one by one. Of the butchers and floorsmen, the beef-boners and trimmers, and all those who used knives, you could scarcely find a person who had the use of his thumb; time and time again the base of it had been slashed, till it was a mere lump of flesh against which the man pressed the knife to hold it. The hands of these men would be criss-crossed with cuts, until you could no longer pretend to count them or to trace them. They would have no nails,—they had worn them off pulling hides; their knuckles were swollen so that their fingers spread out like a fan. There were men who worked in the cooking rooms, in the midst of steam and sickening odors, by artificial light; in these rooms the germs of tuberculosis might live for two years, but the supply was renewed every hour. There were the beef-luggers, who carried two-hundred-pound quarters into the refrigerator-cars; a fearful kind of work, that began at four o'clock in the morning, and that wore out the most powerful men in a few years. There were those who worked in the chilling rooms, and whose special disease was rheumatism; the time limit that a man could work in the chilling rooms was said to be five years. There were the wool-pluckers, whose hands went to pieces even sooner than the hands of the pickle men; for the pelts of the sheep had to be painted with acid to loosen the wool, and then the pluckers had to pull out this wool with their bare hands, till the acid had eaten their fingers off. There were those who made the tins for the canned meat; and their hands, too, were a maze of cuts, and each cut represented a chance for blood poisoning. Some worked at the stamping machines, and it was very seldom that one could work long there at the pace that was set, and not give out and forget himself, and have a part of his hand chopped off. There were the "hoisters," as they were called, whose task it was to press the lever which lifted the dead cattle off the floor. They ran along upon a rafter, peering down through the damp and the steam; and as old Durham's architects had not built the killing room for the convenience of the hoisters, at every few feet they would have to stoop under a beam, say four feet above the one they ran on; which got them into the habit of stooping, so that in a few years they would be walking like chimpanzees. Worst of any, however, were the fertilizer men, and those who served in the cooking rooms. These people could not be shown to the visitor,—for the odor of a fertilizer man would scare any ordinary visitor at a hundred yards, and as for the other men, who worked in tank rooms full of steam, and in some of which there were open vats near the level of the floor, their peculiar trouble was that they fell into the vats; and when they were fished out, there was never enough of them left to be worth exhibiting,—sometimes they would be overlooked for days, till all but the bones of them had gone out to the world as Durham's Pure Leaf Lard!

/　　　　　/　　　　　/

It was only when the whole ham was spoiled that it came into the department of Elzbieta. Cut up by the two-thousand-revolutions-a-minute flyers, and mixed with half a ton of other meat, no odor that ever was in a ham could make any difference. There was never the least attention paid to what was cut up for sausage; there would come all the way back from Europe old sausage that had been rejected, and that was moldy and white—it would be dosed with borax and glycerine, and dumped into the hoppers, and made over again for home consumption. There would be meat that had tumbled out on the floor, in the dirt and sawdust, where the workers had tramped and spit uncounted billions of consumption germs. There would be meat stored in great piles in rooms; and the water from leaky roofs would drip over it, and thousands of rats would race about on it. It was too dark in these storage places to see well, but a man could run his hand over these piles of meat and sweep off handfuls of the dried dung of rats. These rats were nuisances, and the packers would put poisoned bread out for them; they would die, and then rats, bread, and meat would go into the hoppers together. This is no fairy story and no joke; the meat would be shoveled into carts, and the man who did the shoveling would not trouble to lift out a rat even when he saw one—there were things that went into the sausage in comparison with which a poisoned rat was a tidbit. There was no place for the men to wash their hands before they ate their dinner, and so they made a practice of washing them in the water that was to be ladled into the sausage. There were the butt-ends of smoked meat, and the scraps of corned beef, and all the odds and ends of the waste of the plants, that would be dumped into old barrels in the cellar and left there. Under the system of rigid economy which the packers enforced, there were some jobs that it only paid to do once in a long time, and among these was the cleaning out of the waste barrels. Every spring they did it; and in the barrels would be dirt and rust and old nails and stale water—and cartload after cartload of it would be taken up and dumped into the hoppers with fresh meat, and sent out to the public's breakfast. Some of it they would make into "smoked" sausage—but as the smoking took time and was therefore expensive, they would call upon their chemistry department, and preserve it with borax and color it with gelatine to make it brown. All of their sausage came out of the same bowl, but when they came to wrap it they would stamp some of it "special," and for this they would charge two cents more a pound.

Such were the new surroundings in which Elzbieta was placed, and such was the work she was compelled to do. It was stupefying, brutalizing work; it left her no time to think, no strength for anything. She was part of the machine she tended, and every faculty that was not needed for the machine was doomed to be crushed out of existence. There was only one mercy about the cruel grind—that it gave her the gift of insensibility. Little by little she sank into a torpor—she fell silent. She would meet Jurgis and Ona in the evening, and the three would walk home together, often without saying a word. Ona, too, was falling into a habit of silence—Ona, who had once gone about singing like a bird. She was sick and miserable, and often she would barely have strength enough to drag herself home. And there they would eat what they had to eat, and afterward, because there was only their misery to talk of, they would crawl into bed and fall into a stupor and never stir until it was time to get up again, and dress by candlelight, and go back to the machines. They were so numbed that they did not even suffer much from hunger, now; only the children continued to fret when the food ran short.

Yet the soul of Ona was not dead—the souls of none of them were dead, but only sleeping; and now and then they would waken, and these were cruel times. The gates of memory would roll open—old joys would stretch out their arms to them, old hopes and dreams would call to them, and they would stir beneath the burden that lay upon them, and feel its forever immeasurable weight. They could not even cry out beneath it; but anguish would seize them, more dreadful than the agony of death. It was a thing scarcely to be spoken—a thing never spoken by all the world, that will not know its own defeat.

They were beaten; they had lost the game, they were swept aside. It was not less tragic because it was so sordid, because it had to do with wages and grocery bills and rents. They had dreamed of freedom; of a chance to look about them and learn something; to be decent and clean, to see their child grow up to be strong. And now it was all gone—it would never be! They had played the game and they had lost. Six years more of toil they had to face before they could expect the least respite, the cessation of the payments upon the house; and how cruelly certain it was that they could never stand six years of such a life as they were living! They were lost, they were going down—and there was no deliverance for them, no hope; for all the help it gave them the vast city in which they lived might have been an ocean waste, a wilderness, a desert, a tomb. So often this mood would come to Ona, in the nighttime, when something wakened her; she would lie, afraid of the beating of her own heart, fronting the blood-red eyes of the old primeval terror of life. Once she cried aloud, and woke Jurgis, who was tired and cross. After that she learned to weep silently—their moods so seldom came together now! It was as if their hopes were buried in separate graves.

Jurgis, being a man, had troubles of his own. There was another specter following him. He had never spoken of it, nor would he allow any one else to speak of it—he had never acknowledged it existence to himself. Yet the battle with it took all the manhood that he had—and once or twice, alas, a little more. Jurgis had discovered drink.

He was working in the steaming pit of hell; day after day, week after week—until now there was not an organ of his body that did its work without pain, until the sound of ocean breakers echoed in his head day and night, and the buildings swayed and danced before him as he went down the street. And from all the unending horror of this there was a respite, a deliverance—he could drink! He could forget the pain, he could slip off the burden; he would see clearly again, he would be master of his brain, of his thoughts, of his will. His dead self would stir in him, and he would find himself laughing and cracking jokes with his companions—he would be a man again, and master of his life.

PAULINE NEWMAN
AND THE NEW YORK WORLD

23 | *The Triangle Fire*

In 1909 the shirtwaist dress makers in New York went on strike for better wages, improved sanitary conditions, and more safety precautions in their workplaces. The strike failed but left in its wake the International Ladies Garment Workers Union. On March 25, 1911, the issues of the strike received renewed meaning when fire broke out in the shop of the Triangle Shirtwaist Company, on the eighth, ninth, and tenth floors of a modern "fireproof" loft building in lower Manhattan. The number of exits was inadequate, doors were locked to prevent pilfering, other doors opened inward, and the stairwell had no exit to the roof; thus, hundreds of workers were trapped. Within half an hour, one-hundred forty-six people had died. They did not, however, die wholly in vain. After the tragedy, New York City created the Bureau of Fire Prevention, and New York State created a Factory Investigation Commission, making New York the most advanced state in the nation in the protection of factory workers. In the first excerpt, Pauline Newman, who became one of the leaders of the garment workers union, recounted what it was like to work at the Triangle Company. The second excerpt is the coverage of the fire in the following morning's edition of the New York World.

PAULINE NEWMAN*

I'd like to tell you about the kind of world we lived in 75 years ago because all of you probably weren't even born then. Seventy-five years is a long time, but I'd like to give you at least a glimpse of that world because it has no resemblance to the world we live in today, in any respect.

That world 75 years ago was a world of incredible exploitation of men, women, and children. I went to work for the Triangle Shirtwaist Company in 1901. The corner of a shop would resemble a kindergarten because we were young, eight, nine, ten years old. It was a world of greed; the human being didn't mean anything. The hours were from 7:30 in the morning to 6:30 at night when it wasn't busy. When the

*From We Were There: The Story of Working Women in America, *by Barbara Wertheimer.* Copyright © 1977 by Barbara Wertheimer, pp. 294–295. Reprinted by permission of Pantheon Books, a Division of Random House, Inc.

season was on we worked until 9 o'clock. No overtime pay, not even supper money. There was a bakery in the garment center that produced little apple pies the size of this ashtray [*holding up ashtray for group to see*] and that was what we got for our overtime instead of money.

My wages as a youngster were $1.50 for a seven-day week. I know it sounds exaggerated, but it isn't; it's true. If you worked there long enough and you were satisfactory you got 50 cents a week increase every year. So by the time I left the Triangle Waist Company in 1909, my wages went up to $5.50, and that was quite a wage in those days.

All shops were as bad as the Triangle Waist Company. When you were told Saturday afternoon, through a sign on the elevator, "If you don't come in on Sunday, you needn't come in on Monday," what choice did you have? You had no choice.

I worked on the 9th floor with a lot of youngsters like myself. Our work was not difficult. When the operators were through with sewing shirtwaists, there was a little thread left, and we youngsters would get a little scissors and trim the threads off.

And when the inspectors came around, do you know what happened? The supervisors made all the children climb into one of those crates that they ship material in, and they covered us over with finished shirtwaists until the inspectors had left, because of course we were too young to be working in the factory legally.

The Triangle Waist Company was a family affair, all relatives of the owner running the place, watching to see that you did your work, watching when you went into the toilet. And if you were two or three minutes longer than foremen or foreladies thought you should be, it was deducted from your pay. If you came five minutes late in the morning because the freight elevator didn't come down to take you up in time, you were sent home for half a day without pay.

Rubber heels came into use around that time and our employers were the first to use them; you never knew when they would sneak up on you, spying, to be sure you did not talk to each other during working hours.

Most of the women rarely took more than $6.00 a week home, most less. The early sweatshops were usually so dark that gas jets (for light) burned day and night. There was no insulation in the winter, only a pot-bellied stove in the middle of the factory. If you were a finisher and could take your work with you (finishing is a hand operation) you could sit next to the stove in winter. But if you were an operator or a trimmer it was very cold indeed. Of course in the summer you suffocated with practically no ventilation.

There was no drinking water, maybe a tap in the hall, warm, dirty. What were you going to do? Drink this water or none at all. Well, in those days there were vendors who came in with bottles of pop for 2 cents, and much as you disliked to spend the two pennies you got the pop instead of the filthy water in the hall.

The condition was no better and no worse than the tenements where we lived. You got out of the workshop, dark and cold in winter, hot in summer, dirty unswept floors, no ventilation, and you would go home. What kind of home did you go to? You won't find the tenements *we* lived in. Some of the rooms didn't have any windows. I lived in a two-room tenement with my mother and two sisters and the bedroom had no windows, the facilities were down in the yard, but that's the way it was in the factories too. In the summer the sidewalk, fire escapes, and the roof of the tenements became bedrooms just to get a breath of air.

We wore cheap clothes, lived in cheap tenements, ate cheap food. There was nothing to look forward to, nothing to expect the next day to be better.

Someone once asked me; "How did you survive?" And I told him, what alternative did we have? You stayed and you survived, that's all.

THE *NEW YORK WORLD**

At 4:35 o'clock yesterday afternoon fire springing from a source that may never be positively identified was discovered in the rear of the eighth floor of the ten-story building at the northwest corner of Washington place and Greene street, the first of three floors occupied as a factory of the Triangle Shirtwaist Company.

At 11:30 o'clock Chief Croker made this statement:

"Every body has been removed. The number taken out, which includes those who jumped from windows, is 141 . . .

At 2 o'clock this morning Chief Croker estimated the total dead as one hundred and fifty-four. He said further: "I expect something of this kind to happen in these so-called fire-proof buildings, which are without adequte protection as far as fire-escapes are concerned."

More than a third of those who lost their lives did so in jumping from windows. The firemen who answered the first of the four alarms turned in found 30 bodies on the pavements of Washington place and Greene street. Almost all of these were girls, as were the great majority of them all. . . .

Inspection by Acting Superintendent of Buildings Ludwig will be made the basis for charges of criminal negligence on the ground that the fire-proof doors leading to one of the inclosed tower stairways were locked. . . . "

It was the most appalling horror since the Slocum disaster and the Iroquois Theater fire in Chicago. Every available ambulance in Manhattan was called upon to cart the dead to the morgue—bodies charred to

*From New York World, *March 26, 1911.*

unrecognizable blackness or reddened to a sickly hue—as was to be seen by shoulders or limbs protruding through flame-eaten clothing. Men and women, boys and girls were of the dead that littered the street; that is actually the condition—the streets were littered.

The fire began in the eighth story. The flames licked and shot their way up through the other two stories. All three floors were occupied by the Triangle Waist Company. The estimate of the number of employees at work is made by Chief Croker at about 1,000. The proprietors of the company say 700 men and girls were in their place. . . .

Before smoke or flame gave signs from the windows, the loss of life was fully under way. The first signs that persons in the street knew that these three top stories had turned into red furnaces in which human creatures were being caught and incinerated was when screaming men and women and boys and girls crowded out on the many window ledges and threw themselves into the streets far below.

They jumped with their clothing ablaze. The hair of some of the girls streamed up aflame as they leaped. Thud after thud sounded on the pavements. It is a ghastly fact that on both the Greene Street and Washington Place sides of the building there grew mounds of the dead and dying.

And the worst horror of all was that in this heap of the dead now and then there stirred a limb or sounded a moan.

Within the three flaming floors it was as frightful. There flames enveloped many so that they died instantly. When Fire Chief Croker could make his way into these three floors, he found sights that utterly staggered him, that sent him, a man used to viewing horrors, back and down into the street with quivering lips.

The floors were black with smoke. And then he saw as the smoke drifted away bodies burned to bare bones. There were skeletons bending over sewing machines.

The elevator boys saved hundreds. They each made twenty trips from the time of the alarm until twenty minutes later when they could do no more. Fire was streaming into the shaft, flames biting at the cables. They fled for their own lives.

Some, about seventy, chose a successful avenue of escape. They clambered up a ladder to the roof. A few remembered the fire escape. Many may have thought of it but only as they uttered cries of dismay.

Wretchedly inadequate was this fire escape—a lone ladder running down to a rear narrow court, which was smoke filled as the fire raged, one narrow door giving access to the ladder. By the score they fought and struggled and breathed fire and died trying to make that needle-eye road to self-preservation. . . .

Shivering at the chasm below them, scorched by the fire behind, there were some that still held positions on the window sills when the first squad of firemen arrived.

The nets were spread below with all promptness. Citizens were commandeered into service, as the firemen necessarily gave their attention to the one engine and hose of the force that first arrived.

The catapult force that the bodies gathered in the long plunges made the nets utterly without avail. Screaming girls and men, as they fell, tore the nets from the grasp of the holders, and the bodies struck the sidewalks and lay just as they fell. Some of the bodies ripped big holes through the life-nets. . . .

Concentrated, the fire burned within. The flames caught all the flimsy lace stuff and linens that go into the making of spring and summer shirtwaists and fed eagerly upon the rolls of silk.

The cutting room was laden with the stuff on long tables. The employees were toiling over such material at the rows and rows of machines. Sinisterly the spring day gave aid to the fire. Many of the window panes facing south and east were drawn down. Draughts had full play.

The experts say that the three floors must each have become a whirlpool of fire. Whichever way the entrapped creatures fled they met a curving sweep of flame. Many swooned and died. Others fought their way to the windows or the elevator or fell fighting for a chance at the fire escape, the single fire escape leading into the blind court that was to be reached from the upper floors by clambering over a window sill!

On all of the three floors, at a narrow window, a crowd met death trying to get out to that one slender fire escape ladder.

It was a fireproof building in which this enormous tragedy occurred. Save for the three stories of blackened windows at the top, you would scarcely have been able to tell where the fire had happened. The walls stood firmly. A thin tongue of flame now and then licked around a window sash. . . .

On the ledge of a ninth-story window two girls stood silently watching the arrival of the first fire apparatus. Twice one of the girls made a move to jump. The other restrained her, tottering in her foothold as she did so. They watched firemen rig the ladders up against the wall. They saw the last ladder lifted and pushed in place. They saw that it reached only the seventh floor.

For the third time, the more frightened girl tried to leap. The bells of arriving fire wagons must have risen to them. The other girl gesticulated in the direction of the sounds. But she talked to ears that could no longer hear. Scarcely turning, her companion dived head first into the street.

The other girl drew herself erect. The crowds in the street were stretching their arms up at her shouting and imploring her not to leap. She made a steady gesture, looking down as if to assure them she would remain brave. But a thin flame shot out of the window at her back and touched her hair. In an instant her head was aflame. She tore at her burning hair, lost her balance, and came shooting down upon the mound of bodies below.

From opposite windows spectators saw again and again pitiable companionships formed in the instant of death—girls who placed their arms around each other as they leaped. In many cases their clothing was flaming or their hair flaring as they fell. . . .

By eight o'clock the available supply of coffins had been exhausted, and those that had already been used began to come back from the morgue. By that time bodies were lowered at the rate of one a minute, and the number of patrol wagons became inadequate, so that four, sometimes six, coffins were loaded upon each.

At intervals throughout the night the very horror of their task overcame the most experienced of the policemen and morgue attendants at work under the moving finger of the searchlight. The crews were completely changed no less than three times. . . .

RICHARD W. O'NEILL

24 | A War Hero

About two million Americans served in the American Expeditionary Force in World War I, and no single person's experience can be called "typical." The war-time experience left some, in Gertrude Stein's words, "a lost generation" whose moorings in the past had been cut loose. The war solidified the patriotism of others. These two visions collided in the 1930s, as the country argued about involvement in another European war. When the writer Henry Berry sought veterans of World War I in the mid-1970s, he found mostly men who saw the war as the central test of the prime of their lives. Memoirs like those of Richard W. O'Neill give the reader a feel for the war-time experience of many who fought. Surely for many of the "doughboys," as the infantrymen were called, the war was the first experience for them of the intimate mixing of American ethnic groups, a theme repeated in memoirs—and motion pictures—about World War II.

SERGEANT RICHARD W. O'NEILL

B Company, 165th Infantry (69th NYNG), 42nd (Rainbow) Division; Holder of the Congressional Medal of Honor

> It is only natural, I suppose, to be proud of being the recipient of our glorious nation's highest military award, but it has always been my honest contention that when an individual is chosen to be the recipient of that award, it is a grateful nation's way of recognizing the overall fighting qualities and selfless sacrifices of *all members* of the Unit in which the recipient served, especially the *sacred combat dead.*
>
> Dick O'Neill

What an outfit we had! Of course, I'm bound to be biased, understand. But really, there was something a little special about the old 69th. Maybe it was because of the large amount of Irish-born in the regiment. They

Henry Berry, Make the Kaiser Dance. *(Doubleday and Company, Garden City, New York, 1978) pp. 327–338. Copyright 1978 by Henry Berry. Reprinted by permission of the author.*

had known how hard it was in Ireland, and they had a particularly strong feeling toward America. I think most of those who had come from the other side felt that way. My mother was a native New Yorker, but my father was a County Clare man. When he first left Ireland, he went to Liverpool, England. Hell, he used to work fourteen, sixteen hours a day, trying to make ends meet there. He did much better in this country, and he appreciated it. And so did most of the men who came over.

Of course, they felt they were a little special. Oh they accepted those who had been born here, but they did call us narrow backs. And were they characters! I remember one time in France, before we went into the trenches. I had just received several packages from home. One of these was a carton of cigarettes. Now, I didn't smoke, and these four or five Irishmen eying me and the cigarettes knew it. They turned their backs and started to talk in hush-hush tones—they sounded like people who had learned to whisper in a boiler factory.

"That Dick O'Neill, he's the finest sergeant in the 69th."

"The 69th, yuh say—in the whole goddamn division, I say!"

"The two of yuh are wrong—it's in the whole American Army. He's a fair man, and a brave one at that. He could chase these damn Heinies back to Germany all alone."

Then they turned around with these surprised looks on their faces.

"Oh Sergeant, darlin', we didn't know yuh were there. But we mean it."

"Indeed, indeed, sure and we do!"

Now, what could you say about men like these? I knew they were putting one over on me. But what the hell could I do? I threw them the cigarettes.

Well, I wanted to tell you that so you'd have some kind of an idea what the 69th was like. I think all of New York's Irish were proud of it. As for myself, I was nineteen when the rumors started about the regiment going down to the Mexican border. It sounded great to me, so I joined up. It was May 22, 1916. And do you know it was exactly three years later to the day—May 22, 1919—that I was mustered out. And what a three years they were!

You see, our regiment was a little different. Most of the National Guard outfits had some time off between the border and the World War. Not the 69th. We stayed in right through.

In March of '17 we went to Washington, D.C., to be in Wilson's Inaugural Parade. By then it seemed quite obvious that Uncle Sam was going to go to war with Germany, so I guess the government felt what the hell, there's no sense in discharging these men now. We went back to New York to guard reservoirs and what have you. I think we even had some men guarding Grand Central Station. Washington was afraid that with all the German Americans we had in this country, there was bound to be some trouble. I can't remember that there was, though.

The border itself was a huge letdown. We ended up spending all those months hiking up and down the Rio Grande. We got in great shape, all right, but if anyone was killed, it was by boredom. The poor newspapermen were just as badly off as we were. They're getting all this pressure from back in New York to get some battle stories.

Then they got a big break. Some nut on the other side of the river took a potshot at one of our patrols. Oh this was great! Our men could shoot back, anything for a little excitement. But it was all over in a few minutes, with no one getting hit. Well, Jeez, one of the papers, I think it was the *Journal,* broke out these huge headlines, "69th in Big Battle with the Mexicans." You can imagine what concern this caused back home. What a mess! Even the governor was upset. It took a long time to straighten that out.

There was one other incident to relieve our boredom. I can't remember the name of the Mexican town this happened in, but it was directly across the river from us. I had binoculars, so I really had a front-row seat.

Well, this band of rebels attacked the town. It wasn't much of a battle—a lot of firing, then the rebels rode away, leaving one of their group stretched out on the ground. Then I'll be damned if every one in the town didn't come out and take a shot at the poor guy. He must have looked like a piece of Swiss cheese; it was sickening.

All in all, though, you have to call the whole border thing a farce except for one thing: It gave the National Guard outfits a military feeling that helped a great deal when Congress did declare war on Germany. Remember, four of the six divisions to be in France by the first of March 1918 were Guard outfits.

Ours was the 42nd, soon to be called the Rainbow. And we owed that name to none other than Douglas MacArthur. What an officer he was, a peach! He commanded the Rainbow, you know, at the very end. But back at the beginning he was chief of staff for the division.

Now, the government wanted to get a division, made up of men from states throughout the country, to France as soon as possible. At that time we had the old square divisions with four infantry regiments, three artillery ones, three machine-gun battalions, and all these other units such as MPs, medical groups, etc.—there were a total of twenty-six different organizations in each division.

Well, according to what we heard, MacArthur and Newton Baker [the Secretary of War] were deciding on how they would set the division up when Mac came up with the name.

"Mr. Secretary," he said, "the 42nd will have National Guard outfits from all these states; it will cross the country like a rainbow. Why not call it 'the Rainbow Division'—a rainbow across the land." And that was it.

We were to be one of the infantry regiments, along with the 4th Ohio, 3rd Iowa, and 4th Alabama. And we all got along fine. I know that movie *The Fighting 69th* shows us having some trouble with the Alabama boys. Maybe so, but I don't remember it. And that movie was the biggest phony that ever came down the pike anyway! None of the old 69th people gave a damn about it.

We were now the 165th U. S. Infantry. Along with the 166th (the Ohioans) we made up the 83rd Brigade—that's the way we did it then, two regiments to a brigade. Hell, we had over seven thousand men in our brigade—it was almost as big as some of the French and British divisions all by itself.

Our gathering place was Camp Mills, Long Island. It was here that they started to turn us into a division. And it was here that I got to know our battalion commander, Major William Joseph Donovan. Now, let me point out that my son is named William Donovan O'Neill; that should tell you what I thought about him. But he surely worked us that summer at Mills. But I ask you, was there any other way to get us ready for what was coming? And it came fast enough. We started our trip for France in September 1917, finally landing at Le Havre on November 1. There'll always be a big controversy over which National Guard division landed first, ours or the 26th. They always told us we were the first complete one there. But what difference does it make? Both the Rainbow and the Yankee were there with plenty of time for the war. And that 26th was a good outfit also.

After we landed they shipped us over to Alsace-Lorraine, and it was here that our troubles really began. The hell of it was the foulup in clothing. Here we were in the Vosges Mountain area, with what was to be one of the worst winters in French history beginning, and half the men didn't have their overcoats. Can you imagine that? Hardly any of them had winter brogans—many were walking around in those light shoes you'd wear in a dress parade during the summer. Why, the next thing you knew a lot of the boys had rags on their feet. And the blankets— we had lightweight summer ones until the first of the year.

I can't say the food supplies were much better. Here, look, this is a diary I kept that winter:

"December 7: hiked 10 kilometers. Food—coffee like water, lukewarm—a few strips of bacon—all we had that day. December 10: hiked ten kilometers—many of the men without shoes—weather freezing. One meal, some kind of stew."

Now, it wasn't that we didn't have equipment in France. They just had trouble getting it to us, that's all. But how the boys did suffer! Nothing was worse than Christmas. We went to Mass in a cathedral Christmas Eve and the next day had one tiny meal, that rotten coffee again, and some kind of meat, and a small portion at that.

At about this time I was sent to a place called Mission. My job was to set up barns and sheds for the enlisted men, and houses, if possible, for the officers. I don't know how far it was but because of the weather, it took me ten days. Most of the time I had to walk, even though I did hitch a ride or two on farmers' wagons. Once I even jumped up on a French caisson for a few miles. All in all, that trip had to be one of the low points of the war for me. At least when we were doing all that marching down at the border, we didn't have to worry about frozen feet.

Well, I set things up as best I could, even recruiting many of the French women to help with the food until the rolling kitchen arrived. A while later the first battalion arrived. There was a little improvement in the weather and we did get a chance for some real training. We needed it.

Then in March we moved into a place called Luneville for our first spell in the trenches. We were to spend our next four months here and over at Baccarat going in and out of the trenches.

I can't say this was pleasant, but the real brutal stuff, for D Company anyway, was still a while away. One of our companies took a real pasting at a place called Rouge Bouquet, where they lost twenty-four men in a cave-in, but all in all, the worst thing about it was the living conditions—the mud, the cooties, the rats—just lousy living, that's all.

One of the few good things about our trench tours was the opportunity it allowed me to really establish a friendship with Major Donovan. It was a friendship that would last through two World Wars until 1959, when Bill died.

You know, they always called him "Wild Bill," but not because he was irrational. There had been a manager of the New York Highlanders [later the Yankees] named "Wild Bill" Donovan—that's where Bill got the nickname. In reality, he was anything but. Actually, he was the calmest man under fire I ever saw. Oh you'd think he was standing at the corner of Broadway and Forty-second Street, not in the middle of a barrage.

And he was always in the middle of everything—Bill was no dugout officer. That's way he was such a great leader. Once the men realized that the major was going to keep calm no matter what happened, they began to count on him to do the right thing.

I'll never forget a conversation we had later on when I had to take over command of the company.

"O'Neill," he said to me, "these are great soldiers; they'll take hell with bayonets if they're properly led." And with Donovan leading us, we might have done just that.

Well, after our time in the trenches, we moved into the Champagne sector, where we really got to fight the war. First, we played our part in stopping the last German drive, then we attacked in an area around the Ourcq River. From then on, the Germans were on the defensive until the Armistice.

First came the Champagne defense. Here we were part of Gouraud's Fourth French Army, holding the center of the line. Gouraud was a real old campaigner, with an empty sleeve and a stiff leg from wounds. I think he lost the arm at Gallipoli.

Now, the way we heard it was that MacArthur gave the French the idea for the defense. We knew the Germans were going to attack, so Mac told the French to leave just a few men in the frontline trenches, but to beef up the second line. The Rainbow was right in the middle, with French on either side. None of our battalion was actually in the first trench line; our job was to wait and see what happened. And that waiting was bad business, particularly when the shelling started.

While we had no way of knowing it, this was to be the end of Ludendorff's final offensive. If we could stop them here, at the road to Chalons-sur-Marne, we could start the counterattack that Foch had planned.

Well, I think it was about seven o'clock the morning of July 15 that the Germans came over. Naturally, they had no trouble at first. Most of our men got out of the first-line trenches in a hurry as planned. And were those Germans happy! They tought they'd won a big battle, you see. We could hear them laughing, cheering, singing—it was really a little sad.

Then our concentrated barrage opened up. Oh my Christ, did it ever shock those Heinies! Our artillery had a field day. They'd measured the exact position of the trenches and knew just where those Germans had stopped. It was like ducks in a shooting gallery.

But these were the Prussian Guards. They weren't quite stopped yet. What was left of them kept coming at us. It varied up and down the line depending on the amount of troops. In several areas they reached the second-line trenches, where it turned into a real vicious hand-to-hand affair.

I think it was our second battalion that took it the worst in the 69th. They had some real rough stuff. And they had a couple of great stories to tell.

In one of them four Germans, each with this huge red cross on his arm, were toting a stretcher up to the lines. When they got close enough to us, they threw this blanket off the stretcher and opened up with a machine gun. You can bet those four never saw ze father in ze Fatherland again. Still another group tried to infiltrate our lines dressed in French uniforms. They were also shot down. All in all, I think the Rainbow held its own that day.

Of course, I've been just talking about our regiment because a frontline soldier rarely gets involved with anything larger. And that's pretty high up at that—usually your thinking doesn't go any higher than your battalion.

My point is that there were probably over two hundred thousand Germans attacking along a line of several miles. In some areas I heard they'd made small breakthroughs, but were shortly driven back. From then on until November 11 the Boche were headed the other way. Let me add one more thing before I go into our move to the Ourcq River— I really should tell you this, as it was just about the most incredible thing I saw in France. I can't tell you the day and the hour, but it did happen while we were there in the Champagne sector.

Now, I'll bet you very few Americans realize that we fought along- side of Polish troops in 1918. Well, we did. They were called the Pade- rewski Brigade because he had raised them. I guess they figured they could have an independent country of their own if they ended up on the winning side. It did turn out that way, but very few of the Polish soldiers that we saw lived to see it—not if what they did at Champagne was any indication of their officers, anyway.

I was standing in a trench when I heard a sound of marching men. I looked over and saw these Polish soldiers moving up the Chalons road. My God, you'd think they were strutting down Fifth Avenue on the seventeenth of March—why, they were actually in close formation in broad daylight. How in the hell they ever thought they'd get away with it I'll never know.

The Germans spotted them, of course, probably from a balloon or a plane. Then they opened up with their artillery. It was plain suicide—I doubt like hell if more than 10 per cent of them weren't hit. And the saddest part was they accomplished absolutely nothing. What a waste!

Well, as I've said, our next stop was over near the Ourcq. Oh we had a few days to recuperate, but the first thing we knew they loaded us on those 40 and 8's for a short ride down near Château-Thierry. They'd been fighting like hell here just a few days before, and we had a first-hand view of the destruction. The area looked as if a cyclone had hit it.

I can't remember where they let us off, but wherever it was they piled us onto these camions for our jaunt to where the Germans were. These camions seemed to be a cross between a bus and a truck. They were driven by Vietnamese. Naturally, we called them Chinks—I doubt if any of the boys had even heard of Vietnamese then.

Now, the Ourcq itself was what we'd call a creek back home. I can particularly remember one of our boys taking one look at it with disgust.

"If this is a river," he croaked, "the Hudson must be an ocean."

River or not, the Germans thought enough of it to have some very tough *hombres*, including the 4th Imperial Prussian Footguard, trying to hold it. Between working our way up to it and finally crossing the damn thing, the 69th experienced just about as tough a fight as it ever had. It was attack, face their counterattack, and attack again. It may be almost sixty years ago, but there are many little things that still stick in my mind about that last week in July of '18.

One of them concerns this grand old Irish sergeant, Tom O'Malley. It happened at Dead Man's Curve just as we were ready to hit the Ger- mans, not far from Meurcy Farm. We were taking a little rest when a

couple of officers came by and asked Tom for Company D's commanding officer.

"Sure and there're no officers here," O'Malley told them. "Oh
we'd see them all the time back at the camp; Christ, you'd be tripping
over 'em! But here, none atall."

"Then we'd better give you a temporary commission, O'Malley.
These men can't go against the Germans without an officer."

"What, Tom O'Malley an officer, the devil you say? No Sam Browne
belt for me! Now, take that nice young man Dick O'Neill—we'll make
Dick the acting captain. I'll see the boys do what he says."

And that's how I was given temporary command of Company D. I
was twenty years of age. Hell, O'Malley knew much more about soldier-
ing than I did—I wanted him to have command myself. But we all got
a kick out of his crack, "No Sam Browne belt for me!"

Of course, it's the events of the thirtieth of July that have stayed
with me the longest, even though my actual fight with the twenty-five
Germans is a little hazy. Then again, it always was. When you keep
getting hit with bullets and you're fighting as hard as you can to stay
alive, you're reacting by instinct.

Strangely enough, one of the things that stands out in my mind is
what a beautiful morning it was and how nice it would have been to
take a walk through that French countryside. What a contrast between
the scenic beauty and the shelling! I said to myself, "Dick, this is a hell
of a morning to pick to get killed!"

My pessimism was due to the job Donovan had given us. We knew
there were machine guns up ahead but not how many or where. We
were to find out where they had them so our artillery could zero in. It
was, however, the major's final words that stuck in my mind.

"Dick," he said, "it would be a lot better if your boys could knock
out those guns. We could move faster."

Well, we found their machine guns soon enough and went after
them; I had thirty-two men with me.

It didn't take the Germans long to open up on us. Christ, there were
bullets flying all around. One of them knocked the rifle out of my hand,
but being a sergeant, I still had my pistol. I didn't realize it at the time,
but I was running so fast that I was way out in front of the men I was
leading.

The first thing I knew I climbed this ridge and almost fell into this
large gravel pit. Then I got the shock of my life. The hole was filled with
about twenty-five Germans and several machine guns. The only thing
that saved me was the fact that they were as surprised as I was. I threw
a grenade or two and started firing my pistol—of course, they started
firing at the same time. They hit me with four or five shots, maybe six,
but they weren't bad enough to knock me over; amazingly enough, they
were all flesh wounds.

I knew I'd been doing better against them because I could see these gray-clad figures falling over. They later told me there were five dead Germans in the gravel pit—two of them being noncoms. I guess this panicked the rest because they all started to surrender.

Oh, it all sounds great, all right, but put yourself in my place. Here I am with twenty or so Heinie prisoners smack on top of the German lines. They're all jabbering away a mile a minute while I'm pointing a pistol at them that probably didn't have any rounds left in it. I was the one in a hell of a spot, but I guess these Krauts didn't know it.

Anyway, I figured the only thing to do was hike them back to our lines. It seemed like a good idea at the time, but Jeez, we'd no sooner started when whack, a couple of other German machine gunners over on my left opened up on us. They knocked the bejesus out of me, but they also chopped down their own men like cordwood.

Hell, I'd already been hit in one of my legs in the gravel pit—now they really punctured the other one. I couldn't walk, couldn't even crawl. But I could roll—so over and over I barreled down the ridge with their machine-gun fire bouncing all around me. And two more of those damn German bullets didn't miss!

I finally reached the cover of some woods, where some of our men grabbed me. One of my Irish buddies, named Pat, took one look at me and sighed.

"Jee-sus, Dick me boy, you're leaking all over the place! I should carry yuh back on me back."

Well, I knew he wanted to get out of the fighting. Then another Irishman came over.

"And where the hell do yuh think you're going?"

"Oh I want to take care of the sergeant."

"And not yourself, Pat—get back over there. Someone will get the sergeant."

So poor Pat went back over where he belonged, and wouldn't you know it, Pat was killed within the hour.

A short time later two men rolled me in a blanket and headed for a dressing station. Oh I wanted to get patched up, all right, but not before I told Major Donovan precisely where those German machine guns were. The 2nd Battalion was going to attack in that area, and I figured they wouldn't spot them until they'd lost a lot of men. The boys carrying me in the blanket started to argue with me about it.

"I'm not going anywhere," I told them, "until I tell the major where those machine guns are." So they took me to Donovan. I gave him a report, and then I think I collapsed.

My next step landed me in a damn good hospital run by a Jewish group from back home. I think it was connected with New York Hospital. And what a great job they did on me! I was lucky in one respect: None of the bullets had really injured a vital spot. I was also young and healthy, which greatly aided my recovery. The first thing I knew I reached a point where I was really itching to get back with the 69th.

When the word came back on how rough things were up in the Argonne, I couldn't take it any longer, so I cornered my doctor.

"Look," I told him, "I could go ten rounds with Jess Willard; I want to get back with my outfit."

"Oh for Christ's sake, O'Neill," he answered, "you looked like a pincushion when they brought you in. You've had your war!"

Well, it went on like this for a few days until I wore him down; then he finally gave up.

"All right, all right," he said, "you're driving us all nuts. If you want to kill yourself, go ahead, but I won't be responsible for you." I moved out as quickly as I could and headed for the 69th.[1]

I joined the boys sometime in October, right in the middle of that donneybrook called the Meuse-Argonne. I was shocked to find so few of the old-timers left. And with that nasty grinding-out stuff, it was fewer every day. The Germans even badly wounded my old friend Sergeant Tom O'Malley. There he was, lying there calmly smoking his pipe.

"Don't worry none about me, boys," he said, "I'll be foine, just foine." And he did make it back home.

It was beginning to get to me also. I took some shrapnel wounds up there, but compared to what happened at the Ourcq, I always figured they didn't count. I did start to occasionally get dizzy spells, but I was determined to stick it out.

Then, on November 8, when we were all tangled up in that mess to see who was going to take Sedan, I collapsed and was out cold for days. When I finally woke up, I was in a hospital bed with clean white sheets, looking out a window right into a beautifully bright dawning. When I turned my head, I saw this smiling nurse with a sparkling starched white uniform.

"Well, holy Christ," I said to myself, "I'm finally dead, and here's an angel. Thank God I'm in heaven and not the other place!" Then the angel started to talk.

"Good morning, Sergeant, I know you'll be glad to know it's all over."

"What's over?"

"Why, the war, of course."

"It is not. Why . . . " Then I began to realize where I was.

---

1. One report says that the sergeant went AWOL to get back to the 69th. Dick did not say this, only that they did not want him to go back.

25 | Campaigning for the War

During World War I, the job of the federal Committee on Public Information, as its director, George Creel, explained, was "to sell the war to America." Creel had been a journalist. In the year and a half that the United States was in the war, the committee arranged for more than seven-million propaganda speeches and distributed huge quantities of pamphlets and posters. Movies were made that extolled America's war effort. Creel even enlisted the Boy Scouts to aid in spreading the word. The Boy Scouts organization took up the task enthusiastically and in a highly American fashion.

To the Members of the Boy Scouts of America!

Attention, Scouts! We are again called upon to do active service for our country! Every one of the 285,661 Scouts and 76,957 Scout Officials has been summoned by President Woodrow Wilson, Commander-in-Chief of the Army and Navy, to serve as a dispatch bearer from the Government at Washington to the American people all over the country. The prompt, enthusiastic, and hearty response of every one of us has been pledged by our [Scout] President, Mr. Livingstone. Our splended record of accomplishments in war activities promises full success in this new job.

This patriotic service will be rendered under the slogan

"EVERY SCOUT TO BOOST AMERICA"
AS A GOVERNMENT DISPATCH BEARER

The World War is for liberty and democracy.

America has long been recognized as the leader among nations standing for liberty and democracy.

America entered the war as a sacred duty to uphold the principles of liberty and democracy.

As a democracy, our country faces great danger—not so much from submarines, battleships and armies, because, thanks to our allies, our enemies have apparently little chance of reaching our shores.

From a pamphet entitled Committee on Public Information, Boy Scouts of America, *1917.*

Our danger is from within.

Our enemies have representatives everywhere; they tell lies; they mispresent the truth; they deceive our own people; they are a real menace to our country.

Already we have seen how poor Russia has been made to suffer because her people do not know the truth. Representatives of the enemy have been very effective in their deceitful efforts to make trouble for the Government.

Fortunately here in America our people are better educated—they want the truth. Our President recognized the justice and wisdom of this demand when in the early stages of the war he created the Committee on Public Information. He knew that the Government would need the confidence, enthusiasm and willing service of every man and woman, every boy and girl in the nation. He knew that the only possible way to create a genuine feeling of partnership between the people and its representatives in Washington was to take the people into his confidence by full, frank statements concerning the reasons for our entering the war, the various steps taken during the war and the ultimate aims of the war.

Neither the President as Commander-in-Chief, nor our army and navy by land and sea, can alone win the war.

At this moment the best defense that America has is an enlightened and loyal citizenship. Therefore, we as scouts are going to have the opportunity of rendering real patriotic service under our slogan

"EVERY SCOUT TO BOOST AMERICA"
AS A GOVERNMENT DISPATCH BEARER

Here is where our service begins.

We are to help spread the facts about America and America's part in the World War.

We are to fight lies with truth.

We are to help create public opinion "just as effective in helping to bring victory as ships and guns," to stir patriotism, the great force behind the ships and guns. Isn't that a challenge for every loyal Scout?

SPECIAL WORD TO SCOUTS

A Scout Is Clean. Again you are the messenger of the Government to the people. *Look the part.* See that your face and hands are clean, shoes polished, badge on your hat, uniform correct and spotless. What you have to say will count more if you make a good impression.

A Scout Is Courteous. Again you are the President's messenger, with a big message to carry. *Act the part.* Remember that politeness pays every time.

A Scout Is Prepared. Know what the Committee on Public Information stands for and what it is working for. Know what that Committee wants you to do. Know what is in the series of pamphlets yourself as listed on pages 12–15, so you can tell other people what is in them. Know how the pamphlets are obtained, so as to explain to other people how to get them. Remember, the public wants just the information you have to give.

Know whom you are to interview. Your Scoutmaster will arrange your territory. Get your instructions from him. Cover your territory. Get people interested, if they aren't interested. Give them the information they want, not something they don't want. Get everybody to read the Flag Day Speech. The chances are they won't be willing to stop there, but will want to know more about how war came to America.

It is for you to keep your eyes and ears open. Find out what the public wants to know. The Government may later ask you just this question. Be prepared to answer.

"EVERY SCOUT TO BOOST AMERICA" AS A GOVERNMENT DISPATCH BEARER: HOW?

As Mr. George Creel, the Chairman of the Committee on Public Information, says in his letter, scouts are to serve as direct special representatives of the Committee on Public Information to keep the people informed about the War and its causes and progress. The Committee has already prepared a number of special pamphlets and others will be prepared. It places upon the members of the Boy Scouts of America the responsibility of putting the information in these pamphlets in the homes of the American people. Every Scout will be furnished a credential card by his Scoutmaster. Under the direction of our leaders, the Boy Scouts of America are to serve as an intelligence division of the citizen's army, always prepared and alert to respond to any call which may come from the President of the United States and the Committee on Public Information at Washington.

Every Home to Be Reached. The Boy Scouts of America as now organized, have troops of scouts in practically every part of this great country of ours. Over a third of our troops are in rural communities. In such places the Scoutmasters will work out a definite plan so that all of the homes of the community will be reached. In our larger cities where there are two or more troops, and therefore local council organizations, Scout Commissioners and Scout Executives will assign to each troop definite territory to cover. All scouts will be expected to work in full harmony with such arrangements.

Scouts to Get 15 Adult "Boosters." It will be the duty of every scout official and every scout to know his territory well. Each scout should discover at least fifteen people who will be influential in boosting the cause of America. Friendly relationship should be established with these people as soon as possible. From time to time as official bulletins or pamphlets are sent out from Washington by the Committee on Public Information for distribution by scouts as dispatch bearers of the government, the scouts will deliver such pamphlets to the list of people whom they have selected as being good boosters for America in the community. The pamphlets will be delivered whenever possible upon the condition that the person receiving the same will not only read the publication himself, but agrees to place each copy in the hands of some other person where it is most likely to do practical good in boosting the cause of America. In all cases where possible have the person receiving the pamphlet sign his or her name on your record sheet. In some cases the pamphlets may well be passed on to more than one person—the more the better, naturally.

Other Free Pamphlets Available. Each scout is to be furnished with a list of all of the publications available without charge from the Committee on Public Information at Washington, D. C., through the Scoutmasters. These reports will give the scouts and scout officials an opportunity to make available to the Committee on Public Information from time to time, not only facts about their work, but suggestions as to additional publications which might be helpful.

A Scout Is Thrifty. Avoid waste. A scout is thrifty, he wastes nothing, and in this special responsibility all scouts will be particularly careful to avoid the wasting of any printed matter.

"EVERY SCOUT TO BOOST AMERICA" RESULTS

If each of the 285,661 scouts does his job well and reaches on an average of fifteen persons, who will join with him in working under the slogan "EVERY SCOUT TO BOOST AMERICA," and if each of these fifteen in turn places important printed matter in the hands of at least one other person, it will mean that through the Boy Scouts of America the Committee on Public Information will have an audience of over eight million people. Worth working for? We should say so!

GENERAL INFORMATION

A supply of franked postal cards is to be given to each Scoutmaster so that the persons who have been selected for the honor list of influential persons may have the opportunity of selecting from the available government publications any or all of these publications that they wish to read, provided they will agree after reading the same to pass them on where they will serve the purpose of public enlightenment.

Each Scoutmaster is to be furnished with a complete set of all of the government publications, in order that all of the members of his troop may be completely informed. Each scout and scout official is expected to seize every opportunity to serve the Committee on Public Information by making available authoritative information. It is up to the Boy Scouts to see that as many people as possible have an intelligent understanding of any and all facts incident to our present national crisis and the World War.

REPORTS

Each scout is to be furnished with a blank report on which he will write the name and address of the persons to whom he distributes any of the government publications. These reports are to be sent to the Committee on Public Information, through the Scoutmasters or scout officials.

POINTS TO REMEMBER

A Brief Review

1. Get your district assigned by Scoutmaster.
2. Make up your list of influential persons with the aid of your Scoutmaster.
3. Read this book of instructions and study the list of other pamphlets available for free distribution, as shown on pages 12–15.
4. Go to the person or persons whom you have agreed to interview. Ask directly for such person or persons.
5. Tell them, simply and courteously, why you are there. Show them President Wilson's letter on the back of your credential card.
6. Tell them what the Committee on Public Information is for.
7. Tell them what the Committee on Public Information has to give them. Explain what is in the pamphlets.
8. Tell them where and how they can get the pamphlets. Show them the post cards which will order the pamphlets. Offer to mail the post cards.
9. Tell them you will, if desired, get any of the free publications for them.
10. When you deliver any of the pamphlets, get the persons to whom you deliver them, to promise not only to read the pamphlets but to place them in the hands of some person where they will likely do good.
11. If anybody asks you questions you cannot answer, find out the answer and go back with it.
12. Go to your Scoutmaster for information. If he wants more particu-

lars he will be able to get them from National Headquarters, Boy Scouts of America.

13. Don't waste pamphlets. They keep alive the spirit of the Declaration of Independence.

14. Be proud of your job. Enthusiasm catches like fire. "Boost America."

Sincerely yours,
James E. West,
Chief Scout Executive

PAMPHLETS NOW READY FOR CIRCULATION

Note:—A set will be sent to every Scoutmaster. You will need to know what is in these pamphlets so as to act as a serviceable bureau of information and be able to give each person the particular intelligence he seeks.

Series I. (Red, White and Blue Covers.)

No. 1. How the War Came to America. This is what a good many people want to know. They realize that war is here, knocking at the gates, but how it came to be here—as to that they are a little hazy in their minds. They know it has something to do with the Monroe Doctrine and the freedom of the seas and a meeting held at the Hague, but just what—well, that is what the pamphlet can tell them. Then there are the people who wish they had saved the President's speech to the Senate last January and his great war message to Congress, last April, which fired another shot "heard round the world," and his almost equally significant Flag Day speech last June. And here they are gathered together in this pamphlet in convenient form. The pamphlet has been also translated into German, Polish, Bohemian, Italian, Spanish, Swedish, Yiddish and Portuguese and stands the Melting Pot process very well too.

/   /   /

No. 4. The President's Flag Day Speech with Evidence of Germany's Plans. In this address, with the accompanying notes, are marshalled forth an impressive array of facts as to how Germany—or rather, "Germany's military masters" forced us into the war. By their own mouths they are condemned. Why they wanted war, what price they were willing to pay for it, the scope and treachery of the scheme involved is all here for him to read who will and many will be interested to read the record.

Note.—This is the pamphlet Scouts are asked to deliver in person to those interested.

No. 5. Conquest and Kultur. This pamphlet, too, deals searchingly with Germany's war aims and dreams of a "Deutschland uber Alles" with a vengeance. It contains a statement of Germany's attitude toward America and a considerable body of quotations from the pens and lips of some of the German war lords, given without comment. No comment is necessary. The evidence of Kultur is all in. Germany meant to swallow the world as its oyster. Her benevolent intention is disclosed in the pamphlet.

No. 6. German War Practices. A calm statement of facts for those who really want to know just how the German military machine worked in Belgium and Northern France, based solely upon American and German evidence. The pamphlet is cool, but does not leave the reader in that condition.

Series II. (Plain Black Covers.)

No. 101. The War Message and the Facts behind It. The President's War Message, with the explanatory notes, makes a brief document—only 32 pages—but it contains the Bed Rock Facts every citizen of these United States ought to know.

No. 103. The Government of Germany. We hear often that Germany is liberal and democratic. This study of the German Constitution and the actual workings of government under the Prussian rule of thumb is likely to upset that theory.

No. 105. The War of Self Defense. Another expression of how war was thrust upon us, containing addresses by Lansing, Secretary of State, and Post, the Assistant Secretary of Labor.

No. 106. American Loyalty. An interesting pamphlet for and by the open minded, written by Americans of German descent who, having found their ideal of political liberty in this country, believe with President Wilson—and don't mind saying so—that we are fighting for and not against the German people in this war.

No. 107. A German Translation of the Above.

No. 108. American Interest in Popular Government Abroad. A pamphlet of particular appeal to historians and others interested in proof from historic utterances and government records that America is only living true to her destiny and the ideals of her great leaders in helping to make the "world safe for Democracy."

EMMA GOLDMAN

26 | Opposing the Draft

Emma Goldman, who emigrated from Lithuania to the United States in 1885,
was a major influence among American literary and political radicals from the
early 1890s until her arrest in 1917 and her subsequent deportation. With her
fellow anarchist, Alexander Berkman ("Sasha" in the excerpt below), her publi-
cations and lectures became an important conduit for European ideas of political
anarchism and literary modernism as well as for a variety of related reforms,
such as birth control and social welfare issues. Leon Czolgosz, who assassinated
President McKinley in 1901, claimed to have been inspired by her speeches.

   Goldman's opposition to the draft after the entry of the United States into
World War I led to her arrest, conviction, and deportation, despite the lack of
evidence that any of her activities had interfered with conscription. Her fate was
more highly publicized than that of many others who criticized America's role
in the war. The nation, sharply divided about entry into the European conflict,
nonetheless showed scant tolerance for dissent even from speakers far more con-
servative than Emma Goldman.

In the spirit of her military preparations America was rivalling the most
despotic countries of the Old World. Conscription, resorted to by Great
Britain only after eighteen months of war, was decided upon by Wilson
within one month after the United States had decided to enter the European conflict. Washington was not so squeamish about the rights of its
citizens as the British Parliament had been. The academic author of *The
New Freedom* [Woodrow Wilson] did not hesitate to destroy every democratic principle at one blow. He had assured the world that America was
moved by the highest humanitarian motives, her aim being to democra-
tize Germany. What if he had to Prussianize the United States in order
to achieve it? Free-born Americans had to be forcibly pressed into the
military mould, herded like cattle, and shipped across the waters to fer-
tilize the fields of France. Their sacrifice would earn them the glory of
having demonstrated the superiority of *My Country, 'Tis of Thee* over *Die
Wacht am Rhein*. No American president had ever before succeeded in

From Living My Life *by Emma Goldman. Copyright 1931 by Alfred A. Knopf, Inc. Reprinted by*
permission of Alfred A. Knopf, Inc., pp. 597–601, 604–607 of Volume 2.

so humbugging the people as Woodrow Wilson, who wrote and talked democracy, acted despotically, privately and officially, and yet managed to keep up the myth that he was championing humanity and freedom.

We had no illusions about the outcome of the conscription bill pending before Congress. We regarded the measure as a complete denial of every human right, the death-knell to liberty of conscience, and we determined to fight it unconditionally. We did not expect to be able to stem the tidal wave of hatred and violence which compulsory service was bound to bring, but we felt that we had at least to make known at large that there were some in the United States who owned their souls and who meant to preserve their integrity, no matter what the cost.

We decided to call a conference in the *Mother Earth* office to broach the organization of a No-Conscription League and draw up a manifesto to clarify to the people of America the menace of conscription. We also planned a large mass meeting as a protest against compelling American men to sign their own death-warrants in the form of forced military registration.

Because of previously arranged lecture dates in Springfield, Massachusetts, I was unfortunately not able to be present at the conference, set for May 9. But as Sasha, Fitzi,* Leonard D. Abbott, and other clearheaded friends would attend, I felt no anxiety about the outcome. It was suggested that the conference should take up the question of whether the No-Conscription League should urge men not to register. *En route* to Springfield I wrote a short statement giving my attitude on the matter. I sent it with a note to Fitzi asking her to read it at the gathering. I took the position that, as a woman and therefore myself not subject to military service, I could not advise people on the matter. Whether or not one is to lend oneself as a tool for the business of killing should properly be left to the individual conscience. As an anarchist I could not presume to decide the fate of others, I wrote. But I could say to those who refused to be coerced into military service that I would plead their cause and stand by their act against all odds.

By the time I returned from Springfield the No-Conscription League had been organized and the Harlem River Casino rented for a mass meeting to take place on May 18. Those who had participated at the conference had agreed with my attitude regarding registration.

Almost ten thousand people filled the place, among them many newly rigged-out soldiers and their woman friends, a very boisterous lot indeed. Several hundred policemen and detectives were scattered through the hall. When the session opened, a few young "patriots" tried to rush the stage entrance. Their attempt was foiled, because we had prepared for such a contingency.

Leonard D. Abbott presided, and on the platform were Harry Wein-

---

* [M. Eleanor Fitzgerald, Office Secretary]

berger, Louis Fraina, Sasha, myself, and a number of other opponents of forced military service. Men and women of varying political views supported our stand on this occasion. Every speaker vigorously denounced the conscription bill which was awaiting the President's signature. Sasha was particularly splendid. Resting his injured leg on a chair and supporting himself with one hand on the table, he breathed strength and defiance. Always a man of great self-control, his poise on this occasion was remarkable. No one in the vast audience could have guessed that he was in pain, or that he gave a single thought to his helpless condition if we should fail to carry the meeting to a peaceful end. With great clarity and sustained power Sasha spoke as I had never heard him before.

The future heroes were noisy all through the speeches, but when I stepped on the platform, pandemonium broke loose. They jeered and hooted, intoned *The Star-Spangled Banner,* and frantically waved small American flags. Above the din the voice of a recruit shouted: "I want the floor!" The patience of the audience had been sorely tried all evening by the interrupters. Now men rose from every part of the house and called to the disturber to shut up or be kicked out. I knew what such a thing would lead to, with the police waiting for a chance to aid the patriotic ruffians. Moreover, I did not want to deny free speech even to the soldier. Raising my voice, I appealed to the assembly to permit the man to speak. "We who have come here to protest against coercion and to demand the right to think and act in accordance with our consciences," I urged, "should recognize the right of an opponent to speak and we should listen quietly and grant him the respect we demand for ourselves. The young man no doubt believes in the justice of his cause as we do in ours, and he has pledged his life for it. I suggest therefore that we all rise in appreciation of his evident sincerity and that we hear him out in silence." The audience rose to a man.

The soldier had probably never before faced such a large assembly. He looked frightened and he began in a quavering voice that barely carried to the platform, although he was sitting near it. He stammered something about "German money" and "traitors," got confused, and came to a sudden stop. Then, turning to his comrades, he cried: "Oh, hell! Let's get out of here!" Out the whole gang slunk, waving their little flags and followed by laughter and applause.

Returning from the meeting home we heard newsboys shouting extra night editions—the conscription bill had become a law! Registration day was set for June 4. The thought struck me that on that day American democracy would be carried to its grave.

/   /   /

Streams of callers besieged our office from morning till late at night; young men, mostly, seeking advice on whether they should register.

We knew, of course, that among them were also decoys sent to trick us into saying that they should not. The majority, however, were frightened youths, fearfully wrought up and at sea as to what to do. They were helpless creatures about to be sacrificed to Moloch. Our sympathies were with them, but we felt that we had no right to decide the vital issue for them. There were also distracted mothers, imploring us to save their boys. By the hundreds they came, wrote, or telephoned. All day long our telephone rang; our offices were filled with people, and stacks of mail arrived from every part of the country asking for information about the No-Conscription League, pledging support and urging us to go on with the work. In this bedlam we had to prepare copy for the current issues of *Mother Earth* and the *Blast*, write our manifesto, and send out circulars announcing our forthcoming meeting. At night, when trying to get some sleep, we would be rung out of bed by reporters wanting to know our next step.

Anti-conscription meetings were also taking place outside of New York and I was busy organizing branches of the No-Conscription League. At such a gathering in Philadelphia the police came down with drawn clubs and threatened to beat up the audience if I dared mention conscription. I proceeded to talk about the freedom the masses in Russia had gained. At the close of the meeting fifty persons retired to a private place, where we organized a No-Conscription League. Similar experiences were repeated in many cities.

/   /   /

The June issue of *Mother Earth* appeared draped in black, its cover representing a tomb bearing the inscription: "IN MEMORIAM—AMERICAN DEMOCRACY." The sombre attire of the magazine was striking and effective. No words could express more eloquently the tragedy that turned America, the erstwhile torch-bearer of freedom, into a grave-digger of her former ideals.

We strained our capital to the last penny to issue an extra large edition. We wanted to mail copies to every Federal officer, to every editor, in the country and to distribute the magazine among young workers and college students. Our twenty thousand copies barely sufficed to supply our own needs. It made us feel our poverty more than ever before. Fortunately an unexpected ally came to our assistance: the New York newspapers! They had reprinted whole passages from our anti-conscription manifesto, some even reproducing the entire text and thus bringing it to the attention of millions of readers. Now they copiously quoted from our June issue and editorially commented at length on its contents.

The press throughout the country raved at our defiance of law and presidential orders. We duly appreciated their help in making our voices resound through the land, our voices that but yesterday had called in vain. Incidentally the papers also gave wide publicity to our meeting scheduled for June 4.

/   /   /

When we got within half a dozen blocks of Hunt's Point Palace, our taxi had to come to a stop. Before us was a human dam, as far as the eye could see, a densely packed, swaying mass, counting tens of thousands. On the outskirts were police on horse and on foot, and great numbers of soldiers in khaki. They were shouting orders, swearing, and pushing the crowd from the sidewalks to the street and back again. The taxi could not proceed, and it was hopeless to try to get Sasha to the hall on his crutches. We had to make a detour around vacant lots until we reached the back entrance of the Palace. There we came upon a score of patrol wagons armed with search-lights and machine-guns. The officers stationed at the stage door, failing to recognize us, refused to let us pass. A reporter who knew us whispered to the police sergeant in charge. "Oh, all right," he shouted, "but nobody else will be admitted. The place is overcrowded."

The sergeant had lied; the house was only half filled. The police were keeping the people from getting in, and at seven o'clock they had ordered the doors locked. While they were denying the right of entry to workers, they permitted scores of half-drunken sailors and soldiers to enter the hall. The balcony and the front seats were filled with them. They talked loudly, made vulgar remarks, jeered, hooted, and otherwise behaved as befits men who are preparing to make the world safe for democracy.

In the room behind the stage were officials from the Department of Justice, members of the Federal attorney's office, United States marshals, detectives from the "Anarchist Squad," and reporters. The scene looked as if set for bloodshed. The representatives of law and order were obviously keyed up for trouble.

When the meeting was opened and Leonard D. Abbott took the chair, he was greeted by the soldiers and sailors with catcalls, whistles, and stamping of feet. This failing of the desired effect, the uniformed men in the gallery began throwing on the platform electric lamps which they had unscrewed from the fixtures. Several bulbs struck a vase holding a bunch of red carnations, sending vase and flowers crashing to the floor. Confusion followed, the audience rising in indignant protest and demanding that the police put the ruffians out. John Reed, who was with us, called on the police captain to order the disturbers removed, but that official declined to intervene.

After repeated appeals from the chairman, supported by some women in the audience, comparative quiet was restored. But not for long. Every speaker had to go through the same ordeal. Even the mothers of prospective soldiers, who poured out their anguish and wrath, were jeered by the savages in Uncle Sam's uniform.

Stella was one of the mothers to address the audience. It was the first time she had to face such an assembly and endure insults. Her own son was still too young to be subject to conscription, but she shared the woe and grief of other, less fortunate, parents, and she could articulate the protest of those who had no opportunity to speak. She held her own against the interruptions and carried the audience with her by the earnestness and fervour of her talk.

Sasha was the next speaker; others were to follow him, and I was to speak last. Sasha refused to be helped to the platform. Slowly and with great effort he managed to climb up the several steps and then walked across the stage to the chair placed for him near the footlights. Again, as on May 18, he had to stand on one leg, resting the other on the chair and supporting himself with one hand on the table. He stood erect, his head held high, his jaw set, his eyes clear and unflinchingly turned on the disturbers. The audience rose and greeted Sasha with prolonged applause, a token of their appreciation of his appearance in spite of his injury. The enthusiastic demonstration seemed to enrage the patriots, most of whom were obviously under the influence of drink. Renewed shouts, whistles, stamping, and hysterical cries of the women accompanying the soldiers greeted Sasha. Above the clamour a hoarse voice cried: "No more! We've had enough!" But Sasha would not be daunted. He began to speak, louder and louder, berating the hoodlums, now reasoning with them, now holding them up to scorn. His words seemed to impress them. They became quiet. Then, suddenly, a husky brute in front shouted; "Let's charge the platform! Let's get the slacker!" In an instant the audience were on their feet. Some ran up to grab the soldier. I rushed to Sasha's side. In my highest pitch I cried: "Friends, friends—wait, wait!" The suddenness of my appearance attracted everyone's attention. "The soldiers and sailors have been sent here to cause trouble," I admonished the people, "and the police are in league with them. If we lose our heads there will be bloodshed, and it will be our blood they will shed!" There were cries of "She's right!" "It's true!" I took advantage of the momentous pause. "Your presence here," I continued, "and the presence of the multitude outside shouting their approval of every word they can catch, are convincing proof that you do not believe in violence, and it equally proves that you understand that war is the most fiendish violence. War kills deliberately, ruthlessly, and destroys innocent lives. No, it is not we who have come to create a riot here. We must refuse to be provoked to it. Intelligence and a passionate faith are more convincing than armed police, machine-guns, and rowdies in soldiers' coats. We have demonstrated it tonight. We still have many speakers, some of them with illustrious American names. But nothing they or I could say will add to the splendid example you have given. Therefore I declare the meeting closed. File out orderly, intone our inspiring revolutionary songs, and leave the soldiers to their tragic fate, which at present they are too ignorant to realize.''

The strains of the *Internationale* rose above the approval shouted by the audience, and the song was taken up by the many-throated mass outside. Patiently they had waited for five hours and every word that had reached them through the open windows had found a strong echo in their hearts. All through the meeting their applause had thundered back to us, and now their jubilant song.

In the committee room a reporter of the New York *World* rushed up to me. "Your presence of mind saved the situation," he congratulated me. "But what will you report in your paper?" I asked. "Will you tell of the rough-house the soldiers tried to make, and the refusal of the police to stop them?" He would, he said, but I was certain that no truthful report would be published, even if he should have the courage to write it.

The next morning the *World* proclaimed that "Rioting accompanied the meeting of the No-Conscription League at Hunt's Point Palace. Many were injured and twelve arrests made. Soldiers in uniform sneered at the speakers. After adjournment the real riot began in the adjacent streets."

The alleged riot was of editorial making and seemed a deliberate attempt to stop further protests against conscription. The police took the hint. They issued orders to the hall-keepers not to rent their premises for any meeting to be addressed by Alexander Berkman or Emma Goldman. Not even the owners of places we had been using for years dared disobey. They were sorry, they said; they did not fear arrest, but the soldiers had threatened their lives and property. We secured Forward Hall, on East Broadway, which belonged to the Jewish Socialist Party. It was small for our purpose, barely big enough to seat a thousand people, but no other place was to be had in entire New York. The awed silence of the pacifist and anti-military organizations which followed the passing of the registration bill made it doubly imperative for us to continue the work. We scheduled a mass meeting for June 14.

It was not necessary for us to print announcements. We merely called up the newspapers, and they did the rest. They denounced our impudence in continuing anti-war activities, and they sharply criticized the authorities for failing to stop us. As a matter of fact, the police were working overtime waylaying draft-evaders. They arrested thousands, but many more had refused to register. The press did not report the actual state of affairs; it did not care to make it known that large numbers of Americans had the manhood to defy the government. We knew through our own channels that thousands had determined not to shoulder a gun against people who were as innocent as themselves in causing the world-slaughter.

EMMETT J. SCOTT

27 | Letters from the Great Migration

The following letters, collected by Emmett J. Scott, a distinguished black educator and editor, reflect one of the great events of American social history: the "great migration" of blacks from southern to northern cities during World War I. The war-fueled economy created opportunities, and the widespread circulation of Chicago newspapers, particularly the Chicago Defender, *gave southern blacks a picture of the opportunities in Chicago and other northern cities. The letters are, for the most part, practical requests to the* Defender *for information about jobs and the treatment of blacks.*

The "Great Migration" was dwarfed by the similar, but far larger, migration of blacks to the northern cities between 1940 and 1965. During the twentieth century, black Americans went from being preponderantly the most rural Americans to the most urban. This had enormous consequences for American politics, cities, and culture.

Sherman, Ga., Nov. 28, 1916.
Dear sir: This letter comes to ask for all infirmations concerning employment in your connection in the warmest climate. Now I am in a family of (11) eleven more or less boys and girls (men and women) mixed sizes who want to go north as soon as arrangements can be made and employment given places for shelter and so en (etc) now this are farming people they were raised on the farm and are good farm hands I of course have some experience and qualefication as a coman school teacher and hotel waiter and along few other lines.

I wish you would write me at your first chance and tell me if you can give us employment at what time and about what wages will you pay and what kind of arrangement can be made for our shelter. Tell me when can you best use us now or later.

Will you send us tickets if so on what terms and at what price what is the cost per head and by what route should we come. We are Negroes and try to show ourselves worthy of all we may get from any friendly source we endeavor to be true to all good causes, if you can we thank you to help us to come north as soon as you can.

/   /   /

Sanford, Fla., April 27, 1917.
Dear sir: I have seen through the Chicago Defender that you and the people of Chicago are helping newcomers. I am asking you for some information about conditions in some small town near Chicago.

There are some families here thinking of moving up, and are desirous of knowing what to expect before leaving. Please state about treatment, work, rent and schools. Please answer at some spare time.

Anniston, Ala., April 23, 1917.
Dear sir: Please gave me some infamation about coming north i can do any kind of work from a truck gardin to farming i would like to leave here and i cant make no money to leave I ust make enought to live one please let me here from you at once i want to get where i can put my children in schol.

Cedar Grove, La., April 23, 1917
Dear Sir: to day I was advise by the defendent offices in your city to communicate with you in regards to the labor for the colored of the south as I was lead to beleave that you was in position of firms of your city & your near by surrounding towns of Chicago. Please state me how is the times in & around Chicago place to locate having a family dependent on me for support. I am informed by the Chicago Defender a very valuable paper which has for its purpose the Uplifting of my race, and of which I am a constant reader and real lover, that you were in position to show some light to one in my condition.

Seeking a Northern Home. If this is true Kindly inform me by next mail the next best thing to do Being a poor man with a family to care for, I am not coming to live on flowry Beds of ease for I am a man who works and wish to make the best I can out of life I do not wish to come there hoodwinked now knowing where to go or what to do so I Solicite your help in this matter and thanking you in advance for what advice you may be pleased to Give I am yours for success.

P.S. I am presently imployed in the I C RR. Mail Department at Union Station this city.

Brookhaven, Miss., April 24, 1917.
Gents: The cane growers of Louisiana have stopped the exodus from New Orleans, claiming shortage of labor which will result in a sugar famine.

Now these laborers thus employed receive only 85 cents a day and the high cost of living makes it a serious question to live.

There is a great many race people around here who desires to come north but have waited rather late to avoid car fare, which they have not got. isnt there some way to get the concerns who wants labor, to send passes here or elsewhere so they can come even if they have to pay out of the first months wages? Please done publish this letter but do what you can towards helping them to get away. If the R. R. Co. would run a low rate excursion they could leave that way. Please ans.

Savannah, Ga., April 24, 1917.
Sir: I saw an advertisement in the Chicago Ledger where you would send tickets to any one desireing to come up there. I am a married man with a wife only, and I am 38 years of age, and both of us have so far splendid health, and would like very much to come out there provided we could get good employment regarding the advertisement.

Fullerton, La., April 28, 1917
Dear sir: I was reading about you was neading labor ninety miles of Chicago what is the name of the place and what R R extends ther i wants to come north and i wants a stedy employment ther what doe you pay per day i dont no anything about molding works but have been working around machinery for 10 years. Let me no what doe you pay for such work and can you give me a job of that kind or a job at common labor and let me no your prices and how many hours for a day.

De Ridder, La., April 29, 1917.
Dear Sir: there is lots of us southern mens wants transportation and we want to leave ratway as soon as you let us here from you some of us is married mens who need work we would like to bring our wife with us there is 20 head of good mens want transportation and if you need us let us no by return mail we all are redy only wants here from you there may be more all of our peoples wont to leave here and I want you to send as much as 20 tickets any way I will get you up plenty hands to do most any kind of work all you have to do is to send for them. looking to here from you. This is among us collerd.

Atlanta, Ga., April 30, 1917.
Dear Sir: In reading the Chicago Defender I find that there are many jobs open for workmen, I wish that you would or can secure me a position in some of the northern cities; as a workman and not as a loafer. One who is willing to do any kind of hard in side or public work, have had broad experience in machinery and other work of the kind. A some what alround man can also cook, well trained devuloped man; have travel extensively through the western and southern states; A good strong *morial religious* man no habits. I will accept transportation on advance and deducted from my wages later. It does not matter where, that is; as to city, country, town or state since you secure the positions. I am

quite sure you will be delighted in securing a position for a man of this description. I'll assure you will not regret of so doing. Hoping to hear from you soon.

Houston, Tx., April 30, 1917
Dear Sir: wanted to leave the South and Go and Place where a man will be any thing Except a Ker I thought would write you for Advise as where would be a Good Place for a Comporedly young man That want to Better his Standing who has a very Promising young Family.

I am 30 years old and have Good Experience in Freight Handler and Can fill Position from Truck to Agt.

would like Chicago or Philadelphia But I dont Care where so long as I Go where a man is a man.

Beaumont, Texas, May 7, 1917.
Dear Sir: I see in one of your recent issue of collored men woanted in the North I wish you would help me to get a position in the North I have no trade I have been working for one company eight years and there is no advancement here for me and I would like to come where I can better my condition I woant work and not affraid to work all I wish is a chance to make good. I believe I would like machinist helper or Molder helper. If you can help me in any way it will be highly appreciate hoping to hear from you soon

28 | Observations of the Middle Class

Sinclair Lewis, the first American to win a Nobel Prize for literature, was one of the most notable of the intellectuals who lived through the disillusionment accompanying World War I and who ever after saw through—or thought they saw through—the pretentions of contemporary society. Lewis's 1922 novel, Babbitt, is one of the most enduring of American attempts to make a judgment about the materialistic passions of the 1920s.

There were two sides to the culture of the 1920s. One is shown in the world of George Babbitt—the decade is portrayed as a new consumer paradise, in which cars and radios, mass-produced household items, and all the personal adornments we now take for granted were new and exciting. The other side is seen in the attitudes about George Babbitt. It is represented by the music, painting, and literature of the 1920s—described from an artistic, anti-middle class perspective that was, in fact, a reaction to this consumer culture that seemed to threaten all values of aesthetics. Present in the early novels of Sinclair Lewis and in the work of a generation of new American artists is a satiric—even savage—criticism of all that was dear to the emerging consumer culture.

Before he followed his wife, Babbitt stood at the western-most window of their room. This residential settlement, Floral Heights, was on a rise; and though the center of the city was three miles away—Zenith had between three and four hundred thousand inhabitants now—he could see the top of the Second National Tower, an Indiana limestone building of thirty-five stories.

Its shining walls rose against April sky to a simple cornice like a streak of white fire. Integrity was in the tower, and decision. It bore its strength lightly as a tall soldier. As Babbitt stared, the nervousness was soothed from his face, his slack chin lifted in reverence. All he articulated was "That's one lovely sight!" but he was inspired by the rhythm of the city; his love of it renewed. He beheld the tower as a temple-spire of the religion of business, a faith passionate, exalted, surpassing common men; and as he clumped down to breakfast he whistled the ballad "Oh, by gee, by gosh, by jingo" as though it were a hymn melancholy and noble.

Relieved of Babbitt's bumbling and the soft grunts with which his wife expressed the sympathy she was too experienced to feel and much too experienced not to show, their bedroom settled instantly into impersonality.

It gave on the sleeping-porch. It served both of them as dressing-room, and on the coldest nights Babbitt luxuriously gave up the duty of being manly and retreated to the bed inside, to curl his toes in the warmth and laugh at the January gale.

The room displayed a modest and pleasant color-scheme, after one of the best standard designs of the decorator who "did the interiors" for most of the speculative-builders' houses in Zenith. The walls were gray, the woodwork white, the rug a serene blue; and very much like mahogany was the furniture—the bureau with its great clear mirror, Mrs. Babbitt's dressing-table with toilet-articles of almost solid silver, the plain twin beds, between them a small table holding a standard electric bedside lamp, a glass for water, and a standard bedside book with colored illustrations—what particular book it was cannot be ascertained, since no one had ever opened it. The mattresses were firm but not hard, triumphant modern mattresses which had cost a great deal of money; the hot-water radiator was of exactly the proper scientific surface for the cubic contents of the room. The windows were large and easily opened, with the best catches and cords, and Holland roller-shades guaranteed not to crack. It was a masterpiece among bedrooms, right out of Cheerful Modern Houses for Medium Incomes. Only it had nothing to do with the Babbitts, nor with any one else. If people had ever lived and loved here, read thrillers at midnight and lain in beautiful indolence on a Sunday morning, there were no signs of it. It had the air of being a very good room in a very good hotel. One expected the chambermaid to come in and make it ready for people who would stay but one night, go without looking back, and never think of it again.

Every second house in Floral Heights had a bedroom precisely like this.

The Babbitt's house was five years old. It was all as competent and glossy as this bedroom. It had the best of taste, the best of inexpensive rugs, a simple and laudable architecture, and the latest conveniences. Throughout, electricity took the place of candles and slatternly hearth-fires. Along the bedroom baseboard were three plugs for electric lamps, concealed by little brass doors. In the halls were plugs for the vacuum cleaner, and in the living-room plugs for the piano lamp, for the electric fan. The trim dining-room (with its admirable oak buffet, its leaded-glass cupboard, its creamy plaster walls, its modest scene of a salmon expiring upon a pile of oysters) had plugs which supplied the electric percolator and the electric toaster.

In fact there was but one thing wrong with the Babbitt house: It was not a home.

/   /   /

Often of a morning Babbitt came bouncing and jesting in to breakfast. But things were mysteriously awry to-day. As he pontifically tread the upper hall he looked into Verona's bedroom and protested, "What's the use of giving the family a high-class house when they don't appreciate it and tend to business and get down to brass tacks?"

He marched upon them: Verona, a dumpy brown-haired girl of twenty-two, just out of Bryn Mawr, given to solicitudes about duty and sex and God and the unconquerable bagginess of the gray sports-suit she was now wearing. Ted—Theodore Roosevelt Babbitt—a decorative boy of seventeen. Tinka—Katherine—still a baby at ten, with radiant red hair and a thin skin which hinted of too much candy and too many ice cream sodas. Babbitt did not show his vague irritation as he tramped in. He really disliked being a family tyrant, and his nagging was as meaningless as it was frequent. He shouted at Tinka, "Well, kittiedoolie!" It was the only pet name in his vocabulary, except the "dear" and "hon." with which he recognized his wife, and he flung it at Tinka every morning.

He gulped a cup of coffee in the hope of pacifying his stomach and his soul. His stomach ceased to feel as though it did not belong to him, but Verona began to be conscientious and annoying, and abruptly there returned to Babbitt the doubts regarding life and families and business which had clawed at him when his dream-life and the slim fairy girl had fled.

Verona had for six months been filing-clerk at the Gruensberg Leather Company offices, with a prospect of becoming secretary to Mr. Gruensberg and thus, as Babbitt defined it, "getting some good out of your expensive college education till you're ready to marry and settle down."

But now said Verona: "Father! I was talking to a classmate of mine that's working for the Associated Charities—oh, Dad, there's the sweetest little babies that come to the milk-station there!—and I feel as though I ought to be doing something worth while like that."

"What do you mean 'worth while'? If you get to be Gruensberg's secretary—and maybe you would, if you kept up your shorthand and didn't go sneaking off to concerts and talkfests every evening—I guess you'll find thirty-five or forty bones a week worth while!"

"I know, but—oh, I want to—contribute— I wish I were working in a settlement-house. I wonder if I could get one of the department-stores to let me put in a welfare-department with a nice rest-room and chintzes and wicker chairs and so on and so forth. Or I could—"

"Now you look here! The first thing you got to understand is that all this uplift and flipflop and settlement-work and recreation is nothing in God's world but the entering wedge for socialism. The sooner a man learns he isn't going to be coddled, and he needn't expect a lot of free grub and, uh, all these free classes and flipflop and doodads for his kids unless he earns 'em, why, the sooner he'll get on the job and produce— produce—produce! That's what the country needs, and not all this fancy stuff that just enfeebles the will-power of the working man and gives his kids a lot of notions above their class. And you—if you'd tend to business instead of fooling and fussing— All the time! When I was a young man I made up my mind what I wanted to do, and stuck to it through thick and thin, and that's why I'm where I am to-day, and— Myra! What do you let the girl chop the toast up into these dinky little chunks for? Can't get your fist onto 'em. Half cold, anyway!''

Ted Babbitt, junior in the great East Side High School, had been making hiccup-like sounds of interruption. He blurted now, "Say, Rone, you going to—"

Verona whirled. "Ted! Will you kindly not interrupt us when we're talking about serious matters!"

"Aw punk," said Ted judicially. "Ever since somebody slipped up and let you out of college, Ammonia, you been pulling these nut conversations about what-nots and so-on-and-so-forths. Are you going to— I want to use the car tonight."

Babbitt snorted, "Oh, you do! May want it myself!" Verona protested, "Oh, you do, Mr. Smarty! I'm going to take it myself!" Tinka wailed, "Oh, papa, you said maybe you'd drive us down to Rosedale!" and Mrs. Babbitt, "Careful, Tinka, your sleeve is in the butter." They glared, and Verona hurled, "Ted, you're a perfect pig about the car!''

"Course you're not! Not a-tall!" Ted could be maddeningly bland. "You just want to grab it off, right after dinner, and leave it in front of some shirt's house all evening while you sit and gas about lite'ature and the highbrows you're going to marry—if they only propose!"

"Well, Dad oughtn't to *ever* let you have it! You and those beastly Jones boys drive like maniacs. The idea of your taking the turn on Chautauqua Place at forty miles an hour!"

"Aw, where do you get that stuff! You're so darn scared of the car that you drive up-hill with the emergency brake on!"

"I do not! And you— Always talking about how much you know about motors, and Eunice Littlefield told me you said the battery fed the generator!"

"You—why, my good woman, you don't know a generator from a differential." Not unreasonably was Ted lofty with her. He was a natural mechanic, a maker and tinkerer of machines; he lisped in blueprints for the blueprints came.

"That'll do now!" Babbitt flung in mechanically, as he lighted the gloriously satisfying first cigar of the day and tasted the exhilarating drug of the *Advocate-Times* headlines.

Ted negotiated: "Gee, honest, Rone, I don't want to take the old boat, but I promised couple o' girls in my class I'd drive 'em down to the rehearsal of the school chorus, and, gee, I don't want to, but a gentleman's got to keep his social engagements."

"Well, upon my word! You and your social engagements! In high school!"

"Oh, ain't we select since we went to that hen college! Let me tell you there isn't a private school in the state that's got as swell a bunch as we got in Gamma Digamma this year. There's two fellows that their dads are millionaires. Say, gee, I ought to have a car of my own, like lots of the fellows."

Babbitt almost rose. "A car of your own! Don't you want a yacht, and a house and lot? That pretty nearly takes the cake! A boy that can't pass his Latin examinations, like any other boy ought to, and he expects me to give him a motor-car, and I suppose a chauffeur, and an aeroplane maybe, as a reward for the hard work he puts in going to the movies with Eunice Littlefield! Well, when you see me giving you—"

Somewhat later, after diplomacies, Ted persuaded Verona to admit that she was merely going to the Armory, that evening, to see the dog and cat show. She was then, Ted planned, to park the car in front of the candy-store across from the Armory and he would pick it up. There were masterly arrangements regarding leaving the key, and having the gasoline tank filled; and passionately, devotees of the Great God Motor, they hymned the patch on the spare inner-tube, and the lost jack-handle.

Their truce dissolving, Ted observed that her friends were "a scream of a bunch—stuck-up gabby four-flushers." His friends, she indicated, were "disgusting imitation sports, and horrid little shrieking ignorant girls." Further: "It's disgusting of you to smoke cigarettes, and so on and so forth, and those clothes you've got on this morning, they're too utterly ridiculous—honestly, simply disgusting."

Ted balanced over to the low beveled mirror in the buffet, regarded his charms, and smirked. His suit, the latest thing in Old Eli Togs, was skin-tight, with skimpy trousers to the tops of his glaring tan boots, a chorus-man waistline, pattern of an agitated check, and across the back a belt which belted nothing. His scarf was an enormous black silk wad. His flaxen hair was ice-smooth, pasted back without parting. When he went to school he would add a cap with a long vizor like a shovel-blade. Proudest of all was his waistcoat, saved for, begged for, plotted for; a real Fancy Vest of fawn with polka dots of a decayed red, the points astoundingly long. On the lower edge of it he wore a high-school button, a class button, and a fraternity pin.

And none of it mattered. He was supple and swift and flushed; his eyes (which he believed to be cynical) were candidly eager. But he was not over-gentle. He waved his hand at poor dumpy Verona and drawled: "Yes, I guess we're pretty ridiculous and disgusticulus, and I rather guess our new necktie is some smear!"

Babbitt barked: "It is! And while you're admiring yourself, let me tell you it might add to your manly beauty if you wiped some of that egg off your mouth!"

Verona giggled, momentary victor in the greatest of Great Wars, which is the family war. Ted looked at her hopelessly, then shrieked at Tinka: "For the love o' Pete, quite pouring the whole sugar bowl on your corn flakes!"

When Verona and Ted were gone and Tinka upstairs, Babbitt groaned to his wife: "Nice family, I must say! I don't pretend to be any baa-lamb, and maybe I'm a little cross-grained at breakfast sometimes, but the way they go on jab-jab-jabbering, I simply can't stand it. I swear, I feel like going off some place where I can get a little peace. I do think after a man's spent his lifetime trying to give his kids a chance and a decent education, it's pretty discouraging to hear them all the time scrapping like a bunch of hyenas and never—and never— Curious; here in the paper it says—Never silent for one mom— Seen the morning paper yet?"

"No, dear." In twenty-three years of married life, Mrs. Babbitt had seen the paper before her husband just sixty-seven times.

"Lots of news. Terrible big tornado in the South. Hard luck, all right. But this, say, this is corking! Beginning of the end for those fellows! New York Assembly has passed some bills that ought to completely outlaw the socialists! And there's an elevator-runners' strike in New York and a lot of college boys are taking their places. That's the stuff! And a mass-meeting in Birmingham's demanded that this Mick agitator, this fellow De Valera, be deported. Dead right, by golly! All these agitators paid with German gold anyway. And we got no business interfering with the Irish or any other foreign government. Keep our hands strictly off. And there's another well-authenticated rumor from Russia that Lenin is dead. That's fine. It's beyond me why we don't just step in there and kick those Bolshevik cusses out."

"That's so," said Mrs. Babbitt.

"And it says here a fellow was inaugurated mayor in overalls—a preacher, too! What do you think of that!"

"Humph! Well!"

He searched for an attitude, but neither as a Republican, a Presbyterian, an Elk, nor a real-estate broker did he have any doctrine about preacher-mayors laid down for him, so he grunted and went on. She looked sympathetic and did not hear a word. Later she would read the headlines, the society columns, and the department-store advertisements.

"What do you know about this! Charley McKelvey still doing the sassiety stunt as heavy as ever. Here's what that gushy woman reporter says about last night:

Never is society with the big, big S more flattered than when they are bidden to partake of good cheer at the distinguished and hospitable residence of Mr. and Mrs. Charles L. McKelvey as they were last night. Set in its spacious lawns and landscaping, one of the notable sights crowning Royal Ridge, but merry and homelike despite its mighty stone walls and its vast rooms famed for their decoration, their home was thrown open last night for a dance in honor of Mrs. McKelvey's notable guest, Miss J. Sneeth of Washington. The wide hall is so generous in its proportions that it made a perfect ballroom, its hardwood floor reflecting the charming pageant above its polished surface. Even the delights of dancing paled before the alluring opportunities for tête-à-têtes that invited the soul to loaf in the long library before the baronial fireplace, or in the drawing-room with its deep comfy armchairs, its shaded lamps just made for a sly whisper of pretty nothings all a deux; or even in the billiard room where one could take a cue and show a prowess at still another game than that sponsored by Cupid and Terpsichore.

There was more, a great deal more, in the best urban journalistic style of Miss Elnora Pearl Bates, the popular society editor of the *Advocate-Times*. But Babbitt could not abide it. He grunted. He wrinkled the newspaper. He protested: "Can you beat it! I'm willing to hand a lot of credit to Charley McKelvey. When we were in college together, he was just as hard up as any of us, and he's made a million good bucks out of contracting and hasn't been any dishonester or bought any more city councils than was necessary. And that's a good house of his—though it ain't any 'mighty stone walls' and it ain't worth the ninety thousand it cost him. But when it comes to talking as though Charley McKelvey and all that booze-hoisting set of his are any blooming bunch of of, of Vanderbilts, why, it makes me tired!"

Timidly from Mrs. Babbitt; "I would like to see the inside of their house though. It must be lovely. I've never been inside."

"Well, I have! Lots of—couple of times. To see Chaz about business deals, in the evening. It's not so much. I wouldn't *want* to go there to dinner with that gang of, of high-binders. And I'll bet I make a whole lot more money than some of those tin-horns that spend all they got on dress-suits and haven't got a decent suit of underwear to their name! Hey! What do you think of this!"

Mrs. Babbitt was strangely unmoved by the tidings from the Real Estate and Building column of the *Advocate-Times:*

> Ashtabula Street, 496—J. K. Dawson to Thomas Mullally, April 17, 15.7 x 112.2, mtg. $4000 . . . . Nom.

And this morning Babbitt was too disquieted to entertain her with items from Mechanics' Liens, Mortgages Recorded, and Contracts Awarded. He rose. As he looked at her his eyebrows seemed shaggier than usual. Suddenly:

"Yes, maybe— Kind of shame to not keep in touch with folks like the McKelveys. We might try inviting them to dinner, some evening.

Oh, thunder, let's not waste our good time thinking about 'em! Our little bunch has a lot liver times than all those plutes. Just compare a real human like you with these neurotic birds like Lucile McKelvey—all highbrow talk and dressed up like a plush horse! You're a great old girl, hon.!''

He covered his betrayal of softness with a complaining: "Say, don't let Tinka go and eat any more of that poison nut-fudge. For Heaven's sake, try to keep her from ruining her digestion. I tell you, most folks don't appreciate how important it is to have a good digestion and regular habits. Be back 'bout usual time, I guess.''

He kissed her—he didn't quite kiss her—he laid unmoving lips against her unflushing cheek. He hurried out to the garage, muttering: "Lord, what a family! And now Myra is going to get pathetic on me because we don't train with this millionaire outfit. Oh, Lord, sometimes I'd like to quit the whole game. And the office worry and detail just as bad. And I act cranky and— I don't mean to, but I get— So darn tired!''

29 | Advertising, the Civilizer

Americans seriously began worrying about the effects of advertising in the 1920s, the era in which advertising became a profession, and that fear has never quite been stilled. In the following reading, from the period, an advertising professional offers a defense of his industry. Calkins argues that advertising helps create a market for the labor-saving devices of the modern age. Advertising creates better-educated consumers, who, by their support of industry, encourage even more new products and, through the volume of their demand, help provide incentive for cheaper, more efficient means of production.

The Rising Generation Asks a Question

A young man who had just joined the staff of one of the larger advertising agencies sought his boss in some perturbation. "I wish you would tell me the truth about this advertising business, chief. Is it all bunk?" To which his employer replied, "There is just as much bunk in advertising as there is in law or medicine, or for that matter, in literature and life, but it is never necessary to use bunk to practise advertising successfully."

That young man's state of mind was the natural result of his reading. He had been recruited from the profession of writing, and he still followed the ultra-intellectual world, which has lately concerned itself with the inconsistencies, the waste, and the smugness of advertising. In short, with the bunk.

The pages of those delightful magazines which are distinguished by good writing, distinctive typography, small circulation, and no advertising, offer some interesting points of view to the professional advertising man—who unfortunately does not as a rule read them.

/ / /

William McFee finds the floor of his post office at Westport littered knee-deep with circulars cast off by disdainful recipients, and deplores the destruction of forests to make the paper for so futile an end. And Joseph Pennell, who was pleased with few things apparently despised

Earnest Elmo Calkins, Business the Civilizer (*Boston, Atlantic Monthly Press Publication, Little, Brown, and Company, 1928) pp. 1–3, 12–18.*

advertising more cordially and with stronger adjectives than any other manifestation of our commercial civilization.

Then there are the fiction makers, with less restriction and more imagination. The younger men, most of them after brief experiences inside advertising organizations, have seized the excellent oportunity for satire which modern business affords, and we have . . . Scott Fitzgerald's *The Great Gatsby*, Christopher Morley's *Ginger Cubes*, Sinclair Lewis's *Babbitt*, Sherwood Anderson's *Story-teller's Story*, and *Bunk, Lottery*, and *Bread and Circuses* by William Woodward, all presenting advertising as a sort of gigantic conspiracy, fostered and maintained by highly paid advertising men whose interests, like those of the priests of ancient religions, lie in keeping up the great illusion, and who go about their work with their tongues in their cheeks. Sometimes the conspiracy is imagined as directed against the business man, but the popular conception is that the public is the victim, and that manufacturer and agent are working together to put something over. This something may be higher prices for worthless goods, creating unnecessary wants and desires, or exterminating a competitor making a better article at a lower price, but generally just misleading people with bunk about memory courses, or hair restorers, or correspondence universities.

/ / /

The slogan "It pays to advertise" acquired its currency from George M. Cohan's play. Admitting that advertising pays, whom does it pay? It pays the professional advertising man, beyond doubt. It also pays the manufacturer who uses it to increase his business. But the crucial question is, does it pay the public? Are the people as a whole better off for it? Is it a benefit to mankind? And who pays for it? Is it added to the cost of the goods? Would it be desirable, as writers have suggested, to remove advertising from our commercial fabric, and would we be better off without it?

/ / /

THE AMELIORATION OF THE HOUSEWIFE'S LOT

When I was a boy, about fifty years ago more or less, mother used to buy a bar of Castile soap half a yard long and four inches square and saw it up into cakes an inch thick. The cake was hard as Stonehenge, the corners sharper than a serpent's tooth. It took weeks of use to wear it down so that it comfortably fitted the hand.

To-day we have a cake of toilet soap—a great many of them, in fact— just the right shape to fit the hand, just as pure as Castile, scented if we like, tinted to match the bathroom decorations if we prefer, reasonable in price; and when we want another cake we go to the nearest grocery or drug store, and there it is.

And not only toilet soap. We have seen the evolution of shaving creams, safety razors, and tooth pastes, as well as soap powders, laundry chips, washing machines, vegetable shortenings, self-rising flours, electric sadirons, vacuum cleaners, hot-water taps, aluminum cooking utensils, refrigerators, kitchen cabinets—everything, in short, that constitutes the difference between our mothers' kitchens and our wives'.

The amount of sheer drudgery that has been taken out of housekeeping in fifty years can be realized only by comparison, by drawing the illuminating parallel. An iron, soft-coal cook-stove; a reservoir at the back the only source of hot-water supply; the green-painted iron pump in the wooden corner sink for cold; drinking water from the pump outside; saleratus instead of baking powder; hog lard instead of vegetable shortening; butter and milk hung down the well by a string to keep them cold; heavy iron pots and skillets to be lifted, to say nothing of the coalhod; dishes washed by hand; no device to alleviate the frightful labor—no rubber scrapers, scouring mops, metal-ring dishrags, no wire brushes, or drying racks, or cleansing powders; baked beans an eighteen-hour job; oatmeal an overnight operation; sugar, salt, dried fruit, pickles, crackers, rice, coffee, pepper, spices, lard, bought in bulk, scooped out of open boxes or barrels or tierces, exposed until sold, dumped on a sheet of paper laid on the scales. Molasses and vinegar drawn from the wood, and between whiles the gallon measures standing around, proving the adage that molasses attracts more flies than vinegar. Food was unclean, there was no sponsor for its quality, and it came to the kitchen almost in a state of nature. The housemother became a miniature manufacturing plant before the food was ready for the family to eat. And the preparation of meals was but a small portion of the housewife's burden. There was cleaning with no other implements but a rag, a broom, and a turkey wing. Clothes were washed with a rub-rub-rub that wore the zinc from the washboard.

Put such a kitchen beside the one pictured in most advertisements selling kitchen equipment, or those complete ones shown in the housekeeping departments of the women's magazines, "How to Furnish the Ideal Kitchen." Better still, take a modern housewife, not the delicatessen and can-opener type, but a real housekeeper, who keeps her house and takes pride in it,—there are such even to-day,—and put her in an old-fashioned kitchen like that described above. She could not do in a week what my mother did every day of her toil-bound life. To keep house with what was available half a century ago was an art handed down from generation to generation, which happily has been lost, except among the newly arrived foreign-born.

/   /   /

The amelioration that has come about in fifty years is due directly
and indirectly to advertising. These things did not come into existence
because women demanded them. Women did not know that they were
possible. They exist because there was a method of distributing them,
of teaching possible buyers what a help they would be, of educating the
housewife while offering her the means of applying what she learned,
and of doing it on a large scale. And the strongest urge to invent desirable labor-saving devices has been this same possibility of distributing
them—that is, selling enough of them to make it worth while.

Sometimes advertising supplies a demand, but in most cases it creates demand for things that were beyond even the imagination of those
who would be most benefited by them. A woman knew the use of a
broom, but she could not imagine a vacuum cleaner. Therefore she
could not demand one, save with that vague unspoken desire which
has existed from the beginning for some lightening of the terrible drudgery of keeping a house livable. The vacuum cleaner was introduced by
educational advertising. The advertising was done partly by manufacturers anxious to sell vacuum cleaners, and partly by electric-light companies anxious to sell current. The spread of electrical housekeeping devices has followed the increase in the number of houses wired for
electricity, and that too has been brought about by advertising, by the
selfish desire to do more business, to sell more goods. But the result has
been a public benefit, an increasing willingness to spend money to
lighten the human burden, to cut down the waste of human energy
spent in the operation of living.

No vacuum-cleaner factory could do business as a neighborhood
proposition. Only a national market would furnish enough business to
make the manufacture economically possible. And a national market is
possible only through advertising. And that advertising must be educational. It must teach the sound economy of paying more to get the
greater benefit. The woman's time and health and strength are worth
more than the difference in cost between a broom and a cleaner. But not
all of these improvements are in the vacuum-cleaner class. Most of them
add nothing to the cost of upkeep. The greater number lower it. They
teach the use of something better that costs less.

I do not think I am claiming too much in giving to advertising the
credit of the great change in housekeeping that we have seen. I have
had to observe it very closely for thirty years, and I have to some extent
helped to bring it about. Some may be inclined to think it is due to
the women's magazines. It is true that they have directed their editorial
energies to the same ends and with remarkable results.

But it should not be forgotten that it is advertising that makes such
magazines possible. It is the revenue from the advertisers that pays for
the services of domestic economists, physicians, interior decorators,
cooks, dressmakers, and other experts who teach women better ways

of doing things. More than that, while such departments are conducted with the primary purpose of being helpful to readers, they furnish an excellent background for the advertising. Magazines with constructive departments on the care of babies, cooking, furnishing, housekeeping, dressmaking, laundry work, and all the other activities which go into home-making are preparing audiences to listen to manufacturers who sell sanitary nursing bottles, infants' wear, prepared foods, salad oils, paints, fabrics, wall papers, electric mangles, and washing powders.

/   /   /

Behind the successful and intelligently conducted magazine is the advertiser, who buys space and makes the magazine profitable; and so the educational work of home-making magazines should be credited largely to him.

Advertising is not an end. It is a means to an end. So the question is not, Is advertising desirable, but Are those ends desirable, and is advertising too great a price to pay for them? To those who look upon advertising as merely the selfish effort of manufacturers to induce them to buy more goods it seems that the world could easily do without it. People say to themselves, "I do not want to be persuaded to buy more goods," and that should settle it. As far as they are concerned advertising is unnecessary. For the manufacturer who uses it, advertising is a means of selling goods, but its present proportions are due not to the manufacturer's desire to sell goods, but to the real public need it supplies.

A familiar paradox is the man who tells you with much earnestness that he never reads advertising, and does not believe in it. And as he sits there he is dressed from head to foot in advertised goods. His office is equipped and his home is furnished with advertised goods. How did they get there? Because they were the things most accessible, the ones for sale in the stores where he bought, the ones the salesman showed him, and the ones that most exactly met his needs. It was not necessary for him to read the advertising. The advertising he did not read distributed the goods, brought them within his reach geographically and financially, and keeps them there for his benefit—better things than he could buy for the same money were it not for the tremendous savings that quantity production brings about. And most of them would not even exist, to say nothing of being distributed, if there had not been advertising.

But advertising adds to the cost of the goods! You still hear that. So does production add to the cost of the goods, and traveling salesmen, and retail stores, and jobbers' percentages. Everything that is done to a manufactured article and all handling of natural products must be added to the price that the customer pays. But nothing is so well established as the simple fact that the more you make the less the cost of each. And not only is cost of making lessened, but also the cost of selling, including cost of advertising. And the cost of selling can be and is lessened until the advertising costs nothing. Why does a tailor-made suit cost more than a ready-made? Why do custom-made shoes cost more than the product of the factories? It is difficult to prove these things by tables of statistics because prices of all things have advanced so in the years since the war.

But consider the motor car. Nearly everyone is interested in this product of advertising. Nearly everyone is aware of the continual improvement in the cars and the steady lowering of price, due to quantity production. Some are as much concerned over the congestion of motor cars as they are over the congestion of advertising. They feel that there is too much of both. Granted in both cases; but the only alternative is to turn back the page to mediaeval times, when each village was self-contained, or forward to one of the many Utopias which promise enough of everything and not too much of anything.

The point is that we cannot eat our cake of accessible and convenient apparatus of living and still have our cake of freedom from advertising, freight trains, industrial villages, steel and cement construction, riveting hammers, congested highways, and the many other annoyances of a prosperous, material, and mercantile age. It's a fair question whether or not our modern life is worth while, but it has nothing to do with this question, which is, If our modern life is worth while and we want to continue it, is advertising necessary to that end?

30 | Advice for Raising Children

*Childrearing manuals have a long history in the United States. From Cotton
Mather's* The Family Well Ordered or An Essay to Render Parents and
Children Happy in One Another, *published in 1699, to the current edition of
Dr. Benjamin Spock's* Baby and Child Care, *first published in 1946, American
parents have not lacked advice. In the 1920s and 1930s, the Children's Bureau
of the Department of Labor widely distributed pamphlets essentially intended to
inculcate "American" styles of childrearing among presumably ignorant immigrant parents. "Are You Training Your Child to Be Happy?" illustrates the
emphasis on strictness and the inculcation of good habits that dominated thinking on this subject in the 1920s before the movement toward more "permissive"
childrearing during the era of the "baby boom" of the late 1940s and 1950s.*

DO YOU HAVE A HAPPY BABY?

Does he laugh and coo while you work?
Does he play quietly by himself while you work?
Does your little child like the food you give him?
Is he ready and willing to go to bed at bedtime?
Does he love the new baby?
Does he play happily with other children?
Then he is happy and good.

Does your baby cry all day?
Does he get mad and kick and scream?
Does your little child spit out the food he does not like?
Does he beg you not to put him to bed?
Does he tease the new baby?
Of course, you do not want these things.

United States Department of Labor, Are You Training Your Child to Be Happy? Lesson Material in Child Management. *(Washington, D.C., Government Printing Office, 1930) Department
of Labor Bureau Publication No. 202, pp. v, 1–3, 23–26.*

We can help you to make your baby happy, but you must help, too.
You must try very hard.
You must never stop trying.
You are tired and busy some day. Your baby is crying. You say,
"This one time does not matter. I will pick him up. Then he will stop
crying."
Then your smart little baby says to himself, "Hurrah, I was the boss
that time! I can be boss next time."
Before you know it, he will cry again. Will you pick him up again?
Do you always give him what he wants?
Then he will not be happy long.
Read this little book. It will help you to keep your baby happy and good.

LESSON NO. 1.—HOW CAN YOU HELP YOUR CHILD TO FORM GOOD HABITS?

Do You Want Your Child to Form Good Habits?

The first time you do something new it is hard.
Next time it is easier.
Next time it is very easy.
Soon you can do it and not think about it at all.
Then we call it a *habit*.

You have learned everything that way.
You learned to feed yourself that way when you were little.
You learned to dress yourself that way.
You have the *habit* of dressing yourself.
You have the *habit* of feeding yourself.

Your child is learning everything that way.
He is *forming habits*.
He can learn a *good* way to do things.
But he can learn a *bad* way instead.
He learns the way *you* teach him.

Do you want to teach him the good way or the bad way?
Do you want him to form good habits or bad habits?
This lesson will tell you how to teach him good habits.

Begin When He Is Born

Feed him at exactly the same hours every day.
Do not feed him at any other time.

Let him sleep after every feeding.
Do not feed him just because he cries.
Let him wait until the right time.
If you make him wait, his stomach will learn to wait.
His mind will learn that he can not get things by crying.
You do two things for your baby at the same time. You teach his body good habits and you teach his mind good habits.

You Can Teach Him Not To be a Cross Baby, Too

When he cries, do not pick him up to stop his crying.
See that no pin hurts him.
See that he is warm and dry.
Turn him over.
Then let him alone.
In that way you teach him not to fuss and cry. If mothers pick up their babies when they cry, the babies learn to cry for things. The mothers teach them to cry for things.

Pick up the Baby When He Is Awake and Not Crying

Play with him to talk to him quietly.
In a little while put him down again.
Do this at the same hours every day.
This will show him that he will get attention when he does not cry.
He will learn to wait for the right time.
This saves you time for your work and it is good for your baby.
Do not let other people pick the baby up or talk to him too much.
A little baby should be quiet most of the time.

/   /   /

Start Your Baby with Good Habits. Then the Bad Ones Will Not Form Easily.

Write to the Children's Bureau at Washington, D. C., asking for Infant Care and The Baby's Daily Time Cards. These are free. They will help you to teach your baby good habits.

HOW CAN YOU HELP YOUR CHILD FORM GOOD HABITS?

Mrs. Guerra and Her Two Babies

Mrs. Guerra had her first baby at home.
A neighbor came in to help her.

The doctor told her to feed the baby every four hours.
The baby cried.
Mrs. Guerra and her friend said, "The baby is hungry; we must feed him."
The baby cried soon again. Mrs. Guerra fed him again.
She fed him many times.
Soon the baby got sick and cross.
His stomach was tired of working.
The mother said, "What is the matter with my baby?"
The baby cried all the time.

Mrs. Guerra had her second baby at the hospital.
The nurses took care of him.
They fed him every four hours.
They bathed him at the same time every day.
They kept him clean and comfortable.
They did not pick him up when he cried.
They knew that babies get exercise when they cry. Babies need exercise.
This baby was well and happy.
The nurses said to Mrs. Guerra, "When you go home, do as we do. Then your baby will be well and happy and good."
Mrs. Guerra went home in two weeks. She did what the nurses told her.
The baby was always good and happy. He was always well.
She said: "I made a mistake before. The nurses are right. Now, I will see what I can do with my big baby to keep him well, too."

/   /   /

LESSON NO. 6.—WHY AND HOW DO YOU PUNISH YOUR CHILD?

Why Do You Punish Your Child?

Do you punish him because *you think* he is naughty and you want to make him good? Are you sure that he is really naughty and not just playing some game or trying to help?

Do you punish him because what he is doing annoys you and you want him to stop?

Do you punish him just to "pay him back" because he has done something naughty?

Do you punish him just because you are tired, and so get angry easily?

These are not good reasons for punishing him.

They are not fair to the child.

They do not make him good.

They do not make him want to be good

They only teach him to keep out of your way when you are tired or angry.

There is only one good reason to punish a child. That is to make him understand that he must not do the naughty thing again.

But before you punish you must be sure that what he is doing is *really* naughty. It is not naughty for a child to be noisy. It is not naughty for him to want to move about. It is not naughty for him to want to get hold of things.

Children need to move and make a noise. They need to hold things in their hands to find out about them.

Of course they do not need to be *too* noisy. They do not need to be rough. You must stop them if they do these things too much, but you must be very sure they *are* too much before you stop them.

Do you punish your child again and again for doing the same naughty thing? Do you have to punish your child often for different things? If so, *he is probably being naughty just to attract your attention.* If you will give him attention when he is good and pay no attention to him when he is naughty, he will stop being naughty to get attention.

Do you punish him when he is fretful because he is sleepy? Perhaps he has not been going to bed early enough; or perhaps he does not sleep in the afternoons.

Many times children are punished because their mothers are tired and cross. Is that fair?

When people are tired, little things make them cross. The baby plays with the kitchen pans one day, and his mother is glad. She says, "What a good baby! He plays all alone so nicely!"

Next day mother has done much washing and is very tired. Baby is playing with the pans again; the noise makes her cross. Perhaps she takes the pans away; or perhaps she slaps the baby.

Is that fair? The baby was doing the same to-day as he was yesterday, when mother said he was good. He was not banging the pans too much.

Did that mother punish because the baby was naughty or because she herself was tired and nervous?

A mother should take time for some rest each day. Then she will not be tired and nervous. Then she will not punish the baby so much.

A mother was whipping her boy very hard. A friend said to her, "Does it do him any good to whip him so hard?"

The mother answered, "Maybe it doesn't do *him* any good, but it does *me* lots of good."

Is that the way we ought to think about punishment?

Children understand that they must be punished when they are naughty. They know when a punishment is fair.

They know it is fair to have to play alone if they have been teasing the other children.

They know it is fair not to have a new toy when they have been careless with the old one and broken it.

They know it is fair not to be given dessert or candy when they have not eaten their vegetables.

They know it is fair not to be allowed to go to town with mother if they have not stopped playing in time to get ready.

They do not like these punishments, of course, but they do know that they are fair.

HOW DO YOU PUNISH YOUR CHILD?

Some punishments are better than others.
Do you spank your child?
Do you scold and scream at him?
Do you shut him in the closet?
Do you keep him from outdoor play?
—or—
Do you put him in his room all by himself and shut the door?
Do you send him to bed if he is tired?
Do you pay no attention to him?
Do you refuse to let him have some pleasure or treat?

A wise mother does not need to spank or slap her child very often. She does not shut her child in the closet. She does not scold or scream at him. She does not keep him from outdoor play.

She knows better ways than that.

Perhaps her Johnny has been hurting the children he plays with. Then he can not play with them until he is ready to play nicely. If he forgets and hurts them again, he has to play alone some more.

Johnny's mother will do this again and again until he learns he must not hurt the children he plays with. He will learn this after a while because, of course, he wants to play with them. Children do not like to be alone.

Perhaps Johnny has not come straight home from school; or perhaps he does not come in when mother calls him. When he does come, she says, "You did not come in on time, so you can not have any dessert to-night."

She does not say, "To-morrow you can not go out to play," because she knows Johnny needs to play out in the fresh air. It would be bad for him to go without play, and it would be bad for him to go without fresh air. It will not be bad for him to go without dessert.

Sometimes children do naughty things because they are tired. A tired child is like a sick child. He needs to go to bed. Then he can rest and be quiet. He will not be naughty when he is rested.

A baby who cries because he is hungry is not naughty. He stops crying when he is fed. It is just the same with a tired child.

Some children are naughty just to get attention. The best punishment for them is not to pay attention to them. That is the way to punish temper tantrums and fussiness about food.

The best way of all is to keep your child from needing to be punished.

You can do this if you start right when your child is a baby.

Pay attention to him when he is good. Do not wait until he is naughty.

Always do what you promise.

Speak and act the truth to your child.

Do not threaten even a baby with punishments that can not be carried out.

Always be consistent in treatment of a child. Do not laugh at or praise him for something to-day and scold or punish for the same thing to-morrow.

Be sure your child is really naughty before you punish him.

Do not expect him to sit still or be quiet all the time. Let him have plenty of outdoor play where he can run and jump and climb.

If you need to punish him, the best way is to take some pleasure or treat away from him, or to leave him in a room by himself and pay no attention to him. He should understand that he must not do the naughty thing again. Do not laugh at him when he is naughty

/   /   /

31 | In Its Own Words

The "platform" of the Ku Klux Klan of the 1920s consisted of organized bigotry against Catholics, Jews, blacks, Orientals, and southern- and eastern-European immigrants. For the small-town and small-city inhabitants who made up its ranks, though, membership was also an expression of piety and a badge of respectability. In this sense, the Klan was a descendant of the fraternal orders that had been popular, particularly since the 1870s. These orders compensated for a disruptive, modernizing social environment and allowed men an opportunity to relate to one another and to find a social home. The name "Ku Klux Klan" was the same as that of Southern vigilante groups during Reconstruction, which were organized to intimidate blacks and preserve political power for whites. The new Klan, however, was an anti-Catholic and anti-Jewish national group, a product of the cultural changes that the war and the new consumer society brought about. In addition, the new Klan was a business that, through modern advertising and enterprise, was highly profitable for its promoters. The Klansman's Manual *and* Klan Komment *illustrate these different but closely intertwined tendencies.*

KLANSMAN'S MANUAL, 1925

The Order

I. *The Name*
"Knights of the Ku Klux Klan."
"Forever hereafter it shall be known as KNIGHTS OF THE KU KLUX KLAN."

II. *Its Divisions*
"There shall be four Kloranic Orders of this Order, namely:

1. "The order of citizenship or K-UNO (Probationary)."
2. "Knight Kamellia or K-DUO (Primary Order of Knighthood)."

3. "Knights of the great Forrest or K-TRIO (The Order of American Chivalry)."
4. "Knights of the Midnight Mystery or K-Quad (Superior Order of Knighthood and Spiritual Philosophies)."

III. Its Nature

1. *Patriotic.* One of the paramount purposes of this order is to "exemplify a pure patriotism toward our country." Every Klansman is taught from the beginning of his connection with the movement that it is his duty "to be patriotic toward our country."

2. *Military.* This characteristic feature applies to its form of organization and its method of operations. It is so organized on a military plan that the whole power of the whole order, or of any part of it, may be used in quick, united action for the execution of the purposes of the order.

3. *Benevolent.* This means that the movement is also committed to a program of sacrificial service for the benefit of others. As a benevolent institution, the Knights of the Ku Klux Klan must give itself to the task of relieving and helping the suffering and distressed, the unfortunate and oppressed.

4. *Ritualistic.* In common with other orders, the Knights of the Ku Klux Klan confers ritualistic degrees and obligations, and commits its grips, signs, words, and other secret work to those persons who so meet its requirements as to find membership in the order. The ritualistic devices become the ceremonial ties that bind Klansmen to one another.

5. *Social.* The Knights of the Ku Klux Klan endeavors to unite in companionable relationship and congenial association those men who possess the essential qualifications for membership. It is so designed that kinship of race, belief, spirit, character, and purpose will engender a real, vital, and enduring fellowship among Klansmen.

6. *Fraternal.* The order is designed to be a real brotherhood.

Klansmen have committed themselves to the practice of "Klannishness toward fellow-Klansmen." By this commitment they have agreed to treat one another as brothers. Fraternal love has become the bond of union. And this requires the development of such a spirit of active good will as will impel every Klansman to seek to promote the well-being of his fellow-Klansmen "socially, physically, morally, and vocationally."

IV. Its Government

The Constitution provides for and establishes that form of government that will best further the interests of the movement and develop to the highest possible efficiency all of its component elements.

1. *This form of government is military in character.* It will suffice to compare the Klan's form of government to the government of an army. As the United States Army is duly organized with its various officers and

troops, so is the Knights of the Ku Klux Klan welded together as an organized force for the fulfillment of its patriotic mission. The Commander-in-Chief is the Imperial Wizard. The Divisional Commanders are the Grand Dragons. The Brigade Commanders are the Great Titans. The Regimental Commanders are the Exalted Cyclops. All of these Commanders have their respective staffs and other subordinate officers and aides.

2. *This form of government is necessary.* (a) For efficient administration: (b) For effectiveness in method and operation: (c) For the preservation of the order.

Fraternal order history records the failure of many patriotic societies that were organized on a so-called democratic basis. Without this feature of the military form of government which is designed to provide efficient leadership, effective discipline, intelligent cooperation, active functioning, uniform methods, and unified operation, quickly responsive to the call to put over the immediate task at hand, even the Knights of the Ku Klux Klan would degenerate into a mere passive, inefficient, social order. The military form of government must and will be preserved for the sake of true, patriotic Americanism, because it is the only form of government that gives any guarantee of success. We must avoid the fate of the other organizations that have split on the rock of democracy.

V. Its Authority

Is "Vested primarily in the Imperial Wizard." The organization of the Knights of the Ku Klux Klan provides, and its principle of government demands, that there shall always be *one* individual, senior in rank to all other Klansmen of whatever rank, on whom shall rest the responsibility of command, and whose leadership will be recognized and accepted by all other loyal Klansmen.

The whole movement, fraught with its tremendous responsibilities and rich in its magnificent possibilities, make stirring appeal to red-blooded American manhood. Every Klansman is an important, necessary, and vital factor in the movement. In this crusade there are few occasions for "individual plays." Success is possible only through the most unselfish "playing for the team."

Objects and Purposes (Article II, The Constitution)

I. Mobilization

This is its primary purpose: "To unite white male persons, native-born, Gentile citizens of the United States of America, who owe no allegiance of any nature or degree to any foreign government, nation, institution, sect, ruler, person, or people; whose morals are good; whose reputations and vocations are respectable; whose habits are exemplary;

who are of sound minds and eighteen years or more of age, under a common oath into a brotherhood of strict regulations."

II. Cultural

The Knights of the Ku Klux Klan is a movement devoting itself to the needed task of developing a genuine spirit of American patriotism. Klansmen are to be examples of pure patriotism. They are to organize the patriotic sentiment of native-born white, Protestant Americans for the defense of distinctively American institutions. Klansmen are dedicated to the principle that America shall be made American through the promulgation of American doctrines, the dissemination of American ideals, the creation of wholesome American sentiment, the preservation of American institutions.

III. Fraternal

The movement is designed to create a real brotherhood among men who are akin in race, belief, spirit, character, interest, and purpose. The teachings of the order indicate very clearly the attitude and conduct that make for real expression of brotherhood, or, "the practice of Klannishness."

IV. Beneficient

"To relieve the injured and the oppressed; to succor the suffering and unfortunate, especially widows and orphans."

The supreme pattern for all true Klansmen is their Criterion of Character, Jesus Christ, "who went about doing good." The movement accepts the full Christian program of unselfish helpfulness, and will seek to carry it on in the manner commanded by the one Master of Men, Christ Jesus.

V. Protective

1. *The Home.* "*To shield the sanctity of the home.*" The American home is fundamental to all that is best in life, in society, in church, and in the nation. It is the most sacred of human institutions. Its sanctity is to be preserved, its interests are to be safeguarded, and its well-being is to be promoted. Every influence that seeks to disrupt the home must itself be destroyed. The Knights of the Ku Klux Klan would protect the home by promoting whatever would make for its stability, its betterment, its safety, and its inviolability.

2. *Womanhood.* The Knights of the Ku Klux Klan declare that it is committed to "the sacred duty of protecting womanhood"; and announces that one of its purposes is "to shield . . . the chastity of womanhood."

The degradation of women is a violation of the sacredness of human personality, a sin against the race, a crime against society, a menace to our country, and a prostitution of all that is best, and noblest, and highest in life. No race, or society, or country, can rise higher than its womanhood.

3. *The Helpless.* "To protect the weak, the innocent, and the defenseless from the indignities, wrongs, and outrages of the lawless, the violent, and the brutal."

Children, the disabled, and other helpless ones are to know the protective, sheltering arms of the Klan.

4. *American Interests.* "To protect and defend the Constitution of the United States of America, and all laws passed in conformity thereto, and to protect the states and the people thereof from all invasion of their right from any source whatsoever."

VI. Racial

"To maintain forever white supremacy." "To maintain forever the God-given supremacy of the white race."

Every Klansman has unqualifiedly affirmed that he will "faithfully strive for the eternal maintenance of white supremacy."

Offenses and Penalties

I. Two Classes of Offenses

"Offenses against this order shall be divided into two classes—major and minor offenses."

II. Major Offenses

"Major offenses shall consist of:
1. *"Treason against the United States of America."*
2. *"Violating the oath of allegiance to this order or any supplementary oath of obligation thereof."*
3. *"Disrespect of virtuous womanhood."*

III. *"Violation of the Constitution or laws of this order."*

(a) By conspiracy:
(b) Relinquishment or forfeiture of citizenship:
(c) Support of any foreign power against the United States of America:
(d) Violating the bylaws of a Klan of this Order.
(e) Habitual drunkenness:
(f) Habitual profanity or vulgarity:
5. *Unworthy racial or Klan conduct:* "Being responsible for the polluting of Caucasian blood through miscegenation, or the commission of any act unworthy of a Klansman."

White men must not mix their blood with that of colored or other inferior races.

6. *The repeated commission of a minor offense:* "The repeated commission of a minor offense shall in itself constitute a major offense."

Minor Offenses

1. *Drunkenness.*
2. *Profanity or vulgarity.*
3. *Actions inimical to interests of the order.*
4. *Refusal or failure to obey.*
5. *Refusal or failure to respond.*
6. *Refusal or failure to surrender credentials.*

/ / /

KLAN KOMMENT, 1923

At a recent meeting addressed by two members of the Imperial Kloncilium at Kansas City, Mo., and which was attended by ten thousand Klansmen a novel feature was introduced. Powerful searchlights suddenly illuminated a white-robed horseman, on a white steed standing on a hill near the meeting while an airplane bearing a huge fiery cross swooped low above the celebration.

/ / /

A great Klan meeting was held at Clinton, Mo., a few days ago when Senator Zach Harris addressed seventy-five hundred people on the principles of the order. The meeting was under the direction of Clinton Klan, a very progressive organization.

/ / /

Jacksonville Klan, Realm of Florida, is now one of the most active Klans in that section of the country. A few days ago representatives of the Klan called at the Calvary Baptist Church revival tent and expressed appreciation on the part of the order of the work of Evangelist Allen C. Shuler.

Bloxom Klan, Realm of Virginia, a few days ago presented an American Flag and a forty-foot flagpole to Bloxom High School. The presentation speech was made by a local minister and the flag was accepted by the principal of the school.

/ / /

Members of the Quincy, Ill., Klan visited Woodlawn Cemetery on the night of May 30 with the fiery cross and American flag. They laid a cross of red carnations on the grave of Virgil Johnson as hundreds of people watched them.

York Klan Number I, Realm of Pennsylvania, recently conducted the funeral services of Horace H. Heiney, a prominent and respected citizen and the first member of their Klan to pass on into the empire invisible. At the graveside a committee of Klansmen bore fiery crosses of roses, and one of the members in full regalia, who is a well-known York minister, offered prayer. The services in the cemetery were witnessed by a large number of people.

Klansmen Should Stop at the Sisson Hotel

Klansmen who visit Chicago will make no mistake if they register at the Hotel Sisson, Lake Michigan at Fifty-third Street.

When the Unity League recently published a list of alleged Chicago Klansmen the name of Harry W. Sisson, proprietor of the hotel, appeared upon it.

As a consequence his hotel is boycotted by Jews and Catholics.

32 | Experiences of the Great Depression

The journalist Studs Terkel has spent much of an interesting lifetime talking to Americans and recording what they say. Hard Times, *from which the following selections are taken, is his oral history of the Great Depression. The people he interviewed with a portable tape recorder in the late 1960s talk about experiences they had more than thirty years earlier, and allowance must be made for the tricks an individual's memory can play with historical fact. Nonetheless, the memories of participants offer unique, sharply contrasting insights into the feel and shape of past experience.*

SIDNEY J. WEINBERG

Senior partner, Goldman-Sachs Company, a leading investment house. He served during Roosevelt's first two Administrations as an industrial adviser.

October 29, 1929—I remember that day very intimately. I stayed in the office a week without going home. The tape was running, I've forgotten how long that night. It must have been ten, eleven o'clock before we got the final reports. It was like a thunder clap. Everybody was stunned. Nobody knew what it was all about. The Street had general confusion. They didn't understand it any more than anybody else. They thought something would be announced.

Prominent people were making statements. John D. Rockefeller, Jr., announced on the steps of J. P. Morgan, I think, that he and his sons were buying common stock. Immediately, the market went down again. Pools combined to support the market, to no avail. The public got scared and sold. It was a very trying period for me. Our investment company went up to two, three hundred, and then went down to practically nothing. As all investment companies did.

Over-speculation was the cause, a reckless disregard of economics.

From Hard Times: An Oral History of the Great Depression *by Studs Terkel, pp. 72–75. Copyright © 1970 by Studs Terkel. Reprinted by permission of Pantheon Books, a Division of Random House, Inc.*

There was a group ruthlessly selling short. You could sell anything and depress the market unduly. The more you depressed it, the more you created panic. Today we have protections against it. Call money went up—was it twenty percent?

No one was so sage that he saw this thing coming. You can be a Sunday morning quarterback. A lot of people have said afterwards, "I saw it coming, I sold all my securities." There's a credibility gap there. There are always some people who are conservative, who did sell out. I didn't know any of these.

I don't know anybody that jumped out of the window. But I know many who threatened to jump. They ended up in nursing homes and insane asylums and things like that. These were people who were trading in the market or in banking houses. They broke down physically, as well as financially.

Roosevelt saved the system. It's trite to say the system would have gone out the window. But certainly a lot of institutions would have changed. We were on the verge of something. You could have had a rebellion; you could have had a civil war.

The Street* was against Roosevelt. Only me and Joe Kennedy, of those I know, were for Roosevelt in 1932. I was Assistant Treasurer of the Democratic National Committee. I did not support him after the first two terms. I had a great argument with him. I didn't think any man should serve any more than two terms. I was getting a little tired, too, of all the New Deal things. When I was asked to work with the War Production Board in 1940, he delayed initialing my employment paper. Later on, we had a rapprochement and were friendly again.

Confidence ended the Depression in 1934. We had a recession in 1937. People got a little too gay on the way up, and you had to have a little leveling off. The war had a great deal of stimulus in 1939.

A Depression could not happen again, not to the extent of the one in '29. Unless inflation went out of hand and values went beyond true worth. A deep stock market reaction could bring a Depression, yes. There would be immediate Government action, of course. A moratorium. But in panic, people sell regardless of worth. Today you've got twenty-odd million stockholders owning stock. At that time you had probably a million and a half. You could have a sharper decline now than you had in 1929.

Most of the net worth of people today is in values. They haven't got it in cash. In a panic, values go down regardless of worth. A house worth $30,000, the minute you have a panic, isn't worth anything. Everybody feels good because the stock they bought at fifty is now selling at eighty. So they have a good feeling. But it's all on paper.

*[Wall Street]

MARTIN DEVRIES

People were speculating. Now who are they gonna blame aside from themselves? It's their fault. See my point? If you gamble and make a mistake, why pick on somebody else? It's your fault, don't you see?

It's like many people on the bread lines. I certainly felt sorry for them. But many of them hadn't lived properly when they were making it. They hadn't saved anything. Many of them wouldn't have been in the shape they were in, if they had been living in a reasonable way. Way back in the '29s, people were wearing $20 silk shirts and throwing their money around like crazy. If they had been buying Arrow $2 shirts and putting the other eighteen in the bank, when the trouble came, they wouldn't have been in the condition they were in.

In 1929, I had a friend who speculated. He'd say, "What's good?" I'd say, "We're selling high-grade first mortgage bonds on Common-wealth Edison." "Oh, hell," he'd say, "five percent. I make ten percent on the stock market." He was buying on margin. He thought he was rich. Know what happened to him? He blew his brains out. The Government had nothing to do with that. It's people.

Most people today are living beyond their means. They don't give a damn. The Government'll take care of them. People today don't want to work. We had a nice colored woman that worked for us fifteen years. She had a grandson. We offered to pay him $2 an hour to take the paper off our bedroom wall. Nothing to it. One coat of paper. We'd provide the bucket and sponge and the ladder. Do you think he'd do it? No. We couldn't get anybody to do it. So I did it myself. Nothing to it.

Do you think the New Deal is responsible . . . ?

Certainly. This huge relief program they began. What do you think brings all the colored people to Chicago and New York?

So when I say F.D.R.—

—my blood begins to boil. The New Deal immediately attacked Wall Street. As far as the country was concerned, Wall Street was responsible for all the upheavals. They set up the Securities and Exchange Commission. That was all right. I know there were some evils. But these fellas Roosevelt put in the SEC were a bunch of young Harvard theorists. Except for old Joe Kennedy. He was a robber baron. These New Dealers felt they had a mission to perform. Roosevelt attacked people—with some reason. But without justice. All people on Wall Street are not crooks.

My friends and I often spoke about it. Especially after his hammy fire-side chats. Here we were paying taxes and not asking for anything. Everybody else was asking for relief, for our money to help them out. . . . A certain amount of that is O.K., but when they strip you clean and still don't accomplish much, it's unfair.

They were do-gooders, trying to accomplish something. I give them credit for that. But they didn't listen to anybody who had any sense.

Hoover happened to be in a bad spot. The Depression came on, and there he was. If Jesus Christ had been there, he'd have had the same problem. It's too bad for poor old Herbie that he happened to be there. This was a world-wide Depression. It wasn't Hoover's fault. In 1932, a Chinaman or a monkey could have been elected against him, no question about it.

/   /   /

HARRY TERRELL: A FARMER IN THE 1930s

Three-hundred and twenty acres of farm land, fine land, that my uncle owned and cleared, he lost it. 'Cause they foreclosed the mortgage. Some of the best in the state, and he couldn't borrow a dime.

The farmers didn't have anything they could borrow on. He came down here to see me, because he knew that a fellow that had a job could get credit. He wanted to borrow $850. I knew my banker would give it to me. So I told him I'd get it.

He said, "Harry, I want to give you a mortgage to support this loan." I said I'd never take a mortgage from my mother's brother. But here's what he put up: a John Deere combine and tractor, about sixteen head of cattle, a team of mules and wagons and farm implements. For $850. So you can see how far this had gone. He couldn't get a loan, a man who lived in this state from the time he was two years old.

I was born across the road from the farm of Herbert Hoover's uncle. I knew the Hoover family, distant cousins of the President. My folks sold hogs for 'em, thoroughbred, pure Chester White hogs at two cents a pound. Even people like them, they had times just like the rest of us. That's the way it was going. Corn was going for eight cents a bushel. One county insisted on burning corn to heat the courthouse, 'cause it was cheaper than coal.

This was at the time that mortgaging of farms was getting home to us. So they was having ten cent sales. They'd put up a farmer's property and have a sale and all the neighbors'd come in, and they got the idea of spending twenty-five cents for a horse. They was paying ten cents for a plow. And when it was all over, they'd all give it back to him. It was legal and anybody that bid against that thing, that was trying to get that man's land, they would be dealt with seriously, as it were.

That infuriated all the people that wanted to carry on business as usual. It might be a bank or an implement dealer or a private elevator or something like that. They had their investments in this. The implement dealer, he was on the line, too. The only place he had of getting it was from the fellow who owed him. And they'd have a sheriff's sale.

The people were desperate. They came very near hanging that judge. Because they caught this judge foreclosing farm mortgages, and they had no other way of stopping it. He had issued the whole bunch of foreclosures on his docket.

It all happened in Le Mars. They took the judge out of his court and took him to the fairgrounds and they had a rope around his neck, and they had the rope over the limb of a tree. They were gonna string him up in the old horse thief fashion. But somebody had sense enough to stop the thing before it got too far.

They had marches, just like we have the marches nowadays. They came from all over the state. That was the time of the Farm Holiday. There was a picket line. The Farm Holiday movement was to hold the stuff off the market, to increase the price. It saw its violence, too.

They stopped milk wagons, dumped milk. They stopped farmers hauling their hay to market. They undertook to stop the whole agriculture process. They thought if they could block the highways and access to the packing plants, they couldn't buy these hogs at two cents a pound.

They'd say: we're gonna meet, just east of Cherokee, at the fork of the road, and so on. Now they spread it around the country that they were gonna stop everything from going through. And believe me, they stopped it. They had whatever was necessary to stop them with. Some of 'em had pitchforks. (Laughs.) You can fix the auto tire good with a pitchfork. There were blockades.

The country was getting up in arms about taking a man's property away from him. It was his livelihood. When you took a man's horses and his plow away, you denied him food, you just convicted his family to starvation. It was just that real.

I remember one man, as devout a man as I ever met, a Catholic. He was mixed up in it, too—the violence. His priest tried to cool him down. He says, "My God, Father, we're desperate. We don't know what to do." He was the most old, established man you could find. He was in the state legislature.

I remember in court when they were going to indict a Norwegian Quaker, when they were offering them lighter sentences if they'd plead guilty, his wife said, "Simon, thee must go to jail."

Did they ever talk about changing the society . . . ?

No, the nearer to the ground you get, the nearer you are to conservative. His land is his life. And he's not for anything that might alter the situation. I never found anything in the Iowa farmer to indicate he would accept any form of government but his own. If my family, grandfather, great-grandfather, ever heard my political beliefs, why, they'd turn over in their graves. I don't think that without the Depression this farm country would be anything by McKinley Republican.

You know, Hitler's men were awfully interested that I'd been through a farm strike in northern Iowa. I was in Germany, with my wife, as a tourist in 1937. I had been to Geneva for a disarmament conference. I met Hitler's agricultural attaché in Berlin. They were just putting controls on their farmers. He wanted to know how this violence was handled. He kept getting madder and madder. I said: "What do you do with these people?" He said: "They've got to come to terms with the government or we'll just wipe them out."

LOUIS BANKS: UNEMPLOYED VETERAN

I got to be fourteen years old, I went to work on the Great Lakes at $41.50 a month. I thought: Someday I'm gonna be a great chef. Rough times, though. It was the year 1929. I would work from five in the morning till seven at night. Washing dishes, peeling potatoes, carrying heavy garbage. We would get to Detroit.

They was sleepin' on the docks and be drunk. Next day he'd be dead. I'd see 'em floatin' on the river where they would commit suicide because they didn't have anything. White guys and colored.

I'd get paid off, I'd draw $21 every two weeks and then comin' back I'd have to see where I was goin'. 'Cause I would get robbed. One fella named Scotty, he worked down there, he was firin' a boiler. He was tryin' to send some money home. He'd work so hard and sweat, the hot fire was cookin' his stomach. I felt sorry for him. They killed 'im and throwed 'im in the river, trying to get the $15 or $20 from him. They'd steal and kill each other for fifty cents.

1929 was pretty hard. I hoboed, I bummed, I begged for a nickel to get somethin' to eat. Go get a job, oh, at the foundry there. They didn't hire me because I didn't belong to the right kind of race. 'Nother time I went into Saginaw, it was two white fellas and myself made three. The fella there hired the two men and didn't hire me. I was back out on the streets. That hurt me pretty bad, the race part.

When I was hoboing, I would lay on the side of the tracks and wait until I could see the train comin'. I would always carry a bottle of water in my pocket and a piece of tape or rag to keep it from bustin' and put a piece of bread in my pocket, so I wouldn't starve on the way. I would ride all day and all night long in the hot sun.

I'd ride atop a boxcar and went to Los Angeles, four days and four nights. The Santa Fe, we'd go all the way with Santa Fe. I was goin' over the hump and I was so hungry and weak 'cause I was goin' into the d.t.'s, and I could see snakes draggin' through the smoke. I was sayin', "Lord, help me, Oh Lord, help me," until a white hobo named Callahan, he was a great big guy, looked like Jack Dempsey, and he got a scissors on me, took his legs and wrapped 'em around me. Otherwise, I was about to fall off the Flyer into a cornfield there. I was sick as a dog until I got into Long Beach, California.

Black and white, it didn't make any difference who you were, 'cause everybody was poor. All friendly, sleep in a jungle. We used to take a big pot and cook food, cabbage, meat and beans all together. We all set together, we made a tent. Twenty-five or thirty would be out on the side of the rail, white and colored. They didn't have no mothers or sisters, they didn't have no home, they were dirty, they had overalls on, they didn't have no food, they didn't have anything.

Sometimes we sent one hobo to walk, to see if there were any jobs open. He'd come back and say: Detroit, no jobs. He'd say: they're hirin' in New York City. So we went to New York City. Sometimes ten or fifteen of us would be on the train. And I'd hear one of 'em holler. He'd fall off, he'd get killed. He was trying' to get off the train, he thought he was gettin' home there. He heard a sound. (Imitates train whistle, a low, long, mournful sound.)

And then I saw a railroad police, a white police. They call him Texas Slim. He shoots you off all trains. We come out of Lima, Ohio . . . Lima Slim, he would kill you if he catch you on any train. Sheep train or any kind of merchandise train. He would shoot you off, he wouldn't ask you to get off.

I was in chain gangs and been in jail all over the country. I was in a chain gang in Georgia. I had to pick cotton for four months, for just hoboin' on a train. Just for vag. They gave me thirty-five cents and a pair of overalls when I got out. Just took me off the train, the guard. 1930, during the Depression, in the summertime. Yes, sir, thirty-five cents, that's what they gave me.

I knocked on people's doors. They'd say, "What do you want? I'll call the police." And they'd put you in jail for vag. They'd make you milk cows, thirty or ninety days. Up in Wisconsin, they'd do the same thing. Alabama, they'd do the same thing. California, anywhere you'd go. Always in jail, and I never did nothin'.

A man had to be on the road. Had to leave his wife, had to leave his mother, leave his family just to try to get money to live on. But he think: my dear mother, tryin' to send her money, worryin' how she's starvin'.

The shame I was feeling. I walked out because I didn't have a job. I said, "I'm going' out in the world and get me a job." And God help me, I couldn't get anything. I wouldn't let them see me dirty and ragged and I hadn't shaved. I wouldn't send 'em no picture.

I'd write: "Dear Mother, I'm doin' wonderful and wish you're all fine." That was in Los Angeles and I was sleeping under some steps and there was some paper over me. This is the slum part, Negroes lived down there. And my ma, she'd say, "Oh, my son is in Los Angeles, he's doin' pretty fair."

And I was with a bunch of hoboes, drinkin' canned heat. I wouldn't eat two or three days, 'cause I was too sick to eat. It's a wonder I didn't die. But I believe in God.

I went to the hospital there in Los Angeles. They said, "Where do you live?" I'd say, "Travelers Aid, please send me home." Police says, "O.K., put him in jail." I'd get ninety days for vag. When I was hoboing I was in jail two-thirds of the time. Instead of sayin' five or ten days, they'd say sixty or ninety days. 'Cause that's free labor. Pick the fruit or pick the cotton, then they'd turn you loose.

I had fifteen or twenty jobs. Each job I would have it would be so hard. From six o'clock in the morning till seven o'clock at night. I was fixin' the meat, cookin', washin' dishes and cleaning up. Just like you throwed the ball at one end and run down and catch it on the other. You're jack of all trade, you're doin' it all. White chefs were getting' $40 a week, but I was getting' $21 for doin' what they were doin' and everything else. The poor people had it rough. The rich people was livin' off the poor.

'Cause I picked cotton down in Arkansas when I was a little bitty boy and I saw my dad, he was workin' all day long. $2 is what one day the poor man would make. A piece of salt pork and a barrel of flour for us and that was McGehee, Arkansas.

God knows, when he'd get that sack he would pick up maybe two, three hundred pounds of cotton a day, gettin' snake bit and everything in that hot sun. And all he had was a little house and a tub to keep the water. 'Cause I went down there to see him in 1930. I got tired of hoboing and went down to see him and my daddy was all gray and didn't have no bank account and no Blue Cross. He didn't have nothin', and he worked himself to death. (Weeps.) And the white man, he would drive a tractor in there. . . . It seems like yesterday to me, but it was 1930.

'33 in Chicago they had the World's Fair. A big hotel was hirin' colored fellas as bellboys. The bellboys could make more money as a white boy for the next ten or fifteen years. I worked as a bellhop on the North Side at a hotel, lots of gangsters there. They don't have no colored bellboys at no exclusive hotels now. I guess maybe in the small ones they may have some.

Jobs were doing a little better after '35, after the World's Fair. You could get dishwashin' jobs, little porter jobs.

Work on the WPA, earn $27.50. We just dig a ditch and cover it back up. You thought you was rich. You could buy a suit of clothes. Before that, you wanted money, you didn't have any. No clothes for the kids. My little niece and my little kids had to have hand-down clothes. Couldn't steal. If you did, you went to the penitentiary. You had to shoot pool, walk all night and all day, the best you could make was $15. I raised up all my kids during the Depression. Scuffled . . . a hard way to go.

No kindness. Except for Callahan, the hobo—only reason I'm alive is 'cause Callahan helped me on that train. And the hobo jungle. Everybody else was evil to each other. There was no friendships. Everybody was worried and sad looking. It was pitiful.

When the war came, I was so glad when I got in the army. I knew I was safe. I put a uniform on, and I said, "Now I'm safe." I had money comin', I had food comin', and I had a lot of gang around me. I knew on the streets or hoboing, I might be killed any time.

I'd rather be in the army than outside where I was so raggedy and didn't have no jobs. I was glad to put on a United States Army uniform and get some food. I didn't care about the rifle what scared me. In the army, I wasn't gettin' killed on a train, I wasn't gonna starve. I felt proud to salute and look around and see all the good soldiers of the United States. I was a good soldier and got five battle stars. I'd rather be in the army now than see another Depression.

BEN YORITA AND
PHILIP HAYASAKA

33 | Memories of the Internment Camp

Compared with its record in World War I, America was remarkably careful about protecting civil liberties during World War II. There was, however, one giant exception; the internment of 110,000 Japanese-Americans in desert concentration camps, euphemistically called "relocation centers." Internment was rationalized by straightforward racism. The military director of the internment declared, the "Japanese race is an enemy race and while many second and third generation Japanese born on United States soil, possessed of United States Citizenship, have become Americanized, the racial strains are undiluted. . . . It, therefore, follows that along the vital Pacific coast over 112,000 potential enemies, of Japanese extraction, are at large today." These people, 70,000 of them native-born citizens of the United States, were forced to evacuate their homes within forty-eight hours (losing about $500,000,000 in property along with their jobs), and were forced to live in tarpapered barracks behind barbed wire. The Supreme Court of the United States, in two major decisions, supported the constitutionality of internment. Justice Robert Jackson in a dissenting opinion warned that the cases established a precedent that "lays about like a loaded weapon." In 1988, however, Congress appropriated compensation for internees. The following reading, from an interview taken by the writer Archie Satterfield in the 1970s, is about the experiences of two Japanese-Americans who suffered during this tragedy.

BEN YORITA

"Students weren't as aware of national politics then as they are now, and Japanese-Americans were actually apolitical then. Our parents couldn't vote, so we simply weren't interested in politics because there was nothing we could do about it if we were.

"There were two reasons we were living in the ghettos: Birds of a feather flock together, and we had all the traditional aspects of Japanese life—Japanese restaurants, baths, and so forth; and discrimination forced us together. The dominant society prevented us from going elsewhere.

Excerpted from The Home Front: An Oral History of the War Years in America: 1941–45 by Archie Satterfield, pp. 330–338. Published by Playboy Press. Copyright © 1981 by Archie Satterfield.

251

"Right after Pearl Harbor we had no idea what was going to happen, but toward the end of December we started hearing rumors and talk of the evacuation started. We could tell from what we read in the newspapers and the propaganda they were printing—guys like Henry McLemore, who said he hated all Japs and that we should be rounded up, gave us the idea of how strong feelings were against us. So we were expecting something and the evacuation was no great surprise.

"I can't really say what my parents thought about everything because we didn't communicate that well. I never asked them what they thought. We communicated on other things, but not political matters.

"Once the evacuation was decided, we were told we had about a month to get rid of our property or do whatever we wanted to with it. That was a rough time for my brother, who was running a printshop my parents owned. We were still in debt on it and we didn't know what to do with all the equipment. The machines were old but still workable, and we had English type and Japanese type. Japanese characters had to be set by hand and were very hard to replace. Finally, the whole works was sold, and since nobody would buy the Japanese type, we had to sell it as junk lead at 50¢ a pound. We sold the equipment through newspaper classified ads: 'Evacuating: Household goods for sale.' Secondhand dealers and everybody else came in and bought our refrigerator, the piano, and I had a whole bunch of books I sold for $5, which was one of my personal losses. We had to sell our car, and the whole thing was very sad. By the way, it was the first time we had ever had a refrigerator and it had to be sold after only a few months.

"We could take only what we could carry, and most of us were carrying two suitcases or duffel bags. The rest of our stuff that we couldn't sell was stored in the Buddhist church my mother belonged to. When we came back, thieves had broken in and stolen almost everything of value from the church.

"I had a savings account that was left intact, but people who had their money in the Japanese bank in Seattle had their assets frozen from Pearl Harbor until the late 1960s, when the funds were finally released. They received no interest.

"They took all of us down to the Puyallup fairgrounds, Camp Harmony, and everything had been thrown together in haste. They had converted some of the display and exhibit areas into rooms and had put up some barracks on the parking lot. The walls in the barracks were about eight feet high with open space above and with big knotholes in the boards of the partitions. Our family was large, so we had two rooms.

"They had also built barbed-wire fences around the camp with a tower on each corner with military personnel and machine guns, rifles, and searchlights. It was terrifying because we didn't know what was going to happen to us. We didn't know where we were going and we were just doing what we were told. No questions asked. If you get an order, you go ahead and do it.

"There was no fraternization, no contact with the military or any Caucasian except when we were processed into the camp. But the treatment in Camp Harmony was fairly loose in the sense that we were free to roam around in the camp. But it was like buffalo in cages or behind barbed wire.

"There was no privacy whatsoever in the latrines and showers, and it was humiliating for the women because they were much more modest then than today. It wasn't so bad for the men because they were accustomed to open latrines and showers.

"We had no duties in the sense that we were required to work, but you can't expect a camp to manage itself. They had jobs open in the kitchen and stock room, and eventually they opened a school where I helped teach a little. I wasn't a qualified teacher, and I got about $13 a month. We weren't given an allowance while we were in Camp Harmony waiting for the camp at Minidoka to be finished, so it was pretty tight for some families.

"From Camp Harmony on, the family structure was broken down. Children ran everywhere they wanted to in the camp, and parents lost their authority. We could eat in any mess hall we wanted, and kids began ignoring their parents and wandering wherever they pleased.

"Eventually they boarded us on army trucks and took us to trains to be transported to the camps inland. We had been in Camp Harmony from May until September. There was a shortage of transportation at the time and they brought out these old, rusty cars with gaslight fixtures. As soon as we got aboard we pulled the shades down so people couldn't stare at us. The cars were all coaches and we had to sit all the way to camp, which was difficult for some of the older people and the invalids. We made makeshift beds out of the seats for them, and did the best we could.

"When we got to Twin Falls, we were loaded onto trucks again, and we looked around and all we could see was that vast desert with nothing but sagebrush. When the trucks started rolling, it was dusty, and the camp itself wasn't completed yet. The barracks had been built and the kitchen facilities were there, but the laundry room, showers, and latrines were not finished. They had taken a bulldozer in the good old American style and leveled the terrain and then built the camp. When the wind blew, it was dusty and we had to wear face masks to go to the dining hall. When winter came and it rained, the dust turned into gumbo mud. Until the latrines were finished, we had to use outhouses.

"The administrators were civilians and they tried to organize us into a chain of command to make the camp function. Each block of barracks was told to appoint a representative, who were called block managers. Of course we called them the Blockheads.

"When winter came, it was very cold and I began withdrawing my savings to buy clothes because we had none that was suitable for that climate. Montgomery Ward and Sears Roebuck did a landslide business from the camps because we ordered our shoes and warm clothing from them. The people who didn't have savings suffered quite a bit until the camp distributed navy pea coats. Then everybody in camp was wearing outsize pea coats because we were such small people. Other than army blankets, I don't remember any other clothing issues.

"The barracks were just single-wall construction and the only insulation was tar paper nailed on the outside, and they never were improved. The larger rooms had potbellied stoves, and we all slept on army cots. Only the people over sixty years old were able to get metal cots, which had a bit more spring to them than the army cots, which were just stationary hammocks.

"These camps were technically relocation centers and there was no effort to hold us in them, but they didn't try actively to relocate us until much later. On my own initiative I tried to get out as soon as I could, and started writing letters to friends around the country. I found a friend in Salt Lake City who agreed to sponsor me for room and board, and he got his boss to agree to hire me. I got out in May 1943, which was earlier than most. In fact, I was one of the first to leave Minidoka.

"Of course I had to get clearance from Washington, D.C., and they investigated my background. I had to pay my own way from Twin Falls to Salt Lake City, but after I left, the government had a program of per diem for people leaving.

"I got on the bus with my suitcase, all by myself, my first time in the outside world, and paid my fare and began looking for a seat, then this old guy said: 'Hey, Tokyo, sit next to me.'

"I thought, Oh, my God, Tokyo! I sat next to him and he was a friendly old guy who meant well."

Yorita's friend worked in a parking garage across the street from the Mormon tabernacle, and the garage owner let them live in the office, where the two young men cooked their own meals. One nearby grocery-store owner wouldn't let them buy from him, and a barber in the neighborhood hated them on sight. Yorita parked a car once that had a rifle and pair of binoculars in the back seat, and he and his friend took the binoculars out and were looking through them when the barber looked out and saw them studying the Mormon tabernacle. He called the FBI, and two agents were soon in the garage talking to the young men.

Yorita wasn't satisfied with his job in Salt Lake City, and soon left for Cincinnati, then Chicago, which he enjoyed because most Chicago people didn't care what nationality he was. He and a brother were able to find good jobs and a good place to live, and they brought their parents out of the Idaho camp to spend the rest of the war in Chicago.

PHILIP HAYASAKA

Philip Hayasaka was a teen-ager when Pearl Harbor was attacked. Unlike most Japanese-Americans, his parents had been able to find a home in a predominantly Caucasian neighborhood because his father was a wholesale produce dealer and most of his business was conducted with Caucasians. Consequently, when the family was interned, Hayasaka was a stranger to most of the other families.

Still, he and his family understood well the rationale of the Little Tokyos along the West Coast.

"If you could become invisible, you could get along. We were forced into a situation of causing no trouble, of being quiet, not complaining. It was not a matter of our stoic tradition. I've never bought that. We did what we had to do to survive.

"There was a lot of hysteria at the time, a lot of confusion, and the not knowing what was going to happen created such a fear that we became supercautious. We would hear that the FBI was going into different houses and searching, and we would wonder when they were coming to our house. We just knew that they were going to come and knock on the door and that we wouldn't know what to do when they came.

"A lot of people were burning things that didn't need to be burned, but they were afraid suspicion would be attached to those things. All those wonderful old calligraphies were destroyed, priceless things, because they thought someone in authority would believe they represented allegiance to Japan. One time I was with my mother in the house, just the two of us, and there was a knock on the door. My mother had those rosary-type beads that the Buddhists use for prayer, and she put them in my pocket and sent me outside to play and stay out until whoever was at the door left. She was afraid it was the FBI and they would take them away from us. It sounds silly now, but that kind of fear was pervasive then. It was tragic.

"When this happened, my dad's business went to hell. Suddenly all his accounts payable were due immediately, but all the accounts receivable weren't. People knew the guy wasn't going to be around much longer, so they didn't pay him. I knew at one time how much he lost that way—we had to turn in a claim after the war—but I've forgotten now. But it was a considerable amount. Those claims, by the way, didn't give justice to the victims; it only legitimized the government. We got about a nickel on the dollar.

"It was kind of interesting how different people reacted when they came to Camp Harmony to see friends, and how we reacted in return. Friends from Seattle would come down to see me, and we had to talk through the barbed-wire fences. [Note: Nobody was permitted to stand closer than three feet to the fence, which meant conversations were held at least six feet from each other, with people standing and watching]. There was one instance when I saw a close friend from high school just outside the fence, and he had come down to see me. He hadn't seen me inside, so I hid rather than going out to see him. The whole evacuation did funny things to your mind.

"All the leaders of the community were taken away, and my dad was interned before we were and taken to the interrogation camp in Missoula. It was one of the greatest shocks of my life when the FBI came and picked him up. Here was a guy who had followed all the rules, respected authority, and was a leader in the company. And all of the sudden he was behind bars for no reason. He stayed there several months before they let him join us at Minidoka."

/   /   /

When the war ended and the camps were closed, about the only people left in them were young children and the elderly. All who could leave for jobs did so, and the experience had a scattering effect on the Japanese-American communities across the Pacific Coast. Several families settled on the East Coast and in the Midwest, and when those with no other place to go, or who didn't want to migrate away from the Coast, returned to their hometowns, they usually found their former ghettos taken over by other minority groups. Consequently, whether they wanted to or not, they were forced to find housing wherever it was available. It was difficult returning to the cities, however. Everybody dreaded it, and some of the elderly people with no place to go of their own were virtually evacuated from the camps. They had become accustomed to the life there and were afraid to leave.

Some Caucasians, such as Floyd Schmoe and the Reverend Emory Andrews, worked with the returning outcasts to help them resettle as smoothly as possible. A few farms had been saved for the owners, but four years of weeds and brush had accumulated. Schmoe was back teaching at the University of Washington by that time, and he organized groups of his students to go out on weekends and after school to help clear the land for crops again. Some people returning found their former neighbors had turned against them in their absence, and grocery-store owners who had become Jap-haters during the war would not sell them food.

The farmers who did get their crops growing again were often so discriminated against that they could not sell their produce, or get it delivered into the marketplace. Schmoe was able to solve this problem for one farmer by talking a neighbor, a Filipino, into taking the Japanese-American's produce and selling it as his own. Hayasaka's father was able to get back into the wholesale produce business by becoming partners with a young Japanese-American veteran of the famed 442d Regiment, the most highly decorated group in the war. The veteran put up a sign over the office saying the business was operated by a veteran, which made it difficult for buyers to avoid it.

BEN YORITA

"The older people never recovered from the camps. The father was the traditional breadwinner and in total command of the family. But after going into the camps, fathers were no longer the breadwinners; the young sons and daughters were. Most of them couldn't even communicate in English, so all the burdens fell on the second generation. And most of us were just kids, nineteen or twenty. Consequently there was a big turnover of responsibility and authority, and the parents were suddenly totally dependent on their children. When we returned to the cities after the war, it was the second generation again that had to make the decisions and do all the negotiating with landlords, attorneys, and the like."

34 | The Allies Invade Europe

More than through any other single source, Americans during World War II understood the experience of their fighting men and women through the columns of Ernest Taylor Pyle. Ernie Pyle's columns for the Scripps-Howard newspapers and his collected columns, Here is your War (1943) and Brave Men (1944), were published worldwide. Sharing many of the dangers of the common soldiers, Pyle was on the front lines to capture their perspective for a vast audience. He also met the fate of many foot soldiers: death by enemy machine gun fire on a Pacific island in April 1945.

The following excerpt describes the allied invasion of Normandy Beach in June 1944. Pyle's unit left from England.

Shortly after breakfast the Army gave us assault correspondents a semifinal set of instructions and sent us off in jeeps in separate groups, each group to be divided up later until we were all separated.

We still weren't given any details of the coming invasion. We still didn't know where we were to go aboard ship, or what unit we would be with. As each batch left, the oldsters among us would shake hands. And because we weren't feeling very brilliant, almost our only words to each other were ''Take it easy.''

The following morning, at another camp, I was called at four o'clock. All around me officers were cussing and getting up. This was the headquarters of a certain outfit, and they were moving out in a motor convoy at dawn. For months those officers had been living a civilized existence, with good beds, good food, dress-up uniforms, polished desks, and a normal social life. But now once again they were in battle clothes. They wore steel helmets and combat boots, and many carried packs on their backs.

They joked in the sleepy predawn darkness. One said to another, "What are you dressed up for, a masquerade?"

Everybody was overloaded with gear. One officer said, "The Germans will have to come to us. We can never get to them with all this load."

The most-repeated question was: "Is your trip necessary?"

Those men had spent months helping to plan a gigantic invasion. They were relieved to finish the weary routine of paper work at last, and glad to start putting their plans into action. If they had any personal concern about themselves they didn't show it.

I rode with the convoy commander, who was an old friend. We were in an open jeep. It was just starting to get daylight when we pulled out. And just as we left rain began to fall—that dismal, cold, cruel rain of which England is so capable. It had rained like that a year and a half before when we left for Africa.

We drove all day. Motorcycles nursed each of our three sections along. We halted every two hours for a stretch. At noon we opened K rations. It was bitter cold.

Enlisted men had brought along a wire-haired terrier which belonged to one of the sergeants. It wouldn't have been an invasion without a few dogs along. At the rest halts the terrier would get out in the fields to play and chase stones, with never any worry. It seemed wonderful to be a dog.

The English roads had been almost wholly cleared of normal traffic. British civil and military police were at every crossing. As we neared the embarkation point people along the roads stood at their doors and windows and smiled bon voyage to us. Happy children gave us the American O.K. sign—thumb and forefinger in a circle. One boy smilingly pointed a stick at us like a gun, and one of the soldiers pointed his rifle back and asked us with a grin, "Shall I let him have it?"

One little girl, thinking the Lord knows what, made a nasty face at us.

Along toward evening we reached our ship. It was an LST, and it was already nearly loaded with trucks and armored cars and soldiers. Its ramp was down in the water, several yards from shore, and being an old campaigner I just waded aboard. But the officer behind me yelled up at the deck, "Hey, tell the captain to move the ship up closer."

So they waited a few minutes, and the ramp was eased up onto dry ground, and our whole convoy walked aboard. I was the only one in the crowd to get his feet wet.

We had hardly got aboard when the lines were cast off and we pulled out. That evening the colonel commanding the troops on our ship gave me the whole invasion plan in detail—the secret the whole world had waited years to hear. Once a man had heard it he became permanently a part of it. Then he was committed. It was too late to back out, even if his heart failed him.

/   /   /

My devastating sense of fear and depression disappeared when we approached the beachhead. There was the old familiar crack and roar of big guns all around us, and the shore was a great brown haze of smoke and dust, and we knew that bombers would be over us that night. Yet all the haunting premonition, the soul-consuming dread, was gone. The war was prosaic to me again. And I believe that was true of everyone aboard, even those who had never been in combat before.

All of us had dreaded the trip, for we had expected attacks from U-boats, E-boats, and at nighttime from aircraft. Yet nothing whatever happened.

We were at sea for a much longer time than it would ordinarily take to make a bee-line journey from England to France. As we came down, the English Channel was crammed with forces going both ways. Minesweepers had swept wide channels for us all the way. Each channel was miles wide, and marked with buoys.

Surely we saw there before us more ships than any human being had ever seen before at one glance. And going north were other vast convoys, some composed of fast liners speeding back to England for new loads of troops and equipment.

As far as you could see in every direction the ocean was infested with ships. There must have been every type of ocean-going vessel in the world. I even thought I saw a paddlewheel steamer in the distance, but that was probably an illusion.

There were battleships and all other kinds of warships clear down to patrol boats. There were great fleets of Liberty ships. There were fleets of luxury liners turned into troop transports, and fleets of big landing craft and tank carriers and tankers. And in and out through it all were nondescript ships—converted yachts, river boats, tugs, and barges.

The best way I can describe that vast armada and the frantic urgency of the traffic is to suggest that you visualize New York Harbor on its busiest day of the year and then just enlarge that scene until it takes in all the ocean the human eye can reach, clear around the horizon. And over the horizon, imagine dozens of times that many.

Everything was magnificently organized, and every ship, even the tiniest one, was always under exact orders timed to the minute. But at one time our convoy was so pushed along by the wind and the currents that we were five hours ahead of schedule, despite the fact that our engines had been stopped half the time. We adjusted that by circling.

Although we arrived just on time, they weren't ready for us on the beaches and we spent several hours weaving in and out among the multitude of ships just off the beachhead. Finally we just settled down to await our turn.

That was when the most incongruous—to us—part of the invasion came. There we were in a front-row seat at a great military epic. Shells from battleships were whamming over our heads, and occasionally a dead man floated face downward past us. Hundreds and hundreds of ships laden with death milled around us. We could stand at the rail and see both our shells and German shells exploding on the beaches, where struggling men were leaping ashore, desperately hauling guns and equipment through the water.

We were in the very vortex of the war—and yet, as we sat there waiting, Lieutenant Chuck Conick and I played gin rummy in the wardroom and Bing Crosby sang "Sweet Leilani" over the ship's phonograph.

Angry shells hitting near us would make heavy thuds as the concussion carried through the water and struck the hull of our ship. But in our wardroom men in gas-impregnated uniforms and wearing life belts sat reading *Life* and listening to the BBC telling us how the war before our eyes was going.

But it wasn't like that ashore. No, it wasn't like that ashore.

ON THE ROAD TO BERLIN

Owing to a last-minute alteration in the arrangements, I didn't arrive on the beachhead until the morning after D-day, after our first wave of assault troops had hit the shore.

By the time we got there the beaches had been taken and the fighting had moved a couple of miles inland. All that remained on the beach was some sniping and artillery fire, and the occasional startling blast of a mine geysering brown sand into the air. That plus a gigantic and pitiful litter of wreckage along miles of shore line.

Submerged tanks and overturned boats and burned trucks and shell-shattered jeeps and sad little personal belongings were strewn all over those bitter sands. That plus the bodies of soldiers lying in rows covered with blankets, the toes of their shoes sticking up in a line as though on drill. And other bodies, uncollected, still sprawling grotesquely in the sand or half hidden by the high grass beyond the beach. That plus an intense, grim determination of work-weary men to get that chaotic beach organized and get all the vital supplies and the reinforcements moving more rapidly over it from the stacked-up ships standing in droves out to sea.

After it was over it seemed to me a pure miracle that we ever took the beach at all. For some of our units it was easy, but in the special sector where I landed our troops faced such odds that our getting ashore was like my whipping Joe Louis down to a pulp. The men who did it on that beach were men of the First and Twenty-ninth Divisions.

I want to tell you what the opening of the second front in that one sector entailed, so that you can know and appreciate and forever be humbly grateful to those both dead and alive who did it for you.

Ashore, facing us, were more enemy troops than we had in our assault waves. The advantages were all theirs, the disadvantages all ours. The Germans were dug into positions they had been working on for months, although they were not entirely complete. A 100-foot bluff a couple of hundred yards back from the beach had great concrete gun emplacements built right into the hilltop. These opened to the sides instead of to the front, thus making it hard for naval fire from the sea to reach them. They could shoot parallel with the shore and cover every foot of it for miles with artillery fire.

Then they had hidden machine-gun nests on the forward slopes, with crossfire taking in every inch of the beach. These nests were connected by networks of trenches, so that the German gunners could move about without exposing themselves.

Throughout the length of the beach, running zigzag a couple of hundred yards back from the shore line, was an immense V-shaped ditch fifteen feet deep. Nothing could cross it, not even men on foot, until fills had been made. And in other places at the far end of the beach, where the ground was flatter, they had great concrete walls. These were blasted by our naval gunfire or by explosives set by hand after we got ashore.

Our only exits from the beach were several swales or valleys, each about a hundred yards wide. The Germans made the most of those funnellike traps, sowing them with buried mines. They also contained barbed-wire entanglements with mines attached, hidden ditches, and machine guns firing from the slopes.

All this was on the shore. But our men had to go through a maze nearly as deadly before they even got ashore. Underwater obstacles were terrific. Under the water the Germans had whole fields of evil devices to catch our boats. Several days after the landing we had cleared only channels through them and still could not approach the whole length of the beach with our ships. Even then some ship or boat would hit one of those mines and be knocked out of commission.

The Germans had masses of great six-pronged spiders—made of railroad iron and standing shoulder-high—just beneath the surface of the water, for our landing craft to run into. They had huge logs buried in the sand, pointing upward and outward, their tops just below the water. Attached to the logs were mines.

In addition to these obstacles they had floating mines offshore, land mines buried in the sand of the beach, and more mines in checkerboard rows in the tall grass beyond the sand. And the enemy had four men on shore for every three men we had approaching the shore.

And yet we got on.

Beach landings are always planned to a schedule that is set far ahead of time. They all have to be timed, in order for everything to mesh and for the following waves of troops to be standing off the beach and ready to land at the right moment. Some elements of the assault force are to break through quickly, push on inland, and attack the most obvious enemy strong points. It is usually the plan for units to be inland, attacking gun positions from behind, within a matter of minutes after the first men hit the beach.

I have always been amazed at the speed called for in these plans. Schedules will call for engineers to land at H-hour plus 2 minutes, and service troops at H-hour plus 30 minutes, and even for press censors to land at H-hour plus 75 minutes. But in the attack on my special portion of the beach—the toughest spot of all, incidentally—the schedule didn't hold.

Our men simply could not get past the beach. They were pinned down right on the water's edge by an inhuman wall of fire from the bluff. Our first waves were on that beach for hours, instead of a few minutes, before they could begin working inland.

The foxholes were still there—dug at the very edge of the water, in the sand and the small jumbled rocks that formed parts of the beach.

Medical corpsmen attended the wounded as best they could. Men were killed as they stepped out of landing craft. An officer whom I knew got a bullet through the head just as the door of his landing craft was let down. Some men were drowned.

The first crack in the beach defenses was finally accomplished by terrific and wonderful naval gunfire, which knocked out the big emplacements. Epic stories have been told of destroyers that ran right up into shallow water and had it out point-blank with the big guns in those concrete emplacements ashore.

When the heavy fire stopped, our men were organized by their officers and pushed on inland, circling machine-gun nests and taking them from the rear.

As one officer said, the only way to take a beach is to face it and keep going. It is costly at first, but it's the only way. If the men are pinned down on the beach, dug in and out of action, they might as well not be there at all. They hold up the waves behind them, and nothing is being gained.

Our men were pinned down for a while, but finally they stood up and went through, and so we took that beach and accomplished our landing. In the light of a couple of days of retrospection, we sat and talked and called it a miracle that our men ever got on at all or were able to stay on.

They suffered casualties. And yet considering the entire beachhead assault, including other units that had a much easier time, our total casualties in driving that wedge into the Continent of Europe were remarkably low—only a fraction, in fact, of what our commanders had been prepared to accept.

And those units that were so battered and went through such hell pushed on inland without rest, their spirits high, their egotism in victory almost reaching the smart-alecky stage.

Their tails were up. "We've done it again," they said. They figured that the rest of the Army wasn't needed at all. Which proves that, while their judgment in this respect was bad, they certainly had spirit that wins battles, and eventually wars.

/   /   /

I took a walk along the historic coast of Normandy in the country of France. It was a lovely day for strolling along the seashore. Men were sleeping on the sand, some of them sleeping forever. Men were floating in the water, but they didn't know they were in the water, for they were dead.

The water was full of squishy little jellyfish about the size of a man's hand. Millions of them. In the center of each of them was a green design exactly like a four-leafed clover. The good-luck emblem. Sure. Hell, yes.

I walked for a mile and a half along the water's edge of our many-miled invasion beach. I walked slowly, for the detail on that beach was infinite.

The wreckage was vast and startling. The awful waste and destruction of war, even aside from the loss of human life, has always been one of its outstanding features to those who are in it. Anything and everything is expendable. And we did expend on our beachhead in Normandy during those first few hours.

For a mile out from the beach there were scores of tanks and trucks and boats that were not visible, for they were at the bottom of the water—swamped by overloading, or hit by shells, or sunk by mines. Most of their crews were lost.

There were trucks tipped half over and swamped, partly sunken barges, and the angled-up corners of jeeps, and small landing craft half submerged. And at low tide you could still see those vicious six-pronged iron snares that helped snag and wreck them.

On the beach itself, high and dry, were all kinds of wrecked vehicles. There were tanks that had only just made the beach before being knocked out. There were jeeps that had burned to a dull gray. There were big derricks on caterpillar treads that didn't quite make it. There were half-tracks carrying office equipment that had been made into a shambles by a single shell hit, their interiors still holding the useless equipage of smashed typewriters, telephones, office files.

There were LCTs turned completely upside down, and lying on their backs, and how they got that way I don't know. There were boats stacked on top of each other, their sides caved in, their suspension doors knocked off.

In this shore-line museum of carnage there were abandoned rolls of barbed wire and smashed bulldozers and big stacks of thrown-away life belts and piles of shells still waiting to be moved. In the water floated empty life rafts and soldiers' packs and ration boxes, and mysterious oranges. On the beach lay snarled rolls of telephone wire and big rolls of steel matting and stacks of broken, rusting rifles.

On the beach lay, expended, sufficient men and mechanism for a small war. They were gone forever now. And yet we could afford it.

We could afford it because we were on, we had our toe hold, and behind us there were such enormous replacements for this wreckage on the beach that you could hardly conceive of the sum total. Men and equipment were flowing from England in such a gigantic stream that it made the waste on the beachhead seem like nothing at all, really nothing at all.

But there was another and more human litter. It extended in a thin little line, just like a high-water mark, for miles along the beach. This was the strewn personal gear, gear that would never be needed again by those who fought and died to give us our entrance into Europe.

There in a jumbled row for mile on mile were soldiers' packs. There were socks and shoe polish, sewing kits, diaries, Bibles, hand grenades. There were the latest letters from home, with the address on each one neatly razored out—one of the security precautions enforced before the boys embarked.

There were toothbrushes and razors, and snapshots of families back home staring up at you from the sand. There were pocketbooks, metal mirrors, extra trousers, and bloody, abandoned shoes. There were broken-handled shovels, and portable radios smashed almost beyond recognition, and mine detectors twisted and ruined.

There were torn pistol belts and canvas water bukets, first-aid kits, and jumbled heaps of life belts. I picked up a pocket Bible with a soldier's name in it, and put it in my jacket. I carried it half a mile or so and then put it back down on the beach. I don't know why I picked it up, or why I put it down again.

Soldiers carry strange things ashore with them. In every invasion there is at least one soldier hitting the beach at H-hour with a banjo slung over his shoulder. The most ironic piece of equipment marking our beach—this beach first of despair, then of victory—was a tennis racket that some soldier had brought along. It lay lonesomely on the sand, clamped in its press, not a string broken.

Two of the most dominant items in the beach refuse were cigarettes and writing paper. Each soldier was issued a carton of cigarettes just before he started. That day those cartons by the thousand, water-soaked and spilled out, marked the line of our first savage blow.

Writing paper and air-mail envelopes came second. The boys had intended to do a lot of writing in France. The letters—now forever incapable of being written—that might have filled those blank abandoned pages!

Always there are dogs in every invasion. There was a dog still on the beach, still pitifully looking for his masters.

He stayed at the water's edge, near a boat that lay twisted and half sunk at the waterline. He barked appealingly to every soldier who approached, trotted eagerly along with him for a few feet, and then, sensing himself unwanted in all the haste, he would run back to wait in vain for his own people at his own empty boat.

Over and around this long thin line of personal anguish, fresh men were rushing vast supplies to keep our armies pushing on into France. Other squads of men picked amidst the wreckage to salvage ammunition and equipment that was still usable.

Men worked and slept on the beach for days before the last D-day victim was taken away for burial.

I stepped over the form of one youngster whom I thought dead. But when I looked down I saw he was only sleeping. He was very young, and very tired. He lay on one elbow, his hand suspended in the air about six inches from the ground. And in the palm of his hand he held a large, smooth rock.

I stood and looked at him a long time. He seemed in his sleep to hold that rock lovingly, as though it were his last link with a vanishing world. I have no idea at all why he went to sleep with the rock in his hand, or what kept him from dropping it once he was asleep. It was just one of those little things without explanation that a person remembers for a long time.

The strong, swirling tides of the Normandy coast line shifted the contours of the sandy beach as they moved in and out. They carried soldiers' bodies out to sea, and later they returned them. They covered the corpses of heroes with sand, and then in their whims they uncovered them.

As I plowed out over the wet sand, I walked around what seemed to be a couple of pieces of driftwood sticking out of the sand. But they weren't driftwood. They were a soldier's two feet. He was completely covered except for his feet; the toes of his GI shoes pointed toward the land he had come so far to see, and which he saw so briefly.

A few hundred yards back on the beach was a high bluff. Up there we had a tent hospital, and a barbed-wire enclosure for prisoners of war. From up there you could see far up and down the beach, in a spectacular crow's-nest view, and far out to sea.

And standing out there on the water beyond all this wreckage was the greatest armada man has ever seen. You simply could not believe the gigantic collection of ships that lay out there waiting to unload. Looking from the bluff, it lay thick and clear to the far horizon of the sea and on beyond, and it spread out to the sides and was miles wide.

As I stood up there I noticed a group of freshly taken German prisoners standing nearby. They had not yet been put in the prison cage. They were just standing there, a couple of doughboys leisurely guarding them with tommy guns.

The prisoners too were looking out to sea—the same bit of sea that for months and years had been so safely empty before their gaze. Now they stood staring almost as if in a trance. They didn't say a word to each other. They didn't need to. The expression on their faces was something forever unforgettable. In it was the final, horrified acceptance of their doom.

35 | The Black Baseball Leagues

Napoleon said, "History is a myth agreed upon." Historian John Holway uses this quotation as the motto for his 1975 book Voices from the Great Black Baseball Leagues, *a book of interviews of black baseball players and some unusual white team owners. Casey Stengel used to say, "You could look it up." To some extent this is true even of black baseball, since Holway and others have found enough box scores of games in which black teams beat white major-league clubs to confirm the major-league caliber of the black teams. But most of the history of black baseball before 1947—when Jackie Robinson became the first black to play in the majors—comes only in the first person: from interviews with old men whose voices should make us redefine the history of America's national game. It leads on to wonder what other large fractions of American history are missing.*

William "Sug" Cornelius shows America at a crossroads. Against lingering racial prejudice in both the North and South, there was an awareness that segregation was costing whites as well as blacks. The black baseball leagues had their own glorious traditions and legends, and their breakup in the late 1940s and early 50s, as more and more of the best talent was invited to the major leagues, was a bittersweet event. For once, however, the participants in the "American past-time" could be seen not only on the same field, but on the same teams.

WILLIAM "SUG" CORNELIUS SPEAKS . . .

Mrs. Grace Comiskey, the White Sox owner, used to look at me and shake her head and say, "Oh, if you were a white boy, what you'd be worth to my club." I told her, "I'm *not* white, I'm black." And I said, "I don't know whether I'd change to white if I could." I had nothing to do with what color I was. Had I known in the beginning what kind of world I was going to be born into, I may have, but I had nothing to do with being born, I had nothing to do with the color.

I pitched for the Chicago American Giants from 1934 to 1946, and I was told many times what I'd be worth to certain clubs if I was a white boy. Every year, see, I'd win twenty-seven or twenty-eight ball games, that was no problem; I'd win that with ease, because we played more games. . . . Well, we almost had to play, they had to play somewhere every day—and night if they possibly could—in order to meet what measly salaries they were paying.

If you got $500 a month, you were tops. Back in the Depression years those salaries ran from $250 a month to $500 for really top players like this boy Josh Gibson, and I doubt whether they had another man on the ball club who was getting that kind of money. During that time I was getting $350. A little later on I was up to $400, and that was it. There just wasn't any money. The people just didn't have the money, and I think a box seat then was seventy-five cents.

I know Satchel Paige and I used to have some awful pitching duels. Yeah, I remember one particular game I think I pitched nine and two-thirds innings. I had two men out in the tenth inning, and I gave up my first hit. I walked one man in that ball game, I think it was Cool Papa Bell. I remember I walked him, 'cause I picked him off base. Turkey Stearnes was playing right field for us, and he said to me, "You couldn't see yourself pitching, but it was something to behold from where I was." I don't think over three or four balls were hit to the outfield.

They beat me in the tenth inning. Judy Johnson came up with two outs. I doubt whether Judy had five hits off me all the time I pitched against him. He hit a routine fly ball to right center field, and I rolled up my glove and started back to the dugout. But when I looked back, Stearnes was just standing there with his legs crossed. The ball could have been an easy out, but he wasn't expecting it. Jack Marshall at second base went out for it, but it fell between them.

I walked back to the mound. My arm was tightening, and I said, "If I get by this inning, I'm going to tell Dave Malarcher, our manager, to get somebody else ready." The next man up, Josh Gibson, hit me for a single. That pitch was that far outside—three feet—and he threw his bat at it and was lucky enough to make contact and get a single out of it. The next man came up and hit a little pop fly to left center field, and that fell in, so they beat me. After two outs.

A lot of white fans came from the Sox park over there to see that ball game. Back then we outdrew the Sox three-to-one. There was no question of that.

Satchel was something to behold. Show you fast balls here at your knee all day. They looked just like a white dot on a bright sunshiny day— a white dot. I imagine he'd win forty or fifty ball games a year, because his arm was just like rubber. After Paige was way up in the forties he pitched three innings every night for the entire week. And you very seldom beat him. I'll just be frank with you: If Satchel had been in the majors in his prime, Satchel would have broken all records.

I'm not exaggerating. The man could throw in a cup, his control was so fine.

/   /   /

It's no question about it. We had the same thing the whites had. We had good hitting, good fielding; they had good pitching, and we had it over here. Only thing I think: In our baseball, we had better of everything. Let's put it this way: If it wasn't better, it was as good.

We played good baseball—and as bad as we would be cheated. That happened very often. I remember Joe Hauser, who was with the Philadelphia Athletics. He hit sixty-nine home runs in the minors one year. Well, at this time he was playing for Racine, Wisconsin, and we went in there to play them, and he was walking the streets that afternoon before the game: "Joe Hauser's going to do this and Joe Hauser's going to do that." Candy Jim Taylor, my manager then, said "Cornelius, you're pitching tonight." He said, "Joe Hauser's a pretty fair hitter. He tears up that minor-league pitching, but he can't hit when he gets up to the big leagues." Jim says to me, "You keep your fast ball on his knees, and he's not going to do too much with it." And I had a good change-up off of my fast ball.

When Joe Hauser came to bat, everybody in the stands, I think, stood up. Well, I opened up on Joe with my change, right here, a little above the knee on the inside corner—Joe was a left-handed hitter. A beautiful pitch. The umpire says, "Ball one." So I looked at the umpire. My next pitch I threw him my fast ball. This was to the outside corner, and I think it was on Joe so fast he just stopped and looked at *me*. The umpire said, "Ball two." I started down to him, and my catcher met me half-way. He said, "He's not going to call anything unless Joe thinks he can hit it, and Joe's not going to swing."

The next time I took my windup and just rolled the ball on the ground. The umpire looked at me, said, "Do you think you're being funny?" I told him, "No, you are funny." I said, "Now I'm satisfied. I *know* this is a ball." And he was going to put me out of the game. Everybody in the stands said, "Well, we want our money back then."

I don't know what happened, whether Joe talked to the manager or what, but anyway the next time I threw him a fast ball, he swung and he missed, and from then on he would take his cut at it. Anyway, I struck him out three times. On three pitches. I didn't waste anything on him. So he asked me did I ever lose any ball games. I told him, "Sure." He said, "Well, I'd like to see the guys that hit you." I said, "Well, there are guys over in my league that would hit me if I mess around with them."

/   /   /

When we played white clubs we'd get the usual catcalls from the fans: "It's getting dark," or something like that. I remember once, I was in Dayton, Ohio. I had pitched no-hit, no-run baseball through eight innings. And I was in the batting circle, and I heard one of my players say, "Look out, Sug! Look out, Sug!" I naturally just covered up like that. And the ball hit my arm and glanced off the side of my head. You know what had happened? The pitcher had taken his windup, and took a potshot at me and called me a black son of a bitch. Well, this boy Suttles, being a big guy, got between the pitcher and his dugout, and not one of his teammates raised a hand to help him. The fans booed him, and they rushed me to the hospital. Had the ball not hit my arm, maybe I could have been dead. I know I would have had a concussion.

Well, I stayed in the hospital overnight, and it must have been about 1:30 A.M. and the sister let the manager up to see me. He sat down and talked with me, said he was sorry it happened and everything, didn't know what happened to the guy, what made him do a thing like that. I know he was under contract to one of those major league ball clubs, but they just paid him off, period, after that. Dayton didn't use him anymore.

That's just like this guy Jake Powell of the Yankees. I remember one year he was here in Chicago. Bob Elson was interviewing him and asked him what kind of work did he do in the winter. He says, "I'm a policeman, I enjoy whipping niggers' heads in the winter time." Elson cut him off the air like that, and it wasn't three weeks from then that the Yankees sold him to Detroit, and when he went over the Detroit, those fans over there threw so many balls and things at him that he was gone. Now that was a man that had been brought up, had been taught evil all through his young life. That stuff was just embedded in him.

We had problems like that. I remember we had been to New Orleans spring training this particular year, and we were on the way back North. I said to them, "You got an Illinois license on this bus," and I said, "you're going to be stopped, and God knows how much money you're going to have to pay." So we were coming through a little town, Mayersville, Mississippi, on Highway 61, I think. Foster and Powell, their home was in Mississippi. They just had to have something to eat. And they went in a restaurant. The guy wouldn't let them in the front door, but he let them in the back, with the secretary, a guy named Moore. I think Moore got about twelve or fifteen hamburgers. The guy told him, "fifteen dollars"—he don't owe but six. And you know, they had a shotgun on him, locked him up in that place back there until the police came. We had to pay that $15, and then the police fined him for disturbing the peace!

And it wasn't like that just in the South. I was up here in Marietta, Ohio, one morning. We were on our way to Dayton, and I was driving. I guess it was about 4:30 in the morning. Everybody in the bus asleep

but me, and I was kinda tired. Here comes this police, just blaring his
horn, pulled up beside me, asked me, "Where's the fire?"

I said, "Well, I should ask *you*, you're doing all the running."

He was the peace officer of this little small town. He said, "You ran
through a red light." He had me charged with running a red light, talking back to an officer. This was Tuesday. He said the judge wouldn't be
in town until Thursday, did we want to put up a bond or did we want to
wait until Thursday? My secretary asked me, "You have any money?" I
said, "Yeah, but I wouldn't give him a nickel." So he says, "Well, either
you put up bond or you have to go to jail." I told him, "I wouldn't give
you a quarter, now you can put me in jail." The secretary paid him off,
but I wouldn't have given him my money, not a nickel. You ran into
those things.

Every country you go into, you're going to have to pay. You take
the white Mexican, he's the same way toward the black Mexican. You
know some Mexicans are darker than I am. And some Cubans are
darker than I am, and it's the same way.

I was in Cuba in 1939, and I won nine, lost one, and I got the best
salary, $800 a month American money. I went to Mexico that summer—
a lot of major leaguers went down there—and I had a pretty fair season
down in the Mexican League. I was nine and two. The next year I went
back, I couldn't get accommodations at the same hotel I was living in
before in Mexico City. I asked the hotel manager why, and he said,
"Well, you know, we have a lot of tourists that come here, and the
whites say they don't live in the same hotel with you in the United
States." I told him, "If that's the way you want it, that's okay." The
club management got me a nice apartment.

/   /   /

Like we used to play out East—Yankee Stadium, Detroit—we'd have
40,000 to 50,000 people. We could only get in there once on Sunday,
and I think it was the drawing power of those clubs that promoted the
major-league owners to thinking. They said, "Well now those guys here
are drawing 40 to 50,000 in Comiskey Park in their all-star game." The
major-league all-stars would play there, maybe they'd have 34, 35,000
people. We would have standing room. Oh yes, we had whites, they
would come.

But you never picked up a white paper and saw anything in there
about Negro baseball.

Questions for Part III

1 Why does Riis agree that there is no bottom limit to women's wages? What is different in the situation of women today?

2 What makes Philadelphia so interesting to Steffens? What does he mean when he says that citizens of Philadelphia "have no more rights at the polls" than do blacks in the South?

3 Explain "honest graft" as Plunkitt defines it. What are the worthy functions of political machines according to him? What is your opinion of his view?

4 Sometimes, as in the case of the Triangle Fire, terrible disasters lead to much-needed reforms. Can you think of any examples? Report on one or two, describing the tragedy and the resulting reform.

5 What values did Dick O'Neill fight for? How does he feel about his wartime experiences? How do you think he would have viewed Emma Goldman?

6 Do you think it was proper for the government to use the Boy Scouts to support its policy? Would that be possible today?

7 Why did Emma Goldman oppose the draft? What values did she what life was like for blacks in the South? What were the consequences of the population shift?

8 What do the letters from the "great migration" tell you about support that caused her to risk prison or deportation?

9 Why did George Babbit become a figure of fun for American readers? What is comic about him? How is he representative of a consumer culture?

10 What points does Calkins make in his defense of advertising? What are some of the criticisms of advertising?

11 How would you characterize the child-care advice from 1928? Strict? Lenient? Proper? Silly? Why do you think the government issued such a pamphlet?

12 Based on your reading of the Klansman's Manual, what aspects of the Klan would appeal to a man of the 1920s? What aspects appeal to you? What do you find repugnant?

13 If possible, talk to elderly people you know—perhaps your grandparents or other relatives—about their memories of the early 1930's.

Compare what they say with the comments of the people Terkel interviewed.

14   In your textbook or library, look up the Supreme Court decisions concerning the internment of Japanese-Americans during World War II. How did the majority of the Court justices explain their decision? What is your opinion on this issue?

15   Why do you think Ernie Pyle's war reporting was so popular? Interview people who lived through World War II and ask them how they remember hearing about the war and how they felt about it.

16   In addition to baseball, what areas of American life have changed as a result of the integration of blacks and whites?

PART IV AMERICA SINCE 1945

Victory in World II planted seeds of anxiety. Americans feared the return of depression after industry stopped producing tanks, jeeps, and planes. Uncertainties about the American future were accompanied by ideological quarrels with the Soviet Union. They also brought new challenges to American verities. Tom Rath, in The Man in the Gray Flannel Suit, *while trying to fit into the culture of the suburbs, tried to forget the seventeen men he had killed during the war and the woman he had left behind. Young people, dissatisfied with the placid suburban dream, and black Americans, shut out of the dream, found new ways of asserting their rights and needs. New lifestyles were suddenly undermining American attitudes toward money and toward family behavior. Many young people read Kerouac's* On The Road *and took to the road or to drugs. Americans went into debt and experimented with new ways of experiencing their personal lives even while public figures reaffirmed traditional values.*

The black push for equality, unrest among young people, and the awakening of a vocal movement on the political Right were prominent in the growing ferment of the late 1950s. John F. Kennedy captured these trends in the rhetoric of the 1960 presidential campaign and, in his Inaugural Address, issued an urgent call for action. Responses to that call are obvious in many a manifesto of the 1960s, among them the influential Students for a Democratic Society's "Port Huron Statement." We see the idealism of the 1960s in the letters from Mississippi and in the slow steps toward openness and tolerance revealed in the story of an American commune. And overshadowing all American lives was the growing cancer of the nation's longest and strangest war, depicted in the testimony of Dave Baker and Clarence Fitch.

The experimentation in lifestyles as seen in the Twin Oaks Community continued past the 1960s, and the fight for civil liberties continued, most notably in the attempts to pass a constitutional amendment explicitly guaranteeing equal rights and freedom from discrimination for women. However, beginning in the early 1970s, at least a segment of society was calling for order, consolidation, and traditional values, and some of those crying loudest in support of the new conservatism were former members of the left, as seen in the essay by Peter Collier and David Horowitz.

Although to some people the 1980s seemed to be a time of 1920s-style affluence and growth, to others it was a time when husband and wife both had to work in order to simply maintain their standing of living. It was a time when the number of poor, female-headed households increased dramatically, and it brought into focus the problems women faced as they felt pressure to choose between newfound economic opportunities and any interest they had in roles as spouses or parents.

Although the administration of Ronald Reagan was able to intertwine American hopes and memories in a way that no critic could disentangle, the years of his administration were a period during which not all citizens were optimistic about the future. The toxic waste problem at Love Canal was repeated at Times Beach and elsewhere across the nation. All this was less significant, however, to a generation of new immigrants, who, like Jessie de la Cruz, left political and economic instability in their homelands to come to a new land in renewal of the American dream of prosperity and good fortune. To them, America still represented the best hope for a secure future.

36 | Life In Gray Flannel

The Man in the Gray Flannel Suit *became in the mid-1950s a catch phrase for the struggling, security-oriented male suburbanite and corporate climber. These first pages from Sloan Wilson's 1955 novel—made into a movie starring Gregory Peck and Jennifer Jones—present Tom Rath and his wife, Betsy, who are caught between their ideals and the materialism that has marked the suburbanization of American life. Later in the novel, Tom gets the job he applies for at the United Broadcasting Corporation, the job that makes him another man in a gray flannel suit. Later, incidents from his experiences in World War II, briefly alluded to in this excerpt, come back to haunt him.*

1

By the time they had lived seven years in the little house on Greentree Avenue in Westport, Connecticut, they both detested it. There were many reasons, none of them logical, but all of them compelling. For one thing, the house had a kind of evil genius for displaying proof of their weaknesses and wiping out all traces of their strengths. The ragged lawn and weed-filled garden proclaimed to passers-by and the neighbors that Thomas R. Rath and his family disliked ''working around the place'' and couldn't afford to pay someone else to do it. The interior of the house was even more vengeful. In the living room there was a big dent in the plaster near the floor, with a huge crack curving up from it in the shape of a question mark. That wall was damaged in the fall of 1952, when, after struggling for months to pay up the back bills, Tom came home one night to find that Betsy had bought a cut-glass vase for forty dollars. Such an extravagant gesture was utterly unlike her, at least since the war. Betsy was a conscientious household manager, and usually when she did something Tom didn't like, they talked the matter over with careful reasonableness. But on that particular night, Tom was tired and worried because he himself had just spent seventy dollars on a new suit he felt he needed to dress properly for his business, and at

Sloan Wilson, The Man in the Gray Flannel Suit. (New York, Simon and Schuster, 1955) pp. 3–17. Used by permission.

the climax of a heated argument, he picked up the vase and heaved it against the wall. The heavy glass shattered, the plaster cracked, and two of the lathes behind it broke. The next morning, Tom and Betsy worked together on their knees to patch the plaster, and they repainted the whole wall, but when the paint dried, the big dent near the floor with the crack curving up from it almost to the ceiling in the shape of a question mark was still clearly visible. The fact that the crack was in the shape of a question mark did not seem symbolic to Tom and Betsy, nor even amusing—it was just annoying. Its peculiar shape caused people to stare at it abstractedly, and once at a cocktail party one of the guests who had had a little too much to drink said, "Say, that's funny. Did you ever notice that big question mark on your wall?"

"It's only a crack," Tom replied.

"But why should it be in the form of a question mark?"

"It's just coincidence."

"That's funny." the guest said.

Tom and Betsy assured each other that someday they would have the whole wall replastered, but they never did. The crack remained as a perpetual reminder of Betsy's moment of extravagance, Tom's moment of violence, and their inability either to fix walls properly or to pay to have them fixed. It seemed ironic to Tom that the house should preserve a souvenir of such things, while allowing evenings of pleasure and kindness to slip by without a trace.

The crack in the living room was not the only reminder of the worst. An ink stain with hand marks on the wallpaper in Janey's room commemorated one of the few times Janey ever willfully destroyed property, and the only time Betsy ever lost her temper with her and struck her. Janey was five, and the middle one of the three Rath children. She did everything hard: she screamed when she cried, and when she was happy her small face seemed to hold for an instant all the joy in the world. Upon deciding that she wanted to play with ink, she carefully poured ink over both her hands and made neat imprints on the wallpaper, from the floor to as high as she could reach. Betsy was so angry that she slapped both her hands, and Janey, feeling she had simply been interrupted in the midst of an artistic endeavor, lay on the bed for an hour sobbing and rubbing her hands in her eyes until her whole face was covered with ink. Feeling like a murderess, Betsy tried to comfort her, but even holding and rocking her didn't seem to help, and Betsy was shocked to find that the child was shuddering. When Tom came home that night he found mother and daughter asleep on the bed together, tightly locked in each other's arms. Both their faces were covered with ink. All this the wall remembered and recorded.

A thousand petty shabbinesses bore witness to the negligence of the Raths. The front door had been scratched by a dog which had been run over the year before. The hot-water faucet in the bathroom dripped. Almost all the furniture needed to be refinished, reupholstered, or cleaned. And besides that, the house was too small, ugly, and almost precisely like the houses on all sides of it.

The Raths had bought the house in 1946, shortly after Tom had got out of the army and, at the suggestion of his grandmother, become an assistant to the director of the Schanenhauser Foundation, an organization which an elderly millionaire had established to help finance scientific research and the arts. They had told each other that they probably would be in the house only one or two years before they could afford something better. It took them five years to realize that the expense of raising three children was likely to increase at least as fast as Tom's salary at a charitable foundation. If Tom and Betsy had been entirely reasonable, this might have caused them to start painting the place like crazy, but it had the reverse effect. Without talking about it much, they both began to think of the house as a trap, and they no more enjoyed refurbishing it than a prisoner would delight in shining up the bars of his cell. Both of them were aware that their feelings about the house were not admirable.

"I don't know what's the matter with us," Betsy said one night. "Your job is plenty good enough. We've got three nice kids, and lots of people would be glad to have a house like this. We shouldn't be so *discontented* all the time."

"Of course we shouldn't!" Tom said.

Their words sounded hollow. It was curious to believe that that house with the crack in the form of a question mark on the wall and the ink stains on the wallpaper was probably the end of their personal road. It was impossible to believe. Somehow something would have to happen.

Tom thought about his house on that day in June 1953, when a friend of his named Bill Hawthorne mentioned the possibility of a job at the United Broadcasting Corporation. Tom was having lunch with a group of acquaintances in The Golden Horseshoe, a small restaurant and bar near Rockefeller Center.

"I hear we've got a new spot opening up in our public-relations department," Bill, who wrote promotion for United Broadcasting, said. "I think any of you would be crazy to take it, mind you, but if you're interested, there it is. . . . "

Tom unfolded his long legs under the table and shifted his big body on his chair restlessly. "How much would it pay?" he asked casually.

"I don't know," Bill said. "Anywhere from eight to twelve thousand, I'd guess, according to how good a hold-up man you are. If you try for it, ask fifteen. I'd like to see somebody stick the bastards good."

It was fashionable that summer to be cynical about one's employers, and the promotion men were the most cynical of all.

"You can have it," Cliff Otis, a young copy writer for a large advertising agency, said. "I wouldn't want to get into a rat race like that."

Tom glanced into his glass and said nothing. Maybe I could get ten thousand a year, he thought. If I could do that, Betsy and I might be able to buy a better house.

2

When Tom stepped off the train at Westport that night, he stood among a crowd of men and looked toward the corner of the station where Betsy usually waited for him. She was there, and involuntarily his pace quickened at the sight of her. After almost twelve years of marriage, he was still not quite used to his good fortune at having acquired such a pretty wife. Even with her light-brown hair somewhat tousled, as it was now, she looked wonderful to him. The slightly rumpled cotton house dress she was wearing innocently displayed her slim-waisted but full figure to advantage, and although she looked a little tired, her smile was bright and youthful as she waved to him. Because he felt it so genuinely, there was always a temptation for him to say to her, "How beautiful you are!" when he saw her after being away for the day, but he didn't, because long ago he had learned that she was perhaps the one woman in the world who didn't like such compliments. "Don't keep telling me I'm pretty," she had said to him once with real impatience in her voice. "I've been told that ever since I was twelve years old. If you want to compliment me, tell me I'm something I'm not. Tell me that I'm a marvelous housekeeper, or that I don't have a selfish bone in my body."

Now he hurried toward her. "Hi!" he said, "It's good to get home. How did things go with you today?"

"Not so well," she replied ruefully. "Brace yourself."

"Why, what happened?" he said, and kissed her lightly.

"Barbara's got the chicken pox, and the washing machine broke down."

"Chicken pox!" Tom said. "Do they get very sick with that?"

"No, but according to Dr. Spock, it's messy. The other two will probably get it. Poor Barbara feels awful. And I think we're going to have a buy a new washing machine."

/   /   /

Tom went downstairs and mixed a Martini for Betsy and himself. When Betsy came down, they sat in the kitchen, sipping their drinks gratefully while the children played in the living room and watched television. The linoleum on the kitchen floor was beginning to wrinkle. Originally it had been what the builder described as a "bright, basket-weave pattern," but now it was scuffed, and by the sink it was worn through to the wood underneath. "We ought to get some new linoleum," Betsy said. "We could lay it ourselves."

"I heard about a new job today," Tom said. "Public relations. United Broadcasting Corporation."

"How much does it pay?"

"Probably a good deal more than I'm getting now."

There was an instant of silence before she said, "Are you going to try for it?"

"I might."

Betsy finished her drink and poured herself another. "I've never thought of you as a public-relations man," she said soberly. "Would you like it?"

"I'd like the money."

Betsy sighed. "It would be wonderful to get out of this house," she said.

3

The next morning, Tom put on his best suit, a freshly cleaned and pressed gray flannel. On his way to work he stopped in Grand Central Station to buy a clean white handkerchief and to have his shoes shined. During his luncheon hour he set out to visit the United Broadcasting Corporation. As he walked across Rockefeller Plaza, he thought wryly of the days when he and Betsy had assured each other that money didn't matter. They had told each other that when they were married, before the war, and during the war they had repeated it in long letters. "The important thing is to find a kind of work you really like, and something that is useful," Betsy had written him. "The money doesn't matter."

The hell with that, he thought. The real trouble is that up to now we've been kidding ourselves. We might as well admit that what we want is a big house and a new car and trips to Florida in the winter, and plenty of life insurance. When you come right down to it, a man with three children has no damn right to say that money doesn't matter.

There were eighteen elevators in the lobby of the United Broadcasting building. They were all brass colored and looked as though they were made of money. The receptionist in the personnel office was a breathtakingly beautiful girl with money-colored hair—a sort of copper gold. "Yes?" she said.

"I want to apply for a position in the public-relations department."

"If you will sit down in the reception room, I'll arrange an interview for you," she said.

The company had a policy of giving all job applicants an interview. Every year about twenty thousand people, most of them wildly unqualified, applied for jobs there, and it was considered poor public relations to turn them away too abruptly. Beyond the receptionist's desk was a huge waiting room. A rich wine-red carpet was on the floor, and there were dozens of heavy leather armchairs filled with people nervously smoking cigarettes. On the walls were enormous colored photographs of the company's leading radio and television stars. They were all youthful, handsome, and unutterably rich-appearing as they smiled down benignly on the job applicants. Tom picked a chair directly beneath a picture of a big-bosomed blonde. He had to wait only about twenty minutes before the receptionist told him that a Mr. Everett would see him. Mr. Everett's office was a cubicle with walls of opaque glass brick, only about three times as big as a priest's confessional. Everett himself was a man about Tom's age and was also dressed in a gray flannel suit. The uniform of the day, Tom thought. Somebody must have put out an order.

"I understand that you are interested in a position in the public-relations department," Everett said.

"I just want to explore the situation," Tom replied. "I already have a good position with the Schanenhauser Foundation, but I'm considering a change.

It took Everett only about a minute to size Tom up as a "possibility." He gave him a long printed form to fill out and told him he'd hear from the United Broadcasting Corporation in a few days. Tom spent almost an hour filling out all the pages of the form, which, among other things, required a list of the childhood diseases he had had and the names of countries he had visited. When he had finished, he gave it to the girl with the hair of copper gold and rang for one of the golden elevators to take him down.

Five days later Tom got a letter from Everett saying an interview had been arranged for him with Mr. Gordon Walker in Room 3672 the following Monday at 11:00 A.M. In the letter Walker was given no title. Tom didn't know whether he were going to have another routine interview, or whether he were actually being considered for a position. He wondered whether he should tell Dick Haver, the director of the Schanenhauser Foundation, that he was looking for another job. The danger of not telling him was that broadcasting company might call him for references any time, and Dick wouldn't be pleased to find that Tom was applying for another job behind his back. It was important to keep Dick's good will, because the broadcasting company's decision might depend on the recommendation Dick gave him. In any one of a thousand ways, Dick could damn him, without Tom's ever learning about it. All Dick would have to do when the broadcasting company telephoned him would be to say, "Tom Rath? Well, I don't know. I don't think I'd want to go on record one way or the other on Mr. Rath. He's a nice person, you understand, an awfully nice person. I'd be perfectly willing to say that!"

On the other hand, it would be embarrassing to tell Dick he was seeking another job and then be unable to find one. Tom decided to delay seeing Dick until after he had had his next interview.

Walker's outer office was impressive. As soon as Tom saw it, he knew he was being seriously considered for a job, and maybe a pretty good one. Walker had two secretaries, one chosen for looks, apparently, and one for utility. A pale-yellow carpet lay on ᵗʰe floor, and there was a yellow leather armchair for callers. Walker himself was closeted in an inner office which was separated from the rest of the room by a partition of opaque glass brick.

The utilitarian secretary told Tom to wait. It was extremely quiet. Neither of the two girls was typing, and although each had two telephones on her desk and an interoffice communication box, there was no ringing or buzzing. Both the secretaries sat reading typewritten sheets in black notebooks. After Tom had waited about half an hour, the pretty secretary, with no audible or visible cue, suddenly looked up brightly and said, "Mr. Walker will see you now. Just open the door and go in."

Tom opened the door and saw a fat pale man sitting in a highbacked upholstered chair behind a kidney-shaped desk, with nothing on it but a blotter and pen. He was in his shirt sleeves, and he weighed about two hundred and fifty pounds. His face was as white as a marshmallow. He didn't stand up when Tom came in, but he smiled. It was a surprisingly warm, spontaneous smile, as though he had unexpectedly recognized an old friend. "Thomas Rath?" he said. "Sit down! Make yourself comfortable! Take off your coat!"

Tom thanked him and, although it wasn't particularly warm, took off his coat. There wasn't anyplace to put it, so, sitting down in the comfortable chair in front of Walker's desk, he laid the coat awkwardly across his lap.

"I've read the application forms you filled out, and it seems to me you might be qualified for a new position we may have opening up here," Walker said. "There are just a few questions I want to ask you." He was still smiling. Suddenly he touched a button on the arm of his chair and the back of the chair dropped, allowing him to recline, as though he were in an airplane seat. Tom could see only his face across the top of the desk.

"You will excuse me," Walker said, still smiling. "The doctor says I must get plenty of rest, and this is the way I do it."

Tom couldn't think of anything more appropriate to say than "It looks comfortable. . . ."

"Why do you want to work for the United Broadcasting Corporation?" Walker asked abruptly.

"It's a good company . . . " Tom began hesitantly, and was suddenly impatient at the need for hypocrisy. The sole reason he wanted to work for United Broadcasting was that he thought he might be able to make a lot of money there fast, but he felt he couldn't say that. It was sometimes considered fashionable for the employees of foundations to say that they were in it for the money, but people were supposed to work at advertising agencies and broadcasting companies for spiritual reasons.

"I believe," Tom said, "that television is developing into the great-est medium for mass education and entertainment. It has always fasci-nated me, and I would like to work with it. . . . "

"What kind of salary do you have in mind?" Walker asked. Tom hadn't expected the question that soon. Walker was still smiling.

"The salary isn't the primary consideration with me," Tom said, trying desperately to come up with stock answers to stock questions. "I'm mainly interested in finding something useful and worth while to do. I have personal responsibilities, however, and I would hope that something could be worked out to enable me to meet them. . . . "

"Of course," Walker said, beaming more cheerily than ever. "I un-derstand you applied for a position in the public-relations department. Why did you choose that?"

Because I heard there was an opening, Tom wanted to say, but quickly thought better of it and substituted a halting avowal of lifelong interest in public relations. "I think my experience in working with *people* at the Schanenhauser Foundation would be helpful," he con-cluded lamely.

"I see," Walked said kindly. There was a short silence before he added, "Can you write?"

"I do most of the writing at the Schanenhauser Foundation," Tom said. "The annual report to the trustees is my job, and so are most of the reports on individual projects. I used to be editor of my college paper."

"That sounds fine," Walker said casually, "I have a little favor I want to ask of you. I want you to write me your autobiography."

"What?" Tom asked in astonishment.

"Nothing very long," Walker said. "Just as much as you can man-age to type out in an hour. One of my girls will give you a room with a typewriter."

"Is there anything in particular you want me to tell you about?"

"Yourself," Walker said, looking hugely pleased. "Explain yourself to me. Tell me what kind of person you are. Explain why we should hire you."

"I'll try," Tom said weakly.

"You'll have precisely an hour," Walker said. "You see, this is a device I use in employing people—I find it most helpful. For this particu-lar job, I have twenty or thirty applicants. It's hard to tell from a brief interview whom to choose, so I ask them all to write about themselves for an hour. You'd be surprised how revealing the results are. . . . "

He paused, still smiling. Tom said nothing.

"Just a few hints," Walker continued. "Write anything you want, but at the end of your last page, I'd like you to finish this sentence: 'The most significant fact about me is . . . '"

"The most significant fact about me is . . . " Tom repeated idioti-cally.

"The results, of course, will be entirely confidential." Walked lifted a bulky arm and inspected his wrist watch. "It's now five minutes to twelve," he concluded. "I'll expect your paper on my desk at precisely one o'clock."

Tom stood up, put on his coat, said, "Thank you," and went out of the room. The utilitarian secretary already had a stack of typewriting paper ready for him. She led him to a small room a few doors down the hall in which were a typewriter and a hard office chair. There was a large clock on the wall. The room had no windows. Across the ceiling was a glaring fluorescent light which made the bare white plaster walls look yellow. The secretary walked out without a word, shutting the door silently behind her.

Tom sat down in the chair, which had been designed for a stenographer and was far too small for him. Son of a bitch, he thought—I guess the laws about cruel and unusual punishment don't apply to personnel men. He tried to think of something to write, but all he could remember was Betsy and the drab little house and the need to buy a new washing machine, and the time he had thrown a vase that cost forty dollars against the wall. "The most significant fact about me is that I once threw a vase costing forty dollars against a wall." That would be as sensible as anything else he could think of, but he doubted whether it would get him the job. He thought of Janey saying, "It isn't *fair!*" and the worn linoleum on the kitchen floor. "The most significant fact about me is . . . " It was a stupid sentence to ask a man to finish.

I have children, he thought—that's probably the most significant fact about me, the only one that will have much importance for long. Anything about a man can be summed up in numbers. Thomas R. Rath, thirty-three years old, making seven thousand dollars a year, owner of a 1939 Ford, a six-room house, and ten thousand dollars' worth of G.I. Life Insurance which, in case of his death, would pay his widow about forty dollars a month. Six feet one and a half inches tall; weight, 198 pounds. He served four and a half years in the Army, most of it in Europe and the rest in the South Pacific.

Another statistical fact came to him then, a fact which he knew would be ridiculously melodramatic to put into an application for a job at the United Broadcasting Corporation, or to think about at all. He hadn't thought about this for a long while. It wasn't a thing he had deliberately tried to forget—he simply hadn't thought about it for quite a few years. It was the unreal-sounding, probably irrelevant, but quite accurate fact that he had killed seventeen men.

It had been during the war, of course. He had been a paratrooper. Lots of other people had killed more men than he had. Lots of bomber crews and artillerymen had, but, of course, they never really knew it. Lots of infantrymen and lots of paratroopers had, and most of them knew it. Plenty of men had been dropped behind the enemy lines, as Tom had been on five different occasions, and they had had to do some of their killing silently, with blackjacks and knives. They had known what they were doing, and most of them were healthy enough not to be morbid about it, and not to be proud of it, and not to be ashamed of it. Such things were merely part of the war, the war before the Korean one. It was no longer fashionable to talk about the war, and certainly it had never been fashionable to talk about the number of men one had killed. Tom couldn't forget the number, "seventeen," but it didn't seem real any more; it was just a small, isolated statistic that nobody wanted. His mind went blank. Suddenly the word "Maria" flashed into it.

"The most significant fact about me is that I . . . "

Nonsense, he thought, and brought himself back to the present with a jerk. Only masochists can get along without editing their own memories. Maria was a girl he had known in Italy during the war, a long time ago, and he never thought about her any more, just as he never thought about the seventeen men he had killed. It wasn't always easy to forget, but it was certainly necessary to try.

"The most significant fact about me is that for four and a half years my profession was jumping out of airplanes with a gun, and now I want to go into public relations."

That probably wouldn't get him the job, Tom thought. "The most significant fact about me is that I detest the United Broadcasting Corporation, with all its soap operas, commercials, and yammering studio audiences, and the only reason I'm willing to spend my life in such a ridiculous enterprise is that I want to buy a more expensive house and a better brand of gin."

That certainly wouldn't get him the job.

"The most significant fact about me is that I've become a cheap cynic."

That would not be apt to get him the job.

"The most significant fact about me is that as a young man in college, I played the mandolin incessantly. I, champion mandolin player, am applying to you for a position in the public-relations department!"

That would not be likely to get him far. Impatiently he sat down at the typewriter and glanced at his wrist watch. It was a big loud ticking wrist watch with a black face, luminous figures, and a red sweep hand that rapidly ticked off the seconds. He had bought it years ago at an Army post exchange and had worn it all through the war. The watch was the closest thing to a good-luck charm he had ever had, although he never thought of it as such. Now it was more reassuring to look at than the big impersonal clock on the wall, though both said it was almost twelve-thirty. So far he had written nothing. What the hell, he thought. I was a damn fool to think I wanted to work here anyway. Then he thought of Betsy asking, as she would be sure to, "Did you get the job? How did it go?" And he decided to try.

"Anybody's life can be summed up in a paragraph," he wrote. "I was born on November 20, 1920, in my grandmother's house in South Bay, Connecticut. I was graduated from Covington Academy in 1937, and from Harvard College in 1941. I spent four and a half years in the Army, reaching the rank of captain. Since 1946, I have been employed as an assistant to the director of the Schanenhauser Foundation. I live in Westport, Connecticut, with my wife and three children. From the point of view of the United Broadcasting Corporation, the most significant fact about me is that I am applying for a position in its public-relations department, and after an initial period of learning, I probably would do a good job. I will be glad to answer any questions which seem relevant, but after considerable thought, I have decided that I do not wish to attempt an autobiography as part of an application for a job."

He typed this paragraph neatly in the precise center of a clean piece of paper, added his name and address, and carried to into Walker's office. It was only quarter to one, and Walker was obviously surprised to see him. "You've still got fifteen minutes!" he said.

"I've written all I think is necessary," Tom replied, and handed him the almost empty page.

Walker read it slowly, his big pale face expressionless. When he had finished it, he dropped it into a drawer. "We'll let you know our decision in a week or so," he said.

37 | "The Parties Were Enormous"

Unlike major events in politics, diplomacy, or war, those in the history of a culture usually occur unheralded by trumpets, protocol, or newsreporters. The publication of Jack Kerouac's On the Road *in 1957 marked the advent of a new sensibility. Kerouac's novel describes the netherworld of the "beat" generation, which sought redemption and a sense of community in drugs and sex, exotic religion, mystical inspiration, poetry, and jazz, and rejected the materialism and mass culture of American society in the 1950s. Jack Kerouac's prose and Allan Ginsberg's poetry (Ginsberg is the "Carlo Marx" of* On The Road*) influenced a generation of restless and daring young people in the 1960s to experiment with new ways of living and of viewing the world. "Beat" and its condescending derivative "beatnik" rapidly entered the language as the mass media took up the phenomena. The beat lifestyle was parodied and commercialized, the literary works were scorned by professional critics, and the drug culture was attacked by moralists and the police.*

Setting a tone that would continue over the next two decades, America in the 1950s greeted the new challenge to its conventions with curiosity, disdain, and ambivalence. Time Magazine *described beatniks as a "pack of oddballs who celebrate booze, dope, sex, and despair," and in California a hostess could rent a beatnik to add color and surprise to her parties.*

The parties were enormous; there were at least a hundred people at a basement apartment in the West Nineties. People overflowed into the cellar compartments near the furnace. Something was going on in every corner, on every bed and couch—not an orgy but just a New Year's party with frantic screaming and wild radio music. There was even a Chinese girl. Dean ran like Groucho Marx from group to group, digging everybody. Periodically we rushed out to the car to pick up more people. Damion came. Damion is the hero of my New York gang, as Dean is the chief hero of the Western. They immediately took a dislike to each other. Damion's girl suddenly socked Damion on the jaw with a roundhouse

Excerpt from On the Road *by Jack Kerouac. Copyright 1955, 1957 by Jack Kerouac. Copyright renewed © by Stella Kerouac and Jan Kerouac. Reprinted by permission of Viking Penguin-Inc. Pages 104–107, 110–112 of Signet Edition.*

right. He stood reeling. She carried him home. Some of our mad newspaper friends came in from the office with bottles. There was a tremendous and wonderful snowstorm going on outside. Ed Dunkel met
Lucille's sister and disappeared with her; I forgot to say that Ed Dunkel
is a very smooth man with the women. He's six foot four, mild, affable,
agreeable, bland, and delightful. He helps women on with their coats.
That's the way to do things. At five o'clock in the morning we were all
rushing through the backyard of a tenement and climbing in through a
window of an apartment where a huge party was going on. At dawn
we were back at Tom Saybrook's. People were drawing pictures and
drinking stale beer. I slept on a couch with a girl called Mona in my
arms. Great groups filed in from the old Columbia Campus bar. Everything in life, all the faces of life, were piling into the same dank room.
At Ian MacArthur's the party went on. Ian MacArthur is a wonderful
sweet fellow who wears glasses and peers out of them with delight. He
began to learn "Yes!" to everything, just like Dean at this time, and
hasn't stopped since. To the wild sounds of Dexter Gordon and Wardell
Gray blowing "The Hunt," Dean and I played catch with Marylou over
the couch; she was no small doll either. Dean went around with no
undershirt, just his pants, barefoot, till it was time to hit the car and
fetch more people. Everything happened. We found the wild, ecstatic
Rollo Greb and spent a night at his house on Long Island. Rollo lives in
a nice house with his aunt; when she dies the house is all his. Meanwhile she refuses to comply with any of his wishes and hates his friends.
He brought this ragged gang of Dean, Marylou, Ed, and me, and began
a roaring party. The woman prowled upstairs; she threatened to call the
police. "Oh, shut up, you old bag!" yelled Greb. I wondered how he
could live with her like this. He had more books than I've ever seen in
all my life—two libraries, two rooms loaded from floor to ceiling around
all four walls, and such books as the Apocryphal Something-or-Other
in ten volumes. He played Verdi operas and pantomimed them in his
pajamas with a great rip down the back. He didn't give a damn about
anything. He is a great scholar who goes reeling down the New York
waterfront with original seventeenth-century musical manuscripts under his arm, shouting. He crawls like a big spider through the streets.
His excitement blew out of his eyes in stabs of fiendish light. He rolled
his neck in spastic ecstasy. He lisped, he writhed, he flopped, he
moaned, he howled, he fell back in despair. He could hardly get a word
out, he was so excited with life. Dean stood before him with head
bowed, repeating over and over again, "Yes . . . Yes . . . Yes." He took
me into a corner. "That Rollo Greb is the greatest, most wonderful of
all. That's what I was trying to tell you—that's what I want to be. I want
to be like him. He's never hung-up, he goes every direction, he lets it
all out, he knows times, he has nothing to do but rock back and forth.
Man, he's the end! You see, if you go like him all the time you'll finally
get it."

"Get what?"

"IT! IT! I'll tell you—now no time, we have no time now." Dean rushed back to watch Rollo Greb some more.

George Shearing, the great jazz pianist, Dean said, was exactly like Rollo Greb. Dean and I went to see Shearing at Birdland in the midst of the long, mad weekend. The place was deserted, we were the first customers, ten o'clock. Shearing came out, blind, led by the hand to his keyboard. He was a distinguished-looking Englishman with a stiff white collar, slightly beefy, blond, with a delicate English-summer's-night air about him that came out in the first rippling sweet number he played as the bass-player leaned to him reverently and thrummed the beat. The drummer, Denzil Best, sat motionless except for his wrists snapping the brushes. And Shearing began to rock; a smile broke over his ecstatic face; he began to rock in the piano seat, back and forth, slowly at first, then the beat went up, and he began rocking fast, his left foot jumped up with every beat, his neck began to rock crookedly, he brought his face down to the keys, he pushed his hair back, his combed hair dissolved, he began to sweat. The music picked up. The bass-player hunched over and socked it in, faster and faster, it seemed faster and faster, that's all. Shearing began to play his chords; they rolled out of the piano in great rich showers, you'd think the man wouldn't have time to line them up. They rolled and rolled like the sea. Folks yelled for him to "Go!" Dean was sweating; the sweat poured down his collar. "There he is! That's him! Old God! Old God Shearing! Yes! Yes! Yes!" And Shearing was conscious of the madman behind him, he could hear every one of Dean's gasps and imprecations, he could sense it though he couldn't see. "That's right!" Dean said. "Yes!" Shearing smiled; he rocked. Shearing rose from the piano, dripping with sweat; these were his great 1949 days before he became cool and commercial. When he was gone Dean pointed to the empty piano seat. "God's empty chair," he said. On the piano a horn sat; its golden shadow made a strange reflection along the desert caravan painted on the wall behind the drums. God was gone; it was the silence of his departure. It was a rainy night. It was the myth of the rainy night. Dean was popeyed with awe. This madness would lead nowhere. I didn't know what was happening to me, and I suddenly realized it was only the tea that we were smoking; Dean had bought some in New York. It made me think that everything was about to arrive—the moment when you know all and everything is decided forever.

/   /   /

It was drizzling and mysterious at the beginning of our journey. I could see that it was all going to be one big saga of the mist. "Whooee!" yelled Dean. "Here we go!" And he hunched over the wheel and gunned her; he was back in his element, everybody could see that. We were all delighted, we all realized we were leaving confusion and non-sense behind and performing our one and noble function of the time, *move*. And we moved! We flashed past the mysterious white signs in the night somewhere in New Jersey that say SOUTH (with an arrow) and WEST (with an arrow) and took the south one. New Orleans! It burned in our brains. From the dirty snows of "frosty fagtown New York," as Dean called it, all the way to the greeneries and river smells of old New Orleans at the washed-out bottom of America; then west. Ed was in the back seat; Marylou and Dean and I sat in front and had the warmest talk about the goodness and joy of life. Dean suddenly became tender. "Now dammit, look here, all of you, we all must admit that everything is fine and there's no need in the world to worry, and in fact we should realize what it would mean to us to UNDERSTAND that we're not REALLY worried about ANYTHING. Am I right?" We all agreed. "Here we go, we're all together . . . What did we do in New York? Let's forgive." We all had our spats back there. "That's behind us, merely by miles and inclinations. Now we're heading down to New Orleans to dig Old Bull Lee and ain't that going to be kicks and listen will you to this old tenor-man blow his top"—he shot up the radio volume till the car shud-dered—"and listen to him tell the story and put down true relaxation and knowledge."

We all jumped to the music and agreed. The purity of the road. The white line in the middle of the highway unrolled and hugged our left front tire as if glued to our groove. Dean hunched his muscular neck, T-shirted in the winter night, and blasted the car along. He insisted I drive through Baltimore for traffic practice; that was all right, except he and Marylou insisted on steering while they kissed and fooled around. It was crazy; the radio was on full blast. Dean beat drums on the dash-board till a great sag developed in it; I did too. The poor Hudson—the slow boat to China—was receiving her beating.

"Oh man, what kicks!" yelled Dean. "Now Marylou, listen really, honey, you know that I'm hotrock capable of everything at the same time and I have unlimited energy—now in San Francisco we must go on living together. I know just the place for you—at the end of the regu-lar chain-gang run—I'll be home just a cut-hair less than every two days and for twelve hours at a stretch, and *man*, you know what we can do in twelve hours, darling. Meanwhile I'll go right on living at Camille's like nothin, see, she won't know. We can work it, we've done it before." It was all right with Marylou, she was really out for Camille's scalp. The understanding had been that Marylou would switch to me in Frisco, but I now began to see they were going to stick and I was going to be left alone on my butt at the other end of the continent. But why think about that when all the golden land's ahead of you and all kinds of unforeseen events wait lurking to surprise you and make you glad you're alive to see?

JOHN F. KENNEDY

38 | The Obligations of a Free Society

In his first address as president, John F. Kennedy set ambitious goals for his administration. While Jack Kerouac and the beats were tempting the generation that was then coming of age to withdraw—to "drop out,"—from society, Kennedy's 1961 speech summoned that generation and the nation as a whole to a new set of challenges and responsibilities. Two years and ten months later, though, Kennedy lay dead, the victim of an assassin. And within a few more years, the idealism he called forth was for many Americans transformed into terrible bitterness and cynicism by the quagmire of the Vietnam war.

Vice President Johnson, Mr. Speaker, Mr. Chief Justice, President Eisenhower, Vice President Nixon, President Truman, reverend Clergy, fellow citizens:

We observe today not a victory of a party but a celebration of freedom—symbolizing an end as well as a beginning—signifying renewal as well as change. For I have sworn before you and Almighty God the same solemn oath our forebears prescribed nearly a century and three quarters ago.

The world is very different now. For man holds in his mortal hand the power to abolish all forms of human poverty and all forms of human life. And yet the same revolutionary beliefs for which our forebears fought are still at issue around the globe—the belief that the rights of man come not from the generosity of the state but from the hand of God.

We dare not forget today that we are the heirs of that first revolution. Let the word go forth from this time and place, to friend and foe alike, that the torch has been passed to a new generation of Americans—born in this century, tempered by war, disciplined by a hard and bitter peace, proud of our ancient heritage—and unwilling to witness or permit the slow undoing of those human rights to which this Nation has

John F. Kennedy, "Inaugural Address," January 20, 1961. Reprinted from President Kennedy's Program, *published in May, 1961 by Congressional Quarterly Service, p. 1.*

always been committed, and to which we are committed today at home and around the world.

Let every nation know, whether it wishes us well or ill, that we shall pay any price, bear any burden, meet any hardship, support any friend, oppose any foe to assure the survival and success of liberty.

This much we pledge—and more.

To those old allies whose cultural and spiritual origins we share, we pledge the loyalty of faithful friends. United, there is little we cannot do in a host of cooperative ventures. Divided, there is little we can do—for we dare not meet a powerful challenge at odds and split asunder.

To those new states whom we welcome to the ranks of the free, we pledge our word that one form of colonial control shall not have passed away merely to be replaced by a far more iron tyranny. We shall not always expect to find them supporting our view. But we shall always hope to find them strongly supporting their own freedom—and to remember that, in the past, those who foolishly sought power by riding the back of the tiger ended up inside.

To those peoples in the huts and villages of half the globe struggling to break the bonds of mass misery, we pledge our best efforts to help them help themselves, for whatever period is required—not because the Communists may be doing it, not because we seek their votes, but because it is right. If a free society cannot help the many who are poor, it cannot save the few who are rich.

To our sister republics south of our border, we offer a special pledge—to convert our good words into good deeds—in a new alliance for progress—to assist free men and free governments in casting off the chains of poverty. But this peaceful revolution of hope cannot become the prey of hostile powers. Let all our neighbors know that we shall join with them to oppose aggression or subversion anywhere in the Americas. And let every other power know that this hemisphere intends to remain the master of its own house.

To that world assembly of sovereign states, the United Nations, our last best hope in an age where the instruments of war have far outpaced the instruments of peace, we renew our pledge of support—to prevent it from becoming merely a forum for invective—to strengthen its shield of the new and the weak—and to enlarge the area in which its writ may run.

Finally, to those nations who would make themselves our adversary, we offer not a pledge but a request: that both sides begin anew the quest for peace, before the dark powers of destruction unleashed by science engulf all humanity in planned or accidental self-destruction.

We dare not tempt them with weakness. For only when our arms are sufficient beyond doubt can we be certain beyond doubt that they will never be employed.

But neither can two great and powerful groups of nations take comfort from our present course—both sides overburdened by the cost of modern weapons, both rightly alarmed by the steady spread of the deadly atom, yet both racing to alter that uncertain balance of terror that stays the hand of mankind's final war.

So let us being anew—remembering on both sides that civility is not a sign of weakness, and sincerity is always subject to proof. Let us never negotiate out of fear. But let us never fear to negotiate.

Let both sides explore what problems unite us instead of belaboring those problems which divide us. Let both sides, for the first time, formulate serious and precise proposals for the inspection and control of arms—and bring the absolute power to destroy other nations under the absolute control of all nations.

Let both sides seek to invoke the wonders of science instead of its terrors. Together let us explore the stars, conquer the deserts, eradicate disease, tap the ocean depths and encourage the arts and commerce.

Let both sides unite to heed in all corners of the earth the command of Isaiah—to "undo the heavy burdens . . . (and) let the oppressed go free."

And if a beach-head of cooperation may push back the jungle of suspicion, let both sides join in a new endeavor, not a new balance of power, but a new world of law, where the strong are just and the weak secure and the peace preserved.

All this will not be finished in the first one hundred days. Nor will it be finished in the first one thousand days, nor in the life of this Administration, nor even perhaps in our lifetime on this planet. But let us begin.

In your hands, my fellow citizens, more than mine, will rest the final success or failure of our course. Since this country was founded, each generation of Americans has been summoned to give testimony to its national loyalty. The graves of young Americans who answered the call to service surround the globe.

Now the trumpet summons us again—not as a call to bear arms, though arms we need—not as a call to battle, though embattled we are— but a call to bear the burden of a long twilight struggle, year in and year out, "rejoicing in hope, patient in tribulation"—a struggle against the common enemies of man: tyranny, poverty, disease and war itself.

Can we forge against these enemies a grand and global alliance, North and South, East and West, that can assure a more fruitful life for all mankind? Will you join in that historic effort?

In the long history of the world, only a few generations have been granted the role of defending freedom in its hour of maximum danger. I do not shrink from this responsibility—I welcome it. I do not believe that any of us would exchange places with any other people or any other generation. The energy, the faith, the devotion which we bring to this endeavor will light our country and all who serve it—and the glow from that fire can truly light the world.

And so, my fellow Americans: Ask not what your country can do for you—ask what you can do for your country.

My fellow citizens of the world: Ask not what America will do for you, but what together we can do for the freedom of man.

Finally, whether you are citizens of America or citizens of the world, ask of us here the same high standards of strength and sacrifice which we ask of you. With a good conscience our only sure reward, with history the final judge of our deeds, let us go forth to lead the land we love, asking His blessing and His help, but knowing that here on earth God's work must truly be our own.

39 | "Agenda for a Generation"

During the 1960s, Students for a Democratic Society (SDS) came closer than did any other organization to being the leader of the politically left student movement. The organization emerged when two activists at the University of Michigan, Al Haber and Tom Hayden (now the husband of actress and activist Jane Fonda), coordinated groups at numerous campuses and organized a national meeting in 1962. This meeting, held at a United Auto Workers center in Port Huron, Michigan, approved the following manifesto, which was drafted by Hayden. Tentative in its assertions and written in the language of social science, The Port Huron Statement nonetheless touched on most of the themes of 1960s radicalism, giving an "agenda for a generation." And that generation, when pressure from the Vietnam war was added to the idealism and political assertion of the Kennedy era, took its agenda into the streets.

INTRODUCTION: AGENDA FOR A GENERATION

We are people of this generation, bred in at least modest comfort, housed now in universities, looking uncomfortably to the world we inherit.

When we were kids the United States was the wealthiest and strongest country in the world; the only one with the atom bomb, the least scarred by modern war, an initiator of the United Nations that we thought would distribute Western influence throughout the world. Freedom and equality for each individual, government of, by, and for the people—these American values we found good, principles by which we could live as men. Many of us began maturing in complacency.

As we grew, however, our comfort was penetrated by events too troubling to dismiss. First, the permeating and victimizing fact of human degradation, symbolized by the Southern struggle against racial bigotry, compelled most of us from silence to activism. Second, the enclosing fact of the Cold War, symbolized by the presence of the Bomb, brought awareness that we ourselves, and our friends, and millions of abstract "others" we knew more directly because of our common peril, might

Students for a Democratic Society, The Port Huron Statement, *1962.*

die at any time. We might deliberately ignore, or avoid, or fail to feel all other human problems, but not these two, for these were too immediate and crushing in their impact, too challenging in the demand that we as individuals take the responsibility for encounter and resolution.

While these and other problems either directly oppressed us or rankled our consciences and became our own subjective concerns, we began to see complicated and disturbing paradoxes in our surrounding America. The declaration "all men are created equal . . . " rang hollow before the facts of Negro life in the South and the big cities of the North. The proclaimed peaceful intentions of the United States contradicted its economic and military investments in the Cold War status quo.

We witnessed, and continue to witness, other paradoxes. With nuclear energy whole cities can easily be powered, yet the dominant nation-states seem more likely to unleash destruction greater than that incurred in all wars of human history. Although our own technology is destroying old and creating new forms of social organization, men still tolerate meaningless work and idleness. While two-thirds of mankind suffers undernourishment, our own upper classes revel amidst superfluous abundance. Although world population is expected to double in forty years, the nations still tolerate anarchy as a major principle of international conduct and uncontrolled exploitation governs the mapping of the earth's physical resources. Although mankind desperately needs revolutionary leadership, America rests in national stalemate, its goals ambiguous and tradition-bound instead of informed and clear, its democratic system apathetic and manipulated rather than "of, by, and for the people."

Not only did tarnish appear on our image of American virtue, not only did disillusion occur when the hypocrisy of American ideals was discovered, but we began to sense that what we had originally seen as the American Golden Age was actually the decline of an era. The worldwide outbreak of revolution against colonialism and imperialism, the entrenchment of totalitarian states, the menace of war, overpopulation, international disorder, supertechnology—these trends were testing the tenacity of our own commitment to democracy and freedom and our abilities to visualize their application to a world in upheaval.

/ / /

Some would have us believe that Americans feel contentment amidst prosperity—but might it not better be called a glaze above deeply felt anxieties about their role in the new world? And if these anxieties produce a developed indifference to human affairs, do they not as well produce a yearning to believe there *is* an alternative to the present, that something *can* be done to change circumstances in the school, the workplaces, the bureaucracies, the government? It is to this latter yearning, at once the spark and engine of change, that we direct our present appeal. The search for truly democratic alternatives to the present, and a commitment to social experimentation with them, is a worthy and fulfilling human enterprise, one which moves us and, we hope, others today. On such a basis do we offer this document of our convictions and analysis: as an effort in understanding and changing the conditions of humanity in the late twentieth century, an effort rooted in the ancient, still unfulfilled conception of man attaining determining influence over his circumstances of life.

VALUES

Making values explicit—an initial task in establishing alternatives—is an activity that has been devalued and corrupted. The conventional moral terms of the age, the politician moralities—"free world," "people's democracies"—reflect realities poorly, if at all, and seem to function more as ruling myths than as descriptive principles. But neither has our experience in the universities brought us moral enlightenment. Our professors and administrators sacrifice controversy to public relations; their curriculums change more slowly than the living events of the world; their skills and silence are purchased by investors in the arms race; passion is called unscholastic. The questions we might want raised—what is really important? can we live in a different and better way? if we wanted to change society, how would we do it?—are not thought to be questions of a "fruitful, empirical nature," and thus are brushed aside.

/   /   /

Men have unrealized potential for self-cultivation, self-direction, self-understanding, and creativity. It is this potential that we regard as crucial and to which we appeal, not to the human potentiality for violence, unreason, and submission to authority. The goal of man and society should be human independence: a concern not with image of popularity but with finding a meaning in life that is personally authentic; a quality of mind not compulsively driven by a sense of powerlessness, nor one which unthinkingly adopts status values, nor one which represses all threats to its habits, but one which has full, spontaneous access to present and past experiences, one which easily unites the fragmented parts of personal history, one which openly faces problems which are troubling and unresolved; one with an intuitive awareness of possibilities, an active sense of curiosity, an ability and willingness to learn.

This kind of independence does not mean egotistic individualism—the object is not to have one's way so much as it is to have a way that is one's own. Nor do we deify man—we merely have faith in his potential.

Human relationships should involve fraternity and honesty. Human interdependence is contemporary fact; human brotherhood must be willed, however, as a condition of future survival and as the most appropriate form of social relations. Personal links between man and man are needed, especially to go beyond the partial and fragmentary bonds of function that bind men only as worker to worker, employer to employee, teacher to student, American to Russian.

Loneliness, estrangement, isolation describe the vast distance between man and man today. These dominant tendencies cannot be overcome by better personnel management, nor by improved gadgets, but only when a love of man overcomes the idolatrous worship of things by man. As the individualism we affirm is not egoism, the selflessness we affirm is not self-elimination. On the contrary, we believe in generosity of a kind that imprints one's unique individual qualities in the relation to other men, and to all human activity. Further, to dislike isolation is not to favor the abolition of privacy; the latter differs from isolation in that it occurs or is abolished according to individual will.

We would replace power rooted in possession, privilege, or circumstance by power and uniqueness rooted in love, reflectiveness, reason, and creativity. As a *social system* we seek the establishment of a democracy of individual participation, governed by two central aims: that the individual share in those social decisions determining the quality and direction of his life; that society be organized to encourage independence in men and provide the media for their common participation. . . .

THE STUDENTS

In the last few years, thousands of American students demonstrated that they at least felt the urgency of the times. They moved actively and directly against racial injustices, the threat of war, violations of individual rights of conscience and, less frequently, against economic manipulation. They succeeded in restoring a small measure of controversy to the campuses after the stillness of the McCarthy period. They succeeded, too, in gaining some concessions from the people and institutions they opposed, especially in the fight against racial bigotry.

The significance of these scattered movements lies not in their success or failure in gaining objectives—at least not yet. Nor does the significance lie in the intellectual "competence" or "maturity" of the students involved—as some pedantic elders allege. The significance is in the fact the students are breaking the crust of apathy and overcoming the inner alienation that remain the defining characteristics of American college life.

If student movements for change are still rareties on the campus scene, what is commonplace there? The real campus, the familiar campus, is a place of private people, engaged in their notorious "inner emigration." It is a place of commitment to business-as-usual, getting ahead, playing it cool. It is a place of mass affirmation of the Twist, but mass reluctance toward the controversial public stance. Rules are accepted as "inevitable," bureaucracy as "just circumstances," irrelevance as "scholarship," selflessness as "martyrdom," politics as "just another way to make people, and an unprofitable one, too."

Almost no students value activity as citizens. Passive in pubic, they are hardly more idealistic in arranging their private lives: Gallup concludes they will settle for "low success, and won't risk high failure." There is not much willingness to take risks (not even in business), no setting of dangerous goals, no real conception of personal identity except one manufactured in the image of others, no real urge for personal fulfillment except to be almost as successful as the very successful people. Attention is being paid to social status (the quality of shirt collars, meeting people, getting wives or husbands, making solid contacts for later on); much, too, is paid to academic status (grades, honors, the med school rat race). But neglected generally is real intellectual status, the personal cultivation of the mind.

"Students don't even give a damn about the apathy," one has said. Apathy toward apathy begets a privately constructed universe, a place of systematic study schedules, two nights each week for beer, a girl or two, and early marriage; a framework infused with personality, warmth, and under control, no matter how unsatisfying otherwise. . .

The academic life contains reinforcing counterparts to the way in which extracurricular life is organized. The academic world is founded on a teacher-student relation analogous to the parent-child relation which characterizes in loco parentis. Further, academia includes a radical separation of the student from the material of study. That which is studied, the social reality, is "objectified" to sterility, dividing the student from life—just as he is restrained in active involvement by the deans controlling student government. The specialization of function and knowledge, admittedly necessary to our complex technological and social structure, has produced an exaggerated compartmentalization of study and understanding. This has contributed to an overly parochial view, by faculty, of the role of its research and scholarship, to a discontinuous and truncated understanding, by students, of the surrounding social order; and to a loss of personal attachment, by nearly all, to the worth of study as a humanistic enterprise.

There is, finally, the cumbersome academic bureaucracy extending throughout the academic as well as the extracurricular structures, contributing to the sense of outer complexity and inner powerlessness that transforms the honest searching of many students to a ratification of convention and, worse, to a numbness to present and future catastrophes. The size and financing systems of the university enhance the permanent trusteeship of the administrative bureaucracy, their power leading to a shift within the university toward the value standards of business and the administrative mentality. Huge foundations and other private financial interests shape the under-financed colleges and universities, not only making them more commerical, but less disposed to diagnose society critically, less open to dissent. Many social and physical scientists, neglecting the liberating heritage of higher learning, develop "human relations" or "morale-producing" techniques for the corporate economy, while others exercise their intellectual skills to accelerate the arms race.

/ / /

40 | Letters to Home

In the summer of 1964, after nearly a decade of civil rights demonstrations, more than a thousand people, most of them white Northern college students, volunteered to go to Mississippi to help blacks register to vote, and to conduct "freedom schools." The Mississippi Summer Freedom Project was both a high point and nearly the end of the integrated, nonviolent civil rights movement of the 1950s and 1960s. It was a hard summer. One could consider this macabre "score": at least one black and two white civil rights workers were killed, not including an uncertain number of black Mississippians who died mysteriously; more than eighty were wounded; more than a thousand were arrested; thirty-five black churches were burned; and thirty homes and other buildings were bombed. Twelve hundred new black voters registered in the state.

National attention focused on the deaths of three young volunteers who were murdered in Philadelphia, Mississippi: James Chaney, Michael Schwerner, and Andrew Goodman. The letters below, from participants in the project (some supplied without attribution), testify to the intensity of the volunteers' experiences that summer.

Dear folks,   Mileston, August 18
One can't move onto a plantation cold; or canvas a plantation in the same manner as the Negro ghetto in town. It's far too dangerous. Many plantations—homes included—are posted, meaning that no trespassing is permitted, and the owner feels that he has the prerogative to shoot us on sight when we are in the house of one of *his* Negroes.

Before we canvas a plantation, our preparation includes finding out whether the houses are posted, driving through or around the plantation without stopping, meanwhile making a detailed map of the plantation.

We're especially concerned with the number of roads in and out of the plantation. For instance, some houses could be too dangerous to canvas because of their location near the boss man's house and on a dead end road.

In addition to mapping, we attempt to talk to some of the tenants when they are off the plantation, and ask them about conditions. The kids often have contacts, and can get on the plantation unnoticed by the boss man, with the pretense of just visiting friends.

Our canvassing includes not only voter registration, but also extensive reports on conditions—wages, treatment by the boss man, condition of the houses, number of acres of cotton, etc. Much more such work needs to be done. The plantation system is crucial in Delta politics and economics, and the plantation system must be brought to an end if democracy is to be brought to the Delta. . . .

Love,
Joel

July 18

. . . Four of us went to distribute flyers announcing the meeting. I talked to a woman who had been down to register a week before. She was afraid. Her husband had lost his job. Even before we got there a couple of her sons had been man-handled by the police. She was now full of wild rumors about shootings and beatings, etc. I checked out two of them later. They were groundless. This sort of rumorspreading is quite prevalent when people get really scared. . . .

At 6 P.M. we returned to Drew for the meeting, to be held in front of a church (they wouldn't let us meet inside, but hadn't told us not to meet outside). A number of kids collected and stood around in a circle with about 15 of us to sing freedom songs. Across the street perhaps 100 adults stood watching. Since this was the first meeting in town, we passed out mimeoed song sheets. Fred Miller, Negro from Mobile, stepped out to the edge of the street to give somebody a sheet. The cops nabbed him. I was about to follow suit so he wouldn't be alone, but Mac's policy [Charles McLaurin, SNCC—a civil rights group—project director] was to ignore the arrest. We sang on mightily "Ain't going to let no jailing turn me around." A group of girls was sort of leaning against the cars on the periphery of the meeting. Mac went over to encourage them to join us. I gave a couple of song sheets to the girls. A cop rushed across the street and told me to come along. I guess I was sort of aware that my actions would get me arrested, but felt that we had to show these girls that we were not afraid. I was also concerned with what might happen to Fred if he was the only one.

. . . The cop at the station was quite scrupulous about letting me make a phone call. I was then driven to a little concrete structure which looked like a power house. I could hear Fred's courageous, off-key rendition of a freedom song from inside and joined him as we approached. He was very happy to see me. Not long thereafter, four more of our group were driven up to make their calls . . .

The Drew jail consists of three small cells off a wide hall. It was filthy, hot and stuffy. A cop came back to give us some toilet paper. We sang songs for a while, and yelled greetings to Negroes who drove by curiously. One of the staff workers had been in jail 106 times. I asked the cop if he could open another cell as there were not enough beds accessible to us. He mumbled something about how that would be impossible and left. They hadn't confiscated anything and one of the guys had a battered copy of *The Other America*, so we divided up the chapters. I got the dismal one on the problems of the aged . . . To be old and forgotten is certainly a worse sentence than mine (I wouldn't recommend that book for those planning to do time) . . .

Well, the night was spent swatting mosquitoes. An old Negro couple walked by in front of the jail and asked how we were doing. They said they supported us and the old lady said, "God bless you all." This, in the context of a tense town with a pretty constant stream of whites in cars driving by. . . .

Dear Mom and Dad: Holly Spring
The atmosphere in class is unbelievable. It is what every teacher dreams about—real, honest enthusiasm and desire to learn anything and everything. The girls come to class of their own free will. They respond to everything that is said. They are excited about learning. They drain me of everything that I have to offer so that I go home at night completely exhausted but very happy. . . .

I start out at 10:30 teaching what we call the Core Curriculum, which is Negro History and the History and Philosophy of the Movement, to about fifteen girls ranging from 15 to 25 years of age. I have one girl who is married with four children, another who is 23 and a graduate from a white college in Tennessee, also very poorly educated. The majority go to a Roman Catholic High School in Holly Springs and have therefore received a fairly decent education by Mississippi standards. They can, for the most part, express themselves on paper but their skills in no way compare to juniors and seniors in northern suburban schools.

In one of my first classes, I gave a talk on Haiti and the slave revolt which took place there at the end of the eighteenth century. I told them how the French government (during the French Revolution) abolished slavery all over the French Empire. And then I told them that the English decided to invade the island and take it over for a colony of their own. I watched faces fall all around me. They knew that a small island, run by former slaves, could not defeat England. And then I told them that the people of Haiti succeeded in keeping the English out. I watched a smile spread slowly over a girl's face. And I felt girls sit up and look at me intently. Then I told them that Napoleon came to power, reinstated slavery, and sent an expedition to reconquer Haiti. Their faces began to fall again. They waited for me to tell them that France defeated the former slaves, hoping against hope that I would say that they didn't. But when

I told them that the French generals tricked the Haitian leader Toussaint to come aboard their ship, captured him and sent him back to France to die, they knew that there was no hope. They waited for me to spell out the defeat. And when I told them that Haiti did succeed in keeping out the European powers and was recognized finally as an independent republic, they just looked at me and smiled. The room stirred with a gladness and a pride that this could have happened. And I felt so happy and so humble that I could have told them this little story and it could have meant so much.

We have also talked about what it means to be a Southern white who wants to stand up but who is alone, rejected by other whites and not fully accepted by the Negroes. We have talked about their feelings about Southern whites. One day three little white girls came to our school and I asked them to understand how the three girls felt by remembering how it feels when they are around a lot of whites. We agreed that we would not stare at the girls but try to make them feel as normal as possible.

Along with my Core class I teach a religion class at one every afternoon and a class on non-violence at four-fifteen. All my classes are approximately an hour. Both these classes are made up of four to six girls from my morning class and about four boys of the same age group. In religion they are being confronted for the first time with people whom they respect who do not believe in God and with people who believe in God but do not take the Bible literally. It's a challenging class because I have no desire to destroy their belief, whether Roman Catholic or Baptist, but I want them to learn to look at all things critically and to learn to separate fact from interpretation and myth in all areas, not just religion.

Every class is beautiful. The girls respond, respond, respond. And they disagree among themselves. I have no doubt that soon they will be disagreeing with me. At least this is one thing that I am working towards. They are a sharp group. But they are under-educated and starved for knowledge. They know that they have been cheated and they want anything and everything that we can give them.

I have a great deal of faith in these students. They are very mature and very concerned about other people. I really think that they will be able to carry on without us. At least this is my dream . . .

Love,
Pam

Indianola, August 17

I can see the change. The 16-year-old's discovery of poetry, of Whitman and Cummings and above all, the struggle to express thoughts in words, to translate ideas into concrete written words. After two weeks a child finally looks me in the eye, unafraid, acknowledging a bond of trust which 300 years of Mississippians said should never, could never exist. I can feel the growth of self-confidence . . .

Biloxi, Aug. 16
In the Freedom School one day during poetry writing, a 12-year-old
girl handed in this poem to her teacher:

What Is Wrong?
What is wrong with me everywhere I go
  No one seems to look at me.
Sometimes I cry.

I walk through woods and sit on a stone.
I look at the stars and I sometimes wish.

Probably if my wish ever comes true,
  Everyone will look at me.

Then she broke down crying in her sister's arms. The Freedom School
here had given this girl the opportunity of meeting someone she felt she
could express her problems to . . .

To my brother,

Ruleville
    Last night, I was a long time before sleeping, although I was ex-
tremely tired. Every shadow, every noise—the bark of a dog, the sound
of a car—in my fear and exhaustion was turned into a terrorist's approach. And I believed that I heard the back door open and a Klansman
walk in, until he was close by the bed. Almost paralyzed by the fear,
silent, I finally shone my flashlight on the spot where I thought he was
standing . . . I tried consciously to overcome this fear. To relax, I began
to breathe deep, think the words of a song, pull the sheet up close to
my neck . . . still the tension. Then I rethought why I was here, rethought what could be gained in view of what could be lost. All this
was in rather personal terms, and then in larger scope of the whole
Project. I remembered Bob Moses saying he had felt justified in asking
hundreds of students to go to Mississippi because he was not asking
anyone to do something that he would not do . . . I became aware of
the uselessness of fear that immobilizes an individual. Then I began to
relax.
    "We are not afraid. Oh Lord, deep in my heart, I do believe. We
Shall Overcome Someday" and then I think I began to truly understand
what the words meant. Anyone who comes down here and is not afraid
I think must be crazy as well as dangerous to this project where security
is quite important. But the type of feat that they mean when they, when
we, sing "we are not afraid" is the type that immobilizes. . . . The
songs help to dissipate the fear. Some of the words in the songs do not
hold real meaning on their own, others become rather monotonous—

but when they are sung in unison, or sung silently by oneself, they take on new meaning beyond words or rhythm . . . There is almost a religious quality about some of these songs, having little to do with the usual concept of a god. It has to do with the miracle that youth has organized to fight hatred and ignorance. It has to do with the holiness of the dignity of man. The god that makes such miracles is the god I do believe in when we sing "God is on our side." I know I am on that god's side. And I do hope he is on ours.

Jon, please be considerate to Mom and Dad. The fear I just expressed, I am sure they feel much more intensely without the relief of being here to know exactly how things are. Please don't go defending me or attacking them if they are critical of the Project. . . .

They said over the phone "Did you know how much it takes to make a child?" and I thought of how much it took to make a Herbert Lee (or many others whose names I do not know) . . . I thought of how much it took to be a Negro in Mississippi twelve months a year for a lifetime. How can such a thing as a life be weighed? . . .

With constant love,
Heather

Greenwood, June 29
We have heard rumors twice to the effect that the three men were found weighted down in that river. Both stories, though the same, were later completely dropped in an hour or so. How do you like that guy Gov. Johnson saying that they might be hiding in the North or maybe in Cuba for all he knew . . .

Tchula, July 16
Yesterday while the Mississippi River was being dragged looking for the three missing civil rights workers, two bodies of Negroes were found———one cut in half and one without a head. Mississippi is the only state where you can drag a river any time and find bodies you were not expecting. Things are really much better for rabbits—there's a closed season on rabbits.

Como, August 3
About three weeks ago there was a flying rumor that they had been found in a rural jail. Tonight it was said that three graves had been found near Philadelphia. How the ghosts of those three shadow all our work! "Did you know them?" I am constantly asked. Did I need to?

/   /   /

Meridian, August 4
Last night Pete Seeger was giving a concert in Meridian. We sang a lot of freedom songs, and every time a verse like 'No more lynchings'

was sung, or 'before I'd be a slave I'd be buried in my grave,' I had the flash of understanding that sometimes comes when you suddenly think about the meaning of a familiar song . . . I wanted to stand up and shout to them, "Think about what you are singing—people really have died to keep us all from being slaves." Most of the people there still did not know that the bodies had been found. Finally just before the singing of "We Shall Overcome," Pete Seeger made the announcement. "We must sing 'We Shall Overcome' now," said Seeger. "The three boys would not have wanted us to weep now, but to sing and understand this song." That seems to me the best way to explain the greatness of this project—that death can have this meaning. Dying is not an ever-present possibility in Meridian, the way some reports may suggest. Nor do any of us want to die. Yet in a moment like last night, we can feel that anyone who did die for the Project would wish to be remembered not by tributes or grief but by understanding and continuation of what he was doing . . .

As we left the church, we heard on the radio the end of President Johnson's speech announcing the air attacks on Vietnam . . . I could only think "This must not be the beginning of a war. There is still a freedom fight, and we are winning. We must have time to live and help Mississippi to be alive." Half an hour before, I had understood death in a new way. Now I realized that Mississippi, in spite of itself, has given real meaning to life. In Mississippi you never ask, "What is the meaning of life?" or "Is there any point to it all?" but only that we may have enough life to do all that there is to be done. . . .

Meridian, August 5

At the Freedom school and at the community center, many of the kids had known Mickey and almost all knew Jimmy Chaney. Today we asked the kids to describe Mickey and Jimmy because we had never known them.

"Mickey was a big guy. He wore blue jeans all the time" . . . I asked the kids, "What did his eyes look like?" and they told me they were "friendly eyes" "nice eyes" ("nice" is a lovely word in a Mississippi accent). "Mickey was a man who was at home everywhere and with anybody," said the 17-year-old girl I stay with. The littlest kids, the 6, 7, 8 years olds, tell about how he played "Frankenstein" with them or took them for drives or talked with them about Freedom. Many of the teen-age boys were delinquents until Mickey went down to the bars and jails and showed them that one person at least would respect them if they began to fight for something important . . . And the grownups too, trusted him. The lady I stay with tells with pride of how Mickey and Rita came to supper at their house, and police cars circled around the house all during the meal. But Mickey could make them feel glad to take the risk.

People talk less about James Chaney here, but feel more. The kids describe a boy who played with them—whom everyone respected but who never had to join in fights to maintain this respect—a quiet boy but very sharp and very understanding when he did speak. Mostly we know James through his sisters and especially his 12-year-old brother, Ben. Today Ben was in the Freedom School. At lunchtime the kids have a jazz band (piano, washtub bass, cardboard boxes and bongos as drums) and tiny Ben was there leading it all even with his broken arm, with so much energy and rhythm that even Senator Eastland would have had to stop and listen if he'd been walking by. . . .

/ / /

Meridian, August 8
. . . The service was preceded by several silent marches beginning at churches throughout Meridian and converging on the First Union Baptist Church. I have been on a large number of walks, marches, vigils, pickets, etc., in my life, but I can't remember anything which was quite like this one. In the first place, it was completely silent (at least, the march I was on), even though it lasted over 50 minutes, and even though there were a fair number of children involved. . . .

Meridian, August 11
. . . In the line I was in, there were about 150 people—white and Negro—walking solemnly, quietly, and without incident for about a mile and half through white and Negro neighborhoods (segregation is like a checkerboard here). The police held up traffic at the stoplights, and of all the white people watching only one girl heckled. I dislike remembering the service—the photographers with their television cameras were omnipresent, it was really bad. And cameras when people are crying . . . and bright lights. Someone said it was on television later. I suppose it was.

Dave Dennis spoke—it was if he was realizing his anger and feeling only as he spoke. As if the deepest emotion—the bitterness, then hatred—came as he expressed it, and could not have been planned or forethought . . .

Dear Folks,

Laurel, August 11
. . . The memorial service began around 7:30 with over 120 people filling the small, wooden-pew lined church. David Dennis of CORE [a civil rights group], the Assistant Director for the Mississippi Summer Project, spoke for COFO. He talked to the Negro people of Meridian—it was a speech to move people, to end the lethargy, to make people stand up. It went something like this:

"I am not here to memorialize James Chaney, I am not here to pay tribute—I am too sick and tired. Do YOU hear me, I am S-I-C-K and

T-I-R-E-D. I have attended too many memorials, too many funerals. This
has got to stop. Mack Parker, Medgar Evers, Herbert Lee, Lewis Allen,
Emmett Till, four little girls in Birmingham, a 13-year old boy in Birmingham, and the list goes on and on. I have attended these funerals and
memorials and I am SICK and TIRED. But the trouble is that YOU are
NOT sick and tired and for that reason YOU, yes YOU, are to blame,
Everyone of your damn souls. And if you are going to let this continue
now then you are to blame, yes YOU. Just as much as the monsters of
hate who pulled the trigger or brought down the club; just as much to
blame as the sheriff and the chief of police, as the governor in Jackson
who said that he 'did not have time' for Mrs. Schwerner when she went
to see him, and just as much to blame as the President and Attorney
General in Washington who wouldn't provide protection for Chaney,
Goodman and Schwerner when we told them that protection was necessary in Neshoba County . . . Yes, I am angry, I AM. And it's high time
that you got angry too, angry enough to go up to the courthouse Monday and register—everyone of you. Angry enough to take five and then
other people with you. Then and only then can these brutal killings be
stopped. Remember it is your sons and your daughters who have been
killed all these years and you have done nothing about it, and if you
don't do nothing NOW baby, I say God Damn Your Souls. . . .

Dear Blake,

                                                    Mileston, August 9
     . . . Dave finally broke down and couldn't finish and the Chaney
family was moaning and much of the audience and I were also crying.
It's such an impossible thing to describe but suddenly again, as I'd first
realized when I heard the three men were missing when we were still
training up at Oxford, I felt the sacrifice the Negroes have been making
for so long. How the Negro people are able to accept all the abuses of
the whites—all the insults and injustices which make me ashamed to be
white—and then turn around and say they want to love us, is beyond
me. There are Negros who want to kill whites and many Negros have
much bitterness but still the majority seem to have the quality of being
able to look for a future in which whites will love the Negroes. Our kids
talk very critically of all the whites around here and still they have a
dream of freedom in which both races understand and accept each
other. There is such an overpowering task ahead of these kids that
sometimes I can't do anything but cry for them. I hope they are up to
the task, I'm not sure I would be if I were a Mississippi Negro. As a
white northerner I can get involved whenever I feel like it and run home
whenever I get bored or frustrated or scared. I hate the attitude and
position of the Northern whites and despise myself when I think that
way. Lately I've been feeling homesick and longing for pleasant old
Westport and sailing and swimming and my friends. I don't quite know
what to do because I can't ignore my desire to go home and yet I feel I

am a much weaker person than I like to think I am because I do have these emotions. I've always tried to avoid situations which aren't so nice, like arguments and dirty houses and now maybe Mississippi. I asked my father if I could stay down here for a whole year and I was almost glad when he said "no" that we couldn't afford it because it would mean supporting me this year in addition to three more years of college. I have a desire to go home and to read a lot and go to Quaker meetings and be by myself so I can think about all this rather than being in the middle of it all the time. But I know if my emotions run like they have in the past, that I can only take that pacific sort of life for a little while and then I get the desire to be active again and get involved with knowing other people. I guess this all sounds crazy and I seem to always think out my problems as I write to you. I am angry because I have a choice as to whether or not to work in the Movement and I am playing upon that choice and leaving here. I wish I could talk with you 'cause I'd like to know if you ever felt this way about anything. I mean have you ever despised yourself for your weak conviction or something. And what is making it worse is that all those damn northerners are thinking of me as a brave hero. . . .

                                                            Martha

41 | The War in Vietnam

The war in Vietnam was the first war to be broadcast on television into American homes. Constant exposure to the details of the war did not, however, translate into enduring public support for American participation. The justification of the war on grounds other than that of an immediate threat to American security, the strangeness of its setting, and the scope of its violence (its extensive involvement of children and civilians) made the war in Vietnam a particularly disquieting event in the nation's history.

The Americans for whom the Vietnam war was a most personal experience are, of course, those who fought in overseas combat. The readings that follow are from two soldiers: Dave Baker, an Army volunteer, who patrolled a Vietnamese village with a ''killer'' guard dog; and Clarence Fitch, a black Marine, who before and after the war maintained an interest in civil rights.

Baker's testimony is an account common to many soldiers who went to Vietnam and faced gradual disillusionment with the American mission in the war. It also documents the pain faced by a soldier who risked his life overseas and returned to a country that treated him as an outcast or a criminal.

It has long been stated that Vietnam was not a war in which all Americans shared the risks of the nation's involvement. Deferments, disqualifications for combat, and alternative service, it has been argued, meant that those most likely to serve overseas were those who were poor, politically unconnected, or black. Fitch's testimony does not directly address questions about the fairness of the draft, but it does argue that blacks faced the greatest danger of being killed in action (KIA). It also demonstrates that those who fought in Vietnam did not do so in isolation from the greater social discord of the 1960s.

DAVE BAKER

All my life I have hunted. I go deer hunting and I get maybe five or six a year. When I was little, it was squirrels. I think I was twelve years old when my father gave me my first gun. We had about six acres, and behind that there was land that you could hunt and I really enjoyed it.

Joan Morrison and Robert K. Morrison, From Camelot to Kent State: The Sixties Experience in the Words of Those Who Lived it. (New York, Times Books, 1987) pp. 61–65, 67–70, 76–81.

My father always told me, "If you kill it, you eat it. If you don't want to eat it, don't kill it." Nothing was just shot and dropped on the ground.

When the Vietnam War was going on I thought there was a real need for us, and I wanted to sign up. A bunch of friends of mine, five of us who all went to high school together, were going to join the Marines. We were going to go in at the same time, but by the time I got done with my chores at home, some lawn work and stuff like that, I didn't get down until after they were there. They'd already signed up in the Marines, and the Marine Corps recruiter took them out to lunch.

I started to walk out of the Marine recruiting office, because there was no one there, and this Army sergeant said, "Who you looking for?" I explained to him what it was, and he said, "Well, why do you want to go in the Marines? Let me show you what the Army has," Then I took this test, and it turned out I had high enough marks that I could do anything I wanted to. He said, "Well, you get your choice." I remembered a guy I'd met who'd been a dog handler in the Army, and I said, "Can I get to be a dog handler?" And he arranged it, and that's what I got into. You had to be a volunteer for dog handler, and you knew that if you went in, you were going to Vietnam. But that's what I wanted to do.

/   /   /

The dogs are trained to be hateful against human beings, really aggressive. I think if the ASPCA ever found out what you did, they'd be at the government's door so fast. . . . Those dogs are hung by the tail, beaten with barbed wires, their ears are sliced with razor blades. Of course, you don't do it to your own dog, okay? Because then they'll hate you. When you go through the course, there's twenty people altogether. Ten people will tie the dogs up, and they'll be agitators for the ten that are holding their dogs. I'll be hitting someone else's dog with barbed wire, and he'll be hitting mine.

Instructors come by and zip the dogs' ears with razor blades. They know just what to do not to go too far. And they switch them and beat them. You want to stop them, but you don't, because you know that the meaner your dog gets, the better the chance of you staying alive when you get over to Vietnam. So you let it happen, because you want to come out of there with the best poodle to keep you alive and do your job. It's like a weapon. Do you want a piece of junk that jams, or do you want something that really works good? My dog was a really good dog—a very, very aggressive dog.

The village I was sent to in Vietnam had been built earlier by the French and had a few cement buildings, but the majority of it was just sticks with tin roofs. When people went to the bathroom, they just came out and did it in the street. It stunk, it stunk. And on a hot day it *really* stunk. But you go so used to it that it was, after a while, you know, like being home. I mean, you know, it was just a normal thing.

Walking down the street any day you'd see two or three kids with elephantiasis—like a pretty little girl with a leg blown up using two sticks to walk with, and she's pulling the worms out of her. And there's nothing you can do to fix her, either. You think to yourself, Oh my God, what should I do? Shoot her and put an end to all her misery or what? If you felt sorry for everybody you saw in that village there, you'd be a blabbering slob by the time you got to the end.

The dog handler's job was to patrol the bush outside the village at night to make sure none of the VC could sneak up on us. There were tunnels around our unit, and the VC would use them to get close to the fence. Then they'd come up and get through the fence and get to our main communications center. Tried to blow it up a number of times.

/   /   /

In the village I was in and in the villages around, there were just local VC. They'd have maybe two or three bullets allotted to them to shoot for the night, and they'd come out with their single-shot rifles and go *blinkety-blink*. About every two weeks or so, they'd put on a mortar attack, but primarily it was just snipers. You always had to watch your back, because there was no front line there, and you had women and kids as warriors, too, and you really didn't know who was trustworthy and who wasn't. It was all a battlefield.

There'd be accidents, bad accidents. In one village that I had to go through, the kids would play a game: They would try to touch the killer dogs. If they could touch a killer dog, they were big heroes. But this wasn't known to me when I first got there. A lot of the old-timers don't tell you all the tricks of the trade, you know. So I knew nothing of this game of the kids. One night I was working, cutting through the side of the village, and I'm looking into a shack over there and I see a bunch of eyes. I didn't know whose they were. I just figured to myself, Jesus, somebody in there is going to shoot me just when I get to the right spot.

I had my gun on my side with my hand on it, and my dog was pulling ahead real hard, but I wasn't paying too much attention to him. I was looking at those eyes as I walked. And I was on the ready, because if I saw anything that looked wrong, I was going to start shooting. What I didn't know was that those eyes were all little kids watching their buddy, who had dug a ditch and hidden himself under some weeds right by the path. When I came by, he was going to jump up, touch my dog, and then take off, and he would be a hero. And they were watching for him to do it. So as I went by, he jumped up, touched my dog, and my dog took his head off instantly. [*Sharp snap of fingers.*] Just popped it like that. You know, some of these Vietnam people are very,

very thin, especially the young kids. The neck was like a dog bone to him.

I didn't know what to do. I mean, I'm standing there—the head's sitting over there, spitting and gurgling. Oooooh. . . . I get goose bumps now just thinking about it. It was a real ripper for me. I pulled the dog back quick, and I looked this way and that way, and the kid's mother was coming after me. She had something in her hand, and I thought, "It's a grenade. It's cocked. I'm in real trouble now." So I had to pack her down. I shot her. We can't take a gamble, you know. I just blasted her, and I kept shooting as I backed out.

When I got back to my base, they sent an alert out to see what went on, and it turned out she just had a rock in her hand, but I didn't know that. I just thought, She's going to get me, and I'm going to blast her. . . . That was a rough one.

And, you know, it stays with you. When you're that close to them, and you see it happen—it's not like when you're in the dark, and you're shooting, and the next day you hear that somebody fell down dead. Here, you're with them, and you see it, and it stays with you. I imagine a lot of guys who were there don't mention things like that to anybody. They keep it in, because it's hurting them, and it hurts them to keep it in, too.

/   /   /

I got back to the United States in '68 and there was a lot of antiwar movement going on. It hadn't been like that when I left, so I wasn't expecting it. I got off at Kennedy Airport, and I didn't have any money in my pocket because I'd spent it all on my airplane ticket. So I thought, "Oh, well, I'll go out and hitchhike." I thought that in the uniform, you know, they'd pick me up right away. But no one would touch me. You were the kiss of death in a uniform. So I walked and walked. It took me from early in the morning until late at night to get home. I got a few rides, but most of the time I was walking. One time a fellow I knew came by. I'd been to school with him, and he'd been in one of my classes. He came up and slowed his car and looked at me, called me by name and everything, but when he saw the uniform, he just [cursed] and drove away and left me there. And I thought to myself, Boy, some howdy-do this is.

When I got into my hometown, they were burning the American flag at the monument in front of the police station. One of the cops saw me and saw the medals on my uniform and ran down the street and grabbed me and brought me away. He said, "Dave, you don't want to see what's going on here. You don't want to see it." He told me, "The kids don't really know what's going on. It's not aimed directly at you." And, of course, I understood it wasn't, okay? So I went on my way.

When I was about a mile away from home, my next-door neighbor drove by. She slowed down and looked at me, and then *zoom*, she took off. I was tired as hell, you know, walking all this way and carrying a big duffel bag, but she took right off and left me. And this was a lady I'd shoveled the driveway for when it snowed. I was really pissed. Everybody had this stereotype of a Vietnam veteran coming home either a murderer or a cuckoo.

Why did they shun me? I went to do what they wanted to be done, and now, all of a sudden, they change their mind, and they don't want what is being done to be done, and it's my fault. . . .

I didn't feel like getting a job right away when I came back, so I went out to the California, rented a house on the beach, and drank all night and slept all day. I wasn't ready for anything else yet. People back home bothered me. You'd hear them complain about the silliest little thing, like "It's too hot," if it's ninety-two degrees and a little humid. Think about 130 degrees for three or four months at a time, and ninety-eight in the shade. That's tough.

They would complain about everything. There was a water shortage on, and they were complaining about maybe only taking a bath every two days, or a shower just once a day . . . over there we were lucky if we got to take a shower every two weeks or a month. And during the monsoon season, we would go through a month wearing the same clothes, until they rotted off. You couldn't wash, you couldn't change your clothes, it was pouring rain, everything was wet and mucky. And here people complain, "Oooh, it's raining out." Tough. Get an umbrella. Live with it. I just hated people in general. I don't know why. I just hated everybody.

My mother said a different person came back than what went over to Vietnam, different as night and day, and it changed me, no question about it. When my father died, it seemed I could care less, you know. I was standing right there, my mother was crying, and my brother and everybody else was crying, and I could only see that he was dead. Big deal, you know, I've seen that before. What's next?

I have a very thick wall around me now. I don't let anyone come too close. They know a little bit about me, but nobody knows the inside me. I have a girlfriend living with me now. She's been with me for four years, but I don't even let her come that close. I think being over there made me very cold to people.

And yet, you know, I'd go back today to Vietnam if the people wanted help, and we could help them. Because that's what I thought we were going for in the beginning. I would like to give them a good staple food. So much of the inland water has been ruined there, because of the bombing and defoliation, and a lot of the areas where they were raising fish before are history. I'd like to do that, give something to the people. That was supposed to be the reason we were there anyway. I felt cheated after the war, that what the government said we were going over for we weren't doing.

/   /   /

You know, my sport is to kill. And when I go hunting or fishing now, I can't eat all the stuff I get, so I put it in plastic baggies, and I give it away to my Vietnamese friends here. I might get five or six deer a year, and they can't afford to go hunting, so I give them the meat. I stop off at their houses, and I give it to them. And if I go fishing for bluefish, I'll come back with maybe thirty bluefish, and I'll give it to them. Not for thanks, or to make my head swell, you know, but just to see a smile on their faces.

Am I doing it because of what I did over there? Making up for it in my own noodle? It's nothing that I think about. Maybe subconsciously there is something in there telling me to do it, because of what I did over there. Who the hell knows?

CLARENCE FITCH

We weren't living in no vacuum in Vietnam. There was a certain growing black consciousness that was happening in the States, and also over there in Vietnam. People was aware of what was going on. One of the characteristics of this war was that people didn't come over there together. People just had tours of duty, and so every day somebody was going home and you had somebody coming from home, bringing information. And guys that would leave Vietnam would send stuff back. You know, "Okay, send us all the *Ebonys* and *Jets* and black publications you can get your hands on." Like I sent stuff when I got back to guys I left over there.

The militancy really grew after Martin Luther King got killed in '68. It made black people really angry. You remember the riots after Dr. King's death was some of the fiercest, and the brothers took that up in Vietnam. People changed after that. People were saying it doesn't pay to be nonviolent and benevolent. There were a lot of staff NCOs, the type of so-called Negro that would be telling you to be patient, just do your job, pull yourself up by the bootstraps. So we called them Uncle Toms and that was that. People were saying, "I'm black and I'm proud. I'm not going to be no Uncle Tom."

There was a whole Black Power thing. There was Black Power salutes and handshakes and Afros and beads. It was a whole atmosphere. All that was a way of showing our camaraderie, like brothers really hanging together. When a new brother came into the unit, we used to really reach out for the guy, show him the ropes and tell him what's happening. It was like a togetherness that I ain't never seen since.

I think people really listened to Martin Luther King. We didn't hear his speech about Vietnam until much later, but somehow or another we got a copy of the speech, and we was really impressed. He talked about how blacks were dying in Vietnam at a greater rate, and he was the first person we really ever heard say that, even though it was something we knew.

We saw what was going on. I was there for the Tet Offensive of '68, and I was at this aid station. The place was always getting hit, and I got wounded there. It was like ten miles from the DMZ. I saw a lot of blood and a lot of death, and we would be bumping stretchers for all the casualties from all the units operating in the area.

It would still be more Caucasian bodies coming back than black bodies, but what Dr. King said was that blacks was at the time ten percent of the population and thirty percent of the KIAs. It was like more white guys was in the rear with the easy jobs. They were driving trucks and working in the PX and . . . we're out there in the bush, and that's why we was dying. A lot of the line companies over there were mostly black. There were white grunts, too, assigned to infantry units, but there was a *lot* of black grunts.

And then, as jobs became available in the rear, they would pull people back for jobs like company driver, stuff like that. You know, after so much time in the field, they pull you back to rear-area jobs. And we wasn't getting pulled that easy to the rear. Black guys were staying their whole tour in the field. You just looked around you and said, "Well, they're just using us as cannon fodder."

/   /   /

A lot of blacks fought valiantly at points, but a lot of them didn't see the sense dying in this war. It was more honorable to go to jail. People were refusing to go to the field anymore, just refusing and getting locked up. This was a hell of a thing to do, because brig time didn't count on your tour in Vietnam. They called it "bad time." You did your six months in jail, and then you still had to serve your time in the field. But guys did it. Guys were sitting in the Marine brig for long periods of time. I guess they were hoping the war would just end while they're sitting in jail. . . .

/   /   /

There were people that would go so far as to hurt themselves enough to get out of going into the bush. I seen people shoot themselves in the arm or the foot or the legs to get one of those Stateside wounds. I seen people fake injuries. I had this friend of mine, a brother from Birmingham, Alabama, he broke his ankle three different times to stay in the rear. Every time they took the cast off, he would get a hammer and whack it again, and it would swell up, and they'd put another cast on it. He'd be in the rear playing cards for another month or two, and then they would take the cast off, and he couldn't walk. He would play it right out to the max.

The powers that be knew it, but they couldn't prove it. He caught a lot of flak. They would call him a traitor and all this crap. And he said, "Well. . . . I'm not going out there." And that's the way it went down until his rotation date. It wasn't like World War II, where you stayed for the duration. You did have a date, and the thing was to survive until that date and that's what people did. The other brothers supported him. We didn't put him down or ridicule him. We respected him. We knew we was dying at a higher rate, so we felt very much justified not to add to this . . . figure.

There were fragging incidents for the same reason. It didn't happen every day, but after a while it got to be an unwritten rule. A lot of times you get these boot-camp second lieutenants, just out of Quantico, the officer training school, no field experience, and they just give them a platoon. The smart ones would come over and take suggestions, use their NCOs and squad leaders—guys that have been in the bush six, seven, eight months and really know what's going on—to show them until they get the ropes. But you get these guys that want to come over with schoolbook tactics, and they might want to do something that's detrimental to the company. Then you're talking about people's lives. Well, hey, the first firefight you get in, somebody takes him out. "Killed in action."

I seen one fragging incident up close: a new lieutenant, fresh out of Quantico. He was an asshole, very gung-ho. He would run patrols and set up ambushes, and he wasn't very careful. He took a lot of chances, and people didn't like it. They were trying to take him out, but they didn't get in the right kind of firefight that they could fire on him.

One night we were stationed on this bridge to keep Charlie from blowing the bridge up, and I was on radio, monitoring communications. About four or five in the morning, just before dawn, I seen this brother come out with this hand grenade, and he said, "Hey, Fitch, don't say nothing, man." The lieutenant's bunker was maybe ten yards from the bridge, and this guy went over, pulled the pin on the grenade, held it for a couple of seconds, and rolled it into the bunker. I said, "Oh, shit. I don't want to see this."

Then I heard *boom*, and the lieutenant came staggering out of the bunker. They got a medevac helicopter and medevacked him out of there. He was hurt pretty bad, but he survived it. Went back to the States, I guess. . . .

/   /   /

I saw a lot of craziness there. In retrospect, the reason I think so much of it happened was that everyone was just living a violent way of

life. It was a world where everyone carried a gun and had access to all
the ammunition they wanted. There would be fights between GIs that
might begin over a card game, and one guy would just pull out a rifle
and slap in a magazine and say, "I'm going to lock and load on you."
I think this must be the way it was in the Wild West when everyone
carried a gun.

I left Vietnam in January '69, came home, and got stationed in Camp
Lejeune, North Carolina. It was all Vietnam vets there, and people just
wasn't into that Stateside regimentation no more. People were tired of
the whole military scene. There was a lot of discipline problems. It was
pretty hard to keep up haircut regulations in Vietnam, and some brothers hadn't had haircuts in a year. When we returned, they wanted you
to get a military haircut. I think Marine Corps regulations said your hair
can't be longer than three inches. For a white guy, if his hair is longer
than three inches, it looks like a lot of hair. Very seldom does an Afro
go higher than three inches, but they still wanted to make us get a haircut. So it was a lot of struggle around the Afros.

/   /   /

It was a pretty nasty time between blacks and whites. Blacks tended
to stick together in groups, and there were whites going the other extreme. There were Ku Klux Klan chapters. I was glad I was getting out,
because things really got bad. Any small disagreements would be blown
out of proportion. I remember these rednecks started a fight because a
black guy was dancing with a white girl. Then other guys jumped in,
and somebody got stabbed and killed. There were riots.

The media got ahold of it, and I remember the Commandant of the
Marine Corps getting on television and making this big announcement
that Marines would be able to wear Afro haircuts, that there would be
more black music on the jukebox in the enlisted clubs.

But they were still disciplining . . . people, and a lot of black people
got really hurt. People got in a lot of trouble, trouble that they're probably going to have to live with the rest of their lives. The facts show that
blacks got bad discharges—dishonorable or bad conduct or undesirable—that are proportionately higher than white GIs. Guys were getting
kicked out of the service left and right and not really caring, because
when you're young you tend to live for the day. Since then all that bad
paper is coming back to haunt people, because now, if the employer
knows, it can hurt you.

KATHLEEN KINKADE

42 | "Everyone Wants to Visit a Commune"

*The utopian communities that developed in America in the 1960s had their prec-
edents in religious and secular movements that proliferated during the nineteenth century—perhaps the most famous and enduring of which was the
Oneida Community of upstate New York. In the 1960s, with the challenges to
traditional social conventions as strong as they had been at any other time in
American history, there was a growth of experimentation, both organized and
free-form, with new lifestyles. The author of the following selection, Kathleen
Kinkade, was a founder of the Twin Oaks Community, one of the more ambitious
of the experimental communes of the 1960s.*

*The Twin Oaks Community is not necessarily representative of the com-
munes of the 1960s. For one thing, it was founded on the principles outlined by
behavioral psychologist B. F. Skinner in his 1948 book,* Walden Two. *Given
such a pedigree, more planning, deliberation, and science were involved in its
operation than were employed at other communes. As it evolved, however, the
commune was as much a product of the 1960s as it was of the imagination of
Skinner (who did not lend his active support to the project). As seen in the next
reading, the communal leaders themselves were affected by the same forces of
nonconformity that were challenging society at large.*

We had visitors the first day we started the Community. I don't recall
who they were now. We were much too busy getting acquainted with
each other and unpacking our things to bother too much with them. In
one way or another that has been true of our entire history with visitors.
They come here to talk to us, and we're usually too busy. Certainly we
must have been a disappointment and a puzzle to the people who visited us our first year. We paid them no attention at all unless by some
accident we were working with them or discovered a topic of mutual
interest, or unless the visitor went out of his way to make friends. The
shy ones got very little from their visits, I'm afraid. They slept on the
floor in their sleeping bags in whatever spaces we could find for them.

Kathleen Kinkade, A Walden Two Experiment. (*New York, William Morrow and Company,*
*1973) pp. 204–11. Copyright © 1973 by Kathleen Kinkade. Used by permission of William Morrow
and Company, Inc.*

And for this they paid $1.50 a day. Nevertheless, they kept coming. We kept saying in our newsletter that we really welcomed them (in theory we did), and they kept taking us at our word and discovering when they arrived that we were too busy to make them comfortable.

It took us a while even to realize that visitors were always going to be a part of our lives. The first few weeks Carrie would go into a mood whenever a car drove up with strangers in it. She had difficulty enough adjusting to the enlarged family of Community members (what she really wanted was a normal family life), and each group of visitors seemed to her like unexpected company, something a housewife justifiably gets upset about in the outside world. I remember four college students showed up in the middle of the night once, and Carrie found them in the kitchen the next morning, eating pancakes and smoking cigarettes. She stood still and glared at them as if they were beings from outer space, then turned to me and asked, "What are those?"

"Those" were visitors, a prelude of many hundreds yet to come. Carrie adjusted to them eventually, as the rest of us did, primarily by ignoring them. She would just ask, "How many of them are staying for supper?" and multiply the chickens accordingly.

We had been on the farm less than a week when the Rutledges arrived. They had vacation time from their jobs and decided to spend it with us. There were six of them—the two adult Rutledges, two small children, a teen-age son, and a cousin the same age as the son. Carrie and I were in the kitchen making blackberry jam when they arrived. Jenny breezed through the kitchen and said, "There's a family of six just come, and they've got a tent, and they're intending to stay a couple of weeks." And there they were.

The Rutledges brought with them a problem that we have been fighting ever since. The teen-age cousin was obviously high on one drug or another, and we had formed no policy about drugs, nor did we yet have any government structure that could make policy in a hurry. Most of us felt that we did not want dope on the property. What complicated the issue, however, was that the young man had long, wild, curly hair. Remember, this was 1967 when the hippie movement was just getting started. Somehow our reaction to dope and our reaction to long hair got all mixed up. All of our own men wore their hair short, feeling that they owed something to our local reputation. We didn't want to be known as a hippie farm. After a great deal of worried talk about the entire question of drugs and hair, we called a meeting of the whole group to make a decision on it. It wasn't a very good meeting. People voiced a lot of opinions, but there wasn't any mechanism to get a decision made. We talked for two hours and then went away from the meeting not knowing whether we had decided anything or not. The two opposing points brought up at the meeting were these: (1) long hair will make people think we are kooky, and we want to make a good impression; if we accept visitors who look like hippies, other hippies will start visiting, and we will become a place for hippies to visit, and we don't really want that kind of people around; and (2) the length of one's hair is so obviously one's own business that it would be a moral defeat if we made any policy about it.

It was the latter point of view that we eventually opted for. Dope, no; hair, yes. Within a year, almost all of our men had grown long hair or beards or both. We are indeed known as the hippie farm, and it is indeed difficult to persuade our neighbors that we really do not have drugs on the property. But we are pretty sure we made the right decision.

Most visitors come because they want to take part in community life, to try out the life style, either to write a paper about it or perhaps to test whether they might want to join. But some people visit just because they have no place else to go. One pair that I remember particularly well we called the Apple Tree Couple.

They arrived hitchhiking, with packs on their backs. He was bearded and dreamy-eyed. She was vague-looking and about six months pregnant. They asked for a place to pitch their tent. I explained our visitor policy to them—that they work while visiting, pay $1.50 a day, and eat with us. The man (he always spoke for both of them) accepted all of our terms, or seemed to, but called me aside later and asked if they could build a campfire and eat their own meals, because they couldn't really afford the $1.50 a day.

Decisions like that always bother me. On the one hand, we are trying to build a community here, and a policy of letting drifters camp on our land would be disastrous if carried very far. There are people who have a philosophy of providing free land for whoever wants to stay on it, but that is not what Twin Oaks is about. On the other hand, here are these very poor people, one of them a pregnant girl, asking for a small privilege that costs us nothing. I felt the usual conflict between a long-range "no" and a short-range "yes." I said yes.

So they camped under the apple trees and fixed their own meals. He cooked for her and cared for her tenderly. "She was pregnant once before," he confided to me, "but we were on a strictly macrobiotic diet, and she lost the baby because of malnutrition. Now we're being very careful this time." I told him to feel free to pick and eat our spinach, which was all we had in the garden at the time.

When they had been under the apple tree three days, we began to be annoyed that they had not volunteered to do any work. (We were still trying to take the position that they were visiting our community, not just camping on our land.) Carrie took the initiative. She walked up to them and said, "After visitors have been here twenty-four hours, they generally help out with the work. I can use some help in the kitchen, and Fred would be glad to use you in the garden." They listened in silence but did not volunteer. Later that afternoon, though, Fred spotted the man in the potato patch, apparently planting something. Fred went over to investigate, and found that Mr. Apple Tree was carefully planting summer squash seeds between the rows of potato plants. "Look," said Fred carefully, as he might have to a child or mental patient, "if you want to plant those squashes, I can show you a row where we didn't finish out the beans, and they might do all right there." The man kept on planting. "Because," Fred went on, "this is a potato patch, and we bring a cultivator through here, and the cultivator teeth will tear the squash plants to pieces."

"I like to do things on impulse," the man said. He waited until Fred shrugged his shoulders and went away, and then kept on planting.

"Did you get him to do any work?" Carrie asked Fred at supper time. "No, and I'm not going to," Fred told her, "I've got too much to do to be bothered with crazy people. Let him work when he feels the damned impulse.

After five days the annoyance had reached a peak, and the question remained simply one of who would ask them to leave. By this time their campfire had become an institution. Other guests who would ordinarily have spent their time with us, investigating our methods and ideas, were gathering with the Apple Tree Couple and digging their free philosophy. "They're very interesting people," our guests told us. "Well, they're being interesting at our expense," we replied, and it was thus that the Apple Tree Couple heard that they were not welcome. One of our other visitors let them know. They left, and so did our other visitors, none of them liking us very well. It was one of our more miserable failures in human relations.

More difficult still was Ivan, the Magician, who visited in the early part of 1970. By this time we were a well-established community. Our planner-manager system was working, and we had clear ideas about the role a visitor should play. We were long past allowing anyone to camp under our trees. Anyway, Ivan and his girlfriend didn't come to visit. They came, they announced, to stay. He introduced himself to me. "I am a builder," he said, and paused to see what effect that would have. "A builder and a magician."

Arnie was in the room at the time. "What kind of a magician?" Arnie asked. "Do you pull rabbits out of hats or what?"

"Prestidigitators are a dime a dozen," said Ivan loftily. "I do real magic. But don't be afraid. All my magic is white magic." I wasn't afraid of anything at the moment except having to spend time talking with this absurd man, so I escaped as quickly as I could and left Arnie to handle him. Arnie would talk to anybody about any theoretical matter, no matter how ridiculous the subject or how insane the conversationalist. It is one of Arnie's golden virtues. As I walked out I heard Arnie begin, "Well, now, how do you define magic?"

As it turned out, Ivan was indeed a builder. Or at any rate he was a worker. He could and did work three times as hard as any member of our community, and he quickly grew contemptuous of our haphazard, lazy ways. Our grounds were on the unkempt side, and one day he got tired of the mess and decided to clean it up. Within an hour or two he had gathered a huge pile of combustibles and was preparing to set fire to them when a member stopped him and asked him what he was doing.

"This trash has evil spirits in it," Ivan explained. "Evil spirits cannot live in a clean, neat place. If we burn this pile, the spirits will go and seek some other abode."

"But that's our scrap lumber," objected the member. "We make things out of it. And besides, you don't just do things like that without even asking the manager."

Ivan desisted from his fire-making. Perhaps garnering all the evil spirits into one pile satisfied him temporarily.

Evidently the objects that harbored the worst spirits of all were the two defunct automobiles that were sitting in our parking lot with their engines exposed. Ivan decided to put them in a less offensive spot. He hooked the tractor to them and dragged them off to the storage barn, where they still remain. He had hooked the tractor to the crippled school bus and was trying to drag it away, too, when Arnie came out to see what was going on. Ivan explained once more about the spirits. "Look," said Arnie, "you are a visitor. You are supposed to be doing work on the labor credit system. But even if you were a member, you don't just up and decide to move these cars. If you want them moved, you ask the Automobile Manager, who happens to be me."

"You," said Ivan, " are not fit to be a manager. God is my manager, and he tells me to move these cars." Evidently God intended the school bus to stay where it was, because Ivan couldn't budge it with the tractor.

By this time Ivan had moved into the empty furnace room in the new building we were completing. He had decorated it nicely, and had candles and incense burning. We believe he did incantations. He also did beautiful artwork. When he left (we threatened him finally, with civil authorities if he continued to trespass), he did so with a turn-the-other-cheek gesture of giving us the things he had made. To me personally (I was the villain of the piece, who actually delivered the message) he presented a lovely amethyst set in silver, evidently his own work. To other members he gave his paintings and wood carvings, all exquisite. We joke, sometimes, about the objects being cursed, but I think the gifts were meant purely to heap coals of fire upon our heads—a fairly successful device, by the way. We all felt guilt mixed in with our relief.

Most of our visitors aren't crazy, but they often get confused. Take the man who mistook the word "Dishes" printed on his labor credit sheet for "Ditches." The kitchen was shorthanded for two days before the mistake was discovered, but in the meantime, yards of beautifully dug drainage ditches appeared in the cow yard. How did such a mixup go two days without discovery? "Well," says the Cow Manager, "I didn't remember asking for so many hours of ditch digging, but here was this visitor saying he was supposed to dig ditches, and I'd been wanting them dug for a long time, so I didn't argue with him. I just showed him where to plant his shovel.'' And the Kitchen Manager said, ''I saw that he hadn't done his dishwashing shift, but I saw him working out-of-doors and thought perhaps someone had drafted him for emergency work, and being a visitor, he didn't realize that kitchen work takes priority. The second day I finally got up nerve enough to ask.''

Richard had come just out of curiosity, because he didn't have anything much to do on his week's leave from his Navy base. While he was here he read *Walden Two* and all of our material and talked to members. We talk to a lot of people, but I don't recall ever having converted anyone quite the way we did Richard. It was rather like a religious conversion. He saw the communal light, at it were, saw it as the answer to all of society's problems, and began to spread the word zealously. The first thing he did was call his mother on the telephone. ''Hey, Mom,'' he told her, ''I'm a Communist!''

''Yes, dear,'' said his mother, ''we'll talk about it when you get home.''

Richard did talk to his mother when he went home, according to a letter he later sent us. He says he has her almost convinced. We half expect to see the two of them sign up for provisional membership when Richard's tour in the Navy is finished.

/   /   /

GLORIA STEINEM AND
MARGARET HECKLER

43 | Testimony in Favor of the ERA

In recent decades, there has been a growing awareness that women do not share equally with men the rewards that American society has to offer. Indeed, some feminists go further and maintain that American women—although comprising a majority of the population—are treated like a persecuted ethnic or racial minority. The current revival of the movement for women's rights in the United States may be said to have begun with the publication of Betty Friedan's The Feminine Mystique *in 1963. It marked a turnaround after a period of about forty years during which the gains of an earlier feminist movement had been trivialized by a seemingly unquestioned consensus that women's proper roles were mother, homemaker, teacher, or nurse.*

In fact, by the 1960s the percentage of women working outside the home in "nontraditional" occupations had been increasing for several decades—however, these women worked for substandard wages. Thus, with so many other groups reevaluating their places in American society in the 1960s, a revival of feminism was inevitable. It is quite possible that the women's movement may turn out to be the most permanent and sustained of all manifestations of cultural radicalism of recent years, the one that has had the largest impact on American values and that has the greatest likelihood of continuing to change the way the nation lives.

The following excerpts are from hearings held in 1970 by a committee of the U.S. Senate to consider the proposed Equal Rights Amendment (ERA) to the Constitution. Although passed by Congress, the ERA was not ratified by the required three-fourths of the states and did not go into effect. Some opponents of the ERA argued that would force on the nation a social revolution for which it was ill-prepared and which it did not desire. More moderate opponents argued that existing legal statutes protected women in the workplace.

The response to the first argument has been that there is no explicit or implicit language in the ERA calling for a legally mandated reorganization of male and female roles in society. To the second argument the response has been that differences in pay between men and women performing similar jobs persist, despite general antidiscrimination laws. Supporters of the ERA maintain that, in any event, preexisting legislation is no reason in itself to deny women a constitutional reaffirmation of their full rights as human beings.

From "The Equal Rights" Amendment: Hearings Before the Subcommittee on Constitutional Amendments of the Committee on the Judiciary of the United States Senate, *91st Congress, May 5, 6, and 7, 1970 (Washington, D.C., Government Printing Office, 1970) pp. 331–335, 38–41, 575–578.*

STATEMENT OF GLORIA STEINEM, WRITER AND CRITIC

My name is Gloria Steinem. I am a writer and editor, and I am currently a member of the policy council of the Democratic committee. And I work regularly with the lowest-paid workers in the country, the migrant workers, men, women, and children both in California and in my own State of New York.

/   /   /

During 12 years of working for a living, I have experienced much of the legal and social discrimination reserved for women in this country. I have been refused service in public restaurants, ordered out of public gathering places, and turned away from apartment rentals; all for the clearly-stated, sole reason that I am a woman. And all without the legal remedies available to blacks and other minorities. I have been excluded from professional groups, writing assignments on so-called "unfeminine" subjects such as politics, full participation in the Democratic Party, jury duty, and even from such small male privileges as discounts on airline fares. Most important to me, I have been denied a society in which women are encouraged, or even allowed to think of themselves as first-class citizens and responsible human beings.

However, after 2 years of researching the status of American women, I have discovered that in reality, I am very, very lucky. Most women, both wage-earners and housewives, routinely suffer more humiliation and injustice than I do.

As a freelance writer, I don't work in the male-dominated hierarchy of an office. (Women, like blacks and other visibly different minorities, do better in individual professions such as the arts, sports, or domestic work; anything in which they don't have authority over white males.) I am not one of the millions of women who must support a family. Therefore, I haven't had to go on welfare because there are no day-care centers for my children while I work, and I haven't had to submit to the humiliating welfare inquiries about my private and sexual life, inquiries from which men are exempt. I haven't had to brave the sex bias of labor unions and employers, only to see my family subsist on a median salary 40 percent less than the male medial salary.

I hope this committee will hear the personal, daily injustices suffered by many women—professionals and day laborers, women housebound by welfare as well as by suburbia. We have all been silent for too long. But we won't be silent anymore.

The truth is that all our problems stem from the same sex based myths. We may appear before you as white radicals or the middle-aged middleclass or black soul sisters, but we are all sisters in fighting against these outdated myths. Like racial myths, they have been reflected in our laws. Let me list a few.

That women are biologically inferior to men. In fact, an equally good case can be made for the reverse. Women live longer than men, even when the men are not subject to business pressures. Women survived Nazi concentration camps better, keep cooler heads in emergencies currently studied by disaster-researchers, are protected against heart attacks by their female sex hormones, and are so much more durable at every stage of life that nature must conceive 20 to 50 percent more males in order to keep the balance going.

Man's hunting activities are forever being pointed to as tribal proof of superiority. But while he was hunting, women built houses, tilled the fields, developed animal husbandry, and perfected language. Men, being all alone in the bush, often developed into a creature as strong as women, fleeter of foot, but not very bright.

However, I don't want to prove the superiority of one sex to another. That would only be repeating a male mistake. English scientists once definitively proved, after all, that the English were descended from the angels, while the Irish were descended from the apes; it was the rationale for England's domination of Ireland for more than a century. The point is that science is used to support current myth and economics almost as much as the church was.

What we do know is that the difference between two races or two sexes is much smaller than the differences to be found within each group. Therefore, in spite of the slide show on female inferiorities that I understand was shown to you yesterday, the law makes much more sense when it treats individuals, not groups bundled together by some condition of birth.

/   /   /

Another myth, that women are already treated equally in this society. I am sure there has been ample testimony to prove that equal pay for equal work, equal chance for advancement, and equal training or encouragement is obscenely scarce in every field, even those—like food and fashion industries—that are supposedly "feminine."

A deeper result of social and legal injustice, however, is what sociologists refer to as "Internalized Aggression." Victims of aggression absorb the myth of their own inferiority, and come to believe that their group is in fact second class. Even when they themselves realize they are not second class, they may still think their group is, thus the tendency to be the only Jew in the club, the only black woman on the block, the only woman in the office.

Women suffer this second class treatment from the moment they are born. They are expected to be, rather than achieve, to function biologically rather than learn. A brother, whatever his intellect, is more likely to get the family's encouragement and education money, while girls are often pressured to conceal ambition and intelligence, to "Uncle Tom."

I interviewed a New York public school teacher who told me about a black teenager's desire to be a doctor. With all the barriers in mind, she suggested kindly that he be a veterinarian instead.

The same day, a high school teacher mentioned a girl who wanted to be a doctor. The teacher said, "How about a nurse?"

Teachers, parents, and the Supreme Court may exude a protective, well-meaning rationale, but limiting the individual's ambition is doing no one a favor. Certainly not this country; it needs all the talent it can get.

Another myth, that American women hold great economic power. Fifty-one percent of all shareholders in this country are women. That is a favorite male-chauvinist statistic. However, the number of shares they hold is so small that the total is only 18 percent of all the shares. Even those holdings are often controlled by men.

Similarly, only 5 percent of all the people in the country who receive $10,000 a year or more, earned or otherwise, are women. And that includes the famous rich widows.

The constantly repeated myth of our economic power seems less tetimony to our real power than to the resentment of what little power we do have.

Another myth, that children must have full-time mothers. American mothers spend more time with their homes and children than those of any other society we know about. In the past, joint families, servants, a prevalent system in which grandparents raised the children, or family field work in the agrarian systems—all these factors contributed more to child care than the labor-saving devices of which we are so proud.

The truth is that most American children seem to be suffering from too much mother, and too little father. Part of the program of Women's Liberation is a return of fathers to their children. If laws permit women equal work and pay opportunities, men will then be relieved of their role as sole breadwinner. Fewer ulcers, fewer hours of meaningless work, equal responsibility for his own children: these are a few of the reasons that Women's Liberation is Men's Liberation too.

As for psychic health of the children, studies show that the quality of time spent by parents is more important than the quantity. The most damaged children were not those whose mothers worked, but those whose mothers preferred to work but stayed home out of the role-playing desire to be a "good mother."

Another myth, that the women's movement is not political, won't last, or is somehow not "serious."

When black people leave their 19th century roles, they are feared. When women dare to leave theirs, they are ridiculed. We understand this; we accept the burden of ridicule. It won't keep us quiet anymore.

Similarly, it shouldn't deceive male observers into thinking that this is somehow a joke. We are 51 percent of the population; we are essentially united on these issues across boundaries of class or race or age; and we may well end by changing this society more than the civil rights movement. That is an apt parallel. We, too, have our right wing and left wing, our separatists, gradualists, and Uncle Toms. But we are changing our own consciousness, and that of the country. Engels noted the relationship of the authoritarian, nuclear family to capitalism: the father as capitalist, the mother as means of production, and the children as labor. He said the family would change as the economic system did, and that seems to have happened, whether we want to admit it or not. Women's bodies will no longer be owned by the state for the production of workers and soldiers; birth control and abortion are facts of everyday life. The new family is an egalitarian family.

Gunnar Myrdal noted 30 years ago the parallel between women and Negroes in this country. Both suffered from such restricting social myths as: smaller brains, passive natures, inability to govern themselves (and certainly not white men), sex objects only, childlike natures, special skills, and the like. When evaluating a general statement about women, it might be valuable to substitute "black people" for "women"—just to test the prejudice at work.

And it might be valuable to do this constitutionally as well. Neither group is going to be content as a cheap labor pool anymore. And neither is going to be content without full constitutional rights.

Finally, I would like to say one thing about this time in which I am testifying.

I had deep misgivings about discussing this topic when National Guardsmen are occupying our campuses, the country is being turned against itself in a terrible polarization, and America is enlarging an already inhuman and unjustifiable war. But it seems to me that much of the trouble in this country has to do with the "masculine mystique"; with the myth that masculinity somehow depends on the subjugation of other people. It is a bipartisan problem; both our past and current Presidents seem to be victims of this myth, and to behave accordingly.

Women are not more moral than men. We are only uncorrupted by power. But we do not want to imitate men, to join this country as it is, and I think our very participation will change it. Perhaps women elected leaders—and there will be many of them—will not be so likely to dominate black people or yellow people or men; anybody who looks different from us.

After all, we won't have our masculinity to prove.

/   /   /

STATEMENT OF HON. MARGARET M. HECKLER, A REPRESENTATIVE IN CONGRESS FROM THE 10TH DISTRICT OF THE STATE OF MASSACHUSETTS*

Thank you very much, Mr. Chairman and distinguished members of the subcommittee.

It is assumed today by many persons that women were granted equality with the passage of the 14th amendment, ratified in 1868. Only 50 years later, however, was woman suffrage guaranteed by the ratification of the 19th amendment. Half a century of waiting for the vote required a great deal of patience. In the temper of these turbulent times, I do not believe that total equality of opportunity for women can be further postponed.

Thus I speak out in support of the equal rights amendment—a measure that has been before each Congress since 1923. The fast pace of life in the world today fosters impatience. And when much is promised, failure to deliver becomes a matter of critical importance.

I am sure that every woman who has been in the position of "job seeker" identifies in some small measure with the fundamental complaints that have generated the crusade for equality in employment for women. The 42 percent of working women who are heads of household takes a serious economic interest in fair job opportunity, a basic goal in the cause for women's rights. And the women who have contributed their full share to social security, yet who receive the sum allotted widows, certainly have cause for contemplation.

The average woman in America has no seething desire to smoke cigars or to burn the bra—but she does seek equal recognition of her status as a citizen before the courts of law, and she does seek fair and just recognition of her qualifications in the employment market. The American working woman does not want to be limited in advancement by virtue of her sex. She does not want to be prohibited from the job she desires or from the overtime work she needs by "protective" legislation.

These types of discrimination must be stopped, and the forthright means of halting discrimination against women is passage of the equal rights amendment at the earliest possible time. In fact, I have heard it said quite often that the only discrimination that is still fashionable is discrimination against women.

Perhaps, as some say, it is derived from a protective inclination on the part of men. But women seek recognition as individual human beings with abilities useful to society—rather than shelter or protection from the real world.

---

*Margaret Heckler was defeated in her 1982 bid for reelection. In 1983, she began a term as Secretary of Health and Human Services in the Reagan administration. President Reagan and many of his major officials were opposed to the ERA.

John Gardner has said that our Nation's most underdeveloped resource is womanpower. The old saying "you can't keep a good man down" might well serve as a warning. It is safe to say, I think, that women are unlikely to stay down and out of the field of competition for much longer.

Legal remedies are clearly in order, and the equal rights amendment is especially timely. Although changes in social attitudes cannot be legislated, they are guided by the formulation of our Federal laws. This constitutional amendment must be passed so that discriminatory legislation will be overturned. That custom and attitude by subject to a faster pace of evolution is essential if we are to avoid revolution on the part of qualified women who seek equality in the employment world.

Time and again I have heard American men question the fact of discrimination against women in America. "American women," they say, "enjoy greater freedom than women of any other nation." This may be true with regard to freedom from kitchen labor—because the average American housewife enjoys a considerable degree of automation in her kitchen. But once she seeks to fill her leisure time gained from automated kitchen equipment by entering the male world of employment, the picture changes. Many countries we consider "underprivileged" far surpass America in quality and availability of child care available to working mothers, in enlightened attitudes about employment leave for pregnancy, and in guiding women into the professions.

Since World War II, nearly 14 million American women have joined the labor force—double the number of men. Forty percent of our Nation's labor force is now comprised of women. Yet less than 3 percent of our Nation's attorneys are women, only about 7 percent of our doctors, and 9 percent of our scientists are women. Only a slightly higher percentage of our graduate students in these fields of study are women, despite the fact that women characteristically score better on entrance examinations. The average woman college graduate's annual earnings ($6,694) exceed by just a fraction the annual earnings of an average male educated only through the eighth grade ($6,580). An average male college graduate, however, may be expected to earn almost twice as much as the female—$11,795. Twenty percent of the women with 4 years of college training can find employment only in clerical, sales, or factory jobs. The equal pay provision of the Fair Labor Standards Act does not include administrative, executive, or professional positions—a loophole which permits the talents and training of highly qualified women to be obtained more cheaply than those of comparable qualified men.

Of the 7.5 million American college students enrolled in 1968, at least 40 percent were women. American parents are struggling to educate their daughters as well as their sons—and are sending them to the best colleges they can possibly afford. As many of these mothers attend commencement exercises this summer, their hearts will swell with pride as their daughters receive college degrees—and these mothers may realize their daughters will have aspirations far exceeding their own horizons.

Few of the fathers or mothers, enrolling their daughters in college several years ago, were at the time aware of the obstacles to opportunity their daughters would face. But today they are becoming aware that opportunity for their daughters is only half of that available to their sons. And they are justifiably indignant. Young women graduating with degrees in business administration take positions as clerks while their male counterparts become management trainees. Women graduating from law school are often forced to become legal secretaries, while male graduates from the same class survey a panorama of exciting possibilities.

To frustrate the aspirations of the competent young women graduating from our institutions of higher learning would be a dangerous and foolish thing. The youth of today are inspired with a passion to improve the quality of life around us—an admirable and essential goal, indeed. The job is a mammoth one, however; and it would be ill-advised to assume that the role of women in the crusade of the future will not be a significant one. To the contrary, never before has our Nation and our world cried out for talent and creative energy with greater need. To deny full participation of the resources of women, who compose over half the population of our country, would be a serious form of neglect. The contributions of women have always been intrinsic in our national development. With the increasing complexity of our world, it becomes all the more essential to tap every conceivable resource at our command.

The time is thus ripe for passage of the equal rights amendment. The women of America are demanding full rights and full responsibilities in developing their individual potential as human beings in relationship to the world as well as to the home and in contributing in an active way to the improvement of society.

In this day of the urban crisis, when we seem to be running out of clean air and water, when the quantity of our rubbish defies our current disposal methods, when crime on the streets is rampant, when our world commitments seem at odds with our obligations here at home, when breaking the cycle of ongoing poverty requires new and innovative approaches, when increased lifespan generates a whole new series of gerontological problems—in these complicated and critical times, our Nation needs the fully developed resources of all our citizens—both men and women—in order to meet the demands of society today.

Women are not requesting special privilege—but rather a full measure of responsibility, a fair share of the load in the effort to improve life in America. The upcoming generation is no longer asking for full opportunity to contribute, however—they are demanding this opportunity.

The equal rights amendment is necessary to establish unequivocally the American commitment to full and equal recognition of the rights of all its citizens. Stopgap measures and delays will no longer be acceptable—firm guarantees are now required. The seventies mark an era of great promise if the untapped resource of womanpower is brought forth into the open and allowed to flourish so that women may take their rightful place in the mainstream of American life. Both men and women have a great deal to gain.

Thank you, Mr. Chairman.

PETER COLLIER AND
DAVID HOROWITZ

44 | "Lefties for Reagan"

The extent to which the administration of Ronald Reagan represented a "revolution" in politics and social values is a matter of debate. For example, perspec-
tives on the conservatism of recent decades depends in part on differing views of
the 1960s. In the early 1970s, Richard Nixon used the phrase "silent majority"
to refer to an enduring, core base of support for conservative United States domestic and foreign policy. Was all the protest of the 1960s raised by a radical
fringe? Was opposition to the war in Vietnam as pervasive as one might remember it?

As America evaluates the political and social movements of the 1960s, some
people approve of the mission of the American left, and some challenge its tactics and strategies. Others renounce both mission and method, claiming that
the operations of the left were guided by hypocrisy, naivete, and shallow commitment.

Peter Collier and David Horowitz, who were editors of the radical magazine
Ramparts, belong to the group that criticizes the American Left most severely.
They, like their "hero" Ronald Reagan, who once was an idealistic New-Deal
Democrat, are converts to conservatism.

It can be argued that Collier and Horowitz have changed less than might
appear, that their writing illustrates a continuity of anger as they move from
the fury they felt toward capitalism in the 1960s to a fury toward communism
in the 1980s. They repeat the experience of the 1930s Left, which produced
many of the vigorous anticommunists of the 1950s and 1960s. Indeed, in the
essay that follows, the battle with communism replaces all the domestic issues
that were at the center of the New Left in the first half of the 1960s: racism,
poverty, social welfare, and the quality of life. In their vision, as in the vision
that emerged among many on the Left in the 1960s, there is no middle ground,
only capitalism or communism, Right or Left. The liberalism that defined much
of the 1960s, which arose from attempts to deal with real social problems, is
forgotten. A dirty word to the Left in the late 1960s—for its supposedly moderate, uncritical outlook—liberalism, ironically, became the unspeakable "L-word"
in the 1980s for its association with a radical and indiscriminate ideology.

Peter Collier and David Horowitz, "Lefties for Reagan," In The Washington Post Magazine,
March 17, 1985. Used by permission of Peter Collier and David Horowitz. © Peter Collier and
David Horowitz, 1985.

When we tell our old radical friends that we voted for Ronald Reagan last November, the response is usually one of annoyed incredulity. After making sure that we are not putting them on, our old friends make nervous jokes about Jerry Falwell and Phyllis Schlafly, about gods that have failed, about aging yuppies ascending to consumer heaven in their BMWs. We remind them of an old adage: "Anyone under 40 who isn't a socialist has no heart; anyone over 40 who is a socialist has no brain."

Inevitably the talk becomes bitter. One old comrade, after a tirade in which she had denounced us as reactionaries and crypto-fascists, finally sputtered, "And the worst thing is that you've turned your back on the *Sixties!*" That was exactly right: casting our ballots for Ronald Reagan was indeed a way of finally saying goodbye to all that—to the self-aggrandizing romance with corrupt Third Worldism; to the casual indulgence of Soviet totalitarianism; to the hypocritical and self-dramatizing anti-Americanism which is the New Left's bequest to mainstream politics.

The instruments of popular culture may perhaps be forgiven for continuing to portray the '60s as a time of infectious idealism, but those of us who were active then have no excuse for abetting this banality. If in some ways it was the best of times, it was also the worst of times, an era of bloodthirsty fantasies as well as spiritual ones. We ourselves experienced both aspects, starting as civil rights and antiwar activists and ending as coeditors of the New Left magazine *Ramparts*. The magazine post allowed us to write about the rough beast slouching through America and also to urge it on through noneditorial activities we thought of as clandestine until we later read about them in the FBI and CIA files we both accumulated.

Like other radicals in those days, we were against electoral politics, regarding voting as one of those charades used by the ruling class to legitimate its power. We were even more against Reagan, then governor of California, having been roughed up by his troopers during the People's Park demonstrations in Berkeley and tear-gassed by his National Guard helicopters during the University of California's Third World Liberation Front Strike. But neither elections nor elected officials seemed particularly important compared with the auguries of revolution the left saw everywhere by the end of the decade—in the way the nefarious Richard Nixon was widening the war in Indochina; in the unprovoked attacks by paramilitary police against the Black Panther Party; in the formation of the Weather Underground, a group willing to pick up the gun or the bomb. It was a time when the apocalypse struggling to be born seemed to need only the slightest assist from the radical midwife.

When we were in the voting booth this past November (in different precincts but of the same mind) we both thought back to the day in 1969 when Tom Hayden came by the office and, after getting a Ramparts donation to buy gas masks and other combat issue for Black Panther "guerrillas," announced portentously: "Fascism is here, and we're all going to be in jail by the end of the year." We agreed wholeheartedly with this apocalyptic vision and in fact had just written in an editorial: "The system cannot be revitalized. It must be overthrown. As humanely as possible, but by any means necessary."

Every thought and perception in those days was filtered through the dark and distorting glass of the Vietnam war. The left was hooked on Vietnam. It was an addictive drug whose rush was a potent mix of melodrama, self-importance and moral rectitude. Vietnam was a universal solvent—the explanation for every evil we saw and the justification for every excess we committed. Trashing the windows of merchants on the main streets of America seemed warranted by the notion that these petty bourgeois shopkeepers were cogs in the system of capitalist exploitation that was obliterating Vietnam. Fantasizing the death of local cops seemed warranted by the role they played as an occupying army in America's black ghettos, those mini-Vietnams we yearned to see explode in domestic wars of liberation. Vietnam caused us to acquire a new appreciation for foreign tyrants like Kim Il Sung of North Korea. Vietnam also caused us to support the domestic extortionism and violence of groups like the Black Panthers, and to dismiss derisively Martin Luther King Jr. as an "Uncle Tom." (The left has conveniently forgotten this fact now that it finds it expedient to involve King's name and reputation to further its domestic politics.)

How naive the New Left was can be debated, but by the end of the '60s we were not political novices. We knew that bad news from Southeast Asia—the reports of bogged-down campaigns and the weekly body counts announced by Walter Cronkite—was good for the radical agenda. The more repressive our government in dealing with dissent at home, the more recruits for our cause and the sooner the appearance of the revolutionary Armageddon.

Our assumption that Vietnam would be the political and moral fulcrum by which we would tip this country toward revolution foresaw every possibility except one: that the United States would pull out. Never had we thought that the United States, the archimperial power, would of its own volition withdraw from Indochina. This development violated a primary article of our hand-me-down Marxism: that political action through normal channels could not alter the course of the war. The system we had wanted to overthrow worked tardily and only at great cost, but it worked.

When American troops finally came home, some of us took the occasion to begin a long and painful reexamination of our political assumptions and beliefs. Others did not. For the diehards, there was a post-Vietnam syndrome in its own way as debilitating as that suffered by people who had fought there—a sense of emptiness rather than exhilaration, a paradoxical desire to hold onto and breathe life back into the experience that had been their high for so many years.

As the post-Vietnam decade progressed, the diehards on the left ignored conclusions about the viability of democratic traditions that might have been drawn from America's exit from Vietnam and from the Watergate crisis that followed it, a time when the man whose ambitions they had feared most was removed from office by the Constitution rather than by a coup. The only "lessons" of Vietnam the left seemed interested in were those that emphasized the danger of American power abroad and the need to diminish it, a view that was injected into the Democratic Party with the triumph of the McGovernite wing. The problem with this use of Vietnam as a moral text for American policy, however, was that the pages following the fall of Saigon had been whited out.

No lesson, for instance, was seen in Hanoi's ruthless conquest of the South, the establishment of a police state in Saigon and the political oblivion of the National Liberation Front, whose struggle we on the left had so passionately supported. It was not that credible information was lacking. Jean Lacouture wrote in 1976: "Never before have we had such proof of so many detained after a war. Not in Moscow in 1917. Not in Madrid in 1939, not in Paris and Rome in 1944, nor in Havana in 1959 . . . " But this eminent French journalist, who had been regarded as something of an oracle when he was reporting America's derelictions during the war, was dismissed as a "sellout."

In 1977, when some former antiwar activists signed an Appeal to the Conscience of Vietnam because of the more than 200,000 prisoners languishing in "reeducation centers" and the new round of self-immolations by Buddhist monks, they were chastised by activist David Dellinger, Institute for Policy Studies fellow Richard Barnet and other keepers of the flame in a New York times advertisement that said in part: "The present government of Vietnam should be hailed for its moderation and for its extraordinary effort to achieve reconciliation among all of its people."

When tens of thousands of unreconciled "boat people" began to flee the repression of their communist rulers, Joan Baez and others who spoke out in their behalf were attacked for breaking ranks with Hanoi.

Something might also have been learned from the fate of wretched Cambodia. But leftists seemed so addicted to finding an American cause at the root of every problem that they couldn't recognize indigenous evils. As the Khmer Rouge were about to take over, Noam Chomsky wrote that their advent heralded a Cambodian liberation, "a new era of economic development and social justice." The new era turned out to be the killing fields that took the lives of 2 million Cambodians.

Finally, Vietnam emerged as an imperialist power, taking control of Laos, invading Cambodia and threatening Thailand. But in a recent editorial, The Nation explains that the Vietnamese invaded Cambodia "to stop the killing and restore some semblance of civilized government to the devastated country." This bloody occupation is actually a "rescue mission," and what has happened should not "obscure the responsibility of the United States for the disasters in Indochina," disasters that are being caused by playing the "China card" and refusing to normalize relations with Vietnam. These acts on the part of the United States "make Vietnamese withdrawal from Cambodia unlikely"; only the White House can "remove the pressures on Vietman from all sides [that] would bring peace to a ravaged land." Such reasoning recalls the wonderful line from the Costa-Gavras film "Z": "Always blame the Americans. Even when you're wrong, you're right."

Another unacknowledged lesson from Indochina involves the way in which Vietnam has become a satellite of the Soviet Union (paying for foreign aid by sending labor brigades to its benefactor). This development doesn't mesh well with the left's on-going romantic vision of Hanoi. It also threatens the left's obstinate refusal to admit that during the mid-'70s—a time when American democracy was trying to heal itself from the twin traumas of the war and Watergate—the U.S.S.R. was demonstrating that totalitarianism abhors a vacuum by moving into Africa, Central America, Southeast Asia and elsewhere. Instead of evaluating the Soviets because of the change in what we used to call "the objective conditions," the left rationalizes Soviet aggression as the spasms of a petrified bureaucracy whose policies are annoying mainly because they distract attention from U.S. malfeasance around the world.

If they were capable of looking intently at the Soviet Union, leftists and liberals alike would have to concur with Susan Sontag's contention (which many of them jeered at when she announced it) that communism is simply left-wing fascism.

One of the reasons the left has been so cautious in its reassessments of the Soviets is the fiction that the U.S.S.R. is on the side of "history." This assumption is echoed in Fred Halliday's euphoric claim, in a recent issue of New Left Review, that Soviet support was crucial to 14 Third World revolutions during the era of "detente" (including such triumphs of human progress as Iran and South Yemen), and in Andrew Kopkind's fatuous observation that "the Soviet Union has almost always sided with the revolutionists, the liberationists, the insurgents." In Ethiopia? Propped up by 20,000 Cuban legionnaires, the Marxist government of Mengistu Haile Mariam has as its main accomplishment a "Red Campaign of Terror" (its official designation) that killed thousands of people. Where were those who cheer the Soviets' work in behalf of the socialist zeitgeist when this episode took place? Or this past fall when the Marxist liberator squandered more than $40 million on a party celebrating the 10th anniversary of his murderous rule while his people starved? Where were they to point out the moral when capitalist. America rushed in 250 million metric tons of grain to help allay the Ethiopian starvation while the Soviets' were managing to contribute only 10 million metric tons? Where are they now that Mengistu withholds emergency food supplies from the starving provinces of Eritrea and Tigre because the people there are in rebellion against his tyranny?

Reagan is often upbraided for having described the Soviet Union as an evil empire. Those opposed to this term seem to be offended esthetically rather than politically. Just how wide of the mark is the president? Oppressing an array of nationalities whose populations far outnumber its own, Russia is the last of the old European empires, keeping in subjugation not only formerly independent states such as Estonia, Latvia and Lithuania (Hitler's gift to Stalin), but also the nations of Eastern Europe. Every country "liberated" into the Soviet bloc has been transformed into a national prison, where the borders are guarded to keep the inmates in rather than the foreigners out.

The war in Afghanistan is much more a metaphor for the Soviets' view of the world than Vietnam ever was for America's. Of the approximately 16 million people living in Afghanistan at the time of the Soviet invasion, an estimated 1 million have already been killed and wounded. There are now about 4 million refugees, a figure that does not include "internal" refugees—the hundreds of thousands of villagers forced to leave their scorched earth for the Soviet-controlled big cities, the only places where food is available. Or the thousands of Afghan children who have been taken to the Soviet Union to be "educated" and who will eventually be returned to their native land as spies and quislings.

Soviet strategy is based on a brutal rejoinder to Mao's poetic notion (which we old New Leftists used to enjoy citing) about guerrillas being like fish swimming in a sea of popular support. The Soviet solution is to boil the sea and ultimately drain it, leaving the fish exposed and gasping on barren land. The Russian presence is characterized by systematic destruction of crops and medical facilities, indiscriminate terror against the civilian population, carpet bombings and the deadly "yellow rain" that even the leftist Peoples' Tribunal in Paris (successor to the Bertrand Russell War Crimes Tribunal) has said is being used in Afghanistan.

During each December anniversary of the Soviet invasion, when liberal politicians rediscover the mujaheddin guerrillas in the hills, after 11 months of moral amnesia, there are blithe references to Afghanistan as "Russia's Vietnam." Those who invoke the analogy seem to think that simply by doing so they have doomed the Russian storm troopers to defeat. But this analogy is based on a misunderstanding of what Vietnam was and what Afghanistan is. Unlike America's high-tech television war, Afghanistan is one of those old-fashioned encounters that take place in the dark. The Soviets make no attempt to win hearts and minds; the My Lais that are daily occurrences there cause no shock because they do not appear on Moscow TV; there are no scenes of the peasant children whose hands and faces have been destroyed by antipersonnel bombs in the shapes of toy trucks and butterflies a Los Angeles physician we know saw strewn over the Afghan countryside; there are no images of body bags being offloaded from Soviet transports. Because there is no media coverage, there can be no growing revulsion on the home front, no protests on Soviet campuses and in Soviet streets, no clamor to bring the boys home.

Afghanistan is not Russia's Vietnam not only because the nation committing the atrocities never sees them, but because the rest of the world is blacked out, too. At the height of the Vietnam war there was a noncombatant army of foreign journalists present to witness its conduct. In Afghanistan they are forbidden, as are the Red Cross and all other international relief agencies that were integral to what happened in Vietnam. And without these witnesses, Afghanistan is a matter of "out of sight, out of mind."

In Vietnam we waged a war against ourselves and lost. The Soviets will not let that happen to them. The truth of the Vietnam analogy is not that guerrillas must inevitably bog down and defeat a superior force of invaders, but that war against indigenous forces by a superpower can be won if it is waged against a backdrop of international ignorance and apathy. The proper analogy for Afghanistan is not Vietnam at all but rather Spain—not in the nature of the war, but in the symbolic value it has for our time—or should—in terms of democracy's will to resist aggression. Aid to the mujaheddin should not be a dirty little secret of the CIA, but a matter of public policy and national honor as well.

Perhaps the leading feature of the left today is the moral selectivity that French social critic Jean-Francois Revel has identified as "the syndrome of the cross-eyed left." Leftists can describe Vietnam's conquest and colonization of Cambodia as a "rescue mission," while reviling Ronald Reagan for applying the same term to the Grenada operation, although better than 90 percent of the island's population told independent pollsters they were grateful for the arrival of U.S. troops. Forgetting for a moment that Afghanistan is "Russia's Vietnam," leftists call Grenada "America's Afghanistan," although people in Afghanistan (as one member of the resistance there told us) would literally die for the elections held in Grenada.

The left's memory can be as selective as its morality. When it comes to past commitments that have failed, the leftist mentality is utterly unable to produce a coherent balance sheet, let alone a profit-and-loss statement. The attitude toward Soviet penetration of the Americas is a good example. Current enthusiasm for the Sandinista regime in Nicaragua should recall to those of us old enough to remember a previous enthusiasm for Cuba 25 years ago. Many of us began our New Leftism with the Fair Play for Cuba demonstrations. We raised our voices and chanted, "Cuba, Si! Yanqui, No!" We embraced Fidel Castro not only because of the flamboyant personal style of the barbudos of his 26th of July Movement but also because Castro assured the world that his revolution belonged to neither communists nor capitalists, that it was neither red nor black, but Cuban olive green.

We attributed Castro's expanding links with Moscow to the U.S.-sponsored invasion of the Bay of Pigs, and then to the "secret war" waged against Cuba by U.S. intelligence and paramilitary organizations. But while Castro's apologists in the United States may find it expedient to maintain these fictions, Carlos Franqui and other old Fidelistas now in exile have made it clear that Castro embraced the Soviets even before the U.S. hostility became decisive, and that he steered his country into an alliance with the Soviets with considerable enthusiasm. Before the Bay of Pigs he put a Soviet general in charge of Cuban forces. Before the Bay of Pigs he destroyed Cuba's democratic trade union movement, although its elected leadership was drawn from his own 26th of July Movement. He did so because he knew that the Stalinists of Cuba's Communist Party would be dependable cheerleaders and efficient policemen of his emerging dictatorship.

One symbolic event along the way that many of us missed was Castro's imprisonment of his old comrade Huber Matos, liberator of Matanzas Province, and one of the four key military leaders of the revolution. Matos' crime: criticizing the growing influence of Cuban communists (thereby jeopardizing Castro's plans to use them as his palace guard). Matos' sentence: 20 years in a 4-by-11 concrete box. Given such a precedent, how can we fail to support Eden Pastora for taking up arms against early signs of similar totalitarianism in Nicaragua?

What has come of Cuba's revolution to break the chains of American imperialism? Soviets administer the still one-crop Cuban economy; Soviets train the Cuban army; and Soviet subsidies, fully one-quarter of Cuba's gross national product, prevent the Cuban treasury from going broke. Before the revolution, there were more than 35 independent newspapers and radio stations in Havana. Now, there is only the official voice of Granma, the Cuban Pravda, and a handful of other outlets spouting the same party line. Today Cuba is a more abject and deformed colony of the Soviet empire than it ever was of America. The archrebel of our youth, Fidel Castro, has become a party hack who cheerfully endorsed the rape of Czechoslovakia in 1968 and endorses the ongoing plunder of Afghanistan today, an aging pimp who sells his young men to the Russians for use in their military adventures in return for $10 billion a year.

In leftist circles, of course, such arguments are anathema, and no historical precedent, however daunting, can prevent outbreaks of radical chic. Epidemics of radical chic cannot be prevented by referring to historical precedents. That perennial delinquent Abbie Hoffman will lead his Potemkin village tours of Managua. The Hollywood stars will dish up Nicaraguan president Daniel Ortega as an exotic hors d'oeuvre on the Beverly Hills cocktail circuit. In the self-righteous moral glow accompanying such gatherings, it will be forgotten that, through the offices of the U.S. government, more economic and military aid was provided the Sandinistas in the first 18 months following their takeover than was given to Somoza in the previous 20 years, and that this aid was cut off primarily because of the clear signs that political pluralism in Nicaragua was being terminated.

Adherents of today's version of radical chic may never take seriously the words of Sandinista directorate member Bayardo Arce when he says that elections are a "hindrance" to the goal of "a dictatorship of the proletariat" and necessary only "as an expedient to deprive our enemies of an argument." They will ignore former Sandinista hero and now contra leader Eden Pastora who sees the junta as traitors who have sold out the revolutionary dream ("now that we are occupied by foreign forces from Cuba and Russia, now that we are governed by a dictatorial government of nine men, now more than ever the Sandinista struggle is justified"). They will ignore opposition leader Arturo Cruz, an early supporter of the Sandinista revolution and previously critical of the contras, when the worsening situation makes him change his mind and ask the Reagan administration to support them in a statement that should have the same weight as Andrei Sakharov's plea to the West to match the Soviet arms buildup.

American leftists propose solutions for the people of Central America that they wouldn't dare propose for themselves. These armchair revolutionaries project their self-hatred and their contempt for the privileges of democracy—which allow them to live well and to think badly— onto people who would be only too grateful for the luxuries they disdain. Dismissing "bourgeois" rights as a decadent frill that the peoples of the Third World can't afford, leftists spreadeagle the Central Americans between the dictators of the right and the dictators of the left. The latter, of course, are their chosen instruments for bringing social justice and economic well-being, although no leftist revolution has yet provided impressive returns on either of these qualities and most have made the lives of their people considerably more wretched than they were before.

Voting is symbolic behavior, a way of evaluating what one's country has been as well as what it might become. We do not accept Reagan's policies chapter and verse (especially in domestic policy, which we haven't discussed here), but we agree with his vision of the world as a place increasingly inhospitable to democracy and increasingly dangerous for America.

One of the few saving graces of age is a deeper perspective on the passions of youth. Looking back on the left's revolutionary enthusiasms of the last 25 years, we have painfully learned what should have been obvious all along: that we live in an imperfect world that is bettered only with great difficulty and easily made worse—much worse. This is a conservative assessment, but on the basis of half a lifetime's experience, it seems about right.

LOIS GIBBS

45 | A Toxic Neighborhood

When the environmental movement first gained momentum in the 1960s, many of its goals—the protection of endangered species of animals and plants, over-population in third world nations—seemed esoteric and distant to large segments of the American public. In more recent years, however, environmental issues have begun to hit home. To those injured as a result of exposure to chemicals at their jobs, to those who have had to abandon their houses because of environmental hazards inside or nearby, the argument that economic self-interest is in harmony with an acrid smell in the air no longer makes sense.

Love Canal was the first toxic waste dump-site to be identified as a major environmental hazard. The Environmental Protection Agency has estimated that there are tens of thousands of such dumps in the United States. Located in the center of the town of Niagara Falls, New York, this long trench is part of an unfinished canal begun in 1892 by William T. Love. In 1920, the Hooker Chemical Corporation, along with the City of Niagara Falls and the U.S. Army, began to use Love Canal as a disposal site for chemical wastes.

In 1953, the Hooker Company filled the canal and sold it to the Niagara Falls Board of Education for $1.00, stipulating that, if buried wastes there caused any physical harm, the corporation would not be responsible. During the suburban boom of the 1950s, houses and an elementary school were built on the site. Despite complaints about odors, corrosive substances, and black sludge, it was only in the late 1970s that the State of New York began to investigate the environmental problem.

A series of relocation steps, began on August 2, 1978, involving the moving of increasing numbers of people in close and then less close proximity to the canal. Finally, on October 1, 1980, President Jimmy Carter signed a bill evacuating all families permanently from the canal.

What follows is the bare outline of the beginning of community awareness of the dangers of Love Canal. Lois Gibbs was a major force in mobilizing citizens in the face of what seemed to be bureaucratic indifference or outright callousness.

Such issues as toxic waste dumps, the greenhouse effect, and nuclear waste disposal promise to be important factors in local, national, and international politics well into the next century. In social terms, the story of Lois Gibbs might become all too representative. With the publication in 1906 of The Jungle, Americans began to fear what might be contained in the processed food that lay before them at the breakfast or dinner table. In the 1980s, along with dismaying

From Lois Marie Gibbs, as told to Murray Levine, Love Canal: My Story (Albany, SUNY Press, 1982) pp. 9–19, 22–26.

disclosures about the healthfulness of what they eat, Americans face, on what might seem to be a daily basis, disheartening information about the air they breathe, the water they drink, the cars they drive, and the soil on which they build their homes.

MY SON ATTENDING THAT SCHOOL

Love Canal actually began for me in June 1978 with Mike Brown's articles in the Niagara Falls *Gazette*. At first, I didn't realize where the canal was. Niagara Falls has two sets of streets numbered the same. Brown's articles said Love Canal was between 99th and 97th streets, but I didn't think he meant the place where my children went to school or where I took them to play on the jungle gyms and swings. Although I read the articles, I didn't pay much attention to them. One article did stand out, though. In it, Mike Brown wrote about monkeys subjected to PCB's having miscarriages and deformed offspring.

One of his later articles pointed out that the school had been built over the canal. Still, I paid little attention. It didn't affect me, Lois Gibbs. I thought it was terrible; but I lived on the other side of Pine Avenue. Those poor people over there on the other side were the ones who had to worry. The problem didn't affect me, so I wasn't going to bother doing anything about it, and I certainly wasn't going to speak out about it. Then when I found out the 99th Street School was indeed on top of it, I was alarmed. My son attended that school. He was in kindergarten that year. I decided I needed to do some investigating.

I went to my brother-in-law, Wayne Hadley, a biologist and, at the time, a professor at the State University of New York at Buffalo. He had worked on environmental problems and knew a lot about chemicals. I asked him to translate some of that jibber-jabber in the articles into English. I showed Wayne, Mike Brown's articles listing the chemicals in the canal and asked what they were. I was really alarmed by his answer. Some of the chemicals, he said, can affect the nervous system. Just a little bit, even the amount that's in paint or gasoline, can kill brain cells. I still couldn't believe it; but if it *were* true, I wanted to get Michael out of that 99th Street School.

I went down to the offices of the *Gazette* and was surprised to learn how many articles there were on Love Canal. It not only surprised me, it panicked me! The articles listed the chemicals and described some reactions to them. One is damage to the central nervous system. (Michael had begun having seizures after he started school.) Another is leukemia and other blood diseases. (Michael's white blood cell count had gone down.) The doctor said that might have been caused by the medication he took for his epilepsy, but now I wasn't so sure. Michael had started school in September and had developed epilepsy in December; in February his white blood count dropped

All of a sudden, everything seemed to fall into place. There's no history of epilepsy in either my family or my husband's. So why should Michael develop it? He had always been sensitive to medication. I could never give him an aspirin like a normal baby because he would get sick to his stomach or break out in a rash. I couldn't give him *anything* because of that sensitivity. If it were true that Michael was more sensitive than most other children, then whatever chemicals were buried under the school would affect him more than they did other children in the school, or even more than my daughter Missy, who has always been a strong, lively child. The chemicals probably would not affect Missy, at least not right away. I wasn't thinking then about long-term effects. (A year and a half later, Missy was hospitalized for a blood-platelet disorder, but later she was fine.)

I went over all the articles with Wayne, and decided Michael definitely should not attend that school—nor, for that matter, should any child. They shouldn't even play on that playground. Wayne was worried about his son Eric. He and my sister Kathy used to leave Eric for me to baby-sit while they were at work.

I was stunned that the school board had allowed a school to be built on such a location. Even today, it doesn't seem possible that, knowing there were dangerous chemicals buried there, someone could put up a *school* on the site. The 99th Street School had over 400 children that year, one of its lowest annual enrollments. . . .

/   /   /

I was furious. [Her son could not be transferred to another school.] I wasn't going to send my child to a place that was poisoned. The thoughts that can go through a person's head. I thought that I, as a person, had rights, that I ought to have a choice, and that one of those choices was not to send my child to school in a contaminated place. Like many people, I can be stubborn when I get angry. I decided to go door-to-door and see if the other parents in the neighborhood felt the same way. That way, maybe something could be done. At the time, though, I didn't really think of it as "organizing."

It wasn't just the phone call with the superintendent that convinced me I had to do something. I called the president of the 99th Street School PTA and asked her if she could help me, or if she could at least tell me whom to go to or what to do. She said she was about to go on vacation. I got the feeling she wasn't interested. She seemed to be pushing me away, as if she didn't want to have anything to do with me.

I was disappointed and angry. School would open again in two months, and I wasn't going to let my child go back to that school. I didn't care what I had to do to prevent it. I wasn't going to send him to a private school, either. First of all, we couldn't afford it; and second, I thought parents had the right to send their children to schools that were safe.

KNOCKING ON DOORS

As I said, I decided to go door-to-door with a petition. It seemed like a good idea to start near the school, to talk to the mothers nearest it. I had already heard that a lot of the residents near the school had been upset about the chemicals for the past couple of years. I thought they might help me. I had never done anything like this, however, and I was frightened. I was afraid a lot of doors would be slammed in my face, that people would think I was some crazy fanatic. But I decided to do it anyway. I went to 99th and Wheatfield and knocked on my first door. There was no answer. I just stood there, not knowing what to do. It was an usually warm June day and I was perspiring. I thought: *What am I doing here? I must be crazy. People are going to think I am. Go home, you fool!* And that's just what I did.

It was one of those times when I had to sit down and face myself. I was afraid of making a fool of myself, I had scared myself, and I had gone home. When I got there, I sat at the kitchen table with my petition in my hand, thinking. *Wait. What if people do slam doors in your face? People may think you're crazy. But what's more important—what people think or your child's health? Either you're going to do something or you're going to have to admit you're a coward and not do it.* I decided to wait until the next day— partly to figure out exactly how I was going to do this but more, I think, to build my self-confidence.

/   /   /

At first, I went to my friend's houses.* I went to the back door, as I always did when I visited a neighbor. Each house took about twenty or twenty-five minutes. They wanted to know about Love Canal. Many of the people who lived farther from the canal than 97th or 99th streets didn't even know the canal existed; they thought the area was a field. Some had heard about Love Canal, but they didn't realize where it was, and they didn't pay much attention to the issue—just as I hadn't. So I spent a lot of time giving them the background, explaining what Love Canal was. Something began to happen to me as I went around talking

---

*In this book I am going to write as though people were actually saying certain things, because that's the way I remember what was said. I can't guarantee that they used exactly those words, but what they did say was similar to the way I have written it, and the meaning is the same.

to these people. It was hot and humid that summer. My mother kept saying I was crazy to do it. I was losing weight, mainly because I didn't have much time to eat. My house was a mess because I wasn't home. Dinner was late, and Harry sometimes was upset. Between the kids and the heat, I was getting very tired. But something drove me on. I kept going door-to-door, still on my own street. When I finished 101st, I did 102d; when I finished those two streets, I felt ready to go back to 99th Street, where I had begun by running home afraid of looking foolish.

Just before going back to 99th Street, I called a woman who lived on 97th Street. Her backyard abutted the canal. I had read about her in the newspaper. She was one of the people who had been organizing others. She said she would be willing to help, but nothing ever happened. Somehow something about her voice didn't sound right. Although I didn't realize it at the time, I was getting another lesson: even though we all have common problems, we don't always work together.

I shouldn't have been too surprised when I discovered later that emergencies like this bring out the best and the worst in people. Sometimes people have honest differences about the best way to solve a problem. Sometimes, however, people have big egos; it's more important for them to be up front and draw attention to themselves than cooperate with others in working for a cause. I really did have a lot to learn. At the time, there were a lot of small groups organizing. Tom Heisner and Karen Schroeder, who lived right on the canal, had started getting people together, and they were doing a good job, though we later had our differences.

/ / /

A SICK COMMUNITY

As I proceeded down 99th Street, I developed a set speech. I would tell people what I wanted. But the speech wasn't all that necessary. It seemed as though every home on 99th Street had someone with an illness. One family had a young daughter with arthritis. They couldn't understand why she had it at her age. Another daughter had had a miscarriage. The father, still a fairly young man, had had a heart attack. I went to the next house, and there, people would tell me *their* troubles. People were reaching out; they were telling me their troubles in hopes I would do something. But I didn't know anything to do. I was also confused. I just wanted to stop children from going to that school. Now look at all those other health problems! Maybe they were related to the canal. But even if they were, what could I do?

As I continued going door-to-door, I heard more. The more I heard, the more frightened I became. This problem involved much more than the 99th Street School. The entire community seemed to be sick! Then I remembered my own neighbors. One who lived on the left of my husband and me was suffering from severe migraines and had been hospitalized three or four times that year. Her daughter had kidney problems and bleeding. A woman on the other side of us had gastrointestinal problems. A man in the next house down was dying of lung cancer and he didn't even work in industry. The man across the street had just had lung surgery. I thought about Michael; maybe there *was* more to it than just the school. I didn't understand how chemicals could get all the way over to 101st Street from 99th; but the more I thought about it, the more frightened I became—for my family and for the whole neighborhood.

Everything was unbelievable. I worried that I was exaggerating, or that people were exaggerating their complaints. I talked it over with Wayne. Luckily, he knew someone who might be able to help us—a Dr. Beverly Paigen, who is a biologist, geneticist, and cancer research scientist at the Roswell Park Memorial Institute, a world-famous research hospital in Buffalo. We went to see Dr. Paigen. She is a wonderful, brave person who, like Wayne, had been involved in environmental-pollution fights. She asked us to bring some soil samples so she could do an Ames test. The Ames test is a quick way of determining potentially dangerous effects of chemicals. When bacteria are exposed to mutagenic chemicals, Dr. Paigen told us, they reproduce abnormally.

I continued to go door-to-door. I was becoming more worried because of the many families with children who had birth defects. Then I learned something even more frightening: there had been five crib deaths within a few short blocks. . . .

/   /   /

A REAL PROBLEM?

The New York State Health Department held a public meeting in June 1978. It was the first one I attended. Dr. Nicholas Vianna and some of his staff explained that they were going to do environmental and health studies. They wanted to take samples—of blood, air, and soil, as well as from sump pumps. They wanted to find out if there really was a problem. They would study only the first ring of houses, though, the ones with backyards abutting Love Canal. Bob Matthews, Niagara Falls city engineer, was there to explain the city's plan for remedial construction. They all sat in front of a big, green chalkboard on the stage in the auditorium of the 99th Street School.

I didn't understand everything that was said, especially about determining whether there was a problem. A pretty young woman carefully dressed, with a lovely scarf, spoke articulately. Her dog's nose had been burned when it sniffed the ground in her yard. She kept asking Dr.

Vianna: "What does this mean? How did he burn his nose?" She said the dog was suffering, that her children loved the dog and loved playing with him; but she was willing to have the dog put away if Dr. Vianna would first test the dog.

That was a new reaction to me, one I hadn't come across in my canvassing. How *did* the dog burn his nose? Did that mean chemicals were on the surface? I knew there were health problems, and I felt the school should be closed; but I hadn't actually *seen* any chemicals. I felt a chill. This was a new danger, and a more ominous one. A man got up and said he couldn't put his daughter out in his own backyard because if he did, the soles of her feet would burn. The man thought chemicals were causing it. His daughter was with him. She was a cute little thing, only eighteen months old, with curly dark hair. Imagine he couldn't let her play in his own backyard, and he didn't know why!

/ / /

I asked Dr. Vianna if the 99th Street School was safe. He answered that the air readings on the school had come back clean. But there we were sitting in the school auditorium, smelling chemicals! I said: "You are telling me there are chemicals there. You are going to build this big, elaborate system to . . . collect all this overflow. You tell us the air tests clean. But you also tell us we can't eat the vegetables. How can these kids be safe walking on the playground? How can it be safe?" "Have the children walk on the sidewalk," Dr. Vianna said. "Make sure they don't cut across the canal or walk on the canal itself."

I couldn't believe what I was hearing. I asked again: "How can you say all that when the playground is on the canal?" He didn't have an answer. He just said: "You are their mother. You can limit the time they play on the canal." I wondered if he had any children.

By now the audience was really frustrated, and so was I. People began walking out, muttering, furious. There were no answers. They didn't understand, and they were becoming frightened.

RAPIDLY LOSING MY FAITH

Every time I went to another house, I learned something new. In one home, I met a graying, heavyset man with a pitted face. He couldn't walk very well. He had worked for Hooker at one time, and now he had chloracne, a condition that results from exposure to certain chemicals. I didn't know it then but chloracne is also a symptom of dioxin poisoning. Dioxin is toxic in parts per trillion. Later we learned that it was in Love Canal. The man was as nice and pleasant as he could be, but his face looked awful. It was all I could do to look at him. He wanted to go ahead with a class-action suit; but he was afraid to jeopardize his pension from Hooker.

I thought to myself: *How could you be so concerned about your pension? The law will protect you. Who cares about Hooker? Look what they've done to you in the plant, let alone what they've done to your family living here on one of their dump sites.* It was hard to understand why people were so afraid of Hooker, of what the company might do to them. Why weren't they angrier?

There were so many unbelievable things about the situation. In one house, a divorced woman with four children showed me a letter from the New York State Health Department. It was a thank-you letter, and a check was enclosed. I asked the woman what the check was for. She said the health department had contacted her and asked if her son would go onto Love Canal proper, find two "hot" rocks, and put them in the jars they sent her. She had been instructed to give the rocks to Dr. Vianna or to someone at the 99th Street School headquarters of the health department. The so-called hot rocks were phosphorous rocks that the children would pick up and throw against cement, and, in the process, burn themselves. The rocks would pop like firecrackers. It amused the kids; but some had been burned on the eyes and skin. I just couldn't understand how a supposedly responsible agency would send an eleven-year-old child into a potentially dangerous area such as Love Canal and ask him to pick up something there that could harm him. To get the rocks, he had to climb a snow fence put there to keep children out. It amazed me that the health department would do such a thing. They are supposed to protect people's health, and here they were jeopardizing an innocent child. I used to have a lot of faith in officials, especially doctors and experts. Now I was losing that faith—fast!

/   /   /

I wanted Harry [her husband] to be tested also. I was worried that we were being affected even over there on 101st Street. Some of my neighbors thought it was silly to think we could be affected that far from the canal; but it was only a block and a half farther away. Most people on 101st said they wouldn't take the blood test. If I wanted to shut down the school, fine; but let's not carry it too far. "There's no problem over here," some said. "You have no business going over there. You're not a resident of 97th or 99th. Why don't you stay home and behave yourself!" Some of the women in the neighborhood would get together at a neighbor's house and gossip. "She's just doing it for publicity." But the gossip didn't bother me much. I was developing a pretty thick skin.

After weeks of carrying the petition door-to-door, one door *was* slammed in my face. It wasn't as bad as I had feared, though. The woman who answered my knock recognized me immediately. She really laid it on: "What are you out here for? Why are you doing this? Look what you're doing to property values. When did you put your house up for sale?" She was a bitter woman, but her attack wasn't on me personally. She was just letting me know how she felt. She wouldn't sign my petition. That was the worst encounter I had with a neighbor. By then, such a rebuff made almost no difference. I was disappointed that she wouldn't sign, but I didn't lose any sleep over it.

/   /   /

One woman, divorced and with three sick children, looked at the piece of paper* with numbers and started crying hysterically: "No wonder my children are sick. Am I going to die? What's going to happen to my children?" No one could answer. The health department didn't even give her the OSHA standards provided by the Occupational Safety and Health Administration. I went over to calm her down. I told her that, based on what I had learned from Dr. Paigen and from Wayne, it might be a good idea for her to stay with a relative until the health department finished evaluating the area. She calmed down somewhat, but she was already very nervous and this uncertainty didn't help.

The night was very warm and humid, and the air was stagnant. On a night like that, the smell of Love Canal is hard to describe. It's all around you. It's as though it were about to envelop you and smother you. By now, we were outside, standing in the parking lot. The woman's panic caught on, starting a chain reaction. Soon, many people there were hysterical.

/   /   /

The meeting had one good effect: it brought people together. People who had been feuding because little Johnny hit little Billy were now talking to each other. They had air readings in common or a dead plant or a dead tree. They compared readings, saying, "Hey, this is what I've got. What have you got?" The word spread fast and the community became close-knit. Everywhere you looked, there were people in little groups talking and wondering and worrying.

*Containing air-sample results for her home.

46 | Painful Choices

In the 1970s and 1980s, economic realities converged with feminist efforts to move more women into the workplace in a full range of white-collar and blue-collar occupations.

Whether they worked out of necessity (because real family income in the 1970s and 1980s suffered a gradual decline) or to achieve independence and a new self-respect, women faced difficult choices as they attempted to balance their professional and personal lives. The following selection, from Sylvia Ann Hewlett's book, A Lesser Life, *relates the experiences of several women who tried to exercise the best options available to them. (To document that men's and women's choices in the 1980s are not based on equality, Hewlett considers whether women, more frequently than men, feel that success in their careers means they must forgo the option to have children. She refers to an October 30, 1984* Wall Street Journal *article that cites a study showing that 52% of high-level women executives are childless, compared with 7% of their male counterparts.)*

Reports on American society in the 1970s and 1980s include examinations of the impact of the high-income, dual-wage-earner family; the family in which both spouses must work in order to break even; and the single-parent household, created by accident, choice, or divorce. The long-term impact of these phenomena on the nation's social structure and economy has yet to be fully evaluated. Meanwhile, conflicts over traditional versus modern values are played out in the lives of millions of contemporary Americans.

At 8:00 P.M. on September 21, 1984, my apartment filled with excited young women greeting long-lost classmates.* They ranged in age from twenty-three to thirty-three, and half were married. Some were self-consciously businesslike in skirted suits, little string ties, and cropped hair. But even the more feminine members of the group, in elegant dresses and clever makeup, carried bulging briefcases. Most of them had come straight from work, two brought spouses, and one woman was con-

*[of Barnard College]

spicuously pregnant. After an hour of eating, drinking, gossiping, and cuddling my children (my third child, Adam, was just five months old and particularly popular, despite a tendency to dribble down silk blouses) the serious business of the evening began. We sat around in a big circle, and after some encouragement (I, after all, was an old hand at conducting seminars) everyone started to talk. The first topic these women gravitated toward was how to combine careers with children (a rather surprising choice, for although one of these women was pregnant, *none* had yet had children).

Marion,* age twenty-four, class of '81, one of the most able students of her year, now holds an entry-level position at an investment banking firm, a job she took after completing a master's degree in economics. Marion likes her work and looks forward to building a career in international finance. Marion is getting married in the spring, and her one great worry is: "Can I make room in this career for children?" She recognizes that she has chosen a very time-intensive profession: "Ten to twelve hours a day plus a lot of travel. Not only does my job require me to travel abroad ten days of each month, but I have a ninety-minute commute, which means that I never get home until eight in the evening." Marion particularly regrets that there are no role models in her field. "In my firm there are a hundred partners, only three of them are women, and none of these are in my department, so I don't know them." In the larger financial world Marion has found some women, "but if they are married, they tend to be childless."

Marion does not see herself attempting to have children for at least five years, yet, as she freely admits, "it is a question I think about a lot." Her great hope is that by then "I will be in control of my career and have much more ability to dictate my terms to it."

At this point Marion was interrupted by Laura,** age twenty-nine, class of '77, who said quietly but with conviction, "It's not as easy as that. Things don't resolve themselves. In some ways the choices get harder.

"My situation is typical. I'll be thirty in July and am beginning to feel enormous pressure to have a child. I read somewhere that infertility problems begin to mount in your early thirties, and I would very much like to avoid that kind of trouble. Besides, I've been married for seven years, and both of us want a child quite badly. The other day Michael told me that he 'needed' a child. Yet I cannot decide how to reconcile a family with my work. The basic problem is that my career cannot be put on hold for a few years. If I were to take time out, there would be no way of picking up the threads two or three years down the line."

Everyone in the room was listening very closely to Laura. She was seen by her classmates as an immensely efficient woman thoroughly in

*Pseudonym.

**Pseudonym.

control of her life. If she was encountering problems, they were surely significant ones. Marion pushed Laura to be more explicit. "I don't understand. I thought it was OK to slow down once your career was established."

Laura decided to tell of her experience in some detail, and as she talked, her voice rose and became filled with emotion. Clearly her dilemma was causing considerable pain.

"Professional careers do not become easier or plateau out in your late twenties or early thirties. At these critical early stages there is always *the next step*. I work in a commercial bank. When I started seven years ago, my first goal was to become an officer. Then I wanted to become a higher-level officer, then assistant vice-president. And now I am waiting for my vice-presidency.

"I put in twelve- to fourteen-hour days. I have taken only four sick days in seven years, and I have earned my medals; but that does not mean that I can relax a whole lot now. There just isn't much flexibility in my career. Citibank thinks it has a decent maternity policy—three months' leave—but the kid is not even sleeping through the night by then. The bank will not tolerate part-time work or flextime and has no child-care facilities. Besides, as soon as you get pregnant, people at work start viewing you differently. They assume your priorities have changed and you will have less energy for your job.

"We bought a house in the suburbs a year and a half ago, and since my husband wants to be a neurosurgeon and has four years of specialized training in front of him, there is no way we could keep the house if I stopped work.

"So you see, despite the fact that I have launched my career, delayed childbearing, and done all the things I was supposed to do, I face some very tough choices.

"When we have a child, I can do one of three things. I can continue my career by hiring enough help for full-time coverage at home. I have priced it out; it would cost twenty thousand dollars a year. The snag is I would have to resign myself to seeing my baby only an hour or two a day. Or I can opt out of my banking career and work part time for my father (who has a small business). This way I can make enough money to pay the mortgage and still have time to see my child and manage the house. Or, finally, we could sell the house, move into an apartment, and I can take time out of the work force and become a traditional homemaker.

"All three options entail huge costs for me. I can already visualize the massive guilt I would feel if I took option number one. I had a very traditional upbringing, and an important part of me believes that mothers should be with their children. I have nightmares about my child forgetting that I am its mother, preferring the baby-sitter to me. I can deal with hard work and crazy hours, I would even get up at five A.M.

to spend some quality time with my child, but can I cope with the guilt? I don't think so.

"Option number two would kill my career—at least any ambitious version of my career. If I took even a few years out of banking, there is no way I could get back on the fast track in my mid or late thirties. In other words, if I opted to work part time for my father, I would have to permanently lower my expectations of money, status, and power.

"Option number three is the least attractive to me. I would not like losing the house; I have worked hard for my creature comforts and value them. But more than that, if I were to stay at home all day, I would more than likely go crazy. I thrive on stimulus and love my work. I am now a formed person and cannot change my personality or temperament because it's convenient to do so.". . . .

/   /   /

Debbie,* class of '80 and an associate editor at a top women's magazine, was six months pregnant. She tried to rise to the challenge that had been thrown her and said with some irony, "I wish I did have some solutions, but in many ways my options are more limited than Laura's. You see we face a Catch-twenty-two situation. Both John and I work in low-paying fields, so I need to earn money for us to survive. And I mean, survive. We rent a small apartment in Brooklyn, we don't own a car, yet we barely get by on our two salaries. Despite this need to earn money, which will become more acute when we have a child, it will be impossible for me to keep my job. My maternity benefits are far from good—four weeks of partially paid leave before the birth and four weeks afterward. But even if I could cope with so little time off, full-time high-quality child care would consume all my salary. So my solution (if you can call it that) is to leave my job after the birth of my child and become a free-lance writer. This way I can do a large part of the child care myself and continue to earn at least some money.

"But it's scary. I'm afraid of becoming isolated and unproductive—at home all day with a tiny child. And I'm afraid that John and I will lose the equality we have so carefully built up. If he begins to earn much more than I, it will obviously be difficult to maintain an equal division of household tasks, and I think I will become resentful if I end up with all the cooking and cleaning."

Debbie paused and then added reflectively, "You know, there are a lot of women on the creative, editorial side of the company [the Hearst organization, which owns several magazines including the one Debbie works for], but in management, upper management, I don't think there is one woman, and it is in management that the high salaries are. Even

*Pseudonym.

Helen Gurley Brown has no clout; she is not even on the board. All these women's magazines are supposedly setting up role models for women, but good role models don't exist at the source."

Debbie had one final comment: "This past summer I have been troubled by the fact that I could not work up much enthusiasm for Geraldine Ferraro.* Somehow I felt guilty about not giving her more support. I think the problem is that her life has been so unreal. She took thirteen years off to have her children and then was able to jump back into the work force and get back on track as a lawyer and a politician. I guess I don't believe that you can do that unless you are married to a wealthy man and have great political connections. Most of us need to earn money in order to survive, and many of us are in competitive professions, where it just isn't possible to take a few years off to have a family, let alone thirteen years off. Ferraro talks a lot about her hard life, but she really hasn't faced the toughest issue—rearing children and building a career at one and the same time. I suppose that makes it hard for me to see her as a role model."

/   /   /

*The 1984 vice-presidential nominee of the Democratic Party.

47 | "Hope Dies Last," A Migrant Worker's Story

The prospect of owning land is the original American dream. Although fewer and fewer families actually work the land in the United States, the ideal continues and often is translated into the ownership of a home on a small plot. However, the hopes of migrant workers, to own their own independent farms, recall those of earlier generations, because the migrant workers continue to till the soil on others' land.

Following the crops from Florida or Texas or California to upstate New York or Idaho or Washington—to name a few of the prevalent routes—migrant workers (usually from Mexico) constitute a substantial portion of the agricultural labor force. Studs Terkel's interview with Jessie de la Cruz provides the opportunity to see more deeply into an enduring dream.

Throughout the 1960s, 1970s, and 1980s, people from nations facing economic strife and political oppression came to America, echoing past waves of immigration. This new generation of immigrants includes individuals from Central and South America, Asia, and Africa. It includes migrant farm workers, such as Jesse de la Cruz, but also factory workers, service workers, and skilled laborers in the health professions and advanced technology.

My husband was born in Mexico. He came with his parents when he was two and a half years old. He was irrigating when he was twelve years old, doing a man's work. Twelve hours for a dollar twenty. Ten cents an hour. I met him in 1933. Our first year we stayed in the labor camps.

All farm workers I know, they're always talking: "If I had my own place, I'd know how to run it. I'd be there all the time. My kids would help me." This is one thing that all Chicano families talked about. We worked the land all our lives, so if we ever owned a piece of land, we knew that we could make it.

Mexicans have this thing about a close family, so they wanted to buy some land where they could raise a family. That's what my grandfather kept talkin' about, but his dream was never realized.

We followed the crops till around 1966. We went up north around the Sacramento area to pick prunes. We had a big truck, and we were able to take our refrigerator and my washing machine and beds and kitchen pots and pans and our clothing. It wasn't a hardship any more. We wanted our children to pick in the shade, under a tree, instead of picking out in the vines, where it's very hot. When I picked grapes, I could hardly stand it. I felt sorry for twelve-, thirteen-year-old kids. My husband said: "Let's go up north and pick prunes."

We stopped migrating when Cesar Chavez formed a union. We became members, and I was the first woman organizer. I organized people everywhere I went. When my husband and I started working under a signed contract, there was no need to migrate after that.

I knew how to organize. My husband and I talked to other families. What if we could buy some land? We moved to Fresno and talked to a large group of families. And have meetings. Each of us would borrow, and what little savings we had, maybe a hundred dollars, we would go together and buy some land. We were talkin' about a community, two hundred families.

We made plans of how we'd set up our own little school for preschool children and the older children could be taken into town to attend public school. I came up with the idea of having our own rest home for the elderly. The Chicano people who couldn't work any more and needed to be taken care of. A clinic was discussed too.

A committee was formed to talk to these big growers. We went in a group of five to this man's office. We hear his land was up. He had to sell because of the 1902 law. Nobody ever told us about a law or anything. Where anyone that lived within the Westlands district, they used federally subsidized water. A big project was built. Before, all the irrigating was done by pumps. These farmers were pumping themselves dry. So they asked the government to build a big canal there. They got it. They had a lot of money, and congressmen were helping them.

To me, this law meant helping small farms. It was for small family farms. They had to live on the land. It was a hundred sixty for the wife. A hundred sixty for the husband. And a hundred sixty for two children, no more than two children. That was six hundred forty acres. Who needs more than that?

I told this grower we had families interested in buying some of his land. He didn't even let me go any further. He asked me if we had half a million dollars. (Laughs.) He was paying us seventy-five cents an hour, picking cotton and cantaloupes for him for nine, ten years. Before I worked for even less. And he asked if we had a half-million as a down payment.

They were selling old tractors, levelers, the cotton gin. They were selling it with the land. We weren't interested in any landing strip. He wanted to include that, but we didn't have any private airplane. We feel as farmers you don't have to own these great big huge machines to do the work. There's plenty of people to do it.

At our next meeting, we told them what the answer had been. They became discouraged. All of the families left except six. We heard about this man who had some land he wanted to get rid of because he needed tax money. We were able to buy forty acres at a very reasonable price.

Six families on forty acres. That first year we couldn't plant. It needed to be leveled. It didn't have a pump. We didn't have the water. The land had just been sitting there for years. That winter we started pulling those tumbleweeds out and piling them up. It rained very hard that year and we couldn't do it.

A friend of ours said: "I'll rent you six acres." We started farming those six acres. We were out there from morning till late, on our hands and knees, planting tomatoes. There was the risk of a cold wave coming and killing our plants. So we had to use hot caps.

One day we had finished planting and said: "Tomorrow we'll put the hot caps on." They're cap-shaped papers with wire. Around two or three o'clock I heard on the radio—I always carry a little portable—I heard the weather was gonna be twenty-three degrees. It was gonna kill our plants. I was scared. I ran back to the group and said: "Hey, it's gonna freeze tonight, we're gonna lose our plants." Right away we started putting the hot caps on.

We put dirt around it to hold it down. We had them by the thousands. It was very windy and very cold. We started out there on our hands and knees. I was crying. It was beautiful. I'm not calling it beautiful, my crying. But to have little children five, six years old helping us, because they knew how important it was to save those plants. The wind was very strong, it was just ripping those paper caps off of our hands, and you could see them rolling. (Laughs.) We ran out of caps. Okay, each of us got a hoe and started pulling dirt over our plants, very gently. We covered all of them. We came home, it was dark, cold, and wet.

The next morning we were all anxious to find out what had happened during the night. Oh, it was great to go out there and remove the dirt from those plants and watch 'em shoot straight up like anything. We saved every one of 'em. It took hard work to do it.

If it had been one of the big growers, what would have happened? The farmer would just go out there and look and see all the dead plants, and he'd say: "Oh, what the heck." He'd go home and forget about everything. He would get on his pickup, push a button, lift up a telephone, and call the nursery to bring over this certain amount of thousands of plants and call the workers to plant them over again. That's his way of farming.

When we own land and we're working it for ourselves, we're gonna save everything that we can. We're not about to waste anything or lose anything. We keep on working every day. There's no holidays. We're picking until, oh, November. That is work and income. That first year, we sorted our tomatoes and we took 'em to the shipper and we ended up making sixty-four thousand dollars. Six acres between six families.

Before we divided the money, we saw there was a problem. We had
to have the right amount for each family. My husband and I were only
two of us and my daughter. How could we compare the work of three
to a family that had eight? So we said: "We're gonna divide these rows
between us all." It worked out fine. There were no fights about who's
doing more work, who's getting more money. When you sit down with
a group of people and discuss how you're gonna do things, things will
work out fine. The following year we were working our own forty acres.

When some other family needs help or when we need help, they'll
come over and help us. My husband is a mechanic. Whenever something breaks in one of those tractors, he fixes it in exchange for services
we'll need. We need a tractor, the neighbor comes over and does the
work for us. This is how we share.

We're in very marginal land. We survive by hard work and sacrifices. We're out of the Westland district, where the government supplies
the water. There's acres and acres of land that if you go out there you
can see green from one end to the other, like a green ocean. No houses,
nothing. Trees or just cotton and alfalfa. It's land that is irrigated with
taxpayers' money.

These growers that have been using this water signed a contract that
they would sell, within ten years, in small parcels. It's not happening.
If the law has been enforced, we would be out there right now.

It's the very, very best land. I worked it there. You could grow anything: tomatoes, corn, cantaloupes, vegetables, bell peppers. But they
just grow one or two crops because they just don't want to hire any
people. They have big machines that do the picking. Instead of planting
a few acres of one crop and a few acres of another, they just go to one
crop. What they're looking at, when they see the land and the water,
all they can see is dollar signs. They don't see human beings out there.

We're not thinking about getting a lot of land so we can take European trips and buy a new car a year. That's not what we're talking
about. I never hope to own an airplane. Not those machines that are
worth thousands of dollars. We don't need these things. Everybody
managed before these things were invented. So why can't we?

These farmers aren't thinking about putting food on your table.
They're thinking how much money they're gonna make per acre.
They're putting a lot of chemicals and pesticides into the soil in order
to have a bigger yield of crop. They call it—what?—progress? With their
progress, they're gonna kill the whole planet. Even themselves. In the
not too long.

They're thinking: Well, I'm alive. I'm gonna enjoy life. I'm gonna
have millions of dollars. We're thinking about our future generation.
My children, my grandchildren, my great-grandchildren. We want a
place for them. We don't want them to end up with land that won't
grow things.

There are some big companies, individuals, who own land not only in California but in Arizona, Mexico, all over. They don't even know anything about the land. They know nothing about farming. They don't even live on the farm.

A young couple owns thousands of head of cattle and land. And big steakhouses. They felt they weren't getting enough money, and they wanted to make more. They come out to the hearings and going out to the people, and they say we're trying to take their land away from them. We're not trying to take it away from them. They can still keep on farming enough land. Just sell the rest of it. They lease a lot of acreage from Southern Pacific. They call themselves family farmers. Sixteen thousand acres . . .

One senator said: "These are third-generation farmers with calluses on their hands." How can they have calluses when they never held a hoe in their hand? Maybe they do have calluses from a golf club (laughs) but not from a hoe handle. This one young woman who testified said: "I don't want to go back to stoop, to back-breaking labor." I can almost bet my life she's never done a day's work. She and her husband own the biggest feed lot in the world.

I've gone to Washington a few times. I've never been shy talking to these people. I feel comfortable talking to anyone because what I'm talking about is the truth. I believe in standing up for what I believe in.

I was given a shot in the arm by Cesar Chavez. (Laughs.) All of the things I always felt, like I wanted to say, I held back because of fear of losing a job, of being thought not a very good woman, or some kind of fear inside me that had been instilled in me by my grandmother, who always warned us whenever we did something, the police would come. Always being scared by a neighbor: "I'm gonna call the police and take you to juvenile. We always heard these. So when Cesar Chavez started talking to us and sayin' women have to become involved, they have to speak, they're farm workers, too, then, I just, oh, had a good feeling. I said: "Boy, now!"

I kept learning. I kept writing everything down. So I said: "Here I come." (Laughs.) And everywhere I go I'll talk about the hopes we have of owning our own land. We haven't been the landowners, we've been the farmers. We've been farming the land for somebody else. Until this time, I was very quiet.

My husband attended meetings; I didn't. I always sat back. Until one time I told him I want to go. The first few meetings I went to, I just listened and listened. And then one time Cesar says: "Does anyone have anything to say?" I lifted my arm and I said: "The way I see it" and I started. And he said: "That's the kind of people I want, people that will talk. It's not my union, it's your union."

A big meeting here in Fresno, that was my first public appearance. I was nervous. I remember that hearing. It was on—what was it?—wages for women. It was at Fresno High. I knew I was going to speak. I kept thinking: What am I going to say? I started writing something. I have to make a note of what I'm going to say.

I looked around, and there were all these big growers. And these big businessmen that had stores out in the vacation areas up in the mountains. They were there because they were against raising wages for women. I heard my name and I got up there. My knees were shaking. (Laughs.) I got up before these microphones and I looked around and saw my notes. The only thing I said out of my notes was "Ladies and Gentlemen," I said: "My name is Jessie de la Cruz, and I'm here as a farm worker." And then I started.

I said: "We are forced to go out and work in the fields alongside our husbands, not through choice and not because we love to be out in the sun working so hard ten hours, but because of the need. Us women have to go out there and help support our families." And I said: "I have six children, my husband and I raised, and we never had to go on welfare." Oh, they applauded. Good for you. Oh, it was great that I never had to go on welfare. And I said: "These men here who are growers and businessmen and restaurant owners, if they pay higher wages, they could just close down the welfare doors." Oh, I felt in the pit of my stomach, right there in the pit of my stomach, pain. It was a hard ball right there. I forget what I was saying and my hands were behind me. And I hear somebody in our group say: "Go on, Jessie, tell 'em, tell 'em." And I said: "What I'm gonna tell you is not something I read. It's something that's engraved in my heart and in my brain because it's something that I've lived and many other farm workers' families have done the same." So I went on and on and on and on. (Laughs.) I was congratulated, but for about three or four days, there was a pain right here, a sore spot in my stomach. But I managed to tell 'em off. (Laughs.)
. . .

I'm making it. It's hard work. But I'm not satified, not until I see a lot of farm workers settle on their own farms. Then I'll say it's happening.

Is America progressing toward the better? No, the country will never do anything for us. We're the ones that are gonna do it. We have to keep on struggling. I feel there's going to be a change. With us, there's a saying: *La esperanza muere al último.* Hope dies last. You can't lose hope. If you lose hope, that's losing everything.

Questions for Part IV

1 In *The Man in the Gray Flannel Suit,* why does Tom want the new job? Do you think he will be comfortable with it? What do you think the author is trying to say about suburbia in the 1950s?

2 Compare the Sloan Wilson and Jack Kerouac readings. How does the culture represented by the narrator of *On The Road* differ from that symbolized by the United Broadcasting Corporation? How are women depicted in each reading? Who or what, if anything, in today's America seems closely related to Kerouac's beatniks?

3 What challenges did President Kennedy make in his inaugural address? How did the nation respond? Does he refer to the Soviet Union in his speech? How? In what connection and in what tone?

4 What is the agenda set forth in the Port Huron statement? How much of it has been realized?

5 Many of the volunteers in the Mississippi Project obviously had great courage. What other participants in the civil rights movement were extremely courageous? Why do you think there was such strong—at times violent—opposition to the civil rights movement?

6 How did the attitudes of David Baker and Clarence Fitch about the Vietnam war change as a result of their experiences overseas? How were their views changed by their awareness of events that were taking place in the United States?

7 What challenges were presented to the founders of the Twin Oaks Community? Why was the commune a microcosm of the larger world that it had originally sought to reject?

8 What injustices are cited by the women testifying in favor of the Equal Rights Amendment? What were the main issues in the "human nature" argument against the ERA? How did Gloria Steinem and Margaret Heckler respond to the claims of their opponents?

9 What were the failings of liberalism as identified by Peter Collier and David Horowitz? Contrast their view of the potential for social change with that of the authors of the Port Huron Statement.

365

10   What were the essential elements in Lois Gibbs's success as a
     grassroots organizer? What other issues have developed into
     causes for popular organizing in the 1970s and 1980s?

11   What are the major trade-offs faced by the women in Sylvia Ann
     Hewett's book?

12   How are the ambitions of Jesse de la Cruz similar to those of ear-
     lier immigrants (including those presented earlier in this book)?
     Are the obstacles to her goals significantly different from those
     existing in the past?